BORDERLINE CITIZENS
Women, Gender, and Political Culture in Britain
1815–1867

BORDERLINE CITIZENS
Women, Gender, and Political Culture in Britain
1815–1867

by
Kathryn Gleadle

A British Academy
Postdoctoral Fellowship Monograph

Published for THE BRITISH ACADEMY
by OXFORD UNIVERSITY PRESS

Oxford University Press, Great Clarendon Street, Oxford OX2 6DP

Oxford New York

Auckland Cape Town Dar es Salaam Hong Kong Karachi
Kuala Lumpur Madrid Melbourne Mexico City Nairobi
New Delhi Shanghai Taipei Toronto

With offices in
Argentina Austria Brazil Chile Czech Republic France Greece
Guatemala Hungary Italy Japan Poland Portugal Singapore
South Korea Switzerland Thailand Turkey Ukraine Vietnam

Published in the United States
by Oxford University Press Inc., New York

British Library Cataloguing in Publication Data
Data available

Library of Congress Cataloging in Publication Data
Data available

Typeset by
J&L Composition Ltd, Scarborough, North Yorkshire
Printed in Great Britain
on acid-free paper by
CPI Antony Rowe
Chippenham, Wiltshire

ISBN 978-0-19-726449-2

Contents

Acknowledgements

This study arose from a British Academy Postdoctoral Fellowship which I held at London Guildhall University. The final stages of the book were completed during the tenure of a Philip Leverhulme prize. I am immensely grateful to both the British Academy and to the Leverhulme Trust for their continuing and generous support of this project. In addition, the British Academy have been most considerate and helpful as I have prepared the book for publication. London Guildhall University provided a welcoming home for research, and more recently, Mansfield College have been extremely flexible in granting leave to enable me to finish this book.

My debt to the numerous specialist libraries and record offices which facilitated my research will be apparent from the bibliography. In particular I would like to thank the following for permission to quote from their manuscripts: Bodleian Library, University of Oxford; Cornwall Record Office; the Syndics of Cambridge University Library; East Sussex Record Office; Earl of Lytton and Pollinger Ltd; the Trustees of the National Library of Scotland; Rhodes House Library, University of Oxford; the County Archivist, West Sussex Record Office; Wedgwood Museum Trust; and The Women's Library, London Metropolitan University.

This book started out in life as a collaborative project with Sarah Richardson. Sarah's energy, enthusiasm, and intellectual perspectives greatly influenced my approach to the subject. Her own forthcoming book promises to make a critical intervention in the field. My thanks also to Peter Mandler, Amanda Vickery, and Clare Midgley for their encouragement. Christina de Bellaigue, Kathryn Eccles, Chris Waters, William Whyte, and Emma Mason provided a rich intellectual environment through the formation of an Oxford reading group devoted to gender studies when I was in the early stages of planning this publication. Aurelia Spottiswoode Annat, another reading group devotee, performed a heroic service in assisting me with preparing the text for publication. Conversations with Linda Kerber, during her time as a visiting professor at Oxford, provided much-needed encouragement through her warm, yet probing comments for which I am most grateful. Rhian Jones and Jonny Mood patiently tracked down obscure references and their labours enabled me to extend the scope of the research in many ways. Megha Kumar and Eve Colpus kindly assisted in preparing the bibliography. The support, super-efficiency, and friendship of successive lecturers at Mansfield, namely, Zoë Waxman, Katrina Navickas, and Helen Lacey, have greatly facilitated my ability to progress with this project. Helen also responded to my many word-processing queries with noble fortitude. Ella Dzelzainis undertook a most helpful, last-minute reading of the final manuscript which I greatly appreciated.

I was extremely fortunate in having Jane Rendall act as the academic editor for this book. Jane sailed beyond the call of duty in her scrupulous and insightful reading of early drafts and provided almost instantaneous feedback and suggestions. The errors and weaknesses I managed by myself.

David, Jem, and Rowan have been brilliant as always. Rowan and friends thought that the book should be dedicated to Abi, Alice, Ami, Katherine, Leanne, and Rachel, but they will have to make do with this acknowledgement instead.

Abbreviations

7LOT	Papers of Louisa Twining, The Women's Library, London
Brit. Emp. S. 444	Thomas Fowell Buxton papers, Rhodes House Library, University of Oxford
CRO	Cornwall Record Office
CUL	Cambridge University Library
ESRO	East Sussex Record Office
Edgeworth	Edgeworth Papers, Bodleian Library, Oxford, MSS Eng Lit.
EWJ	*Englishwoman's Journal*
HMCO	Harris Manchester College, Oxford
HRO	Hertfordshire Archives and Local Studies
Kenrick Diary	Diary of Rebecca Kenrick, Birmingham City Archives
LF	*Labourers' Friend*
LFM	*Labourers' Friend Magazine*
LFS	Labourers' Friend Society
LRO	Record Office for Leicestershire, Leicester and Rutland
Martineau, 'Transcribed letters'	James Martineau's shorthand commentary of Harriet Martineau's letters, transcribed by W. S. Coloe for R. K. Webb, Harris Manchester College, Oxford
NAPSS	National Association for the Promotion of Social Science
NLS	National Library of Scotland
NRO	Norfolk Record Office
ODNB	*Oxford Dictionary of National Biography*
REAS	Raymond English Anti-Slavery Collection, John Rylands Library, University of Manchester
SICLC	Society for the Improvement of the Condition of the Labouring Classes
SRO	Shropshire Archives
WSRO	Cobden papers, West Sussex Record Office
W/M	Wedgwood Manuscripts, Keele University Library
WVS	Workhouse Visiting Society

Note on the text

Original spellings and punctuation have been retained in quotations. However, contemporary publications tended to be inconsistent regarding apostrophes in their titles (e.g. *Labourer's Friend* and *Labourers' Friend*) and these have been silently standardized.

Authorial signatures have been given as the known author of a text or texts, rather than the pseudonyms or initials under which they were originally published.

Where contemporary publications have particularly long titles the full citation is given in the bibliography, rather than in the footnotes.

In the citation of manuscript sources, data given in square brackets indicate supposed rather than confirmed information (as in the dating of letters, for example).

Introduction

At the heart of this book lies a desire to understand how it *felt* for women of the middle and gentry classes to engage in British politics in the early nineteenth century. It considers the modes of participation and opportunities available to women and in what ways they were able to articulate their activities and interests. There were multiple avenues for female political interaction, including petitioning, publication, pressure groups, and patronage. Given this, the frequency with which women known for their formidable political skills resorted to highly feminine personas in personal correspondence is striking. The Whig poet and pamphleteer Caroline Norton displayed such a sensibility in her correspondence with Edward Bulwer Lytton, 'I will not attempt to *argue* my point; you will perhaps only smile at the attempt'.[1] Such formulaic protestations frequently flew in the face of women's evident abilities. Sara Coleridge (the intellectual daughter of the famous poet) claimed to her correspondent, Professor Reed, that she was 'no politician, and always speak on such subjects with a reserve on account of my inadequate insight', before proceeding to deliver an analysis of Peel's political career.[2] This was not simply a dynamic of female/male correspondence. Despite the fact that Catherine Hutton was a spirited observer of contemporary affairs she is to be found writing to her close friend Ann Coltman that she would not expatiate upon the 'political state of kingdom', noting '[this] I leave to wiser heads than mine'.[3]

An attempt to understand these ambivalent self-representations is the starting-point of this study. I would like to consider how hegemonic gender codes were continually reused (and thus upheld) despite the diversity and

[1] Caroline Norton to Edward Bulwer Lytton [n.d.], Hertfordshire Archives and Local Studies, D/EK C24/99/7.
[2] Sara Coleridge to Professor Henry Reed (3 July 1850), in Sara Coleridge, *Memoir and Letters of Sara Coleridge,* ed. Edith Coleridge (London, 1875), 353–4.
[3] Catherine Hutton to Ann Coltman (10 Nov. 1831), Leicestershire, Leicester and Rutland Record Office (LRO), Coltman MSS, 15D57, 423.

dynamism of women's activities 'on the ground'. In their famous analysis of
Victorian domestic ideology, Leonore Davidoff and Catherine Hall noted
that it was a discourse 'riven with contradictions'. In their richly elaborated
account they excavated the processes whereby provincial families negotiated, subverted, and reworked dominant assumptions of gender roles to
produce a capacious, if unstable, cultural formation.[4] Just as Davidoff and
Hall found the precepts and foundations of domestic ideology to be
comprised of multiple and sometimes conflicting currents, so too, I would
argue, were assumptions of women as political agents. This book focuses on
the period between the ending of the Napoleonic Wars in 1815 and the
expansion of the formal political nation in 1867. During these years the
contours of the British state, and expectations of citizens' roles within it,
underwent momentous changes, but many aspects of political culture
continued to be shaped by older modes of political expression and engagement. This book explores the implications of these complex patterns for
women and analyses the ways in which they themselves were active agents
in these processes.

During this critical period in British history women, it will be
suggested, were 'borderline citizens'.[5] Their status as political actors, as well
as their own political subjectivities, were often fragile and contingent. They
might be conceptualized (and feel) integral to the political process at one
moment—but this could quickly evaporate in the face of other cultural
pressures. Whilst there were particular constellations of circumstances
which could produce less equivocal attitudes towards female participation,
this did not always translate into similar opportunities in other contexts. In
addition, women often had a cultural and personal investment in the
perpetuation of particular codes of femininity and, as in the examples cited
above, it was common for them to project symbolic conformity to a
publicly agreed discourse of women's inferior political acumen. This practice of acquiescing in certain gendered representations should not be seen
simply as a strategic performance. These repeated denials of female political
aptitude were part of the process through which ascendant gender ideas
were upheld. They formed a critical component of the cultural resources

---

[4] Leonore Davidoff and Catherine Hall, *Family Fortunes: Men and Women of the English Middle Class, 1780–1850* (London, 1987), 450. For the theoretical strengths of their treatment of hegemony see Kathryn Gleadle, 'Revisiting *Family Fortunes: Men and Women of the English Middle Class, 1780–1850*', *Women's History Review*, 16 (2007), 773–82.

[5] This term was suggested to me by Brigitte Studer, 'Citizenship as Contingent National Belonging: Married Women and Foreigners in Twentieth-Century Switzerland', *Gender and History*, 13 (2001), 622–54, although Studer uses the term in a different context.

available to women, and their circulation and recurrence had a significant impact upon the processes of subjectivity.

The apparent difficulties women experienced in articulating their political interests stemmed in part from the absence of a widely agreed convention for expressing their interest. It is a phenomenon which therefore needs to be situated within the complicated and fractured potential of the multiple discourses concerning female roles. Amanda Vickery and Linda Colley have suggested that prescriptive literature urging women to fulfil their domestic destinies was a reactive phenomenon—a response to the vibrant culture of female associational activity which appeared to threaten conservative assumptions of a woman's place.[6] However, contemporary prescriptions of female domesticity were far more intricate and complex than this suggests.

As many scholars have recognized, in the wake of the French Revolution progressive thinkers asserted the crucial connections between private and public reformation, arguing for the importance of reformed family manners as a precursor to wider political change.[7] But those of conservative political persuasions were equally alert to the ways in which the domestic site might have significance as a political environment for women. For example, the novelists Frances Burney and Jane West had long insisted that domesticity should be compatible with an active awareness of political affairs.[8] By the 1830s and 1840s commentators from the Chartist preacher Benjamin Parsons to the Tory pamphleteer Sibella Miles explicitly eschewed the notion that women 'should have nothing to do with politics'. As Miles observed, women 'are not immured in convents, nor incarcerated in seraglios; their position is one of *influential, active, intelligent* life'.[9] Even

---

[6] Amanda Vickery, 'Golden Age to Separate Spheres? A Review of the Categories and Chronology of English Women's History', *Historical Journal*, 36 (1993), 383–414, and Linda Colley, *Britons: Forging the Nation, 1707–1837* (New Haven, 1992), ch. 6.

[7] For indicative discussions see Sylvana Tomaselli, 'The Most Public Sphere of All: The Family', in Elizabeth Eger *et al.* (eds), *Women, Writing and the Public Sphere, 1700–1830* (Cambridge, 2001), 239–56; Kathryn Gleadle, 'British Women and Radical Politics in the Late Nonconformist Enlightenment, c.1780–1830', in Amanda Vickery (ed.), *Women, Privilege and Power: British Politics, 1750 to the Present* (Stanford, Calif., 2001), 133–7.

[8] Frances Burney, *Brief Reflections Relative to the Emigrant French Clergy: Earnestly Submitted to the Humane Consideration of the Ladies of Great Britain* (London, 1793), iii; Jane West, *Letters to a Young Lady, in Which the Duties and Character of Women are Considered* (London, 1996; 1st publ. 1811, 3 vols), i. 65.

[9] Original emphasis. Benjamin Parsons, *The Mental and Moral Dignity of Woman* (London, 1842), 343–6; Sibella Miles, *An Essay on the Factory Question, Occasioned by the Recent Votes in the House of Commons* (London, 1844), 27–8. Miles, a West Country poet, had issued a feminist

the most famous domestic ideologues such as Sarah Lewis and Sarah Stickney Ellis were keen to establish the importance of women's political engagement. As Lewis insisted in her *Woman's Mission*, women might fulfil a political purpose through their domestic roles and as 'moral agents':

> It is by no means my intention to assert, that women should be passive and indifferent spectators of the great political questions, which affect the well-being of the community, neither can I repeat the old adage, that 'women have nothing to do with politics;' they have, and ought to have, much to do with politics.[10]

In her various books on women's position Ellis accused young women of being more interested in fashion than foreign affairs and argued that politics was 'a serious subject, and one which ought to appeal to every mother's bosom'.[11] It is not the case then, that prescriptive literature delineated a depoliticized role for women—on the contrary. Nonetheless, as frustrated readers of Ellis, such as the early Victorian writers Geraldine Jewsbury and Elizabeth Barrett Browning were quick to appreciate, her message could be read as highly restrictive.[12] Ellis emphasized the impact which women's improved knowledge of current affairs might have upon their marriages, and noted that women's duty was to 'listen attentively' rather than to converse on such matters.[13]

Recent scholars have emphasized that the lived experience of Ellis and her wider female circle was far more expansive than that delineated in her prescriptive works. Ellis herself was publicly involved in a range of current

---

pamphlet in her youth: S. Hatfield, *Letters on the Importance of the Female Sex: With Observations on their Manners, and on Education* (London, 1803).

[10] Sarah Lewis, *Woman's Mission* (London, 1839, 2nd edn), 51. Lewis was a contemporary Episcopalian of whom little is known. The text was an elaboration upon *Sur l'education des mères* by M. Aimé Martin.

[11] Sarah Ellis, *The Women of England: Their Social Duties, and Domestic Habits* (London, 1839), 352–4, quote at 354. See also Ellis, *The Wives of England: Their Relative Duties, Domestic Influence, and Social Obligations* (London, 1843), 277–8. For revisionist critiques of Ellis's work see Henrietta Twycross-Martin, 'Woman Supportive or Woman Manipulative? The "Mrs Ellis" Woman', in Clarissa Campbell Orr (ed.), *Wollstonecraft's Daughters: Womanhood in England and France, 1780–1920* (Manchester, 1996), 109–20; Simon Morgan, *A Victorian Woman's Place: Public Culture in the Nineteenth Century* (London, 2007), 39–42.

[12] e.g. Geraldine E. Jewsbury to Jane Welsh Carlyle (22 Nov. 1849) and [1849] in Annie E. Ireland (ed.), *Selections from the Letters of Geraldine Endsor Jewsbury to Jane Welsh Carlyle* (London, 1892), 321, 349; Elizabeth Barrett Browning to Henry F. Chorley (1845) in F. G. Kenyon (ed.), *The Letters of Elizabeth Barrett Browning* (London, 1897, 2 vols), i. 235.

[13] Sarah Ellis, *The Daughters of England, their Position in Society, Character and Responsibilities* (London, 1842), 83–5.

affairs. Her friend Ann Taylor Gilbert likewise endorsed the language of domestic influence, rejecting female enfranchisement as she pointed to the many ways in which women might engage in political questions through their domestic and affective roles. Yet Taylor's own public activities were also considerable, including the organization of an anti-Corn Law petition in Nottingham.[14] Nonetheless, whilst the language of domestic influence did not map neatly onto the actualities of women's lives, this does not mean that they were unaffected by it. The cultural landscape of contemporary discourses profoundly shaped women's sensibilities. In describing her labours to friends Ellis reaffirmed the doctrine of female inferiority and made a gendered distinction between different spheres of political pursuits. She referred to elections and French politics as 'weighty matters' 'pertaining unto the great' in contrast to 'my own sphere', in which she included her anti-slavery tract.[15] Gilbert was beset by similar sensitivities. She fretted to one correspondent about the difficulty in 'drawing the line correctly between *in door* and *out of doors* business'.[16] Women might feel constrained to position their political activities as a secondary and explicitly feminine mode; and extant correspondence belies a recurring anxiety that others should not see their actions as unorthodox.

Of course, historians have identified the many ways in which contemporaries appropriated discourses of gender difference to claim a greater public role for women. Within the networks of liberal Anglicanism and Nonconformity, the notions of 'woman's mission' to succour the poor and disadvantaged was used to smooth their inclusion into humanitarian campaigns such as pacifism, anti-slavery, and temperance.[17] And, as scholars of the Chartist movement have established, maternalism in particular could be employed subversively to claim new rights within the public sphere.[18]

---

[14] Alison Twells, 'Missionary Domesticity, Global Reform and "Woman's Sphere" in Early Nineteenth-Century England', *Gender and History*, 18 (2006), 266–84; Josiah Gilbert (ed.), *Autobiography and Other Memorials of Mrs Gilbert* (London, 1874, 2 vols), i. 176–88.

[15] Sarah Stickney Ellis to 'a friend' (13 July 1821) and to 'MC' (Aug. 1830), in Sarah Ellis, *The Home Life and Letters of Mrs Ellis: Compiled by her Nieces* (London, 1893), 14–15, 39.

[16] Cited in Clare Midgley, *Women against Slavery: The British Campaigns, 1780–1870* (London, 1992), 75.

[17] Alex Tyrrell, ' "Woman's Mission" and Pressure Group Politics (1825–60)', *Bulletin of the John Rylands University Library*, 63 (1980), 194–230.

[18] Anna Clark, 'The Rhetoric of Chartist Domesticity: Gender, Language and Class in the 1830s and 1840s', *Journal of British Studies*, 31 (1992), 62–88; Michelle de Larrabeiti, 'Conspicuous before the World: The Political Rhetoric of the Chartist Women', in Eileen J. Yeo (ed.), *Radical Femininity: Women's Self-Representation in the Public Sphere* (Manchester, 1998), 106–26.

Elizabeth Heyrick adopted a gender-neutral tone in her influential anti-slavery tract of 1824, *Immediate Not Gradual Abolition*, but when she wished to appeal to a wider female audience four years later Heyrick (a childless widow) privileged maternal sensibilities.[19] Whilst gendered discourses could be employed in this strategic manner, this does not mean to say that they functioned simply as fluid identities to be enacted or discarded as the occasion required. The persistent reiteration of these gendered tropes of women's familial interests compromised women's ability to claim political agency in their own right.

Moreover, despite the ubiquitous recourse to gendered notions of middle-class femininity in easing women's entry into civic and philanthropic ventures, this was not an uncontested process, and there was no consensus that wider mobilization along these lines was necessarily appropriate. Despite the much-vaunted association between women and charity, these activities were commonly subject to satire and hostile comment. The formation of female auxiliary societies was decried by many churchmen. One Liverpool clergymen derided female members of Bible societies for their 'zeal that knows no limitation', and accused them of acting like a 'theological police'.[20] As Simon Morgan's study of early Victorian Leeds underlines, many contemporaries deemed home visiting to be incompatible with decorous womanhood, and visiting societies themselves sometimes struggled to find sufficient numbers to assist in their work.[21] The Scottish physiologist Alexander Walker (1779–1852) included female charity in his declamation against women's public activity: 'PHILANTHROPY, PATRIOTISM and POLITICS, not being matters of instinct, but of reason, are unsuited to the mind of woman'.[22] These attitudes often had a theological profile, with High Church commentators such as the Tractarian educationist Elizabeth Sewell being particularly quick to critique the evangelizing tendencies of her peers.[23] The circulation of unflattering images of domineering busybodies betrayed a more deeply rooted uneasiness concerning the contours of women's public work, however. As Marianne Thornton, the daughter of

---

[19] Elizabeth Heyrick, *Immediate, Not Gradual Abolition; Or, an Inquiry into the Shortest, Safest, and Most Effectual Means of Getting Rid of West Indian Slavery* (London, 1824); Heyrick, *Appeal to the Hearts and Consciences of British Women* (Leicester, 1828). See also pp. 149–50 below.

[20] 'A Churchman', *A Letter to the Church Members of the Auxiliary Bible Society, Liverpool* (Liverpool, 1819), 7, 10.

[21] Morgan, *Victorian Woman's Place*, 81.

[22] Alexander Walker, *Woman Physiologically Considered as to Mind, Morals, Marriage, Matrimonial Slavery, Infidelity and Divorce* (London, 1840), 67.

[23] Eleanor L. Sewell (ed.), *The Autobiography of Elizabeth Missing Sewell* (London, 1907), 80.

the Evangelical banker, Henry Thornton, wrote to Patty Smith of an initiative in her community, 'Some busy & efficient people (Ladies of course) took it up here in that sort of bustling & violent way which busy Ladies are apt to pursue, & almost *mobbed* the peaceable inhabitants of the commons'.[24] Similarly the poet Caroline Bowles (later wife of Robert Southey) complained that charitable bazaars had a 'detestable exhibiting character'. She also protested that, 'One lady is President of this, another "Vice −" of that association. . . . all womankind is whirling round in a vortex of religious dissipation'.[25] Women themselves might therefore feel ill at ease with the development of female associational activities, and sometimes reinscribe such stereotypes even as they themselves transgressed them. Marianne Thornton alluded thus to the charitable activity of the Stanley family in Hannah More's popular novel, *Coelebs*: 'our Gents complain that we are far beyond the working Ladies in Coelebs, whom *once* we held in abhorrence — but alas! now we imitate and even surpass'.[26]

These ambiguities were further heightened by the existence of alternative counter-discourses, which opened up the potential for more empowering modes of female public engagement. The term 'politician' was used to denote those (men or women) who were distinguished for their detailed understanding of political affairs, although it was only exceptionally used to describe publicly active women.[27] The appellation was most commonly applied to women in private correspondence where it signified intellectual, rather than practical political commitment. Martha Somerville professed to Julia Smith that she was 'almost afraid to venture to say anything about politics to such an able politician as you'.[28]

Meanwhile in the networks of ultra-Protestantism more explicit calls for female public assertion were made. Here, a premillenarian Evangelicalism was in ascendance (in contrast to the moderate Evangelicalism which typified Nonconformist and liberal Anglican circles). Premillenarians urged far-reaching activity to ensure the beneficent judgement of Christ—believed

---

[24] Marianne Thornton to Patty Smith [1827], Cambridge University Library (CUL), ADD 7674/3/A. See also Marianne Thornton to Hannah More (1828), CUL, Add 7674/3/L.

[25] Caroline Bowles to Robert Southey (21 Oct. 1828 and 18 Apr. 1826), in Edward Dowden (ed.), *Correspondence of Robert Southey with Caroline Bowles* (Dublin, 1881), 146, 103–4. Catherine Hutton was similarly scathing of the work of local Bible societies: Catherine Hutton to Miss Greathead (28 June 1812), Birmingham City Archives, Hutton MS, 58.

[26] Marianne Thornton to Hannah More (21 June 1833), CUL, ADD 7621/457.

[27] For one such example see *Isis* (4 Aug. 1832), 385.

[28] Martha Somerville to Julia Smith (21 June 1833), CUL, Add 7621/457.

to be the critical precursor to the millennium.[29] Evangelicals of this persuasion often argued that certain circumstances were so pressing that women
were compelled to involve themselves in political affairs. The Evangelical
pamphleteer Jane Alice Sargant might advise that women were divinely
appointed to 'the secluded scenes of domestic life' in her protest against
female anti-slavery petitions,[30] but during political crises, such as the
Queen Caroline affair, she appealed to Hannah More to act as a 'mother in
Israel' to save the country in its hour of need.[31] Women's magazines like the
Englishwoman's Magazine and the *Christian Lady's Magazine* urged a similar
message. The editor of the latter, Charlotte Elizabeth Tonna, exhorted
women to mobilize against Roman Catholicism and for state intervention
so as to appease divine wrath. Whilst mindful of the need to demonstrate
an adherence to the notion of woman's 'proper sphere', she drew upon Old
Testament examples of dynamic, even militaristic female behaviour alluding
to the exceptional examples provided by Abigail, Deborah, and Esther as
women divinely appointed to lead their communities.[32]

Tonna also evoked the image of a 'mother in Israel'—an appellation
with very different associations to the image of benevolent womanhood
outlined in the works of Ellis, Lewis, and the like. Associated with early
modern Quakers, it was a term enjoying a revival in our period as a means
of signalling the economic authority and religious influence that typified
the community leadership of some contemporary women.[33] Even within

---

[29] Brian Dickey, ' "Going About and Doing Good": Evangelicals and Poverty, c. 1815–1870',
in John Wolffe (ed.), *Evangelical Faith and Public Zeal: Evangelicals and Society in Britain,
1780–1980* (London, 1995), 38–58.

[30] Jane Alice Sargant, *An Address to the Females of Great Britain on the Propriety of their
Petitioning Parliament for the Abolition of Negro Slavery* (London, 1833), 4. It was originally
published in the *John Bull* newspaper. For other examples of Sargant's work see pp. 173–4
below.

[31] Jane Alice Sargant, *An Englishwoman's Letter to Mrs Hannah More, on the Present Crisis*
(London, 1820), 3.

[32] *Christian Lady's Magazine*, 6 (1836), 24–30; 12 (1839), 512–18; 3 (1835), 85. See also
Englishwoman's Magazine (June 1851), 366–70; Kathryn Gleadle, 'Charlotte Elizabeth Tonna
and the Mobilization of Tory Women in Early Victorian England', *Historical Journal*, 50
(2007), 97–117. Clara Lucas Balfour similarly dwelt upon empowering examples of Old
Testament women in *The Women of Scripture* (London, 1847). Old Testament models had the
potential to be appropriated for feminist discourses. A Mrs Wigfield emphasized the example
of the prophetess Miriam at a women's rights meeting held at Leicester Town Hall in 1857:
Liverpool Mercury (24 July 1857).

[33] *Christian Lady's Magazine*, 2 (1834), 199. For earlier articulations of the model: Phyllis
Mack, *Visionary Women: Ecstatic Prophecy in Seventeenth-Century England* (Berkeley, Calif.,
1992), 215–46. See also below pp. 128 and 138.

the premillenarian camp these formulations could be controversial, however. Tonna's friend Mary Ann Stodart, herself the author of a number of works on female education and related themes, protested that the female role was essentially domestic.[34]

Therefore, whilst there were overt claims for female public engagement these did not go unchallenged. Equally, there were usually points of nuance in the opposition to female politics. When the *Edinburgh Review* denounced female public engagement note that local activity was exempted from the critique: 'The less women usually meddle with any thing which can be called public life *out of their village*, we are sure the better for all parties'.[35] Similarly Tory MP George Canning's censure of female politics was quickly followed by caveats: 'a woman has no business at all with politicks, or that if she thinks at all about them, it should be at least in a feminine manner, as wishing for the peace and prosperity of her country—and for the success and credit of those of her family'.[36] Moreover, criticisms of female political involvement did not necessarily provide a simple representation of an individual's own position, but were often marshalled to support a wider political point. The highly contingent nature of these gendered representations emerged clearly during the Queen Caroline controversy of 1820 when the country was divided by the King's attempts to divorce his wife. James McCord discovered that 'all sides deployed gender in political arguments'— thus the loyalist *John Bull* lambasted Whig ladies for their support of the Queen, yet wrote with equanimity of those ladies who were associated with the King's cause.[37] Women were thus widely evoked as political subjects, but ambiguously so. The ubiquity of representations which marginalized female politics in relation to their maternal and wifely roles, or portrayed it as an exceptional phenomenon, could make women cautious about publicly articulating an independent and forthright political identity.

Historical attention has often focused upon specific moments of politicization, sparked by particular campaigns or episodes (such as anti-slavery, the effects of the Napoleonic Wars, or the Queen Caroline affair). Here it

---

[34] M. A. Stodart, *Every Day Duties: In Letters to a Young Lady* (London, 1840), *passim*, but see esp. 20–5.

[35] *Edinburgh Review*, 57 (Apr. 1833), 3; my emphasis.

[36] Amanda Vickery, 'Introduction', in Vickery (ed.), *Women, Privilege and Power*, 17.

[37] James McCord, 'Taming the Female Politician in Early Nineteenth-Century England: *John Bull* versus Lady Jersey', *Journal of Women's History*, 13 (2002), 31–53.

will be emphasized that women's day-to-day political participation was also predicated within a richer, more highly variable, landscape of opportunity. For example, as Chapters 1 and 4 will investigate, as householders and economic agents women commonly intervened in parochial politics. Yet women performed various personas across the sites of political expression to which they had access. Thus Anna Gurney of Overstrand in Norfolk felt empowered to provide the infrastructure for her local community (including roads, the church, a school, lifeboat service, and adult education facilities), was sufficiently confident to preach in the parish church, authored her cousin's parliamentary reports, and yet *still* claimed in private correspondence that she believed a woman's sphere should be a limited one.[38]

We need a theoretical model, therefore, which will enable us to understand the manifold contradictions in women's lives. In particular, in seeking to understand these complex manifestations of individual subjectivity we need to consider the varied and mutable operation of gender. In order to do this, this book is situated within the broad canon of feminist scholarship. As Alexandra Shepard observed in 2004, 'more recent scholarship is beginning to demonstrate [that] gender was not a monolithic category of identity and it interacted in subtle ways with many other determinants of status'.[39] However, feminist scholarship has never been simply about analysing its subjects through the single lens of gender. Thus Jane Rendall argued in 1987 that, 'Gender was not necessarily the primary factor determining women's loyalties and interests. There were other loyalties, most obviously to class and community.'[40]

Inspired in part by the insights of poststructuralist critique, the assumption that gender was but one factor in a complex grid of influences, determinants, and variables became widespread in the wider canon of feminist scholarship from the late 1980s. In the influential collection published in 1990 by Linda J. Nicholson, *Feminism/Postmodernism*, she and Nancy Fraser urged for a feminism that would recognize the 'plural and complexly constructed conceptions of social identity, treating gender as one relevant strand among others, attending also to class, race, ethnicity, age, and sexual

---

[38] See pp. 242–8 below.

[39] Alexandra Shepard, 'Honesty, Worth and Gender in Early Modern England, 1560–1640', in Henry French and Jonathan Barry (eds), *Identity and Agency in England, 1500–1800* (Basingstoke, 2004), 89.

[40] Jane Rendall, 'Introduction', in Rendall (ed.), *Equal or Different: Women's Politics, 1800–1914* (Oxford, 1987), 4.

orientation'.[41] Gender does not operate in a 'pure' form but rather works in combination with other categories.[42]

These were concerns which were echoed across the social sciences. Of particular importance for the current study is the work of feminist social psychologists such as Kay Deaux and Brenda Major. Deaux and Major caution that gender identity is perceived differently by individual agents, who might variously perceive themselves as, say, 'womanly, feminine, or feminist', and even within these broad categories they note that there are likely to be substantial variations. Deaux and Major therefore seek to apply a flexible, contingent concept of gender in their work, pointing to its 'situational' nature and noting that gender will be differently involved in different contexts. In order to plot the flexibility and fluidity of gender across particular social contexts they call for 'micro-level analysis' of interaction 'which would allow for a complex and detailed mapping of the variability and contingency of gendered discourses and behaviour'.[43]

The current book has been closely informed by such an approach. A potential danger, of course, is that meticulous attention to the particular combinations of various social determinants operating in any one context has the effect of muting broader structural factors. Comparable concerns troubled those feminists who queried postmodernism's embrace of the dizzying constellations of mutating identities. Susan Bordo was one of those who, whilst welcoming 'the invaluable insight that gender forms only one axis of a complex heterogeneous construction', feared 'a universe composed entirely of counterexamples, in which the way men and women see the world is purely as *particular* individuals, shaped by the unique configurations that form that particularity'. Bordo worried that 'Too relentless a focus on historical heterogeneity' would serve to disguise the enduring, structural

[41] Nancy Fraser and Linda J. Nicholson, 'Social Criticism without Philosophy: An Encounter between Feminism and Postmodernism', in Linda J. Nicholson (ed.), *Feminism/Postmodernism* (London and New York, 1990), 34–5.

[42] See Susan Bordo, 'Feminism, Postmodernism and Gender-Scepticism', in Nicholson, *Feminism/Postmodernism*, 150; Toril Moi, 'Appropriating Bourdieu: Feminist Theory and Pierre Bourdieu's Sociology of Culture (1990)', in Moi, *What is a Woman? And Other Essays* (Oxford, 1999), 264–99, here at 291.

[43] Kay Deaux and Brenda Major, 'A Social-Psychological Model of Gender', in Deborah L. Rhode (ed.), *Theoretical Perspectives on Sexual Difference* (New Haven and London, 1990), 89–99. See also Bernice Lott, 'Dual Natures or Learned Behaviour: The Challenge to Feminist Psychology', in Rachel T. Hare-Mustin and Jeanne Marecek (eds), *Making a Difference: Psychology and the Construction of Gender* (New Haven and London, 1990), 65–101.

hierarchies of 'white, male privilege'.[44] A central question for historians of gender and women's history today is to reconcile a perspective which recognizes the shifting significance of gender across the discrete aspects of an individual's identity with one which retains a sense of the enduring role of embedded gendered inequalities.

Over the past fifteen years many scholars have sought to square intellectual problems of this nature by embracing the work of the 'new' sociologists who conceptualize society as a process rather than a structure. Thus historians Michael J. Braddick and John Walter urge that in order to understand the 'multiplicity of exchanges by which domination was achieved and subordination negotiated' we need to turn to 'micro-sociologies of power and of social roles'.[45] Two scholars have been particularly influential in developing these 'microtheories' of social power. The first of these is the French sociologist Pierre Bourdieu. His examination of the role played by agents in reproducing social structures, and his insistence on the primacy of cultural and symbolic domains in constituting social relations promises, for many, a plausible means of linking micro and macro. As the feminist critic Toril Moi observes, in Bourdieu's analyses the 'humdrum details of every day life', including individuals' quotidian and unconscious adoption of social and cultural codes, are related to a 'more general social analysis of power'. Moi takes from Bourdieu's 'microtheory of social power' and 'painstaking attentiveness to the particular case', the insight that 'gender is always a socially *variable* entity, one which carries different amounts of symbolic capital in different contexts'.[46]

Secondly, the work of the British sociologist Anthony Giddens, and in particular his theory of 'structuration', has been a critical inspiration. Here social structures are seen as composed of the actions of knowing agents who are both constrained by these frameworks but also themselves reproduce those arrangements in social interaction. Giddens himself has not focused upon the implications of his theory for women or gender.

---

[44] Bordo, 'Feminism, Postmodernism and Gender-Scepticism', 139, 149, 151. See also Kathleen Canning, 'Feminist History After the Linguistic Turn: Historicizing Discourse and Experience', *Signs*, 19 (1994), 368–404.

[45] See the editors' introduction in Michael J. Braddick and John Walter (eds), *Negotiating Power in Early Modern Society: Order, Hierarchy and Subordination in Britain and Ireland* (Cambridge, 2001), here at 16, 1.

[46] Moi, 'Appropriating Bourdieu', 268, 291. For other feminist readings of Bourdieu see Terry Lovell, 'Thinking Feminism with and against Bourdieu', in Bridget Fowler (ed.), *Reading Bourdieu on Society and Culture* (Oxford, 2000), 27–48; Lisa Adkins and Beverley Skeggs (eds), *Feminism After Bourdieu* (Oxford, 2005). For Bourdieu see esp. his *Outline of a Theory of Practice* (Cambridge, 1977) and *Masculine Domination* (Cambridge, 2001).

However, his concerns with the relationship between individual agency and social structure and his emphasis upon language as a social practice have considerable potential for analysing the ways in which women might participate in patriarchal structures whilst simultaneously experiencing selfhood as a creative and dynamic process.[47]

Both these approaches have informed the present work. It is argued that prevailing discourses on gender were upheld and affirmed through the agency of knowing individuals—individuals whose own sense of self was partially constituted by these same cultural resources of gendered ideology. The methodology of the book is to apply extensive empirical research to compile layers of micro-analyses, exploring the decisions made by numerous historical actors within precise social contexts. These detailed analyses are chosen from points of tension within contemporary discourses or practice. They are moments of ambiguity or indeterminacy, examples that stretch the interstitial spaces between convention and innovation, tradition and change.[48] The hope is that these perspectives provide a fruitful framework for understanding both the 'situational' nature of gender, and its varying salience across different contexts; whilst also remaining sensitive to the subtle processes whereby collective representations of femininity became woven into individual subjectivities.[49] Attempts have been made, therefore, to wed these micro-analyses to a broader, more synthetic appreciation of the structural constraints and opportunities within which individual acts may be located.

In dissecting the negotiations, manœuvres, and tensions that micro-studies reveal, the approach taken here is unashamedly eclectic. Back in

[47] Anthony A. Giddens, *The Constitution of Society: Outline of the Theory of Structuration* (Cambridge, 1984). For discussion see Linda Murgatroyd, 'Only Half the Story: Some Blinkering Effects of "Malestream" Sociology', in David Held and John B. Thompson (eds), *Social Theory of Modern Societies: Anthony Giddens and his Critics* (Cambridge, 1989), 147–61; Rita Felski, *Beyond Feminist Aesthetics: Feminist Literature and Social Change* (London, 1989), 55–62.

[48] See Giovanni Levi, 'On Microhistory', in P. Burke (ed.), *New Perspectives on Historical Writing* (Pennsylvania, 2001, 2nd edn), 107.

[49] Deaux and Major, 'A Social-Psychological Model of Gender'; Deborah Baker and Suzanne Skevington (eds), *The Social Identity of Women* (London, 1989); Karyn Stapleton, 'In Search of the Self: Feminism, Postmodernism and Identity', *Feminism and Psychology*, 10 (2000), 463–9; Peggy A. Thoits and Lauren K. Virshup, '"Me's and We's": Forms and Functions of Social Identities', in Richard D. Ashmore and Lee Jussim (eds), *Self and Identity: Fundamental Issues* (Oxford and New York, 1997), 106–33; Patrizia Violi, 'Gender, Subjectivity and Language', in Gisella Bock and Susan James (eds), *Beyond Equality and Difference: Citizenship, Feminist Politics and Female Subjectivity* (London, 1992), 164–76.

1990 Fraser and Nicholson encouraged the development of a feminist theory which 'might tailor its methods and categories to the specific task at hand, using multiple categories when appropriate and forswearing the metaphysical comfort of a single feminist method or feminist epistemology. In short, this theory would look more like a tapestry composed of threads of many different hues than one woven in a single color'.[50] It is not supposed that the present study matches their vision, but it does seek to draw pragmatically upon a range of insights garnered from feminist perspectives across the boundaries of discipline. Fresh dialogue with the social sciences it is proposed—and especially recent departures in sociology and psychology—enables us to refine theoretical formulations of the self and to better conceptualize the relationship between social structure and individual agency.

Focusing upon the concept of women's political subjectivity provides the opportunity to assess critically the precise historical function of gender. Subjectivity is understood here as the process whereby individuals seek to make sense of their own experience and identities through the cultural resources available to them. As feminist historians Kathleen Canning and Sonya Rose put it, 'subjectivity captures the complexities of citizenship as both highly individualised and, at the same time, a collectively invoked social identity and subject position'.[51] Selves are not simply products or effects of discourse but are forged in dialectical relationship with others; and, as recent feminist scholars have emphasized, the experience of the body is also an important site for the construction of subjectivity.[52]

In seeking to explore how it *felt* to be engaged in politics as an early nineteenth-century woman we are reliant upon extant texts such as diaries, pamphlets, and, in particular, letters. Recent accounts of female political epistolarity have tended to use letters as a positive indicator of women's widespread public involvement. For feminist historians they have often

[50] Fraser and Nicholson, 'Social Criticism', 35.
[51] Kathleen Canning and Sonya O. Rose, 'Gender, Citizenship and Subjectivity: Some Historical and Theoretical Considerations', *Gender and History*, 13 (2001), 432.
[52] For helpful discussion: Maureen A. Mahoney and Barbara Yngvesson, 'The Construction of Subjectivity and the Paradox of Resistance: Reintegrating Feminist Anthropology and Psychology', *Signs*, 18 (1992), 44–73; Linda Alcoff, 'Cultural Feminism versus Post-Structuralism: The Identity Crisis in Feminist Theory', in Nicholas B. Dirks *et al.* (eds), *Culture/Power/History: A Reader in Contemporary Social Theory* (Princeton, 1994), 96–122; Angela Woollacott, 'The Fragmentary Subject: Feminist History, Official Records, and Self-Representation', *Women's Studies International Forum*, 21 (1998), 329–39; Rosi Braidotti, *Nomadic Subjects: Embodiment and Sexual Difference in Contemporary Feminist Theory* (New York, 1994), 3–4.

been used as a means of integrating female experience into analyses of the 'public sphere' famously outlined by Jürgen Habermas. For Habermas, the 'public sphere' comprised the variety of forums and sites where individual actors were able to come together to discuss and critique political and intellectual matters, thus forming a critical source of potential opposition to the state. Women's letters have been conceptualized as a critical component of this 'bourgeois' public sphere of rational discussion, facilitating the circulation of political debates and validating political identities in the process.[53] Nonetheless, such texts can also expose the tensions and fragilities which marked the construction of female political subjectivity. Letters functioned as tools for local and political influence but also as sites for the display of female anxieties. The letters of many politically active women reveal not only agency and authority but also striking expressions of disempowerment, uncertainty as to their political views, and a blurring of the contours of their own agency.

Documents of this nature do not provide us with transparent indicators of female identity, therefore, but rather enable us to consider the ways in which women might wish to convey their interest to others, or fashion themselves as political actors in particular circumstances to specific audiences. Equally, our analyses must be informed by a consideration of the ways in which a particular archive might have been constructed and selected. Furthermore, the performance of an identity or identities in a letter or run of letters cannot be read as a simple manifestation of 'subjectivity'. They form part of the tapestry which comprises the various layers and aspects of subjectivity. We need to consider how these textual articulations relate to other utterances, and also to the broader experiences and opportunities of an individual. These facets of subjectivity functioned together in the construction of selfhood.

Therefore, whilst the book is concerned to excavate how self-identities might fluctuate across different contexts and be variously constituted and

[53] Jane Rendall, '"Friends of Liberty & Virtue": Women Radicals and Transatlantic Correspondence, 1789–1848', in Caroline Bland and Máire Cross (eds), *Gender and Politics in the Age of Letter-Writing, 1750–2000* (Aldershot, 2004), 77–92; Catriona Kennedy, '"Womanish Epistles?": Martha McTier, Female Epistolarity and Late Eighteenth-Century Irish Radicalism', *Women's History Review*, 13 (2004), 649–67; Sarah Richardson, '"Well-Neighboured Houses": The Political Networks of Elite Women, 1780–1860', in Kathryn Gleadle and Sarah Richardson (eds), *Women in British Politics, 1760–1860: The Power of the Petticoat* (Basingstoke, 2000), 58–60. Habermas's theories are fully elaborated in his *The Structural Transformation of the Public Sphere* (1989), tr. Thomas Burger (Cambridge, 1992). For debate see Craig Calhoun (ed.), *Habermas and the Public Sphere* (Cambridge, Mass., 1992).

articulated according to circumstance, this is not to subscribe to a view of the essentially fragmentary nature of the self, nor to argue that subjectivity was endlessly fluid. As Braddick and Walter note, individuals could present a 'variety' of selves, nonetheless whilst individuals had 'some tactical freedom', there were limitations to the roles which could be adopted. Social relationships, they observe, were not 'anarchic'.[54] Insights from the field of social psychology assist in further refining these perspectives. As Dan McAdams argues, it is essential to consider how the various selves an individual might present are nonetheless integrated so as to 'retain a certain degree of unity and coherence'.[55] The feminist psychologist Karyn Stapleton agrees, insisting that despite the 'variable and contingent' nature of discursive constructions of the gendered self, 'some form of personal coherence is necessary in formulating "selves"'.[56] So, as we dissect the many and complex manifestations of self-presentation, we also need to keep in our minds the ways in which individuals are distinguishable from each other because of the clustering of core traits.[57]

One of the aims of this study is to consider how individuals reconciled, ordered, aligned, or silenced various aspects of the self so as to retain their own coherence as persons, to project acceptable modes of femininity, or to maximize the success of particular gendered performances. Accordingly the book is structured so that Part I, 'Women, gender and the landscape of politics', probes the different sites of female endeavour and the multiple ways in which women might engage in the political process and exhibit various forms of political identity. Part II, 'Case studies and micro-histories', seeks to bring these together by analysing particular examples in greater depth. Negotiating between the different sites and expression of female public activity were durable behaviour traits and personal sensibilities, but, as we shall see, these shifts in register came at a price. Even confident political actors frequently displayed fractured or uneasy political subjectivities.

In Chapter 1 the multiple ways in which women were considered as political subjects is outlined. Investigating the formal and quasi-formal position of women *vis-à-vis* the functioning of the state (as constituency members, local electors, parliamentary petitioners, or social policy experts)

---

[54] Braddick and Walter, 'Introduction', in *Negotiating Power*, 38.

[55] Dan P. McAdams, 'The Case for Unity in the (Post)Modern Self: A Modest Proposal', in Ashmore and Jussim, *Self and Identity*, 48.

[56] Stapleton, 'In Search of the Self', 464–5.

[57] David A. Jopling, 'A Self of Selves?' in Ulric Neisser and David A. Jopling (eds), *The Conceptual Self in Context: Culture, Experience, Self-Understanding* (Cambridge, 1997), 249–67.

enables us to plot more fully the ways in which citizenship was defined, and the place of women within this imaginary. Whilst this indicates the manifold political sites available to women, their location within them was never entirely secure. Women's rights as citizens were continually in the process of construction and were always vulnerable to challenge and dismissal. As such, women were but 'borderline' citizens.

In Chapters 2–4 the analysis will proceed by considering the divergent ways in which female political agency was configured within the various forums of the home, the community, and the 'public sphere'. Scholars of gender history have criticized the division of individual experience into the dichotomized departments of 'private' and 'public'. We now have much more sophisticated understandings of the blurrings and interdependence of these two notions, and are more sensitive to the multiple—and sometimes contradictory meanings—which they may have held for contemporaries.[58] As Jane Rendall observes, 'a single vision of the public sphere is insufficient to allow us to understand the complicated variety of ways in which women might identify with communities which stretched far beyond the borders—whatever those were—of home and family'. It is argued here that we do need to remain attentive to the differing possibilities and gendered codes which operated in these spaces. As Rendall notes, we should think, in terms of a variety of publics, and analyse women's activities in relation to the vexed interactions between them.[59] One way to develop such an approach is to adopt the model of public spheres advanced by geographers such as Lyn H. Lofland. Lofland distinguishes between the 'public realm' and the 'parochial realm'. Here the public realm includes 'those spaces in a city which tend to be inhabited by persons who are strangers to one another or who "know" one another only in terms of occupational or other non-personal identity categories'. The parochial realm does not refer to the historical construct of the parish, but rather denotes 'the world of the neighbourhood, workplace, or acquaintance networks'—social relationships based upon personal knowledge and close social interaction. These two realms therefore relate not to physical spaces (although the meanings engendered by specific locations are important) but to the nature of the relationships within a given context.[60]

---

[58] See esp. Lawrence Klein, 'Gender and the Public/Private Distinction in the Eighteenth Century: Some Questions about Evidence and Analytic Procedure', *Eighteenth-Century Studies*, 29 (1995), 97–109.

[59] Jane Rendall, 'Women and the Public Sphere', *Gender and History*, 11 (1999), 478–88.

[60] Lofland is following the formulation of Albert Hunter. Lyn H. Lofland, *The Public Realm: Exploring the City's Quintessential Social Territory* (New York, 1998), 11–14.

The argument advanced here is that contemporaries frequently conceived of women's public roles differently in the parochial realm, where they had greater latitude to act as community figures, than they did in the public realm. In this 'community sphere', as delineated in Chapter 4, women could accrue considerable authority as individual agents through philanthropy, economic status, local print culture, family connections, and their own political efforts. Social status and educational privilege were, in these contexts, often more important than gender in structuring the contours of female opportunity. Whilst these parochial realms provided the greatest opportunities for women, they were also the most threatened by broader processes of social, political, and cultural change.

By contrast, Chapter 2 considers the 'public sphere' of bourgeois associational life. This involves an analysis of the construction of gender difference during those occasions where people met together on the basis of their collective identities—as campaigners for a particular cause, for example. Here, their contributions were more constrained and more frequently contested, and even progressive women tended to replicate normative understandings of the hegemony of the masculine public sphere. In this context, where attention was focused upon women as a collective group, the terms of middle-class women's engagement developed similar conventions to those which often shaped and restricted plebeian women's activities (as in the Chartist movement). In contrast, in the parochial sphere their capacity for public action was more similar to elite and gentry women who derived their authority from individual status and authority. In analysing the distinction between the parochial and the public spheres the aim is not to introduce another unhelpful dichotomy. The two categories are not, of course, fixed in meaning, but could be fluid or blurred, thus creating further ambiguity as to the nature of women's public role. Indeed, understanding the interstices between these two fields of social relationships helps to further explain the intricacies surrounding women's public roles.

The other substantive chapter of Part I, Chapter 3, considers the formation and functioning of political identities within the familial domain. Family practices, such as cooperation in elections and home-based political discussions, were extremely significant, but did not necessarily result in the construction of empowering female subjectivities and they could even entrench male dominance. Not all female members were as strongly involved as others in the maintenance of a family political tradition and family political engagement could itself be episodic. Women were particularly likely to articulate their political subjectivity as part of a collective familial identity. The household and notions of collective identity remained central to conceptions of the self. Indeed, attention to these various forms of collective identity (in both the family context and the civic sphere) complicates assumptions as to this supposed emergence of a dominant, individual liberal subject in this period.[61]

Part II develops these arguments through three detailed case studies. Chapter 5 considers the Reform Act of 1832. Its exclusion of women from the franchise has long been argued to symbolize the hegemony of the masculine political subject. It is suggested here that parliamentary assumptions were less clear-cut. For example, cabinet members entertained highly divergent views towards women's political involvement, and female voting was sanctioned in the Vestries Act (1831). A number of parliamentary debates in 1831–2 did consider women's electoral privileges and also female petitions on reform, revealing a wide spectrum of views. The Reform Act affirmed not women's exclusion from the political nation, but rather crystallized their ambivalent positioning within the contemporary political imaginary.

These complexities were played out beyond Westminster. Publishers might market prominent female authors as explicitly political contributions to the debate, but contemporaries made a tacit distinction between these exceptional women and the representation of the rank and file. Widespread female involvement in local political campaigning was marginalized in subsequent reports which reinscribed passive feminine images. These conflicting processes were significant. The reform crisis precipitated an intense politicization which many women could find hard to weave into a feminine self-identity. This often led to the reactive performance of a heightened feminine sensibility, or the recourse to a collective familial identity.

Chapter 6 considers the career of Mary Ann Gilbert (1776–1845). Many studies of female politics focus upon exceptional women. It is argued here that the process whereby some women attained a cultural position where they were 'exempt' from the usual prescriptions of their gender needs to be subject to analytical scrutiny. Gilbert was recognized in her day as a leading agricultural and educational reformer. Her activities had a major impact upon the operations of Eastbourne parochial politics and were widely cited in parliamentary reports. Gilbert and her networks reveal the importance of those women who eschewed free trade politics and defended the agricultural interest. Land, it is suggested, was of enduring

[61] For the argument that the 18th cent. saw the rise of the 'privatized individual', empowered to act in public because of the new configuration of the rational subject created in the family sphere, see Habermas, *Structural Transformation*, esp. 43–53.

significance within political culture. Dynastic subjectivity and the rich resonance of kinship, place, and regional identity were central to Gilbert, revealing further complexities to the relationship between women, the family, and politics.

Finally, Chapter 7 analyses the gendered politics of the family network of Thomas Fowell Buxton. Buxton's speeches and select committee reports were the product of an extraordinary collective endeavour by his wider family. It will be argued here that the name 'Thomas Fowell Buxton' functioned as a corporate persona. It was freely utilized by other family members who might undertake political writing in his name without needing to gain his sanction. The willingness to suspend their individual political identities derived from their self-perception as instruments of Providence—devoted ciphers acting for a higher purpose. Nonetheless, the gendered dynamics of the family network meant that women's collaboration sometimes had an adverse affect upon their own subjectivities. In contrast in the 'parochial realm' of their villages the women of the Buxton network functioned as empowered community leaders, providing and managing much of the local infrastructure. They still found it necessary to maintain highly gendered identities when representing these activities, however. The Buxton women were differently positioned again in the public domain of pressure-group politics, as competing accounts of an anti-slavery meeting they attended in Norwich in 1840 reveal. Extant letters provide illuminating insights into the intricate relationships women might experience between status, identity, and public space. Yet they also reveal that women's participation in anti-slavery remained a possible source of tension. Female reports of their treatment at the meeting were somewhat disingenuous—an indication of the brittle fragility of women's self-positioning in the public sphere. This chapter thus provides the opportunity to analyse synthetically the varying experiences of women across the different domains of political opportunity outlined in Part I.

Excavating female sensibility in this way reveals a range of neglected themes which disrupt many traditional narratives. These include the persistence of early modern articulations of selfhood; familial and collaborative methods of work and authorship; the differing modes which distinguished parochial from other formal political spheres; and the significance of cultural status in the construction of individuals' local political authority. The continuing resonance of land within political subjectivities is a particularly important theme. Whilst recent scholarship has tended to focus on the urban context, for many women it was the local, rural community which provided the canvas for their activities, and land and its management that enabled the exercise of knowledge and ideological agendas. Equally, previous considerations of the political activities of middle-class women have emphasized their commitment to radical and liberal movements.[62] Here I wish to extend the scope of investigation to include a range of conservative political traditions.

The emergence of a distinctive middle-class identity has been viewed as a central factor in analyses of early Victorian political culture. Asa Briggs identified the anti-Corn Law campaign as integral to the crystallization of middle-class consciousness; whilst Robert Morris emphasized the centrality of voluntarist culture to the emerging middle class.[63] Famously, Leonore Davidoff and Catherine Hall have delineated the ways in which the emergence of the British middle class was predicated upon a growing adherence to a set of normative gendered conventions and assumptions. This included an emphasis upon a masculine public sphere which, whilst never hegemonic in its exclusion of women, nonetheless encouraged a powerful identification of the political world with men. It is a perspective which has been subsequently reworked by the likes of Simon Gunn, who also emphasizes the masculinist basis of the bourgeois urban sphere.[64] Compelling though these narratives are, in the present study female public opportunities are detached from broader arguments concerning the nature of class formation *per se*. As Ruth Grayson and Brian Lewis remind us, it is problematic to assume the existence of a homogeneous middle class. Lewis draws attention to the 'competing and conflicting agendas of fractions of the bourgeoisie'.[65] It will be suggested that too great a preoccupation with the distinctiveness of the middle-class experience can blind us to the important commonalities which operated across social strata. Economic status transpires to be a

[62] e.g. Simon Morgan, 'Domestic Economy and Political Agitation: Women and the Anti-Corn Law League, 1839–1846', and Kathryn Gleadle, '"Our Several Spheres": Middle-Class Women and the Feminisms of Early Victorian Radical Politics', in Gleadle and Richardson, *Women in British Politics*, 115–52; Helen Rogers, *Women and the People: Authority, Authorship and the Radical Tradition in Nineteenth-Century England* (Aldershot, 2000), ch. 4.

[63] Asa Briggs, 'Middle-Class Consciousness in English Politics, 1780–1846', *Past and Present*, 9 (1956), 71; R. J. Morris, *Class, Sect and Party: The Making of the British Middle Class: Leeds, 1820–1850* (Manchester, 1990), e.g. at 322.

[64] Simon Gunn, *The Public Culture of the Victorian Middle Class: Ritual and Authority and the English Industrial City, 1840–1914* (Manchester, 2000).

[65] Brian Lewis, '"A Republic of Quakers": The Radical Bourgeoisie, the State and Stability in Lancashire, 1789–1851', in Alan Kidd and David Nicholls (eds), *The Making of the British Middle Class? Studies of Regional and Cultural Diversity since the Eighteenth Century* (Stroud, 1998), 90; Ruth Grayson, 'Who was Master? Class Relationships in Nineteenth-Century Sheffield', ibid. 42–57.

critical factor in women's experience of the public in this study, but focus is placed on the myriad forms of authority which structured the contours of female political opportunity. Therefore, whilst the book is concerned broadly with the experiences of 'middle-class' women, it interprets its brief inclusively. The attention to small rural communities in addition to urban contexts has encouraged such an approach. As Amanda Vickery has demonstrated, at the parish level, there was not a clear-cut demarcation between the layers of the local elite which was composed of the families of the professional and mercantile classes as well as the lesser gentry.[66] The current book does not attempt to redress the current lacuna in the historiography of provincial gentry women in the 1820–70 period. Nonetheless, pointing to the commonalities and overlapping features of some aspects of gentry and middling women's opportunities is in keeping with the broader thematic structure of the book. In contrast to some recent narratives which have proposed an abrupt shift in selfhood in the 1780s,[67] it seeks to act as a reminder of the continuing importance of older, early modern models of selfhood and of social and political interaction well into the Victorian era. Understanding the bases of women's involvement in politics requires us to excavate the intricate links which endured between earlier, elite patterns of public activity, rather than focusing too exclusively upon the social developments of the industrial age.

---

[66] Amanda Vickery, *The Gentleman's Daughter: Women's Lives in Georgian England* (New Haven and London, 1998), ch. 1.
[67] Dror Wahrman, *The Making of the Modern Self: Identity and Culture in Eighteenth-Century England* (New Haven, 2004).

I

WOMEN, GENDER, AND
THE LANDSCAPE OF POLITICS

Borderline citizens:
women and the political process

Introduction

This chapter will consider how, as ratepayers, householders, electors, parliamentary constituents, petitioners, welfare providers, and policy experts, women were commonly treated as political subjects. Nonetheless, opportunities to take advantage of these possibilities—and to configure empowering identities through them—were fraught with complexity. Women were 'borderline citizens' whose status hovered permanently in the interstices of the political nation: their involvement could be evoked and sanctioned as quickly as it could be dismissed and undermined. As Anna Clark has acknowledged, 'the principles of the British constitution were never entirely clear or fixed'.[1]

Here, the focus will be not on episodic campaigns and issues, but rather on the structural qualities of the political process and the ways in which they variously facilitated or limited female participation. During the course of our period there were a number of legislative developments which had critical consequences for the relationship between the individual, the community, and the state. Foremost amongst these were the Whig reforms of the 1830s: in particular the Reform Act (1832) which enfranchised substantial numbers of the middle classes; the Municipal Corporations Act (1835) which ended the oligarchic control of corporations and enfranchised adult male ratepayers to vote in borough council elections; and the Poor Law Amendment Act (1834) which provided for a more centralized system of poor relief and restricted its distribution. It was also during these years that the state began to intervene more strenuously in social and economic

---

[1] Anna Clark, 'Gender, Class, and the Nation: Franchise Reform in England, 1832–1928', in James Vernon (ed.), *Re-reading the Constitution: New Narratives in the Political History of England's Long Nineteenth Century* (Cambridge, 1996), 231.

questions, as legislation limiting the hours of factory labourers (for example, in 1833, 1844, 1847, and 1850) and mine workers (from 1842) testifies, as well as measures such as the 1848 Public Health Act. By the end of our period the formal political nation was further reshaped through the enfranchisement of urban working-class men in 1867, whilst Gladstone's ministry of 1868–74 dealt the first serious blow to traditional patronage structures with its measures facilitating meritocratic advancement in the civil service and the armed forces.[2]

Considering women's relationship to the polity requires an analysis of the uneven implications of these contemporary shifts in the role of the state, and the changing contours of the political nation. Only radical reformers envisaged political representation to involve the enfranchisement of individual political actors: the dominant understanding of parliamentary representation was more capacious. In 1832 towns were enfranchised not by dint of their population size, but whether they could be considered to represent a particular trade or industry.[3] The notion of the vote as a piece of family property—a mechanism which represented not an individual male but rather the interests of a household—ensured a conduit whereby women could be imagined to have a permissible role within the polity.[4] This provided the space for women to be able to construe themselves, and be treated as, parliamentary constituents. Indeed, the ubiquitous trope of 'female influence' became woven into broader rationales for the appropriate exercise of 'legitimate' as opposed to 'illegitimate' political influence during electoral proceedings.

Women's religious identities were central to their sense of involvement in political change. To be a practising Anglican, Dissenter, or Catholic did not involve merely the observance of religious doctrine, it drew the individual into a whole nexus of political, ideological, and cultural concerns. The Nonconformist community, for example, was increasingly mobilized over this period, benefiting from the repeal of the Test and Corporations Acts in 1828, and also the widening of the franchise in 1832. Nonconformity's growing political muscle facilitated not only women's contribution to pressure-group campaigns—it also had implications for

[2] For overviews of these developments see Geoffrey Finlayson, *Citizen, State and Social Welfare in Britain, 1830–1990* (Oxford, 1994); William C. Lubenow, *The Politics of Government Growth: Early Victorian Attitudes towards State Intervention, 1833–1848* (Newton Abbot, 1971).

[3] Norman Gash, *Politics in the Age of Peel: A Study in the Technique of Parliamentary Representation, 1830–50* (London, 1953), ch. 1.

[4] Matthew Cragoe, ' "Jenny Rules the Roost": Women and Electoral Politics, 1832–68', in Gleadle and Richardson, *Women in British Politics*, 153–68.

their involvement in formal political processes. For example, the centrality of religious identity to public issues emerged sharply in the fierce disputes over the church rates. Until their abolition in 1868 rates were levied in the parish to cover the costs of the upkeep of the local Anglican church. Dissenters were bitterly opposed to this taxation and in many vestries succeeded in preventing a rate from being imposed. Women often became involved in these fierce parochial disputes during which all householders, regardless of sex, were able to vote. Religious affiliation forced individuals to consider not only the relationship between church and government (in 1844 the Nonconformist constituency established the Anti-State Church Association) but also the appropriate contours of the state itself.[5] Although philanthropists often cooperated across denominational lines, within their communities women's interventions were commonly situated within distinct ideological traditions. Rational Dissenters such as Rachel Lee and Catharine Cappe related philanthropic concerns to hopes for a more sensitive, enlightened polity;[6] whereas Victorian ultra-Evangelicals like Charlotte Elizabeth Tonna called for greater state intervention as part of a revived paternalism.[7] In contrast, moderate Evangelicals presented poverty as part of God's divine plan, leading them to reject large-scale philanthropic schemes and state intervention and to favour individual alms-giving to the worthy poor.[8] Female religiosity, therefore, affected not only women's spiritual life. It positioned women as political subjects in the various debates and practices concerning philanthropic projects and the role of the state.

The evolving relationship between local and national government was also critical to this narrative, but it had multiple and uneven implications for women. It was in the parish that women enjoyed the most expansive opportunities (a theme explored more fully in Chapter 4) yet parochial authority was increasingly eroded in this period thanks to reforms such as the Poor Law Amendment Act and the Municipal Corporations Act. On the other hand, the evolution of the state occurred hand-in-hand with the

---

[5] For an overview see J. P. Ellens, *Religious Routes to Gladstonian Liberalism: The Church Rate Conflict in England and Wales, 1832–1868* (Pennsylvania, 1994).

[6] Catharine Cappe, *Thoughts on Various Charitable and Other Important Institutions* (York, 1814), 106. Rachel Lee, *An Essay on Government* (London, 1808) outlined an interventionist state at both local and national level. Lee, an advanced radical, was daughter of the outlandish Sir Frances Dashwood. See Gleadle, 'British Women', 132, 145–6.

[7] Gleadle, 'Charlotte Elizabeth Tonna'.

[8] e.g. Priscilla Maurice, *Help and Comfort for the Sick Poor* (London, 1853), 7–11; Maria Louisa Charlesworth, *The Ministry of Life* (London, 1858), e.g. 214–16.

work of voluntary agencies.[9] Accounts of the nineteenth-century state are often cast within narratives of modernization (as epitomized in Gladstone's meritocratic reforms in the 1870s) but older models of patronage remained important in the growth of government. This was an aspect of the political process in which women were able to intervene—albeit with varying degrees of success. It provided the space for women to act as important, sometimes pioneering agents, although the impact of these developments upon female subjectivities was, as we shall see, problematic. A similarly tessellated picture emerges from a consideration of the gendered geographies of formal political institutions, such as the Houses of Parliament, with which the chapter concludes. Women's ambivalent role as parliamentary spectators provided the potential for empowering political possibilities for the well-connected. Nonetheless, these uneven opportunities were symptomatic of the gendered distinctions which shaped women's political actions. This, in turn, had an impact upon how women were able to define and imagine themselves as political citizens.

Parliamentary elections

The continuing importance of landed influence in the political system provided aristocratic women with a wealth of opportunities for electoral involvement well into the nineteenth century—either as landowners themselves or in the support of family interests.[10] Women of the middling and gentry classes also profited from these traditional sources of political authority. Mrs Jones, for instance, was noted for her flamboyant support of her husband's candidacy in Shrewsbury in 1806.[11]

Women also enjoyed some limited electoral privileges in their own right. In burgage boroughs the franchise was attached to the ownership of specific forms of property. This technically gave women who met the qualification a right to vote. Richard Carlile, the free-thought politician, claimed to have known a woman who voted in just such circumstances.[12] This was wholly

[9] See Finlayson, *Citizen, State and Social Welfare*, esp. 80–100, and Lubenow, *Politics of Government Growth*.

[10] Elaine Chalus, *Elite Women in English Political Life, 1754–1790* (Oxford, 2005), esp. chs 5–7; Judith Schneid Lewis, *Sacred to Female Patriotism: Gender, Class and Politics in Late Georgian Britain* (London, 2003); Sarah Richardson, 'The Role of Women in Electoral Politics in Yorkshire during the 1830s', *Northern History*, 32 (1996), 133–51; Cragoe, 'Jenny Rules the Roost', 155–7.

[11] Notebooks of Katherine Plymley, Shropshire Archives, 1066/69 (1806).

[12] *The Prompter* (9 Apr. 1831).

exceptional, but in some areas women customarily nominated a man—typically their husband—to vote in their place. In freeman boroughs marriage to the daughter of a freeman conferred freeman status (and thus often the parliamentary vote) upon the husband.[13] In Grimsby and Bristol stories abounded of marriages conducted purely for political purposes, in which the bride and groom might be barely acquainted.[14] This was a privilege which could be embraced as part of the peculiar identity of a borough, and woven into accounts of its heritage. Provincialism and local culture could therefore form important reservoirs for female politics. There is evidence that until these rights were lost in 1832 they were viewed within some communities as relevant to women's political identities.[15] The poet Robert Southey suggested that in Bristol the practice produced highly politicized women, where they 'enter into the heat of a party even more eagerly than men'.[16] Even so, the gendered asymmetry of the practice, whereby women enjoyed these rights only vicariously through their husbands, meant that they remained an ambivalent source of political agency. No doubt in many cases it was a privilege which would have been viewed as part of a marriage portion, rather than necessarily endowing women with authority in their own right.

Women's positioning as constituency actors extended far beyond ancient franchise entitlements however.[17] Within local communities shop-keepers and tradesmen frequently encountered women as skilful electoral manipulators—refusing to give their custom unless they promised to vote for the right candidate. The liberal politician John A. Roebuck railed against the 'old Tory ladies' who threatened to ruin radical shopkeepers in Bath in the 1837 election. It was a phenomenon which was strengthened by the increasing potency of middle-class pressure groups. Female anti-slavery campaigners proved adept in this respect. They 'ferreted out the quarters of electioneering influence', as anti-slavery activist George Stephen put it. Anti-Corn Law women could be similarly robust in boycotting protec-tionist traders during critical elections.[18] Wily shopkeepers could turn the

[13] Edward Porritt and Annie G. Porritt, *The Unreformed House Of Commons: Parliamentary Representation Before 1832*, i. *England and Wales* (Cambridge, 1903), 79; Chalus, *Elite Women*, 40–3.
[14] George Shaw, *Old Grimsby* (Grimsby and London, 1897), 187–213, and Robert Southey, *Letters from England* (London, 1807, 3 vols), ii. 320–1.
[15] See below pp. 164–9.
[16] Southey, *Letters*, ii. 320.
[17] See James Vernon, *Politics and the People: A Study in English Political Culture, c.1815–1867* (Cambridge, 1993), 91–2, 116.
[18] Cragoe, 'Jenny Rules the Roost,' 161; Morgan, 'Domestic Economy', 119; Dorothy Thompson, 'Women, Work and Politics in Nineteenth-Century England: The Problem of

practice to their advantage: a grocer in Cheapside kept a poll of the voting preferences of his female customers in the 1852 election, declaring he would vote for their most popular candidate.[19]

From the 1830s, it became increasingly common for successful candidates to evoke women as a collective block of constituency opinion. This was probably a result both of the enlarged electorate and more widely circulated notions of female public activity (due to women's success in anti-slavery and philanthropy). In Ipswich the newly elected MP referred in 1835 to the 'ladies of Ipswich, to whose exertions he in a great measure attributed his success'. At his chairing it was reported that ladies wearing his colours 'formed a very considerable proportion of the multitude which had collected'.[20] Robert Peel was quick to recognize the assistance of women in the Tamworth election in 1841, characterizing their intervention as a 'just and legitimate influence' and suggesting that his victory had been largely due to the influence they had exerted over the town's electors.[21]

Peel's comments are telling. 'Legitimate influence' was widely viewed as an important mechanism through which the smooth functioning of the polity was assured. A common argument against the secret ballot, for example, was that it would prohibit the rightful exercise of landed influence upon electors.[22] The argument that women did not need the vote because they were already represented through their male relatives was to become a cliché in anti-suffrage debate.[23] However, it also reflected a widespread perception of the virtues of indirect representation. Contemporary politicians certainly behaved as if they viewed female influence to be a significant factor in the negotiation of political decisions (and electoral customs which enfranchised men by dint of their wife's status no doubt gave added currency to such assumptions). The reciprocal gift-giving and entertaining between female constituents and local MPs suggests that women might equally perceive themselves to have a distinct constitutional relationship with their local parliamentarian. Daniel Whittle Harvey, the

---

Authority', in Rendall, *Equal or Different*, 76–7; George Stephen to Anne Knight (14 Nov. 1834), Friends House Library, London, MS Box W 2/2/37.

[19] *Liverpool Mercury* (22 June 1852).

[20] *The Times* (20 and 22 June 1835).

[21] *The Times* (30 June 1841).

[22] For the exercise of political influence see Gash, *Politics in the Age of Peel*, ch. 8.

[23] e.g. Lucy F. March Phillipps, *Strong and Free: Or First Steps towards Social Science* (London, 1869), 319–25, has a fictional dialogue on the pros and cons of female suffrage which includes a professor pointing to the influence which women already exerted over parliamentary decisions.

Whig member for Colchester, organized mass tea parties for the ladies of his constituency and also mobilized a group of voters' wives to act as campaigners and fund-raisers.[24] The Tory candidate in the 1834 Wakefield election made explicit attempts to appeal to local women, holding a tea party for over 4,000 women. The 'ladies of the Tory party' reciprocated Lascelles's largesse by presenting him with a 'splendid blue flag'.[25] Similarly 'five hundred of the most fashionable and influential ladies of Devonport' presented their Conservative MP with a banner at a public meeting in 1840. In 1841 women in Nottingham raised a substantial subscription to purchase two silver gifts for their MPs, to express their gratitude for the 'zeal with which they had endeavoured to promote the ascendancy of constitutional principles in Nottingham'.[26]

These practices had the potential to facilitate more heterodox female rituals. Over 1,500 Oldham women presented their MP William Johnson Fox with a signet ring and a purse of money at a public ceremony in February 1853 during which one lady read a 'poetical address'.[27] Conversely, during a difficult election campaign in Liverpool in 1818 George Canning apologized at length to his female constituents for failing to earlier acknowledge their important electoral influence. But he reminded them that in debates on parliamentary reform he had always noted the inadequacy of measures which failed to enfranchise duly qualified women.[28]

Canning's assumption that a record of support for female rights had the potential to be a successful line of argument is striking. It was a rare stance, but not unique. In Buckinghamshire, Dr John Lee (to the delight of contemporary feminists) repeatedly pronounced his support for female suffrage during his unsuccessful election campaigns in the early Victorian period. It was a position ridiculed in *The Times* (even though this paper, like many others, often reported without comment on the electoral rights of women in European states).[29] Nonetheless, W. J. Fox, Matthew Davenport

<hr>

[24] A. F. J. Brown, *Colchester 1815–1914* (Chelmsford, 1980), 75–6.

[25] Ann K. Jacques, *Merrie Wakefield Based on Some of the Diaries of Clara Clarkson (1811–89) of Alverthorpe Hall, Wakefield* (Wakefield, 1971), 98.

[26] *The Times* (11 Sept. 1841). For other examples see *Farmers' Journal* (3 Feb. 1840) and also Davidoff and Hall, *Family Fortunes*, 448; Vernon, *Politics and the People*, 238–41.

[27] Robert A. Walling (ed.), *The Diaries of John Bright* (London, 1930), 135; Georgiana Hill, *Women in English Life* (London, 1896, 2 vols), ii. 327.

[28] George Canning, *The Speeches and Public Addresses of the Right Hon. George Canning during the Election in Liverpool* (Liverpool, 1818), 16–18; *Monthly Repository*, 9 (1835), 496–7.

[29] Anne Knight et al., 'Address to the inhabitants of Aylesbury, Beaconsfield, Marlow, Slough and Wycombe on behalf of Dr. Lee and women's rights' [n.d.], Centre for Buckinghamshire Studies, Robert Gibbs papers, D 15/10/5; *The Times* (30 Dec. 1863 and 9 July 1841). For

Hill, Carey Dobbs, and James Silk Buckingham were all elected to parliament despite delivering overtly feminist speeches.[30]

Whilst support for the female parliamentary vote remained exceptional, it would be misleading to treat it as necessarily inimical to mainstream political culture. By the early Victorian period, in addition to the MPs cited above, there were a number (like Henry Hunt, John Wilks, Thomas Barrett-Lennard, Joseph Sturge, George Thompson, John Bowring, and Richard Cobden) who were known for their private sympathies—or at least ambiguity—on the issue. J. A. Roebuck admitted that the 'degrading spectacles' of electoral culture was 'the only argument which I could ever find worth a rush, against giving to women all political rights'.[31]

In addition, politicians from both sides of the political spectrum occasionally rehearsed arguments in favour of female enfranchisement so as to expose the fallacy of universal suffrage. Lord John Russell suggested to parliament that 'persons like Miss Martineau, and many other ladies, are as fitted to give votes for Members of Parliament as many thousands of those who are now called "slaves" on account of their not possessing the privilege of voting'.[32] It was an assertion which at least admitted women's political abilities, and in some cases it signalled a tacit sympathy for their rights. In a speech to the Commons in 1848, Disraeli described Britain as a country,

> governed by a woman—where you allow women to form part of the other estate of the realm—Peeresses in their own right, for example—where you allow a woman not only to hold land, but to be a lady of the manor and hold legal courts,—where a woman by law may be churchwarden—I do not see,

reports of female enfranchisement in Stuttgart, Sweden, and Austria see *Leeds Mercury* (11 Apr. 1861); *Belfast Newsletter* (31 Jan. 1859); *The Times* (25 Sept. 1845).

[30] James Silk Buckingham, *Qualifications and Duties of Members of Parliament, Being the Substance of an Address, Delivered to the Inhabitants of Sheffield* (Nottingham, 1831), esp. 12; Kathryn Gleadle, *The Early Feminists: Radical Unitarians and the Emergence of the Women's Rights Movement, 1831–51* (Basingstoke, 1995), 71; Hill, *Women in English Life*, ii. 327; *Belfast Newsletter* (3 Apr. 1857).

[31] J. A. Roebuck to Alexander P. Falconer (3 Nov. 1832) in Robert E. Leader (ed.), *Life and Letters of John Arthur Roebuck, with Chapters of Autobiography* (London and New York, 1897), 46–7; Clare Taylor, *British and American Abolitionists: An Episode in Transatlantic Understanding* (Edinburgh, 1974), 183–4; Anne Knight annotated her copy of Marion Reid, *A Plea for Woman* (1843) with a list of MPs whom she was given to believe were not hostile to women's suffrage, Friends House, MS vol s.495, 214. For Hunt, Wilks, and Barrett-Lennard, see Ch. 5 below.

[32] *Hansard's Parliamentary History*, 3rd ser. 106 (3 July 1849), col. 1297.

where she has so much to do with State and Church, on what reasons, if you come to right, she has not a right to vote.[33]

Whilst he concluded that 'All this proves that right has nothing to do with the matter', in 1866 he returned to the theme:

I have always been of opinion [sic] that if there is to be universal suffrage, women have as much right to vote as men. And more than that—a woman having property now ought to have a vote in a country, in which she may hold manorial courts and sometimes acts as churchwarden.[34]

The following year Disraeli signalled his support for female suffrage.[35] Attitudes towards female voting, therefore, could be subtle and unpredictable. When taxpaying women decided to test the law in the general election of 1868 and attempt to cast votes, what is striking is the sheer range of local responses to their actions.[36] There was no universal consensus that such action was inimical to the constitution. Perceptions of women's formal constitutional role were fluid. This created the potential for dynamic practices and representations of their political rights.

Even so women, like men, might involve themselves in elections for reasons other than the purely political. For many they provided a focal point for sociability, as friends and kin congregated together. As Mary Coltman explained to her brother in 1826, 'I came here to dinner to meet Sarah & Mrs & Miss Sanders whilst they were hearing the speeches of the candidates'.[37] Similarly Ottilie Augusta Schwabe wrote to her fiancé John McLaren in 1868, 'Do you not get a holiday on election days? & would it not still be possible for you to come to Glasgow with us, if we stayed till the afternoon & so gained two ends, seeing the election & having your society here?'[38] Many women might be interested in politics, but this could be subordinated to other pursuits, such as social networking. Perhaps in some cases this was a comfortable means to accommodate a concern in political affairs with a normative female identity, for not all women would

---

[33] *Hansard*, 3rd ser. 99 (20 June 1848), col. 950.

[34] *Hansard*, 3rd ser. 183 (27 Apr. 1866), col. 99.

[35] Jane Rendall, 'The Citizenship of Women and the Reform Act of 1867', in Catherine Hall *et al., Defining the Victorian Nation: Class, Race, Gender and the British Reform Act of 1867* (Cambridge, 2000), 122, 130–1, 138.

[36] Jane Rendall, 'Who was Lily Maxwell? Women's Suffrage and Manchester Politics, 1866–1867', in June Purvis and Sandra Stanley Holton (eds), *Votes for Women* (London and New York, 2000), 57–83.

[37] Mary Coltman to Samuel Coltman (22 May 1826), LRO, Coltman MSS, 15D57, 186.

[38] Ottilie Augusta Schwabe to John McLaren (12 Nov. 1868), National Library of Scotland, Edinburgh, McLaren family papers, F. Scott Oliver, MS 24789, f and v. 33.

have felt comfortable with taking too forthright a role in elections. During the 1819 election in Shrewsbury, Katherine Plymley learnt of a friend that 'her conscience was concerned in endeavouring to get a good man returned . . . she was scarcely satisfied that she had done enough.—She thought if another such occasion should occur, she would *almost* canvass herself.'[39] For others, exerting influence within their personal relationships remained the more attractive path. Catherine Marsh, the premillenarian Evangelical author, wrote enthusiastically to her friend Caroline Maitland in 1846, 'What are you doing about the elections? Influencing everyone you meet, I trust, to vote only for the candidates who take the Protestant pledge.'[40]

The heterogeneity and vibrancy of contested elections thus produced a diverse range of opportunities for politically interested women. This does mean that women were able, or desirous, of experiencing elections in the same way as men, nor that the majority of women necessarily embraced such opportunities. Whilst individual women of status might have their activities described in terms of direct political influence (Mrs Osbaldeston's Yorkshire constituents toasted her as a 'female patriot' for her vigorous involvement in the election of 1807[41]) descriptions of female collective action tended to be more tightly gendered—as the practice of ladies' 'tea parties' and recurring references to 'female influence' indicates. But this did not preclude the possibility of women being variously implicated in constituency politics, with occasionally radical consequences.

Local elections

Through intervening in contests concerning community bodies like hospitals, schools, and asylums it was also possible for women to feel involved in local governance. Lydia North was a strenuous canvasser for her brother who hoped to secure the position of chaplain at St Bartholomew's Hospital in 1835.[42] Promoting family interests was not always the motivation however. In 1863 a Suffolk farmer's wife, Elizabeth Cotton, was impressed

---

[39] Plymley Notebook, SRO, 1066/120 (1819); my emphasis.
[40] L. E. O' Rorke, *The Life and Friendships of Catherine Marsh* (London, 1917), 55.
[41] E. A. Smith, 'The Yorkshire Elections of 1806 and 1807: A Study in Electoral Management', *Northern History*, 2 (1967), 80.
[42] M. Jeanne Peterson, *Family, Love and Work in the Lives of Victorian Gentlewomen* (Bloomington, Ind., 1989), 165.

by the energy with which her female cousin was campaigning for a candidate seeking a position at a psychiatric asylum and consequently began canvassing herself.[43] The Yorkshire gentlewoman Anne Lister and her partner Ann Walker were similarly involved in a lively contest for a schoolteacher in Hipperholme in 1835. Amelia Opie, the Norwich author, was active in rallying votes for candidates at positions in local schools and hospitals even into her eighties.[44]

Women were also entitled to vote directly in some contests relating to community institutions, although this could provoke controversy. When the parish of St John in Hackney was trying to select a pensioner for the local almshouse, local ladies polled their vote at the vestry meeting. However, this was viewed with some distaste by *The Times*.[45] In Oxford a row erupted in 1864 as to whether female subscribers to the Radcliffe Infirmary should be permitted to vote in elections for the hospital's committee. In the end legal advice confirmed that the women's votes should stand.[46]

Contemporaries were also accustomed to female voting in other kinds of local elections. Charles Dickens's *Sketches by Boz* described an election for a new beadle in which the ladies of the parish chose the candidate with the largest family. Whilst their behaviour and reasoning is satirized, women's right to vote was presented as a routine phenomenon.[47] Certainly contemporary commentators often took it for granted that women acted as electors in parochial contests. The Scottish feminist Marion Reid and the Chartist R. J. Richardson both noted the ease with which women voted for local commissioners and other parish officers. Richardson also observed, in common with Disraeli and Lee, that women frequently held these offices themselves.[48] It was an argument which gained currency from the late 1850s, as women's rights campaigners insisted that these anomalies should

---

[43] Sheila Hardy, *The Diary of a Suffolk Farmer's Wife, 1854–69* (London, 1992), 154.

[44] Jill Liddington, *Female Fortune: Land, Gender and Authority. The Anne Lister Diaries and Other Writings, 1833–1836* (London, 1998), 160–2; Amelia Opie to Joisah Fletcher (7 Dec. 1850), Norfolk Record Office, MS 5252, f. 40; Amelia Opie to Revd J. Alexander (23 June 1845), NRO, MS 6181; Amelia Opie to Lady Catherine Boileau (Mar. 1847), NRO, N.R.S. 24495, Boi 63/5/34.

[45] *The Times* (26 Nov. 1833).

[46] Records of the Radcliffe Infirmary, Oxfordshire Health Archives, RI/II/99 (6); *The Times* (30 Jan. 1865).

[47] Charles Dickens, *Sketches by Boz* (London, 1836, 2 vols), ii, ch. 3.

[48] Marion Reid, *A Plea for Woman Being a Vindication of the Importance and Extent of her Natural Sphere of Action* (Edinburgh, 1988; 1st publ. 1843), 27; R. J. Richardson, *The Rights of Woman* (Edinburgh, 1840) cited in Kathryn Gleadle, *Radical Writing on Women, 1800–1850: An Anthology* (Basingstoke, 2002), 169–71; see also *The Times* (1 Oct. 1829 and 20 June 1831).

become the norm. Barbara Bodichon noted qualified women had the right to 'vote upon parish questions, and for parish officers, overseers, surveyors, vestry clerks, &c'.[49] Jacob Bright made a similar case to the House of Commons in 1869: 'Women held the most important parochial offices. The sister of the Member for Stockport had acted as overseer. Miss Burdett Coutts had been urged to take the office of guardian.'[50] In subsequent decades feminists such as Charlotte Carmichael Stopes, Harriet McIlquham, and Lydia Becker continued to emphasize women's local rights in their disquisitions upon female suffrage.[51]

However, local government remained a highly gendered zone of political practice. I have not come across examples from this period of women acting in the critical county positions of magistrate, justice of the peace, lord lieutenant, high sheriff, or clerk of the peace.[52] Also, the lament of one feminist campaigner in 1838 that women were denied voting rights and the opportunity to hold even parochial local offices, suggests that if women did have such rights then many were unaware of them.[53] In her evidence to the Select Committee on Poor Relief in 1861, the poor law campaigner Louisa Twining intimated that public opinion was not yet 'advanced sufficiently' to allow for the election of female guardians. When MP Richard Monckton Milnes pointed out to her that in some areas the practice was already permitted, she responded that she was aware that it was technically legal but that she had not heard of any such cases.[54]

Two landmark decisions (*Olive v. Ingram*, 1739 and *Rex v. Stubbs*, 1788) had confirmed that women could vote for, and stand as, sextons and as parish overseers, but the exercise of these rights—and other parochial suffrages—depended upon local custom.[55] In Ely a local corporation met

---

[49] Barbara Bodichon, *A Brief Summary in Plain Language of the Most Important Laws Concerning Women* (London, 1854), 3.

[50] *Hansard*, 196 (7 June 1869), appendix, 1.

[51] Lydia Becker, *The Rights and Duties of Women in Local Government* (Manchester, 1879), 5–6; Audrey Kelly, *Lydia Becker and the Cause* (Lancaster, 1992), 33–4; Harriet McIlquham, *The Enfranchisement of Women: An Ancient Right, a Modern Need* (Congleton, 1891), 12; Charlotte Carmichael Stopes, *British Freewomen: Their Historical Privilege* (London, 1907), 152–60.

[52] For an evaluation of these offices see David Eastwood, *Governing Rural England: Tradition and Transformation in Local Government, 1780–1840* (Oxford, 1994), chs 3–4. There were presumably isolated cases of women serving these offices as feminists sometimes argued: Sidney Smith, *The Enfranchisement of Women the Law of the Land* (Manchester, 1879), 4.

[53] *Metropolitan Magazine*, 22 (1838), 17–19.

[54] 'Extracts from the Select Committee on Poor Relief 1861', in Louisa Twining, *A Letter to the President of the Poor Law Board on Workhouse Infirmaries* (London, 1866), 33.

[55] Sidney Webb and Beatrice Webb, *English Local Government from the Revolution to the Municipal Corporations Act* (London, 1906), 15–18, 106–7; Hilda L. Smith, 'Women as Sextons

twice a year to consider applications to parliament for improvement projects. The electorate, formed of those who owned one hundred acres, included women. As one local politician explained, 'It had been decided that the word "person" applied to women as well as men'.[56] During an election for a churchwarden in East Looe in 1825, the town clerk dismissed an objection that one candidate had appealed for the votes of female ratepayers. 'We have our own law here,' he declared.[57] Women's voting privileges could thus form part of a narrative of local tradition and identity. When figures such as Joshua Toulmin Smith sought to oppose centralization in the 1850s, championing parochial authority as a traditional Anglo-Saxon model of governance, it was an argument quickly appropriated by some feminists. As Bessie Rayner Parkes put it, 'A deep inbred principle of local activity and self-government is the very essence of Anglo-Saxon life. . . . It cherishes those traditions which are the truest poetry of a great people.'[58]

It was possible for individual women to claim such rights even if it was not the local custom, but this might require a degree of personal daring, and success was not assured. In Brentford in 1841, a paucity of suitable candidates meant that two women were suggested as parish overseers, but it was decided that 'it was ridiculous to nominate females to such offices'.[59] Female voting was usually less controversial. When a woman in the parish of All Saints, in Newcastle-upon-Tyne, sought to vote in a vestry election, 'although the novelty of the thing caused a little hesitation and demur, the vote was duly recorded'.[60]

Davidoff and Hall suggest that the exercise of women's local votes became increasingly uncommon over this period.[61] Certainly at the start of our period there were isolated attempts to prohibit the practice, but equally it is possible to find pleas that women be given greater responsibility within the parish.[62] Moreover, during close contests the female electorate was liable to be invoked throughout our period (even if women sometimes

---

and Electors: King's Bench and Precedents for Women's Citizenship', in Smith (ed.), *Women Writers and the Early Modern British Political Tradition* (Cambridge, 1998), 324–42.

[56] George Pryme, *Autobiographic Recollections of George Pryme* (Cambridge, 1870), 145.

[57] John Keast, *A History of East and West Looe* (Chichester, 1987), 73.

[58] *EWJ* 4 (Oct. 1859), 116–17.

[59] *Farmers' Journal* (12 Apr. 1841).

[60] *Notes and Queries*, 2nd ser. (31 Jan. 1857).

[61] Davidoff and Hall, *Family Fortunes*, 446.

[62] Webb and Webb, *English Local Government*, 15n., 64n.; *Liverpool Mercury* (10 Jan. 1812) published a letter on just this theme.

preferred to vote through a proxy[63]). This occurred most strikingly during
the heated debates over the church rates in the 1830s and 1840s. When
Nonconformist radicals in Leeds established their candidate as churchwarden local Tories appealed to the parochial community to undertake a
poll, making a somewhat sheepish attempt to flatter female voters: 'Rated
females are entitled to vote as well as males. We do not wish for a
Gynocracy; but we are sufficiently gallant to perceive that too many of the
wayward "lords of the creation" are disposed to make a bad world of it;
therefore the sooner the Ladies interfere the better.'[64] In Manchester, female
voters were provided with a separate polling station.[65] When the church
rate was passed in Edgbaston women's votes were critical to the outcome
(nearly one in four of the pro-rate votes were estimated to be cast by
females). As the *Birmingham Journal* commented however, the votes of the
women 'are usually only called in when the contest becomes severe'.[66]
Liberals in Birmingham accused local Anglicans of resorting to a low Tory
trick when they exhorted women to save the church rate in 1834.[67]
However, it was not only Tories who appealed to the female voter. Anne
Knight, the Quaker anti-slavery activist, was jubilant that in Hackney the
female vote had apparently prevented the imposition of a church rate.[68]

The legislation pertaining to local elections also suggests a more
complex chronology than that delineated by Davidoff and Hall. The
Sturges Bourne Acts (1818 and 1819) which established a weighted voting
system in favour of landholders, did not exclude women from voting and
nor did the Select Vestries Act of 1831, which enfranchised every ratepayer
for vestry elections. The same was true of the Poor Law Amendment Act
(1834) which also provided for weighted voting, benefiting those with
property. In a poor law contest in Lichfield, for example, a Grace Brown
was able to cast four votes.[69] The Act's provision for written votes, with
papers delivered to individual households, may have facilitated female

[63] *Leeds Mercury* (29 Sept. 1857).

[64] *Leeds Intelligencer* (25 Apr. 1835).

[65] *Birmingham Journal* (13 Dec. 1834).

[66] Alex Tyrrell, *Joseph Sturge and the Moral Radical Party in Early Victorian Britain* (London,
1987), 148; *Birmingham Journal* (29 July 1843). See also William Henry Ryland, *Reminiscences
of Thomas Henry Ryland* (Birmingham, 1904), 57–8, 82.

[67] *Birmingham Journal* (13 Dec. 1834). See also Ellens, *Religious Routes*, 31.

[68] Anne Knight's marginalia in her copy of Reid, *A Plea for Woman*, Friends House, MS vol.
s495.

[69] Philip Salmon, *Electoral Reform at Work: Local Politics and National Parties, 1832–1841*
(Woodbridge and Suffolk, 2002), 197.

voting (even though some voting papers referred explicitly to voters as male).[70]

There was confusion too as to whether the new Poor Law permitted women to stand for election. In 1835 Mr Fenn, a churchwarden in St Martin-in-the-Fields, put forward an all-female shortlist of nominees for the new board of guardians. Two years later a carefully compiled list of twenty-two women and two men was proposed by John Newbury. Some perceived this as an attempt to undermine the introduction of the new law which the parish was the first in the capital to implement. For others the matter provoked associations with 'public women', leading to mocking references to local prostitutes. However, the chair of the first meeting took the proposal seriously—he 'saw no reason why ladies should not be elected as guardians of the poor, as it was perfectly clear they were eligible to serve as overseers'. Newbury and Fenn consistently denied local accusations that their (unsuccessful) nominations were a joke. Newbury insisted that those he proposed were women 'of the highest respectability'. Fenn argued that as most of the inmates of the new workhouses would be women it was appropriate that their 'directors and comptrollers' should be female. This met with some support locally. He cited parliamentary authority for this perspective, claiming that poor law commissioners had tried to include a clause that would necessitate a female presence on the board of guardians.[71]

This lack of consensus was symptomatic. William Lumley, a specialist in electoral law, explained in his *Poor Law Election Manual* (1845) that unmarried women who were ratepayers or owners of property might vote, but that they were not qualified to act as guardians. However, in the 1855 edition Lumley had to acknowledge cases where women had been so elected.[72] When a correspondent to *The Times* pointed out in 1867 that married women were commonly elected to such posts in Shropshire, Lumley was quick to query the assertion. In subsequent correspondence the contributor confirmed that the women were in fact widows but tartly observed, 'Mr Lumley's objection does not affect the main purpose of the

[70] e.g. Vernon, *Politics and the People*, 156. The practice of voting papers was noted approvingly by Lucy Aikin who voted in this way: Gleadle, *Radical Writing*, 183.

[71] This discussion is based upon accounts in *The Times* (23 May 1835 and 17 Mar. 1837). I have been unable to trace the parliamentary proposal mentioned.

[72] William Lumley, *The Poor Law Election Manual* (London, 1845), 43–4, 51; Lumley, *The Poor Law Election Manual* (1855), 58. The point was put yet more strongly in the 1877 edn, 59. In contrast Patricia Hollis assumed that the first female guardian was elected in 1875: *Ladies Elect: Women in English Local Government, 1865–1914* (London, 1987), 207.

paragraph, which was to record the fact that the appointment of women to the office of parish overseer is not an unusual custom in country districts.'[73]

Many other pieces of legislation were the subject of similar contestation.[74] The Municipal Corporations Act (1835) explicitly excluded women from the franchise. However, there were dissenting voices. A proposal to enable women to vote in the new incorporated boroughs was defeated by a majority of 66 during committee.[75] The result was that in the newly incorporated boroughs women lost the political rights they had previously enjoyed, yet they remained enfranchised in non-incorporated towns.[76] Some formal avenues did remain available to women after incorporation though, for they continued to be enfranchised in the vestry (rights that were exercised, as we have seen in post-incorporation Birmingham). Indeed Jacob Bright claimed that 'where women had the vote they exercised it to an equal degree with the men'. He cited the case of Manchester where he was informed that men and women voted in equal numbers during the election of overseers.[77] In addition, in some cities moves were made to include women further in urban governance. In Liverpool the Liberal Nonconformist corporation established a ladies' committee to assist in the implementation of its controversial educational policies. (The corporation's decision to open its schools to children of all denominations had caused a furore amongst local Tories.[78]) Mancunian John Roberton suggested that women's legal entitlement to act as parish overseers be extended through an alteration to the by-laws. He envisaged that each ward might have a ladies' committee which would help to spearhead a more proactive form of municipal government.[79] These proposals may reveal a frustration that the new framework did not sufficiently exploit women's civic potential. Certainly when Bright successfully moved that women were entitled to vote in local corporations in 1869 it was seen as an uncontroversial move, provoking little

---

[73] *The Times* (26, 27, and 30 April 1867).

[74] Katherine S. Williams, 'The Public Law and Women's Rights: The Nineteenth Century Experience', *Cambrian Law Review*, 23 (1992), 80–103.

[75] *Hansard*, 29 (16 July 1835), col. 646.

[76] See Bryan Keith-Lucas, *The English Local Government Franchise: A Short History* (Oxford, 1952), 165.

[77] *Hansard*, 196 (7 June 1869), appendix, 1–2.

[78] Philip McCann and Francis A. Young, *Samuel Wilderspin and the Infant School Movement* (London and Canberra, 1982), 201–10; Denis G. Paz, *Popular Anti-Catholicism in Mid-Victorian England* (Stanford, Calif., 1992), 200; Emily A. Rathbone (ed.), *Records of the Rathbone Family* (Edinburgh, 1913), 208–11.

[79] John Roberton, *Suggestions for the Improvement of Municipal Government* (Manchester, 1854), 87–9.

comment in a sparsely attended Commons and only limited debate in a generally favourably disposed House of Lords.[80]

In contrast female ratepayers were not explicitly disqualified from voting under measures such as the Public Health Act (1848) or the Metropolis Management Act (1855)—although the situation remained confused and dependent upon local acquiescence. When commissioners visited Mile-End Old Town to establish wards under the latter, the vestry clerk insisted that women would not be entitled to vote. However a Mr Moody 'did not see why if lady ratepayers could vote at present at parish elections, they should not exercise the same privilege under the new act'. Despite the commissioner's view that 'there was nothing in the act which prevented ladies from voting', the clerk was insistent.[81] Similar debates occurred in Ireland. Here, a judicial decision was required in 1864 to establish that the Towns Improvement Act (1854) enabled women to vote for, but not to sit as, town commissioners. Mr Justice Fitzgerald explained that participating in such elections could hardly be thought to be injurious to women as they already voted for poor law guardians. British colonial legislatures present a similarly chequered picture. In Canada, for example, women did not gain any local voting rights until 1884, with the exception of the post of school trustee.[82]

Women's local political rights were marked by a curious duality. Their existence alerted contemporaries to the possibilities of independent female agency based upon economic status rather than feminine attributes. (As contemporary feminists often pointed out, this included the ability to vote in imperial affairs as shareholders of the East India Company.[83]) Yet the uneven opportunities to exercise such rights simultaneously reaffirmed women as secondary, borderline citizens. The lack of consensus concerning the practices of female voting and officeholding

---

[80] Even so, confusion persisted as to whether the amendment entitled married (and also separated) women to vote until the test case of *Regina v. Harrold* (1872). *Hansard*, 198 (19 July 1869), cols. 145–6; Hollis, *Ladies Elect*, 7; M. Ostrogorski, 'Woman Suffrage in Local Self-Government', *Political Science Quarterly*, 6 (1891), 690.

[81] *The Times* (22 Sept. 1855).

[82] *The Times* (21 Jan. 1864). Women's local political rights were generally more restricted in Ireland than in Scotland, England, and Wales. Ostrogorski, 'Woman Suffrage', 692–3, 705.

[83] Reid, *A Plea*, 27; Hill, *Women in English life*, ii. 327. Although the number of female stock holders declined from the mid-18th cent., in 1836 they still held 17.3% of accounts. Huw V. Bowen, *The Business of Empire: The East India Company and Imperial Britain, 1756–1833* (Cambridge, 2006), 105–9; Susan Staves, 'Investments, Votes, and "Bribes": Women as Shareholders in the Chartered National Companies', in Smith, *Women and the Early Modern British Political Tradition*, 259–78.

meant that local communities and legislators were continually redefining policies on a piecemeal basis. The apparent need to routinely rehearse the legitimacy of female voting rights, combined with the consensus in many areas that they be evoked only in exceptional circumstances, meant that women's citizenship remained a liminal, often ambivalent phenomenon.

Petitions

Men and women had long turned to petitioning during times of heightened political crisis, such as the English Civil War. By the late eighteenth century widespread political agitation over such issues as the American War of Independence meant that legislation restricting the practice to the London Common Council or county meetings became a dead letter (although petitions from the latter continued to be taken the most seriously). By 1831 such was the volume of petitions that parliament imposed curbs on their reception, notably a ban limiting discussion of their contents. That this was derided as 'unconstitutional' in the press shows the extent to which petitioning was now widely construed as the central means through which extra-parliamentary opinion might rightfully be represented.[84]

In recent years historians have drawn attention to widespread petitioning by women in such causes as anti-slavery, the enfranchisement of Roman Catholics in 1829, and the repeal of the Corn Laws.[85] Yet their incorporation into this political phenomenon was fraught with difficulties. The first major incident of our period came in 1820 when women and men protested en masse against the King's attempt to divorce his wife, Caroline.[86] In the agitation which ensued thousands of women called for women's rights to male protection and a stable family life. Large-scale meetings were arranged to organize the numerous 'ladies' petitions' sent in

---

[84] Peter Fraser, 'Public Petitioning and Parliament before 1832', *History*, 46 (1961), 195–211; Colin Leys, 'Petitioning in the Nineteenth and Twentieth Centuries', *Political Studies*, 3 (1955), 45–64.

[85] Midgley, *Women against Slavery*, 23–5, 62–71; Colley, *Britons*, 278–80; Morgan, *Victorian Woman's Place*, 104, 137–9, 153–7; Wendy Hinde, *Catholic Emancipation: A Shake to Men's Minds* (Oxford, 1992), 140–2.

[86] Davidoff and Hall, *Family Fortunes*, 150–5; Anna Clark, *The Struggle for the Breeches: Gender and the Making of the British Working Class* (London, 1995), 164–74; Thomas Laqueur, 'The Queen Caroline Affair: Politics as Art in the Reign of George IV', *Journal of Modern History*, 54 (1982), 417–66.

support of the queen.[87] In contrast, when a cause could not be so obviously presented as having particular interest to women, it was more likely that interested females would simply affix their signatures to primarily 'male' petitions. This made those petitions susceptible to challenge at Westminster, however. Thus in 1834 the ratepayers of Leamington Spa petitioned against a proposal that the town should form a joint borough with Warwick. As in the case of the later Chartist activities, the inclusion of female signatures was seen as damning evidence that this was an irregular petition, adding to other allegations of its impropriety.[88]

Others defended female petitioning of this nature, emphasizing (where applicable) their political status as freemen's daughters, or more commonly, as householders. The high numbers of single and widowed women in this period meant that female householders formed a substantial minority of the population (as high as 23 per cent in one sample from Glasgow in 1851).[89] The radical MP John Cam Hobhouse staunchly defended the inclusion of women's signatures on a petition from the Marylebone Vestry which was requesting its reconstitution as a select vestry: 'It was true that several females had signed the petition, but they, as householders and payers of rates, had an unquestionable right to join in such a demonstration of public opinion.'[90] Attitudes often depended upon whether a particular petition was useful to a politician's cause. In 1829 a number of MPs collected female signatures for anti-Catholic petitions. Robert Waithman, keen to exploit any opportunity to undermine the anti-Catholic cause, urged the house not to accept them. Pronouncing such behaviour to be incommensurate with women's 'proper place' he joked that 'in all probability they were, ladies of a certain description'. The Tory member for Bristol protested, reminding the house that his 'lady constituents' were accustomed

---

[87] e.g. *An Authentic Account of the Whole Proceedings of the Saint Mary-Le-Bone Meeting of the Married Ladies, and Inhabitant Householders of the Parish* (London, 1820).

[88] *Hansard*, 21 (26 Feb.1834), col. 836. See also *Hansard*, 22 (13 Mar. 1834), cols. 181–90. For the petitioning activities of Chartist women: Jutta Schwarzkopf, *Women in the Chartist Movement* (Basingstoke, 1991), 178–80.

[89] Eleanor Gordon and Gwyneth Nair, *Public Lives: Women, Family and Society in Victorian Britain* (New Haven and London, 2003), 169. In 1851 single women comprised 47.6% of the adult female population in Bristol and 45.3% in Liverpool. Mature women of course, were particularly likely to fall into this category (in London two-thirds of women over the age of 60 were single). D. R. Green and A. Owens, 'Gentlewomanly Capitalism? Spinsters, Widows, and Wealth Holding in England and Wales, c. 1800–1860', *Economic History Review*, 56 (2003), 513; Michael Anderson, 'The Social Position of Spinsters in Mid-Victorian Britain', *Journal of Family History*, 9 (1984), 388, 390.

[90] *The Times* (7 June 1828).

to exercising political privileges as freemen's daughters. He alluded to the fact that women might accede to the highest political office as queen and further observed that a female housekeeper had 'as great a right to express the interest she felt in a question of such vital importance'. Mr C. Pallmer who presented a large petition from his London constituents also argued the case for 'female householders' who had 'a right to petition parliament' to uphold the constitution.[91]

Politicians were therefore quite prepared to pose as women's political champions even though mixed-sex petitioning—particularly on constitutional issues—remained controversial. Women-only petitions were increasingly viewed with greater equanimity though. The protest against *sati* (widow burning) in India produced fourteen women's petitions during 1829–30, drawing upon a particular construction of women's Evangelical sympathies for oppressed Indian wives.[92] By the 1830s the practice had also become widespread in the anti-slavery movement. Despite the continuance of some dissenting voices, by 1833 women comprised nearly a third of anti-slavery petitioners and women continued to petition parliament on a wide range of questions. There was also a growing trend for women to publicize causes through signed memorials to the Queen. This was a practice which drew upon long-standing traditions of addressing the monarch with memorials and petitions. The accession of a female monarch clearly facilitated women's confidence in appropriating this for their own campaigns. The ensuing texts drew upon carefully constructed feminine identities, often emphasizing maternal or philanthropic concerns. Over 100,000 women signed an anti-Corn Law memorial to Victoria in 1841 beseeching her to use her influence to relieve the distress of the poor.[93]

Just as petitioners commonly presented themselves as representing 'the people',[94] so many female petitions purported to be from the 'Women of England' or from the women of a particular town or city. This could be an

[91] Ian I. Muirhead, 'Catholic Emancipation: Scottish Reactions in 1829', *Innes Review*, 24 (1973), 26–42, 103–20; *Hansard*, 20 (26 Feb. 1829), col. 572; (27 Feb. 1829), col. 610; and (19 Mar. 1829), col. 1324.

[92] Clare Midgley, 'From Supporting Missions to Petitioning Parliament: British Women and the Evangelical Campaign against *Sati* in India, 1813–30', in Gleadle and Richardson, *Women in British Politics*, 74–92.

[93] Midgley, *Women against Slavery*, 48, 62–71, 100–2, 149, 199; Morgan, *Victorian Woman's Place*, 104, 137–8, 155–8. For disapproval of the practice see p. 8 above and p. 263 below.

[94] See Joanna Innes, 'Legislation and Public Participation, 1760–1830', in David Lemmings (ed.), *The British and their Laws* (Woodbridge, 2005), 115.

[95] Mrs Toll to M. W. Chapman (7 Jan. 1844), Boston Public Library, MS A.9.2.20, 7.

empowering process. Mrs Toll, a Birmingham Dissenter, wrote enthusiastically to her correspondent Maria Weston Chapman (the American abolitionist) that she had 'ardently assisted' in the agitation to prohibit female miners. She rejoiced that with petitions signed by the 'women of Birmingham' they had 'at last . . . gained our point, and obtained the law'.[95]

Nonetheless pressure groups remained highly sensitive to the practice, resulting in divergent, often contradictory practices. Within ultra-Protestantism some local societies disallowed all female signatures, whereas others permitted women's contribution to those which might be construed (however loosely!) as falling within a 'woman's sphere', such as protests against nunneries.[96] On the other hand the ultra-Protestant polemicist Charlotte Elizabeth Tonna urged women to petition on all manner of issues, proclaiming in her *Christian Lady's Magazine*: 'lay before the throne piles of petitions; let the tables of either house groan under their weight'.[97]

The contingency of female petitioning strategies emerges clearly in the debate over affinal marriages. Between 1858 and 1861 parliament received numerous petitions on the legislation prohibiting widowers from marrying their wives' sisters.[98] As a question which could be construed to have particular female interest, both sides in the debate used women as political capital. Lord Dungannon, presenting petitions from the 'Women of Aylesbury and Inhabitants of Droitwich', asserted 'that the strongest repugnance prevailed among the women of England to any change in the law'; whereas Lord Wodehouse referred to a larger petition from Aylesbury women in favour of amendment and declared that were the decision in the hands of 'the ladies of England he was confident that it would be carried'. Female petitioners participated in this process by referring to the impact the legislation would have upon 'the peace of domestic life'.[99] Yet presenting themselves as representatives of their sex elided the religious or political ideologies which underpinned the issue. Within parliament

[96] Paz, *Popular Anti-Catholicism*, 274; *Bulwark*, 2 (1852), 4–5. See also *Englishwoman's Magazine* (June 1851), 369.

[97] *Christian Lady's Magazine*, 13 (1840), 284.

[98] Prior to 1835 if a widower married his deceased wife's sister the marriage could be voided by law, thereafter all such unions were made null and void from the outset. A royal commission in 1847 recommended a relaxation of the law which was finally overturned in 1907: Cynthia F. Behrman, 'The Annual Blister: A Sidelight on Victorian Social and Parliamentary History', *Victorian Studies*, 11 (1968), 483–502; Bruce S. Bennett, 'Banister v. Thompson and Afterwards: The Church of England and the Deceased Wife's Sister's Marriage Act', *Journal of Ecclesiastical History*, 49 (1998), 668–82.

[99] *Hansard*, 156 (27 Feb. 1860), cols. 1823–4; *The Times* (23 Mar. 1859).

debates typically followed denominational loyalties, and the matter struck at
the heart of broader discussions concerning Anglican doctrine and its proper
function within the polity.[100] These distinctions were absent from the claims
of female petitioners who frequently resorted to the appellation of the
'Women of England'. However, contemporaries were alert to the superfi-
ciality of such gendered constructs. In wilfully misreading the epithet as a
literal expression of the female members of the nation, *The Times* exposed
such claims to ridicule, noting that one such petition was signed by only
thirty-one women.[101] If female petitioners wished their interventions to
avoid challenge at Westminster, it was advisable to either confine themselves
to issues which might be construed as appropriate to female interest or to
parade an overtly feminine identity. However, even if they chose the latter,
a respectful response could not be guaranteed.

There was also a disjuncture between parliamentary expectations and
local provincial practice. Whilst scholars' attention has focused upon incidents of mass campaigning on national causes, small petitions, collected
within parishes and covering a diverse range of issues, were an important
facet of this story. Many communities condoned mixed-sex petitions on a
whole variety of questions—including railway maintenance, capital punishment, the Sabbath, and constitutional reform.[102] Nonetheless contemporaries might experience (or present) such conduct as a knowing departure
from usual gendered expectations. As Sarah Ellis wrote to a friend in 1832,
'Ours is a very odd sphere at Ridgmont. I have just had to draw up a petition to Parliament respecting the over-working of children in factories.'[103]
The contours of acceptable practice were therefore highly fluid: politically
active women faced increasing pressure to promote their femininity if they
wished their voices to be heard in national forums. Significant counter-
discourses emphasized women's rights as 'householders', but their comparative rarity underlines the unsettled and uneven imagining of females as
political actors. The easy dismissal of petitions which contained female
signatures when politically expedient exemplified women's peripheral
location within the political nation.

---

[100] For a review of contemporary attitudes and literature on the matter see *Edinburgh Review*
(Apr. 1853), 315–41.

[101] *The Times* (10 Mar. 1859); see also *The Times* (12 Feb. 1861).

[102] *Reports of the Select Committee of the House of Commons on Public Petitions* provide detailed
indices of the petitions presented. Samples from 1833 and 1839 reveal the widespread
practice of small, localized petitions from particular parishes or towns.

[103] Quoted in Ellis, *Home Life*, 47–8.

Female experts and the Victorian state

The advent of female associational life, with its ambitions to provide assistance to the lives of the poor, was a major aspect of British social and cultural development in this period. The implications of charitable giving for parish policies and community institutions meant that women made an ongoing contribution to local governance.[104] Indeed, there were calls across our period for women's activities to be accorded a formal status. This included Catharine Cappe's vision of an institutionalized role for lady visitors in asylums, charitable institutes, hospitals, and schools in the early nineteenth century, and Louisa Twining's efforts to secure lady visitors' access to workhouses in the late 1850s.[105] As we shall see in Chapter 4, women's local interventions were a highly significant facet of contemporary female public activity. However women also made an impact nationally through the emerging phenomenon of the female expert. During the first half of the nineteenth century there was a steady stream of exceptional woman who established themselves in this role. These were women who through personal activities, specialist publications, and the use of elite networking earned national reputations for their contribution to substantial policy issues. Prominent in this respect were the likes of Catharine Cappe; the prison reformer Elizabeth Fry; the poor law campaigner Mary Ann Gilbert; penal reformers Lady Byron and Mary Carpenter; workhouse experts such as Louisa Twining; the nursing pioneer Florence Nightingale; the anti-slavery strategist Elizabeth Heyrick; and political economists like Harriet Martineau.

Such women demonstrated that it was possible to accrue considerable cultural capital to overcome many of the prescriptions of gender within a particular community or field. By the late 1850s the widespread acceptance of female philanthropy, combined with increasingly progressive views on women's public roles in liberal networks, led to projects which gave a national platform to women's expertise. From 1857 the National Association for the Promotion of Social Science (NAPSS) encouraged women of intellectual authority and practical experience to deliver papers

---

[104] The classic overview is F. K. Prochaska, *Women and Philanthropy in Nineteenth-Century England* (Oxford, 1980).

[105] Catharine Cappe, *On the Desirableness and Utility of Ladies Visiting the Female Wards of Hospitals and Lunatic Asylums* (York, 1817) and Cappe, *Thoughts on Various Charitable*, 82–3; see n. 134 below for discussions of Twining's work.

at its conferences held around the country. It was, as *The Times* put it, a 'peripatetic parliament' in which women were 'already enfranchised'.[106]

Eileen Yeo argues that women's involvement in social science was achieved through the reiteration of heavily gendered assumptions, in particular that of 'social mothers'.[107] The well-known feminist Anna Jameson certainly made much of the need to unite male and female qualities in public life when she delivered her own critiques of poor law and parochial administration.[108] Whilst gender was a critical component in the authorial personas of these women, their interventions were also positioned as explicitly political, interrogating the relationship between state intervention, local government, and voluntarism.[109] Margaret Fison, a temperance and sanitary reformer (and author of a 'handbook' for the NAPSS) attacked parish authorities for their failure to implement the recommendations of the Board of Health and called for fundamental reforms to the system of poor relief.[110] Mary Bayly, a temperance campaigner active in the Kensington Potteries, detailed the government's poor record on sanitary reform and housing programmes and pointed to the narrow scope of contemporary legislative agendas.[111] Ellen Barlee, the manager of an innovative women's employment project in Pimlico, outlined policy initiatives to unite 'private benevolence' with parochial systems and urged for investigation into the structural causes of poverty.[112] Despite the humility of its title, Charlotte Ward's *Lending a*

---

[106] Lawrence Goldman, 'A Peculiarity of the English? The Social Science Association and the Absence of Sociology in Nineteenth-Century Britain', *Past and Present*, 114 (1987), 137.

[107] Eileen Janes Yeo, *The Contest for Social Science: Relations and Representations of Gender and Class* (London, 1996), ch. 5.

[108] Anna Jameson, *Sisters of Charity: Catholic and Protestant, Abroad and at Home* (London, 1855), pp. ix–x; Jameson, *The Communion of Labour* (London, 1856).

[109] See Louisa Twining, *Workhouses and Women's Work* (London, 1858); Miss Elliot and Frances Power Cobbe, *Destitute Incurables in Workhouses* (London, 1861); Frances Power Cobbe, *The Sick in Workhouses: Who they are, and How they should be Treated* (London, 1861), 11; Dora Greenwell, *On the Education of the Imbecile* (London, 1869); Florence Davenport Hill, *Children of the State: The Training of Juvenile Paupers* (London, 1868).

[110] Margaret Fison, *Handbook of the National Association for the Promotion of Social Science* (London, 1859), 15–18, 24–5, 190–204. For further references to Fison see *EWJ* 7 (1861), 194–5 and 8 (1861), 19–29.

[111] Mary Bayly, *Ragged Homes and How to Mend them* (London, 1859), 222–30. Bayly's insistence that the poor were to blame for their penury because of improvidence and drunkenness caused much debate in these circles: Bayly, *Workmen and their Difficulties* (London, 1861), 56. *EWJ* 8 (1861), 53, 281–3, and 11 (1863), 176–80; Mary A. Hyde, *How to Win our Workers: A Short Account of the Leeds Sewing School for Factory Girls* (Cambridge, 1862), 70–1.

[112] Ellen Barlee, *Our Homeless Poor; and What we can Do to Help them* (London, 1860); Barlee, *Friendless and Helpless* (London, 1863), esp. 222, 235 and chs 11–12. Barlee moved in the

Hand was a highly authoritative consideration of contemporary philanthropic practice and policy. In common with the other works cited here it displayed the author's credentials through the citation of government data, reports, and statistics, and the display of highly specialist knowledge.[113]

The mounting incidence of female philanthropic activity over the first half of the nineteenth century therefore resulted in a wide-ranging cohort of female experts who made sophisticated contributions to ongoing debates concerning the appropriate boundaries of state intervention. This was a phenomenon which emerged as part of the broader processes of change and debate concerning the role of government and its expansion. As scholars have been at pains to emphasize, the growth of the state occurred gradually and was usually grafted onto older models of elite paternalism and social interaction.[114] Certainly through publications and practical projects many of the women cited made a critical contribution to the development of government policies designed to unite state responsibility with local voluntarism. The Pauper Education Act (1862), for example, provided a legislative framework for projects such as Hannah Archer's pioneering boarding-out scheme for workhouse children in Wiltshire. Similarly an Act of 1863 facilitated the financing of reformatory projects such as those developed by Emmeline Way.[115] But this was also a process which could prove problematic. Way, for example, quickly lost authority over her boarding school for workhouse children when she registered it under the Industrial Schools Act.[116]

Nonetheless these women performed as confident political actors, who felt justified in approaching elite politicians with their views and queries. Elizabeth Fry was frequently in correspondence with successive home secretaries over individual cases and broader policy matters.[117] The Whig minister Lord Morpeth wrote graciously to her in 1841 that, 'I shall ever

---

circles of the Victoria Press and was a contributor to the *EWJ*. She continued her bitter attack upon parochial management in *A Visit to Lancashire in December, 1862* (London, 1863).

[113] Charlotte Ward, *Lending a Hand* (London, 1866). In addition to the other works cited above see Emma Sheppard, *Sunshine in the Workhouse* (London, 1860); M. A. S. Barber, *Earning a Living: Or, from Hand to Mouth, Scenes from the Homes of Working People* (London, 1861), 8, 28.

[114] Lubenow, *Politics of Government Growth*, 188.

[115] Hannah Archer, *A Scheme for Befriending Orphan Pauper Girls* (London, 1861); see also the arguments in Louise Twining, *Metropolitan Workhouses and their Inmates* (London, 1857), 3. This was not a move favoured by all—e.g. Barber insisted that female welfare workers should be paid: *Earning a Living*, 248–50.

[116] Barlee, *Friendless and Helpless*, 247–8.

[117] e.g. Jane Vansittart (ed.), *Katharine Fry's Book* (London, 1966), 71; NRO, MC 234/14.

look upon our intercourse as one of my most gratifying official reminiscences'.[118] This was part of a broader process of interaction between
authoritative women and the establishment. Maria Edgeworth, the Irish
writer and landowner, wrote directly to the prime minister, Lord John
Russell, when she was concerned about the government's implementation
of a parliamentary seed grant to famine-struck Ireland.[119] Amelia Opie,
who had a successful career as a novelist behind her as well as a record of
local philanthropic activism, was delighted with the response of Lord
Brougham, the former Lord Chancellor, to her request for information on
criminal justice reform: 'Lord Brougham has kindly sent me down a large,
thick foglio which I am pleased with . . . it treats of subjects the most
important probably that ever came before a government viz, the Criminal
Law, transportation &c—the evidence before the Committee of the House
of Lords & the opinions of all the judges on these questions.'[120]

Women of such cultural stature could position themselves as authoritative agents who might personally approach key members of state. Those
lacking the necessary credentials were likely to have their approaches
ignored. An obscure feminist, Elizabeth Pickett, was frustrated that her ideas
for 'establishing a more just & efficient system of Law & Government than
at present exists' met with no response from the establishment in 1848: Lord
Morpeth returned her proposals and the Royal Commission on the
Industrial Arts declined to consider them.[121] Similarly Sarah Bowdich
appreciated that as a 'lone woman' she faced considerable obstacles in
persuading politicians to take her plans seriously. In 1829 she was dejected
that Brougham had failed to reply to the prospectuses she had sent him.[122]
To secure a positive response women had to have accrued intellectual or
cultural capital through respect for their activities and publications and to
move in appropriate networks.

Thus, women of proven social and intellectual status benefited from
interstices in the official channels of power. Although this was a declining
source of influence, throughout our period governments continued to draw
upon informal conduits of information and personal networks to advance

[118] Lord Morpeth to Elizabeth Fry (17 June 1841), Rhodes House Library, University of
Oxford, Thomas Fowell Buxton papers, Brit. Emp. S. 444 (20), 267.
[119] Maria Edgeworth to Fanny Wilson (8 Mar. 1847), Edgeworth, c. 711, f. 174.
[120] Amelia Opie to Lady Catherine Boileau (30 Aug. 1847), NRO, N.R.S 24495, Boi
63/5/38.
[121] Elizabeth Pickett to Anne Knight (8 Apr. 1850), Friends House, Temp MSS 725/5/38.
[122] Sarah Bowdich to Thomas Hodgkin (2 May 1829), Wellcome Library for the History and
Understanding of Medicine, London, PP/Ho/D/A1321.

their agendas.[123] The success of Harriet Martineau's *Illustrations of Political Economy* and her evident intellectual strengths led the Whig government to enlist her as an adviser, commissioning such works as *Poor Laws and Paupers Illustrated* (1833) and *Illustrations of Taxation* (1834) to assist in the publicity for their legislative programmes. Unpublished findings of the poor law commissioners were made available to her and Whig politicians sought her opinion on a range of other issues, including educational policy.[124]

To understand these interactions we need to remember the continuing importance of personal contacts and patronage relationships in the functioning of the nineteenth-century state.[125] We still know remarkably little about women's exploitation of these traditional conduits of power relations in this period.[126] It is clear, however, that they could be closely implicated in the construction of the networks and personal relationships which were enmeshed in the workings of the polity. It was a process which could involve women carefully positioning themselves as political agents. The historian Agnes Strickland was active in seeking colonial offices for her brother, Thomas, affirming her own values of 'Christianity, loyalty and true patriotism', in the process.[127] Robert Peel may have had a distaste for patronage and sought to foster a new climate of meritocratic government but during his administration he faced numerous applications by women such as the well-known writers, Maria Edgeworth, Elizabeth Bowles, Caroline Southey, and Caroline Norton.[128] Peel felt obliged to decline their requests, but other women of intellectual stature did succeed in acting as

---

[123] For the continuing role of patronage in 19th-cent. government see Richard Johnson, 'Administrators in Education Before 1870: Patronage, Social Position and Role', and G. Sutherland, 'Administrators in Education After 1870: Patronage, Professionalism and Expertise', in G. Sutherland (ed.), *Studies in the Growth of Government* (London, 1972), 110–38 and 263–85. Both include examples of female patronage.

[124] James Martineau's shorthand commentary of Harriet Martineau's letters, transcribed by W. S. Coloe for R. K. Webb, Harris Manchester College, Oxford (13 Oct. 1832, 14 Nov. 1832, 30 Jan. 1834, Jan. 1844). For Martineau's career see R. K. Webb, *Harriet Martineau: A Radical Victorian* (London, 1960).

[125] J. M. Bourne, *Patronage and Society in Nineteenth Century England* (London, 1986); F. M. L. Thompson, *English Landed Society in the Nineteenth Century* (London, 1963), 74.

[126] See Chalus, *Elite Women*, ch. 4 for elite women as patronage brokers in the Georgian period.

[127] Agnes Strickland to Edward Bulwer Lytton [1858], HRO, D/EK /026/318/2.

[128] Letters to Robert Peel from Maria Edgeworth (28 Jan. 1843), Elizabeth Bowles [n.d.], Caroline Southey (Mar. 1843), Caroline Norton (25 Mar. 1843), British Library, Robert Peel papers, Add MSS 40, 524, fos. 12, 353; Add MSS 40, 526, fos. 182, 312. For Peel's approach to patronage see Philip Harling, 'Rethinking "Old Corruption"', *Past and Present*, 147 (1995), 148–50.

patronage brokers in this manner. Sarah Austin appears to have exercised influence over diplomatic appointments, and it was apparently due to Harriet Martineau's intervention that her close friend Thomas Southwood Smith, the pioneering Unitarian physician, was appointed to the central board of the Factory Commission in 1833.[129]

Therefore, despite growing bureaucratization and professionalism, traditional channels of personal influence and the use of private networks remained an important conduit for women's interaction with the state. Within such processes gender was of intricate and shifting significance. Whilst women of authority could override many of the prescriptions of gender in their dealings with the establishment, these were activities which had to be accommodated within women's own sense of self and this might involve an investment in more traditional modes of femininity. The Unitarian Mary Carpenter wrote numerous works on juvenile delinquency. Drawing on the authority she accrued from her experimental institutions in Bristol, she situated the question of reformatory schools within sophisticated debates on government policy, political economy, and the comparative merits of state responsibility versus the 'fluctuating' nature of voluntary institutions.[130] Despite her position as a national expert and government adviser in these matters, Carpenter exhibited a heightened consciousness of her gender throughout her career. In the early 1850s she declined an invitation to assist the committee drafting the bill on juvenile delinquency, feeling it more judicious to confine her role to reading the drafts they produced. As she explained to a correspondent, 'I feel sure that my work is to be done not by attempting myself any public action, for which my woman's nature quite unfits me, but by a true, earnest, free, simple, loving action of my own soul.' On another occasion she turned down a request that she chair a public meeting of the International Arbitration Association. In personal correspondence she frequently wrestled with her femininity, wondering whether her nature was more masculine or feminine, lamenting and simultaneously celebrating her 'woman's heart'.[131]

[129] Sarah Austin to Sir George Cornewall Lewis (23 May [1850]), National Library of Wales, Harpton Court Collection, C/817; Martineau, Transcribed letters, HMCO (25 Apr. 1833).
[130] Mary Carpenter, *Reformatory Schools, for the Children of the Perishing and Dangerous Classes, and for Juvenile Offenders* (London, 1851), e.g. 56–7, 242; Carpenter, *The Claims of Ragged Schools to Pecuniary Educational Aid from the Annual Parliamentary Grant* (London, 1859). For broader context see Richard Johnson, 'Educational Policy and Social Control in Early Victorian England', *Past and Present*, 49 (1970), 111–13.
[131] J. Estlin Carpenter, *The Life and Work of Mary Carpenter* (London, 1879), see 158, 162, 165, 405, 191.

The invitations Carpenter received indicate that these sensibilities were not shared by her male colleagues. Yet women themselves tended to remain uneasy with the spectre of individual female publicity. Private responses to the work of Florence Nightingale confirm such a view. Marianne Thornton, whilst praising Nightingale as a 'bright particular star born with powers that will enable her to carry out her high aspirations', worried about the 'host of unworthy imitators' that might follow in her wake.[132] Frances Allen who generally entertained rather radical political views was more blunt, writing to her niece Sarah Wedgwood, 'I think she has grievously mistaken her duty, if she sought for it, it lay close to her'.[133] The spectre of independent, active women in the national public eye could seem strange and unpalatable, prompting the reactive assertion of a hegemonic gender ideal. Personal investment in a particular, dominant construct of femininity (or the wish to see it enacted in a younger, female relative) could lead to the rearticulation of conservative views of women's sphere.

The complicated gendered implications involved in women assuming the role of a national expert may be examined more closely in the career of Louisa Twining (1820–1912). Twining, an Evangelical Anglican from the famous tea merchant family, was motivated by family bereavement to become involved in local charity in the late 1840s. By 1854 she had begun to visit workhouses and, by the end of the decade, had seen most of the London institutions and an additional 'thirty to forty' nationwide.[134] By the late 1850s Twining had presented several papers on workhouse reform to the NAPSS, published numerous tracts, and contributed articles and letters to the *Manchester Guardian*, *The Times*, the *Daily News*, *John Bull*, and *Englishwoman's Journal*.[135] She was also founder of the Workhouse Visiting Society (WVS), established to lobby for female access to these institutions,

---

[132] Marianne Thornton to Patty Smith [1854] CUL, ADD 7674/3/A.
[133] Frances Allen to Sarah E. Wedgwood (4 Dec. 1853), Keele University Library, W/M 118. Material from this collection is quoted by kind permission of the Wedgwood Museum Trust.
[134] For Twining's career see Kathleen McCrone, 'Feminism and Philanthropy in Victorian England: The Case of Louisa Twining', Canadian Historical Association, *Historical Papers* (1976), 123–39; Theresa Deane, 'Late Nineteenth-Century Philanthropy: The Case of Louisa Twining', in Ann Digby and John Stewart (eds), *Gender, Health and Welfare* (London and New York, 1996), 166–85; Louisa Twining, *Recollections of Life and Work, Being the Autobiography of Louisa Twining* (London, 1893).
[135] These contributions are discussed in letters to Louisa Twining from Anna Jameson (5 Dec. 1859); N. M. Sturch (4 Jan. [no year]); Revd Edward J. Beck [n.d.]; and the Editor of *John Bull* (8 Aug. 1866): The Women's Library, London, Papers of Louisa Twining (7LOT), 11b, 26c, 59b, and 79.

where she was particularly concerned with the education and training of pauper children and the care of the long-term ill.

Twining cultivated an epistolary network of well-placed, influential experts. This enabled the exchange of views and information, whilst helping her to maintain a high profile in the appropriate channels. Successive presidents of the Poor Law Board, as well as specialists such as Dr Edward Smith (medical officer to the Poor Law Board) and E. C. Tufnell (a workhouse inspector), were invaluable contacts: supporting the work of the WVS, keeping Twining abreast of departmental and government policies, and providing views and advice (when she was to appear before parliamentary committees, for example).[136] Her own lobbying of MPs contributed to the establishment of a government inquiry into workhouse policy.[137] In addition, Twining's work evoked a huge response from other experts in the field, including prominent educationists, public health specialists, and penal reformers. Only very occasionally did her requests for assistance or intervention fall on deaf ears (or at least this is the impression conveyed in the archive of letters she chose to preserve).[138] The majority of her correspondents evinced considerable respect for Twining and her wider network of female experts, praising also the work of two other practitioners in the field: Emma Sheppard and Emmeline Way.[139]

Male experts made little of her gender in their correspondence with her, but Twining's female correspondents revealed considerable anxiety as to whether her projects were sufficiently rooted within a female model of behaviour. Grass-roots activists were evidently grateful for the leadership and inspiration she provided,[140] yet those who had gained prominence

---

[136] e.g. letters to Louisa Twining from T. H. S. Sotheron Estcourt (3 July 1858), (14 July [no year], 7 May 1859, 21 June 1859); Walter Crofton (1 Feb. 1864); John Thornely (on behalf of C. P. Villiers) (24 Dec. 1859); Dr Edward Smith (14 July [no year]); E. C. Tufnell (29 Oct. and 18 May 1860); James Stansfeld (15 Dec. 1871): 7LOT, 3b–c, 5d–e, 15b, 17d, 27a–b; 130b, 94; Twining, *Recollections*, 118.

[137] Letters to Louisa Twining from John V. S. Townshend (4 July 1857); C. N. Neave to Louisa Twining (17 June [no year]): 7LOT, 4c and 98.

[138] Letters to Louisa Twining from Dr Edward H. Sieveking (Sept. 1857); Revd William C. Lake (24 May 1860); Revd Joseph Kingsmill (9 Jan. 1861) and Revd John P Morris (11 Mar. 1867): 7LOT, 24, 28, 37, and 108b. Sir George Nicholls, former Permanent Secretary to the Poor Law Board, declined cooperation with the WVS, claiming it would be 'inconsistent with his position in regard to the Poor Law executive': Sir George Nicholls to Louisa Twining (24 June 1858): 7LOT, 6b.

[139] Letters to Louisa Twining from Sir B. Brodie (19 May 1859) and C. N. Neave (17 June [no year]): 7LOT, 20d, 98.

[140] See Catherine Batten to Louisa Twining (21 Jan. [no year]), and the enthusiastic letter from a committee of ladies in Carrickmacross to Louisa Twining (9 May 1863): 7LOT, 78 and 132.

themselves could be extremely sensitive about the maintenance of gendered proprieties. Ellen Ranyard, founder of the Bible nurse movement whereby working-class women distributed both medical care and Bibles to poor communities, wrote of her hopes that they would be able to keep women's work *'womanly'*.[141] Mrs Peirce, a member of the NAPSS, wrote hopefully, 'perhaps I shall find from you that the Voluntary labour of Christian women supplys [sic] the needed feminine influence without the legal formality that might be disagreeable.'[142] Sarah Austin also downplayed the emerging professionalism of female philanthropy. She praised Twining's scheme of lady superintendants, but added pointedly that she herself did not have time for such projects, as she confined her energies to 'my own special *hobby*'—a home for pauper children.[143] Twining herself was careful to foreground the qualifications of (elite) women in publicly circulated letters. Thus in *A Letter to the President of the Poor Law Board on Workhouse Infirmaries* she asserted, 'surely the care of the sick and helpless and aged is pre-eminently the duty of women'.[144] But the scope of Twining's projects was also a cause for concern to some women. Florence Nightingale and Angela Burdett Coutts both warned Twining of the necessity of confining her projects to small schemes.[145] In contrast, Twining's plans to extend her work to Ireland were supported by Sir Crofton, the commissioner of inquiry into Irish prisons, and Charles Hood offered to give financial support to Twining's proposed institution for the treatment of the terminally ill, only if the project was national, rather than local in scope.[146] Those men who raised anxieties pinpointed not her gender, but the inferior social status and conservatism of local guardians, as the potential stumbling block.[147] Whilst gender was treated as a fairly insignificant consideration by those in authority, women themselves felt anxious to display feminine sensibilities.

---

[141] Ellen Ranyard to Louisa Twining (24 Dec. 1860), 7LOT, 25.

[142] Mrs Peirce to Louisa Twining (16 Feb. [n.y.]), 7LOT, 113.

[143] Sarah Austin to Louisa Twining (5 Nov. 1857), 7LOT, 99b; original emphasis.

[144] Twining, *A Letter to the President of the Poor Law Board*, 3. See also *Journal of the Workhouse Visiting Society: Workhouses and their Inmates* (London, 1859), 8.

[145] Letters to Louisa Twining from J. Bonham Carter (for Florence Nightingale) (22 Mar. 1860); Angela Burdett Coutts (19 Feb. 1860), 7LOT, 18b and 21b.

[146] Letters to Louisa Twining from Walter Crofton (1 Feb. 1864) and Charles Hood (4 Jan. 1861), 7LOT, 17d, 33.

[147] Letters to Louisa Twining from H. G. Bowyer (13 Nov. 1859) and E. C. Tufnell (29 Oct. 1860), 7LOT, 39 and 27a.

Gender and parliamentary spaces

As parliamentary decision-making became more elaborate, the work of select committees and royal commissions provided opportunities for individual women to attend parliament in their own right as respected experts. Elizabeth Fry, Mary Carpenter, Louisa Twining, and Emmeline Way all gave evidence to parliamentary inquiries in this capacity.[148] Therefore although parliament was a pre-eminently masculine site, there were telling exceptions. Harriet Martineau was permitted access to the House of Commons library for research in the early mornings. Before business commenced parliament could be construed as a liminal space, its function as a masculine forum not yet realized. Gendered boundaries could thus be mutable, with spaces carrying different meanings at various times.[149] A female presence was actively encouraged on some occasions. The inclusion of lavishly dressed peeresses at the opening of parliament helped to signal the lustre of the political elite, with observers commenting on their style and glamour.[150] Other parliamentary spaces were accessed by women more routinely. Elizabeth Malkin described how she and a companion had been able to catch a glimpse of the Italian leader Garibaldi 'by the simple expedient of standing in the House of Commons lobby', and Alicia Bayne recalled taking tea in one of the committee rooms.[151]

Women's admission to parliamentary debates was more complicated, however. Colley's assertion that women were banned from the galleries in 1778 is a simplification. It seems to have been taken for granted that during critical debates elite women would still be permitted to the Lords' galleries.[152] Nonetheless, because female access to the Commons' galleries continued to be contentious, a custom developed in the early years of the nineteenth century whereby women were permitted to listen to the

---

[148] Anne Summers, '"In a Few Years we shall None of us that Now Take Care of them be Here": Philanthropy and the State in the Thinking of Elizabeth Fry', *Historical Research*, 67 (1994), 138; Prochaska, *Women and Philanthropy*, 152; Jo Manton, *Mary Carpenter and the Children of the Streets* (London, 1976), 107–11.

[149] Martineau, Transcribed letters, HMCO (30 Jan. 1834). Anthony Giddens suggests that social spaces are 'regionalised', their functions differing according to time and occasion: *Constitution of Society*, 119–32.

[150] Edward Baines to his wife (5 Feb. 1839), West Yorkshire Archives, Leeds, Baines papers, 45/5.

[151] Anthony R. Mills, *Two Victorian Ladies: More Pages from the Journals of Emily and Ellen Hall* (Letchworth, 1969), 107; Pryme, *Autobiographic Recollections*, 210.

[152] Colley, *Britons*, 248–9; P. D. G. Thomas, *The House of Commons in the Eighteenth Century* (Oxford, 1971), 149; *The Times* (6 Apr. 1829).

debates by sitting in the 'ventilator'. This was a cramped and humid space above the debating chamber. As Sarah Richardson explains, it allowed members to maintain 'the fiction of women's absence' for they were not included in the normal rules governing 'strangers' to the house. Following the fire which destroyed the Commons in 1834, a ladies' gallery was eventually agreed upon, although women had to listen to debates from behind a metal grille.[153] Significantly, this decision did not represent a unified male position—there had been considerable divergence in parliamentary opinion over the rationale and propriety of women's access to political debate.[154] Equally, female access to the 'ventilator' had represented diverse and multiple meanings to the women involved. Although it was a confined and stuffy location, some women used it to follow issues which are currently under-represented in the historiography of female politics, such as Jewish civic rights, and colonial policy relating to Canada.[155] For those with the right connections it functioned as a privileged space. Frances (Fanny) Edgeworth referred to her 'ecstasy in being really within the walls of St Stephens', observing 'We have a great privilege in being witnesses to the mysteries of the division which strangers are never allowed to see.' This was a view shared by Frances Verney who proudly affirmed, 'It was the best place for hearing in the House.' Women's personal knowledge of parliamentary orators could enhance their sense of belonging to a political elite. Fanny Edgeworth noted that one member spoke 'exactly as he used to do in the library'.[156] With its organized system of refreshments, this was also a venue for mixed-sex networking. As Priscilla Buxton noted to her aunt in 1833, 'I should have said that there was quite a levee in the Ventilator, so many ladies and Gentlemen too'.[157] Alicia Bayne remembered her love of the old ventilator space where she enjoyed the company of elite male politicians.[158]

[153] Sarah Richardson, *The Political Worlds of Middle-Class Women in Nineteenth-Century Britain* (Palgrave, forthcoming), ch. 5. My thanks to Sarah Richardson for allowing me to read this chapter prior to publication.

[154] *The Times* (17, 18, and 30 July 1835); Grantley F. Berkeley, *My Life and Recollections* (London, 1865–6, 2 vols), i. 359–63.

[155] Patty Smith to Fanny Allen (4 July 1849), Add 7621/359; Frances Mackintosh to Sarah Wedgwood [n.d.], W/M 167.

[156] Frances Edgeworth to Lucy Edgeworth (5 Mar. 1822), Edgeworth, c. 743, f. 171; Frances Parthenhope Verney, *Memoirs of the Verney Family during the Civil War* (London 1892, 2 vols), i. 339.

[157] Priscilla Buxton to Sarah Maria Buxton (16 May 1833), Brit. Emp. S. 444 (2), 282. There is a bill for refreshments taken in the ventilator, ibid. (1), 238.

[158] Pryme, *Autobiographic Recollections*, 209.

Yet cognizance of women's presence in this quasi-public space could be instantly suspended by politicians who performed different, homosocial identities when in the debating chamber. Here, they often acted as if it was a private members' club. This was encouraged by the 'premise of [female] invisibility', with allusions to women frequently prompting smutty humour.[159] The stylized masculinity of debating culture reinforced a sense of the primacy and cohesiveness of parliament as a masculine space. This is not to say that the gendered dichotomies of the Commons could not be challenged or resisted. The restrictions placed upon women, either from their banishment to the ventilator, or their seclusion behind the metal grille, could result in the emergence of a sense of female solidarity. One MP commented on women's 'loud approval and disapproval' from behind the grille during debates over affinal marriages in 1869. Also, women's restriction to this 'cage' became an important icon for suffrage campaigners.[160] Nevertheless, whilst the seeds for resistance and change may have grown from these gendered practices, we should also be mindful of how they simultaneously shaped female subjectivities in less empowering ways. As Helen Hills has suggested, 'space does not simply map existing social relations, but helps to construct them'.[161] The social imaginary of gender relations was reinscribed through parliament's gendered geographies. Women's experience of the ventilator space exemplified the 'paradoxical geography' they experienced.[162] It was a positioning which construed them as both central (by dint of their privileged access to the country's senate) yet simultaneously marginal. Women's habituation to experiencing parliamentary debates through this inhibiting architectural space required them to rehearse bodily their gendered exclusion. As we shall see in Chapter 5, the ventilator space tended to produce a distinctively feminized political

---

[159] Philip J. Waller, 'Laughter in the House: A Late Nineteenth-Century and Early Twentieth-Century Parliamentary Survey', *Twentieth-Century British History*, 5 (1994), 4–37; Silvia Rodgers, 'Women's Space in a Men's House: The British House of Commons', in Shirley Ardener (ed.), *Women and Space: Ground Rules and Social Maps* (London, 1981), 55, 63–4.

[160] Claire Eustance, 'Protests from Behind the Grille: Gender and the Transformation of Parliament, 1867–1918', *Parliamentary History*, 16 (1997), 107–26.

[161] Helen Hills, 'Theorising the Relationship between Architecture and Gender in Early Modern Europe', in Hills (ed.), *Architecture and the Politics of Gender in Early Modern Europe* (Aldershot, 2003), 5; see also Edward Soja and Barbara Hooper, 'The Spaces that Difference Makes: Some Notes on the Geographical Margins of the New Cultural Politics', in Michael Keith and Steve Pile (eds), *Place and the Politics of Identity* (London, 1993), 183–205.

[162] Gillian Rose, *Feminism and Geography: The Limits of Geographical Knowledge* (Cambridge, 1993), ch. 7.

subjectivity which, whilst indicative of women's privileged status, equally underlined their gendered marginalization.

Conclusion

There were a multitude of ways in which women could be conceptualized as citizens. However, they enjoyed but borderline political status as their position could never be assured. Just as the actions of an ambitious parliamentarian, a careful lawyer, or a sympathetic vestry could bring women within the political fold, so too could an obdurate clerk, a hostile chairman, or an antagonistic judge instantly exclude them. Attitudes towards female citizens were thus constantly in the process of being reformed and rearticulated. These micro-decisions provided opportunities for the assertion of new or heterodox practices. But at the macro-level progress was continually halted as the lack of consensus resulted in an uncertain field of action for women, and each contested case prompted the restatement of gendered differences.

Individual women of status, whether their position derived from their economic standing as householders, or from the cultural authority they had accrued, had considerable potential for public involvement and recognition. In contrast, when women's activities were projected to wider publics as a collective phenomenon—in electoral literature, philanthropic texts, or parliamentary petitions—a more restrictive mode of gendered discourse was usually employed. The resultant, ubiquitous images of reified femininity could make it difficult for even politically successful women to reconcile their status as respected experts with deeply embedded expectations of female roles.

This chapter has considered women's political activities through the prism of the nineteenth-century state. This was not a homogeneous entity, but rather an uneven composite of varying practices and institutions. This provided multiple points of entry for women to interject their own views and agendas, both at the local and national level, enabling them to make an active if problematic contribution to the constitution of the state.[163] In so doing it has ranged across a variety of 'publics', including vestry, constituency

---

[163] See Georgina Waylen, 'Gender, Feminism and the State: An Overview', and Vicky Randall, 'Gender and Power: Women Engage the State', in Vicky Randall and Georgina Waylen (eds), *Gender, Politics and the State* (London and New York, 1998), 1–17, 185–205. For the 'porous' nature of citizenship see Canning and Rose, 'Gender, Citizenship', 427–43.

and borough politics, parliament, pressure-group campaigning, and the family. The following chapters will seek to explore further the intricacies of female politicking through approaching our themes via different axes, isolating particular kinds of publics for scrutiny. Thus Chapter 2 considers the constitution of women in the collective identities of nineteenth-century political cultures. It considers women's experience and representations in associational politics and large-scale public meetings where they were defined primarily by their gender. As this chapter has hinted, as the wives of electors, the daughters of freemen, or the relatives of MPs, family relationships provided a web of sometimes conflicting political opportunities for women. Chapter 3 develops this theme, analysing the ambiguous significance of the family as a site for female political involvement. A recurring theme of this chapter has been how individual communities might sanction female voting or petitioning despite the fact that such practices were construed as aberrant in other parts of the polity. Chapter 4 therefore analyses how women were differently positioned in the parochial sphere of their own communities.

Women's political activities in the nineteenth century are often considered within the context of the modernizing impulses of the period, such as the rise of the middle classes, the growth of associational culture, and the moves towards a more democratic system. It is a picture which should be complemented with an awareness of the continuing salience of older modes and structures of political practice. This included local cultures of franchise entitlement, the significance of elite authority figures within the community, and an investment in familial rather than individual political identities. These, as we shall see, had varying implications for women across the different sites of their engagement.

2

Women, the public sphere,
and collective identities

Introduction

The previous chapter considered how women were positioned in relation
to the polity. Here we will develop the analysis by examining many of these
features of female citizenship through a different lens—their experience of
the public sphere. Recent historical inquiry has explored the interconnect-
edness between 'public' and 'private', recognizing the fluid boundaries that
might exist between the two.[1] Many sites of political exchange and sociability defy simple categorization along such a binary. Thus, salons, hydropathic hospitals, and even prisons could function as political sites which
depended upon networks and intimate socializing, blurring the distinction
between public and private.[2] Nonetheless, a recognition of the porosity
between 'public' and 'private' should not blind us to the fact that contemporaries often did make a qualitative distinction between the two. It is
helpful to retain a 'common-sense' understanding of 'public' to refer to
events which took place, say, outside of people's homes and to which access
was not necessarily restricted to acquaintances. When a meeting was held
in a venue which permitted the wide attendance of people beyond one's
acquaintance, such as large-scale meetings of political, religious, or philanthropic societies, contemporaries displayed great sensitivity to the need to
display heightened modes of gendered propriety. This was particularly the

---

[1] For helpful overviews see Rendall, 'Women and the Public Sphere'; Leonore Davidoff,
'Gender and the "Great Divide": Public and Private in British Gender History', *Journal of
Women's History*, 15 (2003), 11–27.

[2] Iain McCalman, 'Newgate in Revolution: Radical Enthusiasm and Romantic
Counterculture', *Eighteenth-Century Life*, 22 (1998), 95–110; Kathryn Gleadle, '"The Age of
Physiological Reformers": Rethinking Gender and Domesticity in the Age of Reform', in
Arthur Burns and Joanna Innes (eds), *Rethinking the Age of Reform* (Cambridge, 2003), 205;
Richardson, 'Well-Neighboured Houses', 56–73.

case when an event was designed to attract or mobilize support for a national cause or could be construed to have national significance. In this chapter we will therefore consider the public sphere of pressure-group campaigns, parliamentary elections, constituency celebrations, and royal visits. The gendered patterns of public conduct which typified gatherings of this nature had, it will be argued, a significant impact upon women's experiences of politics and their own attitudes towards female citizenship.

Despite his acknowledgement of women's contribution to constituency and electoral politics, James Vernon has suggested that by the 1830s women were marginalized from the public sphere and participated as observers rather than as agents in their own right. Even when women were incorporated into the public sphere he asserts that 'the terms of that inclusion were invariably restrictive'. Women's 'public political presence', concludes Vernon, 'was confined to supporting their husbands, sons or brothers in social, rather than overtly political, roles'.[3] Similar assumptions shape Simon Gunn's assessment of gendered publicity in the civic life of the middle class. It was a public sphere, he argues, which was characterized by its predominantly masculine nature.[4] Leonore Davidoff and Catherine Hall have also emphasized the centrality of an exclusive masculinity to the emerging identity of the Victorian middle class, claiming that the 'public world was consistently organized in gendered ways and had little space for women'. They were alert however, to the complexities and fluidities in the picture they evoked: 'Some divisions between men and women were enshrined in bricks and mortar, some in custom and practice and others in association rules and regulations, but *none were so set as not to be open to contestation and negotiation.*'[5]

This chapter proposes to pursue these insights. There were few obvious grounds of demarcation dictating when women were able to attend a public meeting and when they should remain at home. The rituals and routines developed across these settings were marked by unpredictability and instability. Beyond the sphere of private clubs and associations, which might certainly explicitly exclude females, if a woman was of a forthright disposition there appear to have been relatively few public meetings from which she would be openly turned away. Yet the courage it must have taken for a women to enter a meeting composed entirely of men is a factor that would be woven into their consciousness. In measuring the impact of

---

[3] Vernon, *Politics and the People*, 77–8, 91–2, 116, 208, 238–41, 249.
[4] Gunn, *Public Culture*.
[5] Davidoff and Hall, *Family Fortunes*, 416, 429; my emphasis.

restrictive boundaries we need to consider not only the ease with which they might be transgressed. We also need to be sensitive to the subtler, more insidious consequences of inegalitarian practices. This could contribute to the shaping of psyches and attitudes against the grain of individuals' own intellectual rationales.

Historians have often employed a rather literal interpretation of contemporary sources regarding women's attendance at public events. 'Their presence at public meetings was rarely commented upon in the press, which likely means that they were rarely present', wrote D. G. Paz in 1992.[6] Since then others have discovered that women were frequently present at civic events in the eighteenth-century town but rarely commented upon. 'The language of urban politics', concludes Rosemary Sweet, 'was such that women's presence or influence could not be acknowledged.[7] Over the course of our period it was increasingly common for references to be made to female attendance, but mention tended to be restricted to those occasions where special arrangements had been made to allow for differential kinds of access. Typically, at the election dinner held in Kettering in 1832 women were permitted to attend once the meal was over so as to hear the speeches.[8] These gendered distinctions were commonly formalized through the erection of galleries or the reservation of particular seats for women. The anti-slavery campaigner George Thompson described to his daughter how the appearance of her mother and a friend at a meeting in the Town Hall (where they sat in reserved seats in the gallery) 'honoured' the occasion with their presence, claiming they 'shed a lustre over the large assembly'.[9] Such use of space, according to Simon Morgan, 'served to reinforce the physical and symbolic distance between apolitical "Woman", the observer, and political "Man" the active participant'.[10] A similar arrangement was made in Newcastle at a dinner in honour of the Earl of Durham in 1834. Here 'as soon as dinner was over' ladies 'took their seats in the gallery amidst cordial greetings'.[11] Morgan argues that such

[6] Paz, *Popular Anti-Catholicism*, 275.

[7] Rosemary Sweet, 'Women and Civic Life in Eighteenth-Century England', in Rosemary Sweet and Penelope Lane (eds), *Women and Urban Life in Eighteenth-Century England: 'On the Town'* (Aldershot, 2003), 21–41, here at 22. See also Helen Rogers, 'Any Questions? The Gendered Dimensions of the Political Platform', *Nineteenth-Century Prose*, 29 (2002), 117–32.

[8] *The Times* (25 Dec. 1832).

[9] George Thompson to his daughter, Amelia (23 May 1847), John Rylands Library, University of Manchester, Raymond English Anti-Slavery Collection /3/2, 24.

[10] Simon Morgan, ' "A Sort of Land Debatable": Female Influence, Civic Virtue and Middle-Class Identity, c. 1830–1860', *Women's History Review*, 13 (2004), 183–209 here at 197.

[11] *The Times* (21 Nov. 1834).

procedures provided an acceptable means to incorporate women into the civic sphere. He notes that reports tended to focus upon women as a collective entity, emphasizing their feminine characteristics, in keeping with the need to convey the respectability of the bourgeois public sphere.[12]

Morgan's work provides a helpful contribution to our understanding of female public opportunities. Here I would like to suggest three further frames of analysis. The public events with which this chapter is concerned were primarily occasions on which people met together on the basis of their collective identity (as abolitionists, Protestants, or peace activists, for example). This meant that a consciousness of one's gender had the potential to be superseded or suspended, if momentarily, by other frames of identity. In contrast to Morgan, who emphasizes how women participated in a construction of public involvement based upon their femininity, I would suggest we also consider how individuals' own subjectivity involved more manifold elements of identification. Secondly, I would like to consider the effect of discursive representations upon women themselves. When women's presence was described it was usually done in such a way as to reify their status as feminine subjects. There were, as we shall see, telling fissures within such representations. Nonetheless, the tight discursive contours of these portrayals served to marginalize female public engagement. The ubiquity of these limited representations became woven into the subjectivity of even forthright campaigners for women's political rights.[13] Finally, our knowledge of female activity has tended to focus on those within the networks of Nonconformist liberalism, with women's positioning within the anti-slavery, anti-Corn Law, and peace movements receiving considerable attention.[14] Here, I will suggest that it is important to include women's involvement in a broader range of issues—including electoral and civic activities as well as the movements associated with conservative politics. Such an approach suggests that women's access to

[12] Morgan, 'A Sort of Land'. See also Nicholas Rogers, *Crowds, Culture, and Politics in Georgian Britain* (Oxford, 1998), 235–6; Peter Brett, 'Political Dinners in Early Nineteenth-Century Britain: Platform, Meeting Place and Battleground', *History*, 81 (1996), 527–52. Brett notes (530) that Peel's wife complained that she was unable to accompany him to a dinner in 1831. Her sense of pique may have derived from the fact that she commonly attended such events: e.g. *The Times* (16 May 1838).

[13] See Leonore Davidoff, 'Regarding Some "Old Husbands' Tales": Public and Private in Feminist History', in Davidoff, *Worlds Between: Historical Perspectives on Gender and Class* (Cambridge, 1995), 227–76, esp. 262–3.

[14] See Midgley, *Women against Slavery*; Louis and Rosamund Billington, '"A Burning Zeal for Righteousness": Women in the British Anti-Slavery Movement, 1820–1860', in Rendall, *Equal or Different*, 82–111; Morgan, 'Domestic Economy'; Tyrrell, 'Woman's Mission'.

activities beyond the domestic setting was constantly in the process of rene-gotiation. Regional, status, and political differences ensured that decisions as to the inclusion or exclusion of women were continually reinvented at the micro-level. As we shall see, public practices facilitating female atten-dance at meetings depended upon the infinite and myriad decisions constantly being made by historical actors. Gendered distinctions were not static but were continually reinvented. This complicated women's experience of and participation in the public sphere, but it also provided opportunity spaces for innovation and resistance to conventional practices.

Pressure-group politics and the public sphere

Within pressure groups women might consider themselves to be critically involved with the public sphere through their role as petitioners, canvassers, and as producers and consumers of pamphlet literature. The anti-slavery cause in particular has sparked great interest. Seventy-three female anti-slavery societies were established in the period 1825–33, and anti-slavery women made a major contribution to the movement's strategy and debate. Anti-slavery women hired public venues for their own committee meet-ings and often predominated—sometimes in considerable numbers—at mixed-sex public events. Many female societies developed views inde-pendent of those of local male societies on critical issues like the immediate versus the gradual abolition of slavery, and found means to exert leverage over policy through the withholding of funds. Yet they rarely acted in an official capacity at mixed-sex anti-slavery meetings: chairing and public speaking, for example, was confined almost wholly to men.[15] This was symptomatic. George Thompson liked his friend and co-worker, Elizabeth Pease, to attend committee meetings with him on the issues with which they were involved (namely British colonial policy).[16] Yet outside of Owenite circles, the formal inclusion of women was rare. Even organiza-tions such as the People's International League or the Friends of Italy, founded by radical unitarian feminists, had committees composed entirely of men.[17]

---

[15] Famously the British anti-slavery movement refused to allow female American delegates to participate in the 1840 World Anti-Slavery Convention. Midgley, *Women against Slavery*, esp. chs 3–4, and pp. 158–66.

[16] George Thompson to Elizabeth Pease (3 Nov. 1838), REAS/3/6.

[17] Gleadle, 'Our Several Spheres', 140–7; Barbara Taylor, *Eve and the New Jerusalem: Socialism and Feminism in the Nineteenth Century* (London, 1983), ch. 7.

In contrast, at the local level women commonly undertook arduous community activities. Philanthropic visitors, Bible society members, and temperance crusaders carved out districts over which campaigners would assume responsibility for home visiting and the distribution of tracts.[18] Sophia Sturge, a founder member of the female anti-slavery society in Birmingham, undertook extensive door-to-door canvassing, visiting thousands of households to persuade people to join the sugar boycott.[19] Traversing the community in this way could resonate with the sense of local authority which many women assumed. Women's experiences were thus marked by a paradoxical geography.[20] There was a striking disjuncture between local and personal experiences of women's political activities and the practices and representations which tended to dominate at large-scale events and in quasi-official accounts. As we will see in Chapter 4, local communities sometimes championed the work of the anti-slavery women in their midst and identified their civic image with such endeavours. On the other hand, at major meetings organizers commonly reinscribed the sentiment that women were less suited to the demands and bustle of public life. Despite the ceaseless and energetic work of female peace promoters, James Clark, a delegate at the Paris Peace congress in 1850, seemed struck that the women attending 'have borne the fatigue wonderfully'.[21] Sentiments such as these could lead to the careful delineation of gendered space at meetings, in sharp distinction to women's authority over their local terrain. This in turn affected how women themselves might frame their participation. In 1832 Frances Mackintosh attended an anti-slavery meeting held at Exeter Hall from where she wrote a letter to Sarah Wedgwood. Mackintosh noted wryly the provision of a room 'prepared with water for fainting ladies'. Yet Mackintosh herself had found the occasion to be 'vilely crowded' with no seats available. She confessed to her correspondent that she had 'sneaked out' and was now composing her letter in this very room. Whilst mocking the perceived need to cater to women in this manner, that Mackintosh herself sort refuge in the room would have reiterated organizers' assumptions as to the need for special arrangements.[22] These individual decisions comprised a broader sociological process concerning the ongoing construction of contemporary gender difference.

---

[18] See Ch. 4 below; Prochaska, *Women and Philanthropy*, esp. chs 4 and 6.

[19] Tyrrell, *Joseph Sturge*, 50.

[20] Rose, *Feminism and Geography*, ch. 7.

[21] Cited in David Nicholls, 'Richard Cobden and the International Peace Congress Movement, 1848–1853', *Journal of British Studies*, 30 (1991), 374.

[22] Frances Mackintosh to Sarah Wedgwood (May 1832), W/M, 167.

The demarcation of gendered space at public meetings was but one means to highlight their respectability. Another was to represent female audiences within a discourse of highly stylized femininity, emphasizing their decorative presence. Public meetings are a form of performance in which an individual's clothes and demeanour assume a heightened significance.[23] In contrast to the tightly regimented nature of male middle-class apparel, women enjoyed comparative 'aesthetic freedom'—being able to choose from a rich array of fabrics and colours—but they were expected to be finely sensitive to the parameters within which they might exercise this agency.[24] These were subtle codes that had to be learnt—often subconsciously. Too flamboyant an appearance and a woman risked being criticized for her 'love of finery'.[25] The unspoken pressure for women to comport themselves in a particular way at public occasions—neatly dressed, upright, gracious—must have heightened an awareness of their gendered bodies. An important part of that process involved the ways in which women moved through public spaces. Contemporary fashions which emphasized tiny waists through imposing sleeves and shoulders and wide, bell-shaped skirts shaped women's deportment.[26] Feminist scholars have argued that presenting women as the subjects of a male gaze further intensifies a consciousness of their occupation of space.[27] This is germane here, for the trope of 'well dressed ladies' became the most common means to reference women's presence at public meetings, reinforcing an assumption that female spectators formed part of the visual tableau of public moments.[28] A typical example is a report from *The Times* in August 1820 describing the arrangements made for a gathering in support of Queen Caroline. 'Temporary galleries had been erected around the court, or coach-yard, for the accommodation

[23] Consideration has only recently been given to the relationship between women's experience of the public and female corporeality: Carole Turbin, 'Refashioning the Concept of Public/Private: Lessons from Dress Studies', *Journal of Women's History*, 15 (2003), 43–51; Barbara Burman and Carole Turbin (eds), special edn of *Gender and History*, 14 (2002). Simon Gunn does consider some aspects of 'fashionable femininity' in *Public Culture*, e.g. at 144.

[24] Iris Marion Young, *Throwing Like a Girl: And Other Essays in Feminist Philosophy and Social Theory* (Bloomington, Ind., 1990), 186.

[25] Mariana Valverde, 'The Love of Finery: Fashion and the Fallen Woman in Nineteenth-Century Social Discourse', *Victorian Studies*, 32 (1989), 169–88.

[26] For an illustrated overview see Charles H. Gibbs-Smith, *The Fashionable Lady in the Nineteenth Century* (London, 1960).

[27] Young, *Throwing Like a Girl*, 179; Lynda Nead, 'Mapping the Self: Gender, Space and Modernity in Mid-Victorian London', in Roy Porter (ed.), *Rewriting the Self: Histories from the Renaissance to the Present* (London and New York, 1997), 167–85.

[28] Morgan, *Victorian Woman's Place*, ch. 8.

of the ladies who might attend,' the correspondent explained, 'and these were completely filled with well-dressed females.'[29] To focus upon women's attire in this manner could be used to attest to the probity of an occasion, even if separate accommodation had not been arranged. Thus at a Christian Chartist festival held in Birmingham's Town Hall, the meeting was described as 'densely crowded, being principally filled with well-dressed ladies'.[30]

These representations did not provide a literal commentary on women's attire nor simply determine behaviour of course. When the enterprising Rebecca Solly (wife of the Unitarian Chartist preacher, Henry) wished to hear Henry Vincent give an election speech at a hotel in Yeovil in 1843, she extricated herself from the great crush to tend her new baby by climbing a ladder and exiting through a window! Solly came from an unconventional, feminist-minded family—most women would have found it difficult to disregard polite mores so flagrantly.[31] Equally, evocations of 'well-dressed ladies' could mask gender tensions and expunge recognition of women's potential for more robust intervention on the ground. Catherine Hall observes that a 'number of elegantly dressed ladies in the gallery' were noted at the celebration dinner held in Birmingham in February 1839 in honour of the town's recent incorporation. However this had only been agreed after local women had protested bitterly about a proposal that they should be seated in a side gallery where they would not be able to see or hear the speeches.[32] Perpetuating these particular representations of femininity thus required a suspension of contemporaries' practical experience of publicly active females.

Nonetheless, the pervasive nature of these representations contributed to the cultural codification of gendered performance, privileging male public activity as the focal point of political affairs. The constant repetition of practices, such as gendered segregation and the sheer ubiquity of the benign images of women in the public sphere, formed part of the cultural resources of contemporary women (even if some individuals might choose to deliberately flout such prescriptions). As Patrizia Violi has argued,

---

[29] *The Times* (30 Aug. 1820).

[30] *National Association Gazette* (8 Jan. 1842)

[31] Henry Solly, *These Eighty Years: Or, the Story of an Unfinished Life* (London, 1893, 2 vols), i. 416–17. Rebecca Solly's brother was a Unitarian feminist, William Shaen (for whom see Gleadle, *Early Feminists*, passim).

[32] Catherine Hall, 'Private Persons versus Public Someones: Class, Gender and Politics in England, 1780–1850', in Hall, *White, Male and Middle Class: Explorations in Feminism and History* (Cambridge, 1992), 163–4.

'Collective representations of women are significant because they define our gender identity and because the construction of our gendered subjectivity is affected by them.'[33] Certainly Schwarzkopf and Rogers found that the gendered nature of women's inclusion in the Chartist movement reinforced particular feminine identities.[34] Similarly, listen here to Geraldine Jewsbury, a writer of advanced views on the position of women, writing to her great friend Jane Welsh Carlyle of a recent meeting with which she had been involved in support of Hungarian independence:

> I tried to go, but there was not a woman in the place, so it was too strong for me to go as *femme sole*, representative of the women of England. But, really, a meeting all of men looks a deal more imposing than when interspersed with white pocket-handkerchiefs. I had just a glimpse (for tickets were sent me), and such a surface of upturned, rough faces was very stirring . . . The people were very civil, and as I declined going in when I found how it was, a gentleman most gallantly took me and Mrs. —, who was with me, into the Council Room behind the platform, and opened the door; but as we could only hear one word in five, we soon retired.[35]

That Jewsbury was sent tickets for the meeting and that she initially went to the occasion with her friend suggests that at least some of the organizers, and Jewsbury herself, assumed it was appropriate for women to attend. What prevented Jewsbury from entering was not formal prohibition but a lack of confidence in entering a male-only environment and a fear that such behaviour would be interpreted as extreme. The deeply entrenched assumption that the political sphere was essentially masculine was woven into the subjectivities of even progressive women such as Jewsbury. Her emotive evocation of 'upturned, rough faces' and her comment that 'a meeting all of men' was more imposing than one attended also by women reveals that pervasive cultural modes could exert a powerful sway upon the imaginative landscape of even self-styled radicals. That many commentators sometimes disparaged a meeting by adverting to the large numbers of women present undoubtedly heightened such sentiments.[36] Tellingly, Zachary Macaulay recorded that he 'rejoiced to see the proportion of men far exceed that of ladies' at an anti-slavery meeting in 1825, believing this

---

[33] Violi, 'Gender, Subjectivity and Language', 174.

[34] Schwarzkopf, *Women in the Chartist Movement*, *passim*, but see esp. ch. 10; Rogers, *Women and the People*, ch. 3.

[35] Geraldine E. Jewsbury to Jane Welsh Carlyle (20 Aug. 1849) in Ireland, *Selections from the Letters of Geraldine Endsor Jewsbury*, 291.

[36] e.g. report of the SICLC, *The Times* (27 June 1845).

represented a greater adherence to anti-slavery ideas.[37] Despite the many forums which included women, the public sphere was still a male-dominated entity and this could make women feel disinclined to participate in aspects of it.

Finding a public voice

A fundamental difference between women and men's experience of the public sphere was that men, through their status, talents, or activities, commonly accrued sufficient cultural capital (or simply possessed the confidence) to claim the right to speak at public meetings. This was only an exceptional experience for women. Nonetheless, there were small shifts, innovations, and experiments which cut against the grain and fractured the masculine hegemony of the public sphere. In the networks of metropolitan radicalism women such as Eliza Flower, her sister Sarah Flower Adams, and their close associate Sophia Dobson Collet, composed political songs and anthems which were sung at a variety of progressive political events, from Chartist meetings to the annual celebrations for the Swiss national struggle.[38] A more widespread practice was for women to express their opinions at public forums through the medium of a sympathetic male who would read or describe their activities.[39] The Co-operative League, for example, organized public readings of the work of Mary Gillies and Eliza Meteyard ('Silverpen').[40] Less prominent women could also gain a voice at gatherings in this way. At meetings of the Society for the Improvement of the Condition of the Labouring Classes (SICLC), a body founded in 1844 and heavily influenced by 'ultra' Evangelicalism, letters from both men and women detailing the society's projects and agenda were read out.[41] The nature of the vegetarian movement, with its obvious emphasis upon food preparation, appears to have been particularly associated with facilitating women's public contributions. At the annual meeting of the Vegetarian Society in 1865 a Mr Barker positioned himself as a spokesperson for the

---

[37] Emma Pigott, *Memoir of the Honourable Mrs Upcher of Sheringham* (London, 1860), 163.

[38] *The Reasoner*, 5 (1848), 351 and 6 (1849), 19; Sophia Dobson Collet papers (in private hands). My thanks to Collet's descendants for allowing me access to their collection.

[39] The testimony of Fanny Lacy was read, along with letters of male champions of the vegetarian cause, at a conference held in Ramsgate in 1847: *Truth Tester*, 2 (1848), 29; *Dietetic Reformer*, (Jan. 1865), 8.

[40] *Howitt's Journal* (3 July 1847).

[41] See below p. 213.

vegetarian activist, Mrs Smith, of Glasgow, relating her activities to the
meeting whilst noting, 'He was quite sure she could make a very eloquent
speech'.[42] Within these networks there was a progressive strand which
condoned more explicit instances of female public speaking. Elizabeth
Horsell, for example, was accustomed to giving florid speeches at vegetarian
meetings.[43]

Clearly many of these practices capitalized upon particular 'feminine'
associations—music, the epistolary, and catering. Occasionally there were
women who might 'earn' the right to speak in public meetings by dint of
their exceptional authority in certain fields. It was not uncommon for elite
women to address specific constituencies within their own communities or
networks.[44] From the 1840s it would appear that a few exceptional women
were able to do this in wider and more formal public spheres. George Jacob
Holyoake reported that, because of her profound deafness, Harriet
Martineau 'could take no part in public meetings or conferences, save those
of which the business was foreknown to her'.[45] This seems to suggest that
Martineau made active contributions where possible. It is probable that
Martineau's singular standing and contacts in the political world gave her a
particular authority to speak. Lady Byron, an acknowledged expert in such
areas as penal reform and co-operation, was similarly placed. In 1854 she
was invited to the Birmingham court to attend the inauguration of the new
legislation concerning the treatment of juvenile delinquents:

> While waiting for the Recorder, a conversn arose on the subject of the
> J[uvenile] D[elinquents] Bill—& as I had been invited there, I saw not
> reason why I should not say a few words now & then, tho the only Woman
> . . . Rev York gave me his arm & conducted me to the place assigned me
> near the Judge & Mayor—the other Ladies being at a distance—There was
> nothing to be done but to acquiesce—& let myself be stared at.[46]

Not all civic authorities would have been as willing to extend such an invitation and the heightened gender tensions are palpable here. However the
recorder referred to was the radical Unitarian Matthew Davenport Hill,
who had played a major role in the passage of the Act in question. As

[42] *Dietetic Reformer* (Jan. 1865), 8.
[43] *Vegetarian Advocate* (Nov. 1850), 66–8, and (Dec. 1850), 74. See also *Vegetarian Messenger* (June 1851), 45.
[44] See below pp. 127, 139, 142, 144, 151–2.
[45] George Jacob Holyoake, *Bygones Worth Remembering* (London, 1905, 2 vols), i. 171.
[46] Lady Byron, 'Notes Made at Birmingham' (3 Sept. 1854), Bodleian Library, University of Oxford, Lovelace Byron papers, 143. Reproduced by permission of Pollinger Ltd and the Earl of Lytton. See also Byron's letter to Caroline Bathurst (4 Sept. 1854), ibid., f. 144.

recorder of Birmingham since 1839, he had long exhibited the most liberal sentiments regarding women's public role. He was well acquainted with Mary Carpenter, whose projects concerning juvenile reformation had been financed by Byron; and Hill and Carpenter had arranged two conferences on juvenile reformatory schools in Birmingham in 1851 and 1853.[47] Thus the civic sphere was not a monolithic, masculine space but could be moulded and shaped by particular networks to encourage more progressive policies towards women. By the end of our period, as we saw in Chapter 1, women in these circles were gaining access to institutional forums, such as the NAPSS. A rather cautious Mary Carpenter did so, for example, in 1860.[48]

Female lecturing was also a common phenomenon within the circles of radical activism, as the careers of Frances Wright, Anna Wheeler, Eliza Sharples, and Jessie White Mario testify.[49] Mainstream commentators might revile the public lecturing of Owenite women, but even so there was growing sympathy for those speaking on such topics as female education, temperance, and social reform. In Sheffield a Mrs Spurr enlightened local ladies on the subject of infant education in 1836, for example.[50] Despite her rehabilitation of Mary Wollstonecraft, temperance campaigner Clara Lucas Balfour gained wide recognition as a 'respectable' speaker.[51] As Elizabeth Pease observed in 1852, female public speaking on 'behalf of Temperance & other philanthropic questions' had become less contentious.[52] Women of exceptional cultural authority in relevant fields were increasingly 'earning' the right to speak in public on a variety of causes. This did not fundamentally alter the representation or experiences of the generality of female

[47] Rosamond and Florence Davenport Hill, *The Recorder of Birmingham: A Memoir of Matthew Davenport Hill* (London, 1878), in particular 115, 161, 250; *ODNB*.

[48] Lawrence Goldman, *Science, Reform and Politics in Victorian Britain: The Social Science Association, 1857–1886* (Cambridge, 2002), 115–18.

[49] Taylor, *Eve and the New Jerusalem, passim*; Helen Rogers, ' "The Prayer, the Passion and the Reason" of Eliza Sharples: Freethought, Women's Rights and Republicanism, 1832–52', in Yeo, *Radical Femininity*, 52–78. For Mario's lecture tour on Italian nationalism, 1855–6, see Elizabeth Adams Daniels, *Jessie White Mario: Risorgimento Revolutionary* (Athens, Ohio, 1972), 53–4.

[50] Mrs Thomas Spurr, *Course of Lectures on the Physical, Intellectual, and Religious Education of Infant Children: Delivered before the Ladies of Sheffield* (Sheffield, 1836).

[51] Kristin G. Doern, 'Equal Questions: The "Woman Question" and the "Drink Question" in the Writings of Clara Lucas Balfour, 1808–78', in Sue Morgan (ed.), *Women, Religion and Feminism in Britain, 1750–1900* (Basingstoke, 2002), 159–75.

[52] Elizabeth Pease to William Lloyd Garrison (9 July 1852), Boston Public Library, MS.A.1.2.21.50. The Duchess of Sutherland made a similar observation in a letter to Thomas Fowell Buxton (21 Dec. 1840), Brit. Emp. S. 444 (20), 91a.

participants but it did form a significant and growing counter-current within political culture.

Another development that assisted women in gaining access to the public sphere was the adoption of domestic modes of sociability, such as evening soirees and 'conversaziones' for political purposes.[53] Foremost amongst these inclusive forums of campaigning was the tea party. A tactic long employed by parliamentary candidates, it pointed to a conscious politicization of a traditionally female mode of interaction.[54] When Birmingham Dissenters organized an event to celebrate the passage of the Dissenters' Chapels Bill in 1844, their strong temperance leanings combined with a desire to recognize the significance of this Act for all members of the Dissenting community made a tea party an obvious choice.[55] Arranging a tea party could imply a valorization of women's contribution to a particular movement, albeit in highly gendered terms. Social practices such as the tea party therefore created 'female-friendly' zones of political engagement. Their use amongst progressive circles also showed that there was the space to reconfigure such rituals to facilitate further innovations in social practice. As a report of the Co-operative League emphasized in 1847, 'At two of the chief tables Mr. and Mrs. Howitt made tea'. Their shared labour is indicative of the egalitarian policies associated with the Howitt coterie.[56]

This did not go unchallenged, of course. As Catherine Hall observes, the *Quarterly Review* thundered against the Anti-Corn Law League's use of mass tea parties 'for the purposes of *political agitation*'.[57] The association of the tea party with the presence of women enabled it to be portrayed as a lesser form of political organization. *The Times*, for example, referred disparagingly to 'tea party rhetoric' and 'tea party arguments'.[58] The tea party thus provided an inclusive forum for political engagement, facilitating women's participation in a range of political causes. Nonetheless, as an avowedly feminine mode of interaction it could lack the status and cachet of more traditional modes of political sociability.

---

[53] e.g. George Eliot to Clementia Taylor (27 Mar. 1852), Gordon S. Haight, *The George Eliot Letters*, ii. *1852–1858* (London, 1954), 15.

[54] See above p. 31; and Vernon, *Politics and the People*, 240–3. For examples see Plymley Notebook, SRO, 1066/120 (1819); Jacques, *Merrie Wakefield*, 98.

[55] Diary of Rebecca Kenrick (1844), Birmingham City Archives, MS 2024/1/1, 24.

[56] 'Weekly Record', in *Howitt's Journal* (9 Jan. 1847). For the Howitt coterie see Gleadle, *Early Feminists*.

[57] Hall, 'Private Persons', 167–8.

[58] *The Times* (20 Dec. and 24 Nov. 1842).

Ultra-Protestantism

To illustrate more fully the subtle processes of interplay between individual agency, discursive representations, and public practice, let us consider the case study of ultra-Protestantism. This was an important strand of popular Toryism during the 1830s and 1840s. It articulated a vigorous anti-Catholicism, galvanized by the Emancipation Act of 1829 and by continuing political unrest in Ireland.[59] One of the most prominent figures within the Ultra-Protestant camp was the popular writer, Charlotte Elizabeth Tonna, who vigorously championed women's right to intervene in public affairs, particularly over the Irish question.[60] In her *Christian Lady's Magazine* she exhorted women to mobilize on the matter but assumed that their presence at public meetings might be controversial. Describing her attendance at a public meeting at Freemason's Hall in December 1835, she explained how she and a group of female friends had 'boldly entered' the meeting. The use of such language reminded her readership that access to the public sphere might depend upon the audacious actions of individuals. In a rather disingenuous reversal of etiquette she also insisted that she and her friends would have given up their seats to gentlemen attendees were they required to do so. Tonna thus felt the need to defuse potential fears that she was encouraging belligerent female behaviour by hinting at their humility.[61]

By 1852 meetings of this nature usually accommodated women through the erection of a gallery.[62] The provision of galleries for female audience members often had complex motives. When the controversial premillenarian preacher, Hugh McNeile established an auxiliary of the Protestant Association in Liverpool in 1839 women were provided with designated gallery space at its meetings. However, this did not reflect an assumption that women were physically more fragile: the association reported that large numbers of women spent many hours queuing outside the venue to obtain seats before the event began. Nor does it appear to have originated in a desire to segregate women—for they were also seated in the main body of the amphitheatre. (This is only to be expected given that women formed around 70 per cent of the audience at its annual meeting.) The allusion to gallery accommodation for women seems to have been a strategic move to hint that women were welcome to attend and could do

[59] John Wolffe, *The Protestant Crusade in Great Britain, 1829–1860* (Oxford, 1991).
[60] Gleadle, 'Charlotte Elizabeth Tonna'.
[61] *Christian Lady's Magazine*, 5 (1836), 92.
[62] e.g. *Protestant Magazine* (Dec. 1852), 392.

so with propriety.[63] Such policies reinforced the increasing uniformity of discursive representations of public meetings and their gendered use of space, but did not therefore necessarily reflect the circumstances or attitudes of individual bodies which might condone less regimented practices. Even so, female involvement often had to be argued for locally. In Sheffield a request that a ladies' committee be established to emulate the successful pattern of female involvement in the York Protestant Society appears to have stalled. It required local insistence to resuscitate the proposal. One supporter, Mr Bramhall, resorted to reminding the society of the 'influence exerted upon society by woman'.[64]

Throughout the 1840s attitudes and practices towards female public involvement remained uneven within ultra-Protestantism. A meeting to protest against a government grant to the Irish Catholic seminary in Maynooth which took place at Exeter Hall in May 1845 was seen as unusual for its prohibition of women. In his opening speech Sir C. E. Smith declared himself 'struck with the peculiar feature of this meeting'—that ladies were not present. He was then heckled by one attendee who demanded to know why ladies had been excluded. Sir C. E. Smith's response was to argue that a male-only meeting would send a more persuasive signal to 'Parliament and to the Government that this had been a meeting composed exclusively of men—of Englishmen—who came forward to exercise a manly judgment on one of the most important questions that had ever affected the destinies of this nation'.[65] The assumption that formal political communications should be endowed with the import of masculine integrity was clearly powerful, but could be queried, as in this example, by the rank and file. The Evangelical Alliance, a less overtly politicized forum for Protestant mobilization that emerged in the mid-1840s, was also hesitant concerning the involvement of women. In 1847 a leading member, J. W. Massie felt compelled to explain why a ladies' association had only recently been established: 'it has appeared scarcely compatible with the proprieties, or usages of Christian decorum, to extend membership to females in the earlier stages'.[66] Whereas Sir C. E. Smith insisted that a movement was more likely to be taken seriously if it projected a masculine

[63] Fourth Annual Report of the Liverpool Protestant Association (Liverpool, 1839), 7; Third Annual Report of the Liverpool Protestant Association (Liverpool, 1838), 7–8.
[64] The Tocsin (13 May and 13 June 1840).
[65] The Times (2 May 1845).
[66] J. W. Massie, The Evangelical Alliance: Its Origin and Development (London, 1847), 444–5; Evangelical Alliance British Organization, Report of the Proceedings of the Conference of British Members Held at Manchester, 4–9 November 1846 (London, 1847), 103.

image, the Alliance based their argument upon considerations of propriety. These subtle differences underline the unstable nature of discourses and practices of female public involvement in this period—despite the seeming homogeneity of many contemporary accounts.

Another mode adopted by some wings of the movement was to reserve seats for a select number of ladies on the platforms at their meetings, typically those with personal connections to the male speakers. This had been a feature of the radical mass platform since the 1810s and was adopted by a wide range of middle-class reforming and philanthropic networks from the 1840s. Located at the physical centre of the meeting, women's exceptionality would have underlined their difference from the masculine bodies who dominated the occasion. In many cases women were expected to overtly parade their gender through particular attention to dress and comportment. Ultra-Protestant Evangelical women adopted a dress code of high, black, satin dresses and white, lace caps when sitting on the platform at Exeter Hall meetings, thus conforming to expectations concerning the stylized femininity required of women in the public sphere.[67]

A close relationship often existed between ultra-Protestantism and premillenarian Evangelicalism, leading to further subtleties as to the modes and chronologies of women's public activities.[68] During the 1820s and 1830s female public prophecy was condoned by some premillenialists—and female evangelical preaching enjoyed a further recrudescence at the end of our period.[69] More broadly, premillenarians privileged the Old Testament as their scriptural model. This included championing female prophets such as Deborah and Abigail who were celebrated as 'mothers in Israel'. Early Victorian premillenarian campaigners, like Charlotte Elizabeth

---

[67] Mary Somerville, *Personal Recollections: From Early Life to Old Age* (London, 1874), 220–1. It was a practice particularly encouraged in the coteries of metropolitan radicalism: e.g. *The Reasoner*, 3 (1847), 535. By the time of Gladstone's premiership the practice had become widespread. H. C. G. Matthew, 'Rhetoric and Politics in Great Britain, 1860–1950', in Philip J. Waller (ed.), *Politics and Social Change in Modern Britain: Essays Presented to A. F. Thompson* (Brighton, 1987), 42.

[68] For premillenarianism see Boyd Hilton, *The Age of Atonement: The Influence of Evangelicalism on Social and Economic Thought, 1785–1865* (Oxford, 1988); W. H. Oliver, *Prophets and Millennialists: The Uses of Biblical Prophecy in England from the 1790s to the 1840s* (Auckland, 1978); D. N. Hempton, 'Evangelicalism and Eschatology', *Journal of Ecclesiastical History*, 31 (1980), 179–94.

[69] Timothy C. F. Stunt, *From Awakening to Secession: Radical Evangelicals in Switzerland and Britain, 1815–35* (Edinburgh, 2000), 260–7. For the later revival consult Olive Anderson, 'Women Preachers in Mid-Victorian Britain: Some Reflexions on Feminism, Popular Religion and Social Change', *Historical Journal*, 12 (1969), 467–84.

Tonna and the Scottish writer, Margaret Tough, explicitly evoked such a tradition when they urged women to mobilize over current affairs.[70] Thus within the overlapping circles of these movements there was sporadic experience of more overt forms of female publicity. Whilst ultra-Protestantism typified many of the gendered conventions of the public sphere, it also revealed the fissures and nuances in its construction. This reaffirmed a restrictive vision of public femininity, but it also provided the potential for heterodox behaviour and innovation.

Spectatorship and collective identities

It has been argued so far that the perpetuation of a dominant discourse concerning the feminized nature of women's public presence obscured cultural knowledge as to the vigorous activities which women often performed on the ground. Whilst the numerous examples of women speakers may have gradually begun to pull against hegemonic discourses of female public engagement, more generally the repeated emphasis upon a particular feminine mode of public behaviour formed part of the framework of gender difference against which contemporary women defined themselves.[71] There is a further, important strand of analysis to be added to our picture. Although a heightened consciousness of one's gender may well have been a dominant feature of women's experience of the public sphere, participation necessitated the management of different identities—not just an awareness of one's gender but also one's role as patriots, Dissenters, or free-traders, for example.[72]

Simon Morgan has thoughtfully suggested that the careful depiction of gracious ladies at political events tended to construe them as 'apolitical'.[73] However, my own research shows that it was not uncommon for women

[70] e.g. *Christian Lady's Magazine*, 6 (1836), 27. Margaret H. Tough, *A Plain Practical Address to the Ladies of Scotland, Concerning their Church* (Edinburgh, 1840), 4. Tough, a follower of Scottish premillenarian Edward Irving, is a little-known figure whose work articulated a distinctive Scottish public identity for women. See also her *The Offering: A Selection from the Poems, Published and Unpublished of a Minister's Daughter* (Edinburgh, 1851).

[71] Violi, 'Gender, Subjectivity and Language', 173; Dorothy E. Smith, *Texts, Facts, and Femininity: Exploring the Relations of Ruling* (London and New York, 1990), ch. 6.

[72] This reading draws upon Martin Sökefeld, 'Debating Self, Identity, and Culture in Anthropology', *Current Anthropology*, 40 (1999), 417–47.

[73] Simon Morgan, 'Seen But Not Heard? Women's Platforms, Respectability and Female Publics in the Mid-Nineteenth Century', *Nineteenth-Century Prose*, 29 (2002), 50–1.

to be ascribed a specific political identity. When a lavish celebration was held at Lord's Cricket Ground in 1836 to celebrate the anniversary of the Vestries Act, hundreds of ladies attended. The speaker, Mr Hume, declared his hope that the 'ladies present would exert their influence in favour of the Liberal cause'. At a dinner in Rochdale in 1838 the 'conservative ladies of the borough' presented a 'splendid banner' to the Operative Conservative Association. In another example, a toast was given to 'The Conservative ladies of the United Kingdom' at a public dinner in honour of Stephen Lushington in Canterbury in 1835.[74] At a dinner for the late Derby ministry held at the Liverpool Philharmonic Hall in 1859 the ladies attending signified their political support through sporting the Tory colours.[75] The highly gendered appearance of women at public events formed but one facet of their experience. It was possible for women—and those who observed them—to interpret their attendance as an actively engaged political act.

Excavating such sensibilities requires a nuanced account of spectatorship. The act of observing was not simply passive.[76] To appear at a window during a political procession, for example, could form part of the ritualized formation of social hegemonies. As Pamela Graves provocatively remarks, 'there is an active, constitutive role in appearing at the windows'. The common practice of the crowd acknowledging those at the windows meant that they functioned as 'a membrane between the arenas in which different identities were created and reproduced'.[77] Spectating women, then, might feel actively implicated in the social and political meanings of an event; and, within the tight discursive contours of representing female public presence, it is possible to discern some recognition of this. For instance, reporters sometimes sought to discreetly convey women's commitment to the issues represented at public occasions. At a meeting in aid of the infant education movement hosted by the Wakefield reformers Mary and Daniel Gaskell, the *People's Journal* wrote of the 'ladies, who added to the

---

[74] *The Times* (4 Aug. 1836, 8 Oct. 1838, and 12 Nov. 1835). For further examples see above pp. 29–31.

[75] Joseph Meisel, *Public Speech and the Culture of Public Life in the Age of Gladstone* (New York, 2001), 260.

[76] The argument for female passivity is put in Gunn, *Public Culture*, 172, and Howard M. Wach, 'Civil Society, Moral Identity and the Liberal Public Sphere: Manchester and Boston, 1810–1840', *Social History*, 21 (1996), 281–303.

[77] C. Pamela Graves, 'Civic Ritual, Townscape and Social Identity in Seventeenth and Eighteenth-Century Newcastle-upon-Tyne', in Susan Lawrence (ed.), *Archaeologies of the British: Explorations of Identity in Great Britain and its Colonies, 1600–1945* (London, 2003), 40–1.

current eloquence by a speaking silence'.[78] The report of a 'Physiological Conference' held at Ham Common in 1847 for the promotion of vegetarianism referred to the 'approving countenances of many fair sisters [who] enlivened the meeting'.[79] Journalists also sometimes hinted at the genuine interest of women in election proceedings. During the 1841 election the 'elegantly-dressed ladies' of Newton-in-the-Willows in South Lancashire were reported to have 'patiently listened to the whole of the proceedings' despite torrential rain.[80]

Furthermore, there were specific rituals which might be performed by women to signal their active engagement in a political gathering. This was commonly achieved through the waving of handkerchiefs. In a culture highly sensitized to the ritual display of symbols this was not viewed as a superficial or passively 'feminine' action. Parading a handkerchief in a candidate's colour could immediately mobilize an election crowd. The waving of a handkerchief often symbolized the high-water mark of a political event, encapsulating the enthusiasm for a particular issue or figure or providing a dramatic cue for further action.[81] A description of the radical procession in Manchester on the day of Peterloo described how 'on a white handkerchief being waved from a window' the crowd burst into applause.[82] This was not a custom that was confined to women, but they were particularly associated with it. When the radical MP John Cam Hobhouse was released from prison in 1820, following his arrest for breach of privilege, a celebration dinner was held at the Crown and Anchor Tavern. *Cobbett's Evening Post* reported that the 'ladies in the gallery waved their handkerchiefs in sympathy with the emotions of the numerous guests beneath them'.[83] The report of a conservative political meeting in Leicester in 1840 noted that a toast to Earl Howe met 'with the most flattering applause, the gentlemen cheering and the ladies waving their handkerchiefs'.[84] It was a rite which had the potential for women to determine the mood of a meeting and to briefly take control of its flow. In a dinner given for Daniel O'Connell at Covent Garden in 1844, as the chairman gave his toast to him, the women rose en masse and began to wave their handkerchiefs. According to the reporter,

[78] *People's Journal*, 3 (June 1847), appendix, 50.
[79] *Truth Tester*, 1 (1847), 141.
[80] *The Times* (9 July 1841).
[81] See e.g. *The Times* (30 Apr. 1842 and 12 July 1841).
[82] *The Times* (20 Mar. 1820).
[83] Cited in Jonathan Fulcher, 'Gender, Politics and Class in the Early Nineteenth-Century English Reform Movement', *Historical Research*, 67 (1994), 68.
[84] *The Times* (18 Sept. 1840).

'the mass of white, from the floor to the ceiling reminded one of a snow-storm'. It was a 'scene of excitement' which lasted for over five minutes.[85] Conversely when an Ipswich crowd wished to register their disapproval of O'Connell the women refused to wave their handkerchiefs.[86]

As these examples indicate, there was an attempt to ascribe to women a sense of deliberate commitment to the principles of a particular event. *The Times* noticed at an Anti-Corn Law League meeting that of the six or seven thousand present, 'About one-third of the company was composed of women in the middle walks of life, who appeared to take a warm interest in the proceedings.'[87] This was a convention also employed in the reporting of electoral events. At a city election in 1826 *The Times* observed that 'The gallery over the principal entrance was crowded with ladies, who seemed to participate in the feelings which the occasion called forth.'[88] Similarly the *Norwich Mercury* reported of the nomination procedure for the East Norfolk election in 1857 that, 'In the jury box, a number of elegantly-dressed ladies were seated, and seemed to take much interest in the proceedings.'[89]

Formulas such as the 'great interest' exhibited by women depended upon an audience's knowing understanding of wider cultural referents. When newspaper readers perused an account of a public meeting their comprehension of it was filtered through their prior experience and knowledge of likely behaviour. This would include their own familiarity with the multitude of ways in which women conducted themselves in public (as local philanthropists, electoral supporters, door-to-door canvassers, lecturers, and so on). The repeated allusions to women's 'great interest' in an event may well have functioned as a genteel code for noisy participation on the part of women. As Peter Bailey has provocatively suggested, in our focus upon the visual aspects of Victorian culture we have tended to neglect the significance of other sensory experiences. Noise, he asserts, 'is an expressive and communicative resource that registers collective and individual identities'. However, Bailey assumes that 'noise unsexed women', arguing that 'Bravura noise-making was an essential signal of masculine identity for much of this era'.[90] I would agree that noise could form an important means of expressing a

---

[85] *The Times* (13 Mar. 1844).

[86] *The Times* (28 May 1836).

[87] *The Times* (30 Oct. 1845).

[88] *The Times* (10 June 1826).

[89] *Norwich Mercury* (8 Apr. 1857). For other indicative examples: *Durham Chronicle* (17 Sept. 1841); *The Times* (2 Sept. 1819 and 25 Dec. 1850).

[90] Peter Bailey, *Popular Culture and Performance in the Victorian City* (Cambridge, 1998), 209–10.

collective identity, but would suggest that this was a practice to which women contributed.

It certainly appears to be the case that the custom of handkerchief waving could be accompanied by cheering and vocal support from the women. Thus *The Times* wrote of the Queen's visit to Dublin in 1849, that 'Ladies threw aside the old formula of waving a white pocket-handkerchief and cheered for their lives.'[91] Similarly as Hobhouse recorded in his diary in February 1839, 'Her Majesty opened the Parliament. I saw her return from the House. There was a great crowd in the streets, but very little cheering, except from the ladies in the balconies.' Women could also intervene vocally for explicitly political purposes too. Hobhouse noted that the appearance of Daniel O'Connell at the Queen's coronation 'raised a hiss from the ladies and gentlemen in our galleries'.[92] Elections could also provide occasions for such vocal interjections, though it might be discreetly reported. At the Brighton Conservative festival in 1837 a toast to the local candidate, Sir Adolphus Dalrymple, was 'received with the loudest enthusiasm, in which the ladies joined; the waving of the handkerchiefs presenting a most animating spectacle'.[93] On the election of John Bright, the young Elizabeth Blackwell apparently 'shouted herself hoarse at his chairing'.[94]

The generation of collective identities at public meetings relied upon an active audience which engaged in the creation of the meanings of an event. Within the public culture of the early Victorians there were ample opportunities for women to participate in this process. The ritualized nature of such occasions—whether it be the waving of a handkerchief, or sensing the appropriate moment to cheer or groan at an orator's words— provided a cultural framework in which women might experience an exuberant commonality with those present.[95] Gender may have formed the

[91] *The Times* (16 Aug. 1897).

[92] Lady Dorchester (ed.), *Recollections of a Long Life by Lord Broughton (John Cam Hobhouse)* (London, 1911, 6 vols), v. 174, 147.

[93] *The Times* (24 May 1837). See also the report of the conservative meeting in Leicester: *The Times* (18 Sept. 1840).

[94] Dorothy Clarke Wilson, *Lone Woman: The Story of Elizabeth Blackwell, the First Woman Doctor* (London, 1970), 31.

[95] For the importance of aural traditions to 19th-cent. political culture consult: James A. Epstein, 'Rituals of Solidarity: Radical Dining, Toasting and Symbolic Expression', in Epstein, *Radical Expression: Political Language, Ritual and Symbol in England, 1790–1850* (Oxford and New York, 1994), 147–65; Brett, 'Political Dinners'; Vernon, *Politics and the People*, 120–6. An innovative overview of the literature may be found in Matthew Bevis, 'Volumes of Noise', *Victorian Literature and Culture*, 31 (2003), 577–91.

cultural framework shaping the nature of their participation at a public event, including the heightened attention to female dress and appearance, but it did not determine all aspects of that experience. As Nancy Fraser has remarked, 'one is not always a woman in the same degree'.[96] To be interpellated as part of an engaged audience provided women with more empowering modes of identification than simply the decorative feminine mode in which their presence was recorded. Gender was both a central feature of women's participation in the public sphere, but also a mutable and ever-shifting facet of that experience.

Peace and Nonconformity: Lydia Becker and Priscilla McLaren

To probe further how women responded to these forums of political engagement and the varying salience of a gendered identity across these different contexts, we will now explore two contrasting case studies, both drawn from the networks of liberal Nonconformity. Scholars of the peace movement have carefully delineated the complex contours of women's contributions.[97] Whilst the emergence of Olive Leaf Circles in the 1820s enabled a domestic mode of political interaction and networking, women were also present at the movement's congresses. Although they comprised 42 per cent of the British visitors to the Paris Congress in 1850, the Peace Society steadfastly refused to allow women to act as delegates.[98] This could clearly rankle with fervent advocates for women's rights such as Anne Knight (who had herself addressed mixed-sex audiences in France) but these policies did not hamper women's ability to forge a powerful allegiance to the cause.[99]

In her early womanhood, before she achieved fame as a women's suffrage campaigner, Lydia Becker, was a devoted pacifist.[100] On 27 January

---

[96] Nancy Fraser, 'The Uses and Abuses of French Discourse Theories for Feminist Politics', *boundary 2*, 17 (1990), 84.

[97] Jill Liddington, *The Long Road to Greenham: Feminism and Anti-Militarism in Britain since 1820* (London, 1989), 13–22.

[98] Nicholls, 'Richard Cobden', 373–4.

[99] *Glasgow Emancipation Society Sixth Annual Report* (1840), 48–9.

[100] Lydia Becker (1827–90) spent much of her youth in Germany due to ill health. Her family lived in Reddish, now part of Greater Manchester. A brief account of her life and work may be found in Audrey Kelly, *Lydia Becker and the Cause* (Lancaster, 1992). See also Elizabeth Crawford, *The Women's Suffrage Movement: A Reference Guide, 1866–1928* (London, 1999), 42–7.

1848, the 21-year-old Becker attended a peace meeting in Manchester. The occasion centred on the leak of a private letter from the Duke of Wellington to Sir John Burgoyne (the Inspector General of Fortifications) published earlier in the month in the *Morning Chronicle* and suggesting the need to increase Britain's military defences. It had been seized upon by Richard Cobden as proof of the needlessly martial preoccupations of government in the face of what he perceived to be growing international cooperation.[101] Public sentiment was quickly galvanized and a number of protest meetings were held across the country.[102] As it happened, a 'Great Free Trade Banquet' had already been planned at the Free Trade Hall to celebrate the recent return of Anti-Corn Law League members to parliament. This was quickly reconceived as a forum to protest against the Duke's letter. Unsurprisingly the event was deemed a triumph by local liberal journalists. 'The great industrial community of these districts has spoken', the *Manchester Times* proclaimed, 'not only to England—but the world.'[103] Recording the event in her diary, Becker was similarly animated, clearly enthused by the wider public with which she felt she was now engaged. Although the organizers arranged for a ladies' gallery, this was apparently a gesture towards propriety and did not signify a literal separation of men and women. Men were permitted into the galleries, and women (although their tickets were much cheaper) were equally welcome to sit in the main body of the hall.[104] It was the sense of inclusivity of the occasion which appears to have inspired Becker: 'It was a new and delightful feeling', she exclaimed, 'to be in such an assembly to know that my heart beat in union with the thousands around me and that we raised that night a sensation which would be felt more or less all over the civilized world.'[105] The internationalist sentiments expressed here were central to the vision of mid-century peace campaigners. Her diary further reveals the impassioned religious sensibilities which were central to contemporary pacifism. No Christian, she suggested, could wish for war.[106]

---

[101] An interesting account of the debate may be found in *The Times* (2 Feb. 1848).

[102] The *Manchester Times* reported upon gatherings in Exeter and Derby, as well as in Manchester: (29 Jan. 1848).

[103] Ibid.

[104] *Manchester Guardian* (22 and 29 Jan. 1848).

[105] Lydia Becker, 'Notebook' (29 Jan. 1848), The Women's Library, London Metropolitan University, Lydia Becker papers, 7/LEB/1/1. In the following discussion all quotes from Becker are taken from this source, unless otherwise indicated.

[106] For contextualization see Alex Tyrrell, 'Making the Millennium: The Mid-Nineteenth Century Peace Movement', *Historical Journal*, 21 (1978), 75–95.

In the build-up to the meeting the local press had provided further frames of reference, dwelling upon the significance of particular class and regional identities. The *Manchester Times*, arguing that the Duke's proposals amounted to an aristocratic desire to shore up its decaying power through the use of patronage via arms deals, declared its hope that 'Manchester will make a move'.[107] The newspaper thus articulated a collective identity of local citizens which might be subsumed under the metonymic device of the city's name. The significance of the meeting's location at the Free Trade Hall was also critical to the sense of collective identity expressed. The building, erected partially on the site of the Peterloo massacre, was an 1843 rebuild of the original 1840 hall designed to house and support the work of the Anti-Corn Law League. In the words of the *Manchester Times*, those attending were the 'peace promoting Free Traders of this metropolis'.[108] Becker's intense identification with the politics of the occasion was built upon an amalgam of influences, sensibilities, and ideologies which achieved focus through the tight web of associations that were built into the identity of 'Manchester'.

There was one further factor which crystallized Becker's impassioned response to the meeting. The principal speaker at the meeting was the great free trade campaigner, Richard Cobden, who claimed it to be the 'greatest pacific demonstration ever made'.[109] His undoubted gifts as a public speaker were grudgingly recognized by *The Times* who characterized him at this time as a 'laurelled agitator . . . Gifted, too, with those peculiar qualities which win the attention and seize the minds of mixed assemblies.'[110] Fresh from his European tour to promote free trade principles Cobden was a national celebrity who certainly appears to have affected Becker. The meeting further intensified her fervour for this 'noblest advocate of the noblest cause'.[111] Thus a heady combination of factors facilitated an

---

[107] *Manchester Times* (8 Jan. 1848).
[108] Ibid.
[109] *The Times* (5 Feb. 1848).
[110] *The Times* (16 Jan. 1849).
[111] Simon Morgan, 'From Warehouse Clerk to Corn Law Celebrity: The Making of a National Hero', in Anthony Howe and Simon Morgan (eds), *Rethinking Nineteenth-Century Liberalism: Richard Cobden Bicentenary Essays* (Aldershot, 2006), 39–55. For the importance of emotion in the generation of collective identity see Ronald Aminzade and Doug McAdam, 'Emotions and Contentious Politics', in Ronald Aminzade *et al.* (eds), *Silence and Voice in the Study of Contentious Politics* (Cambridge, 2001), 14–50. In contrast to Becker, George Eliot was disappointed with Cobden's oratory: George Eliot to Caroline Bray (28 Feb. 1852), in Haight, *George Eliot Letters*, 12.

emotional and personal attachment to the pacifist movement and enabled her to experience the occasion as inspirational.

As David Nicholls reminds us, however, Cobden did not achieve a consensus amongst Manchester liberals.[112] He himself did not privilege the religious message which was clearly so important to Becker. Moreover, she over-read his enthusiasm for the cause—at this point he was concerned rather to use the issue of military spending to further his central political objectives of free trade and financial reform. But the generation of a collective identity at such a meeting did not require a perfect fit between orator and participants. Rather, listeners needed to be able to invest the occasion with their own meanings and interpretations within a broadly compatible framework.[113] That Cobden had already delivered widely reported speeches in which he had drawn carefully upon the interconnected strands of Mancunian middle-class identity, exhorting Mancunians 'It is your business to make calicoes and cottons, and not to fight', undoubtedly assisted this process.[114]

At the meeting Becker attended, Cobden himself did briefly acknowledge the significance of the cause to women—although as taxpayers rather than through any feminized construct (an interesting detail which later Victorian reprints of the speech silenced).[115] However, it appears to have been Becker's emerging self-identification as a liberal peace campaigner and a member of the Mancunian middle class (her family owned a prosperous industrial bleaching plant) which had greater salience for her at this meeting than her gender *per se*.[116] At this period she appears to have preferred identification with male modes of interaction. Politically engaged females in their late teens often seemed to wish to identify with male subjects who were seen to have greater social and political prestige.[117] In Becker's case this sometimes resulted in a deliberate rejection of specifically female modes of identification. Thus she wrote to her sister in 1845 that 'a party of

---

[112] Nicholls, 'Richard Cobden', 375.

[113] See A. P. Cohen, *Symbolising Boundaries: Identity and Diversity in British Cultures* (Manchester, 1986), 11–16; Martin Ceadel, 'Cobden and Peace', in Howe and Morgan, *Rethinking Nineteenth-Century Liberalism*, 189–207. In the event Cobden's speech, in which he adverted to Wellington's advanced age, was deemed to be a tactical disaster: Nicholas C. Edsall, *Richard Cobden: Independent Radical* (Cambridge, Mass., and London, 1986), 196.

[114] *The Times* (16 Jan. 1849).

[115] Compare *Manchester Times* (29 Jan. 1848) with John Bright and James E. Thorold Rogers (eds.), *Speeches on Questions of Public Policy by Richard Cobden M.P.* (London, 1870), 466.

[116] This discussion draws upon Thoits and Virshup, 'Me's and We's'.

[117] See below pp. 101–3.

ladies alone is my abhorrence'.[118] Later, however, a consciousness of gender became central to her sense of herself as a political subject and this impacted accordingly upon her peace politics. By the late 1860s Becker was involved with the women's rights movement and her pacifism became interwoven with a powerful feminist polemic. As she wrote in 1870, 'War is an essentially masculine pursuit.'[119]

Becker's political trajectory is illuminating as to the processes of identity formation which shaped women's interaction with the public sphere. Investing in a collective identity involved a realignment, a sharpening of certain individual dispositions at the expense of others. Despite the apparent crystallization of identity involved in joining a political movement, strands of subjectivity might continue to alter as new circumstances and influences were encountered. In Becker's case this gradually led to greater significance being placed upon certain facets of her identity.[120] Gender, that is to say, was a shifting facet of women's political subjectivity.

Priscilla McLaren (1815–1906) shared very similar politics to Lydia Becker. A sister of the Quaker politicians Jacob and John Bright, she was a radical Nonconformist who believed fervently in the peace movement, female suffrage, franchise reform, and alternative medicine. In common with Becker, she emerged as a prominent figure in the women's rights movement and was also closely involved in the free trade movement. From 1841 Priscilla lived with her widowed brother, the radical politician John Bright, a leading figure in the anti-Corn Law movement and she clearly felt closely implicated in the politics with which her brother was involved. At the beginning of 1845 she expressed her hopes of attending an Anti-Corn Law League meeting, despite suffering from chronic toothache. She explained she wished to 'witness the enthusiasm of the people by way of stirring up my own nerves a little which are in a very *fine ladyish* sort of state and not at all like my own'.[121] She thus implied that this was an opportunity to distance herself from the heightened feminine sensitivity she had

---

[118] Lydia Becker to her sister, Esther (17 Jan. 1845): 'Reminiscences of Esther Becker', The Women's Library, Box FL448, IND/LEB/1/12, 69.

[119] Cited in Heloise Brown, *'The Truest Form of Patriotism': Pacifist Feminism in Britain, 1870–1902* (Manchester, 2003), 1.

[120] For useful theoretical formulations see Fraser, 'Uses and Abuses'; George J. McCall and J. L. Simmons, *Identities and Interactions* (New York, 1966), ch. 4.

[121] Priscilla McLaren to Catherine Cobden (14 Jan. 1845), West Sussex Record Office, Cobden papers, Add MS 6024; original emphasis. Presumably this was the League's meeting which took place on 15 Jan. in Covent Garden Theatre. *The Times* reported the presence of 'a dozen or two of ladies' (16 Jan. 1845).

been experiencing and which she categorized as alien to her 'real self'. Priscilla clearly felt animated by public meetings, yet this conflicted with aspects of her self-identity. At times she presented such feelings as mildly illicit. As she wrote to Cobden's wife on one occasion, 'We hope to be at the League meeting tomorrow evening—it is something uncommon for us to be so *gay*—ought I to use the word when our engagements are of a sensible kind.'[122]

In 1848 Priscilla married Duncan McLaren a leading Scottish radical liberal who, following a high-profile career in Edinburgh local politics, became an MP for the city in 1865. Public meetings thus continued to be a recurrent feature of Pricilla McLaren's life. The correspondence of her and her children is littered with wide-ranging references to the meetings they attended on matters such as colonial issues, church government, education, and peace politics, and she took for granted her right to attend town council meetings.[123] Yet subtle changes are discernible in her attitudes towards public campaigning. She appears to have been somewhat disillusioned by Edinburgh political culture, characterizing the local peace movement as too 'respectable' to gain results, and believing that local ladies overestimated the role that the church would be willing to play.[124]

Her experience of the public sphere was further complicated by her position as a 'political wife'. Whilst her relationship to Duncan McLaren brought her privileged access to political meetings, this appears to have had the effect of reifying an assumption that it was the masculine public sphere which carried the most gravitas. Although she routinely attended events associated with her husband's politics, the public domain was not experienced by her as a zone of equal or unlimited opportunities. This becomes starkly apparent in her desire to be involved in the campaign for working-class votes. Whilst the 1867 Reform Act has been analysed in terms of its implications for the campaign for female suffrage,[125] it must not be forgotten that many women were exercised by the issue of franchise extension *per se*, as intimated in Priscilla McLaren's heart-felt, detailed correspondence on the issue.[126] Whilst she earnestly wished to be able to attend reform

[122] Priscilla Bright (McLaren) to Catherine Cobden (27 Oct. 1845), WSRO, Add MS 6024.
[123] e.g. Agnes McLaren to John McLaren (13 Dec. 1865), MS 24797, fos. 196–7; Catherine McLaren to Priscilla McLaren (6 July 1859), NLS, MS 24786, v. 74; Priscilla McLaren to John McLaren (22 Dec. 1856), NLS, MS 24793, f. 17.
[124] Priscilla McLaren to John McLaren (1 Apr. 1862), NLS, MS 24793, f. 42.
[125] Rendall, 'The Citizenship of Women', 119–78.
[126] e.g. Priscilla McLaren to John McLaren (11 May 1866), NLS, MS 24793, f. 98; Priscilla McLaren to Agnes McLaren (3 May 1867), NLS, MS 24808, f. 90.

meetings, this was viewed as controversial by her husband. As she wrote to her stepson John just before Christmas in 1856, 'I am looking forward with great interest to the reform meeting as to something of a rousing nature—but Papa as usual discourages the idea of ladies attending it—However if all be well I have made up my mind to be there.'[127] Notwithstanding her husband's disapproval, McLaren did attend a number of reform meetings over the next few years. In the winter of 1858, Priscilla McLaren along with Elizabeth Pease was granted a seat on the platform of a major meeting for parliamentary reform, led by her brother John at the City Hall.[128] More commonly, she appears to have attended meetings in a less official capacity, usually accompanied by her stepdaughter, Agnes, who recorded such events with evident excitement. 'The Reform Meeting was capital', she enthuses of a meeting in 1866, 'Mamma and I were present & enjoyed it very much.'[129] Significantly, all the reform meetings described by either Priscilla or Agnes were occasions on which Duncan McLaren was speaking. It was their family relationship to him which gave them the opportunity to attend and even then—as Duncan's uneasiness hints—this had to be negotiated.

On one occasion Priscilla McLaren recounted to her stepson that a close friend of theirs, a Miss Bird, wished to attend a reform meeting but had assumed that she would be the only lady present. So, reported McLaren, 'she put on a hat as near like a man's as possible and went & remained near the door'.[130] There were in fact three women at the meeting, all close relatives of prominent male campaigners: Priscilla and Agnes McLaren, and Emily Masson (whose husband was a prominent figure in the Scottish reform movement and himself a supporter of female suffrage).[131] Bird's assumption that this would be a male-only event underlines, as suggested above in the case of Geraldine Jewsbury, that central aspects of the public sphere could be perceived as a masculine bastion. Bird did not imagine that this would unequivocally prohibit her from entering—but to do so without a well-connected male required some daring. As we have seen, women's attendance at such affairs tended to require the display of an

---

[127] Priscilla McLaren to John McLaren (22 Dec. 1856), NLS, MS 24793, f. 16.
[128] Anna M. Stoddart, *Elizabeth Pease Nichol* (London, 1899), 226.
[129] Agnes McLaren to John McLaren (16 Jan. 1866), NLS, MS 24797, v. 127. Sometimes Agnes dissented from her father's assessment of these meetings, believing him to over-estimate the enthusiasm with which he was received. Agnes McLaren to John McLaren (2 Feb. 1866), MS 24797, v. 140.
[130] Priscilla McLaren to John McLaren (26 Jan. 1866), NLS, MS 24793, v. 90.
[131] For Professor David Masson see his *Memories of London in the 'Forties* (Edinburgh and London, 1908).

overtly feminine appearance. In contrast, Bird clearly felt that to attend a meeting without explicit sanction required her to physically obscure and de-accentuate her gender.

Increasingly Priscilla McLaren tended to emphasize the discomfort of public meetings, rather than the exhilarating sense of personal empowerment they had clearly represented to her as a young woman. In 1864 she reported of a series of meetings she attended in Bath, 'we have *struggled* through in a most imperfect manner. They are really most uncomfortable affairs—crushing, noisy meetings, I believe two thirds of the people scarcely hear any thing that is said.'[132] McLaren herself was conscious that public meetings no longer held the same excitement for her, recalling rather sadly the 'old times when it took a week to settle down after a successful League meeting'.[133] When her niece Helen Bright Clark experienced fever and illness in October 1866, Priscilla attributed it to her attendance at a dramatic reform meeting in Manchester. In fact Helen was prone to ill health and had been unwell for several days before the event.[134] Perhaps contemporary rhetoric questioning the suitability of public life for women had begun to impact upon her own sensibilities.

Pricilla McLaren's position as Duncan's wife may have permitted her access to the male-dominated sphere of reforming politics but the perception remained that this was an essentially masculine space to which she was granted exceptional access. There are glimpses that this could have a telling impact upon her subconscious attitudes towards political activity. In 1868 she wrote disparagingly of the opening of the Cobden Club in Edinburgh. Criticizing the poor organization of the event, she described it scathingly as 'just a select tea party—half of them ladies'.[135] The previous year Priscilla McLaren and her husband had both supported J. S. Mill's women's suffrage initiative; two years later she was to become the first president of the Edinburgh Society for Women's Suffrage in 1870.[136] Even so, at some level McLaren internalized the notion that 'proper' parliamentary politics should be the preserve of a masculinized public sphere. She did not consider the

---

[132] Priscilla McLaren to Catherine Cobden (20 Sept. 1864), WSRO, Add MS 6024. She was presumably referring to the NAPSS meetings which were held in Bath at this time: see the reports in *The Times* (14–23 Sept. 1864).

[133] Priscilla McLaren to Catherine Cobden (16 Dec. 1864), WSRO, Add MS 6024.

[134] Priscilla McLaren to Catherine Cobden (14 Oct. 1866), WSRO, Add MS 6027. This appears to have been the enormous demonstration held in Manchester on 24 Sept. in torrential rain. *The Times* (24 and 25 Sept. 1866).

[135] Priscilla McLaren to John McLaren (20 Dec. 1868), NLS, MS 24793, f. 139.

[136] For further details see Crawford, *Women's Suffrage*, 400–4.

'tea party'—that feminized version of the public meeting—to represent a serious political occasion.[137] As Leonore Davidoff perceptively notes, 'Examples may be found of women in public but this does not change the underlying way public was and is defined.'[138]

Conclusion

The pressure-group politics of early nineteenth-century Britain were marked by a distinct gender asymmetry. Whilst it was possible for women to be intensively and extensively involved in particular campaigns they could not attain the same degree of public authority or freedom to act within a movement at the national level as men. Their engagement in 'public' politics was typically facilitated through a heightened attention to their gender. As Jutta Schwarzkopf has similarly noted of Chartist women, gendered segregation or female-dominated rituals such as handkerchief-waving shaped the experience and representation of female public activity.[139] These emerging customs betrayed a persistent recognition and valuing of women's contribution to politics—but this was often only obliquely registered in subsequent accounts. Gendered codes were upheld and maintained in complex circuits of cultural interchange in which individual agents responded to wider social practices and discourses and then re-enacted gender differences themselves within the public sphere. Yet in the process different political movements, networks, and public contexts developed subtly discrete conventions and rituals. Despite its seeming homogeneity the public sphere in its many manifestations was porous and multi-layered. This in itself provided interstices for potential female agency. By 1860 the mounting incidence of female preachers, lecturers, radical reformers, suffrage campaigners, and philanthropic experts started to create a critical mass of publicly distinguished female actors.

Certain representations of female public behaviour were dominant in this period, but we must be cognizant of the other frames of identity which constituted female subjectivity at public events. As Dror Wahrman points out, 'collective identities count most' in politics.[140] In considering what it

---

[137] As a later feminist campaigner she was to argue for women-only meetings however. Crawford, *Women's Suffrage*, 402.

[138] Davidoff, 'Gender and the "Great Divide"', 22.

[139] Schwarzkopf, *Women in the Chartist Movement*, ch. 7.

[140] Dror Wahrman, *Imagining the Middle Class: The Political Representation of Class in Britain, c. 1780–1840* (London, 1995), 9.

felt like for a woman to act as a citizen in this period we need to consider the ways in which they were able to express political commitment within the dynamics of mixed-sex public events. This requires a careful reading of the historical record, to note those fissures, those hints of dynamic engagement cast within tactful images of female propriety. Despite the repeated emphasis on a particular presentation of female public behaviour, women 'on the ground' found multiple ways to express and enact their agency. The broader implications were more complicated however. Discursive representations of women's public activities erased tensions and differences that might pertain to a female presence through the privileging of a dominant, harmonious, and decorous image; yet that process in itself simultaneously contributed to the discursive landscape of perceived gender difference. This was a phenomenon which contributed to the multiple and contradictory matrices of female selfhood. McLaren's feminist identity sometimes coexisted with more traditional models of womanhood—such as that of a political wife.[141] Adhering to conventional modes of femininity could be a comfortable and 'safe' stance to maintain, leading even feminists to reiterate conventional codes of gender behaviour.

[141] For the complexities of gender (and feminist) identification see Christine Griffin, '"I'm Not a Women's Libber, But . . .": Feminism, Consciousness and Identity', in Skevington and Baker, *Social Identity of Women*, 173–93; Rhoda K. Unger, 'Imperfect Reflections of Reality: Psychology Constructs Gender', in Hare-Mustin and Marecek, *Making a Difference*, 102–49, esp. 122–3.

3

Women and the family in political culture

Introduction

In the early Victorian period, according to the pioneering feminist historian
Sally Alexander, 'Women fell under the protection of their fathers, husbands
or Parliament and were denied an independent political subjectivity.'[1] Since
Alexander made this assessment in 1984, a generation of women's historians
have attempted to articulate a more positive assessment of women's political
identities. As outlined in Chapters 1 and 2, scholars of pressure-group
movements, electoral politics, and early feminism have indicated the wide
range of independent female political actions and the multiplicity of
discourses and languages within which such activity was cast. One feature
of this reclamation of female agency has been to consider the ways in
which the family environment might operate as a site of politicization.[2]

Historians of feminism, such as Jane Rendall, have demonstrated how
the family was construed as a vital locus of civic virtue in Enlightenment
histories, Evangelical moralizing, and revolutionary politics.[3] More recently,
scholars of elite politics have demonstrated that family networks of patronage
and electoral influence were critical to the functioning of parliamentary
politics.[4] Other analyses have looked at the implications of particular
political movements upon family behaviour. As Clare Midgley has shown,
the anti-slavery sugar boycott politicized the domestic site and provided an

---

[1] Sally Alexander, 'Women, Class and Sexual Difference in the 1830s and 1840s: Some
Reflections on the Writing of a Feminist History' (1984), repr. in Alexander, *Becoming a
Woman: And Other Essays in Nineteenth and Twentieth Century Feminist History* (London, 1994),
125.
[2] For a critical evaluation of scholarship which has attempted to bridge the gap between
family and political history see Katherine A. Lynch, 'The Family and the History of Public
Life', *Journal of Interdisciplinary History*, 24 (1994), 665–84.
[3] Jane Rendall, *The Origins of Modern Feminism: Women in Britain, France and the United States,
1780–1860* (Basingstoke, 1985), chs 1–4.
[4] Chalus, *Elite Women*; Lewis, *Sacred to Female Patriotism*.

accessible means for women to engage in political action.[5] Elsewhere I have observed that some currents within early Victorian progressivism necessitated the adoption of lifestyle choices which directly affected the ways in which women would undertake (or direct) domestic duties within the home. Vegetarianism required a dedicated commitment to ethical consumerism, whilst the alternative health remedies that were commonly practised by contemporary radicals called for particular practices of child-rearing and family-based health management.[6] In addition Lynda Walker has demonstrated how early feminist campaigners, such as Barbara Leigh Smith Bodichon, exploited the potential of the home as a political meeting place to construct dynamic and empowering identities.[7]

Here I wish to refine such analyses further. Families of course, are not monolithic entities. Their functioning is complex: they are subject to the play of personalities, changing fortunes, individual development, and shifts in circumstance. Whilst many aspects of political allegiance required attention to domestic behaviours, such as consumption or child-rearing, this does not mean that the home can be viewed unproblematically as a site of political engagement for women. Moreover, political agendas were subject not only to the unpredictable emotional dynamics of family life. They also had their own discrete chronologies. The widespread interest evoked by events of national significance, such as the 1832 Reform Act, provoked episodic moments of family political engagement. Long-term patterns are also discernible. Whereas in the early years of the French Revolution many British radicals attempted to institute progressive family relationships, these attempts appear to have been short-lived, many presumably abandoning such plans as their own families evolved and revolutionary enthusiasm dissipated. By this period even those families who continued to engage with Wollstonecraft's ideas tended to promote a conservative interpretation of her work. In 1812 the Unitarian minister William Turner wrote to his newly wed daughter, Mary Robberds, with advice as to her marital role. '[Y]ou have perused the strong and often coarse, though too often well-founded,

---

[5] Clare Midgley, 'Slave Sugar Boycotts, Female Activism and the Domestic Base of British Anti-Slavery Culture', *Slavery and Abolition*, 17 (1996), 137–62; Lynne Walker and Vron Ware, 'Political Pincushions: Decorating the Abolitionist Interior, 1787–1865', in Inga Bryden and Janet Floyd (eds), *Domestic Space: Reading the Nineteenth-Century Interior* (Manchester and New York 1999), 58–83.

[6] Gleadle, 'Age of Physiological Reformers', 200–19.

[7] Lynda Walker, 'Home and Away: The Feminist Remapping of Public and Private Space in Victorian London', in Iain Borden *et al.* (eds), *The Unknown City: Contesting Architecture and Social Space; A Strangely Familiar Project* (Cambridge, Mass., 2001), 296–311.

strictures of Mrs Wollstonecraft,' he wrote, 'I need not, therefore, say anything to you on the *general* rights and obligations of Husband and Wife.' He encouraged his daughter to embrace her domestic role but to also entertain an expansive view of her position as a minister's wife, suggesting that in many ways she could act as 'his proxy'. He recommended that she consult Catharine Cappe's works on the management of charitable institutions yet intimated that her fundamental duty was to 'encourage and support your husband' with a 'prevailing cheerfulness'.[8] Our period thus opens just as the radical critique of the family was on the wane.

I would suggest therefore that in the excavation of female political engagement it is helpful to remember that women might be differently empowered in their families at different moments. Empirical examples of political activity which cluster around particular issues or moments of tension do not necessarily provide evidence of durable political identities. Moreover, even progressive men and women commonly replicated patriarchal codes of behaviour within their closest relationships. A woman might dissent from dominant social expectations of femininity, and yet still evaluate herself and others in relation to conventional understandings of gendered behaviour.[9] Within the family, gendered roles which privileged the position of the male head of the household remained remarkably enduring, a factor which complicated the construction of female political subjectivity.

Female political influence and the home

The ubiquitous trope of 'female influence' supposed that, through their activities as wives and mothers, women could exercise a degree of political agency. As Matthew Cragoe has discovered, electoral canvassers not infrequently recorded wives' voting preferences, assuming that their views would hold some sway over the exercise of the vote. Cragoe's sample includes examples of forthright, domineering women who were perceived

---

[8] J. A. V. Chapple and Anita Wilson, *Private Voices: The Diaries of Elizabeth Gaskell and Sophia Holland* (Keele, 1996), 115–18.

[9] I draw here upon Amy Kroska's 'homogeneity hypothesis': that individuals' gender ideologies will not 'significantly override the ongoing effects of socialization into gendered identities': 'Does Gender Ideology Matter? Examining the Relationship between Gender Ideology and Self- and Partner-Meanings', *Social Psychology Quarterly*, 65 (2002), 248–65, here at 248.

to have considerable power in this respect.[10] But of course the complexities of individual relationships meant that there would have been a multitude of ways in which particular married couples negotiated such decisions. Equally, references to 'female influence' during elections may have functioned as an uncontroversial way to register women's lively interest in local parliamentary campaigning and culture, rather than literally referencing their impact upon their husbands' voting decisions. The existence of powerful counter-discourses would have complicated individual women's willingness to perform strong spousal roles. The image of the shrewish, overbearing wife in popular literature such as broadside ballads tapped into a stream of popular misogyny which frequently reviled such behaviour. Others might wish to remain mindful of religious injunctions concerning the appropriate relationship between husband and wife.[11] When Amelia Opie was canvassing support for the election of a particular physician to a local hospital she wrote to Lady Catherine Boileau in Wymondham, Norfolk, clearly hoping that she would influence her husband in favour of her candidate.[12] Yet Lady Boileau's own diary reveals a constant anxiety as to whether she had sufficiently capitulated to the will of her husband.[13]

Evocations of maternal political influence were also ubiquitous, but often unhelpfully bland—as in William Rathbone's pronouncement that 'Justice to Ireland was taken in with my mother's milk'.[14] In contrast, the emphasis upon mothers as infant educators indicated one way in which mothers might be able to conceptualize a more active form of maternal transmission. The innovative pedagogy of the Swiss reformer Johann Pestalozzi (1746–1827) was appropriated by both conservative and radical educationists alike to promote a politicized vision of child-rearing. The conservative Evangelical Elizabeth Mayo promoted Pestalozzian methods, but was insistent on the need to instil deference in children. Another educationist, Mary Ann Stodart, emphasized the importance of a female education which would sensitize its subjects to the dangers of 'infidelity' and

---

[10] Cragoe, 'Jenny Rules the Roost'. For an interesting (and light-hearted) reference to the possibility of female influence at local elections see the Tottenham vestry elections: *The Times* (1 Oct. 1829). See also above pp. 29–31.

[11] Joan Perkin, *Women and Marriage in Nineteenth-Century England* (London, 1989), 157–8, 238–9.

[12] Amelia Opie to Lady Catherine Boileau (Mar. 1847), NRO, Boi 63/5/34.

[13] Jessica Gerard, *Country House Life: Family and Servants, 1815–1914* (Oxford, 1994), 102.

[14] William Rathbone to his daughter, Bessy Paget (23 July 1848) in Rathbone, *Records of the Rathbone Family*, 223.

'liberalism'.[15] Progressive Nonconformists such as Mary Sewell eschewed such an approach. Sewell urged mothers to develop curious, intellectually creative children through a hands-on scientific education in which they were left to experiment and observe. 'I would say again and again', she reasoned, 'foster in bringing up children a [sic] courageous, independent spirit'.[16] It would be mistaken to draw too sharp a divide between these schools of thought, however. Nonconformist liberals, for example, could be equally insistent in securing the compliance of young children. Obedience was believed to be essential for the cultivation of spiritual humility, and presumably many also wished their children to conform to broader social expectations of appropriate behaviour. Equally, the emotional realities of family life could complicate the enactment of ideological precepts. The novelist Elizabeth Gaskell and her husband were liberal Unitarians who wished to raise their daughters as independent, liberal thinkers. Yet they demanded strict obedience; smacking their 3-year-old daughter each time she refused to recite letters of the alphabet.[17]

The confluence between diverse political constituencies on certain aspects of child-rearing means that is difficult to ascertain how far mothers attempted actively to institute ideologically influenced educational methods in practice. Middle-class mothers often kept minute details of their children's development, and in personal correspondence entered into earnest discussions as to the merits of various contemporary educationalists.[18] Nonetheless, individuals' own parenting practices tended not to draw simply upon political precepts, but were a composite of wider influences, including personal experiences and the pressure of wider social expectations. In the matter of education, personal factors might well override political affiliation. The High Church author Elizabeth Sewell recalled a miserable school experience at the hands of Miss Crooke on the Isle of Wight. Although her parents were Tories and Miss Crooke a 'fierce radical',

---

[15] Charles Mayo and Elizabeth Mayo, *Practical Remarks on Infant Education: For the Use of Schools and Private Families* (London, 1837), 51–2; McCann and Young, *Samuel Wilderspin*, 195–7; Mary Ann Stodart, *Principles of Education Practically Considered* (London, 1844), 59.

[16] Mary Bayly, *The Life and Letters of Mrs Sewell* (London, 1889), 109–13. For further discussion of Mary Sewell see pp. 119, 142 below.

[17] Chapple and Wilson, *Private Voices*, 20, 57.

[18] Journal of Caroline Upcher, NRO, UPC 157; Emily H. Duberly to Maria Grey [1840], CUL, Add 7218 (D). Chapple and Wilson, *Private Voices*, 12–18, 52; Helen Heineman, *Restless Angels: The Friendship of Six Victorian Women: Frances Wright, Camilla Wright, Harriet Garnett, Frances Garnett, Julia Garnett Pertz, Frances Trollope* (Athens, Ohio, 1983), 147; Caroline Fox to Isabella Strutt (14 Aug. 1798), Birmingham City Archives, Galton MS 459/4.

her mother and the schoolmistress were friends and this clearly outweighed ideological considerations.[19]

Furthermore, it was commonly the father who assumed the prime responsibility for educational decisions. From the late eighteenth century, fears that overexposure to female care would effeminize boys was one of the factors which led to a reassessment of boys' education. By our period the trend was to educate boys in public schools where possible.[20] As one recent survey of the family has underlined, the legal expectation was that fathers were responsible for child-rearing and educational decisions. Although individual families might negotiate decisions more equitably, legal judgments on contentious cases rearticulated these principles, thus strengthening the possibility of paternal dominance.[21]

A range of other contemporary texts and discourses served to reinforce the political importance of a hierarchical family structure. In her domestic manual *Home Discipline: Or Thoughts on the Origin and Exercise of Domestic Authority* (1841), Adelaide Sophia Kilvert, the wife of an Anglican minister, referred explicitly to the role of 'patriarchs' in structuring both the private and public worlds. Her text construed children's submission to their parents to be essential to the working of the body politic, suggesting that political unrest might be directly traced to the breakdown of household authority.[22] Personal experiences and the interplay of individual personalities could of course complicate a commitment to such principles. The premillenarian Tory, Charlotte Elizabeth Tonna was insistent on the maintenance of a hierarchical family structure, yet articles and letters in her magazine differed as to the appropriate limits of wifely submission. One acknowledged that it created 'severe mental struggles' for women. Tonna herself wrote under a pen name to protect her earnings from her estranged husband.[23] Amanda Vickery and Linda Colley have reminded us that it is mistaken to view contemporary pronouncements of women's role as simply reflective of

---

[19] Sewell, *Autobiography*, 3–4, 14.

[20] Michèle Cohen, 'Gender and the Private/Public Debate on Education in the Long Eighteenth Century', in R. Aldrich (ed.), *Public or Private Education? Lessons from History* (London and Portland, Or., 2004), 15–35.

[21] Leonore Davidoff *et al.*, *The Family Story: Blood, Contract and Intimacy, 1830–1960* (London, 1999), ch. 5.

[22] Adelaide Sophia Kilvert, *Home Discipline: Or Thoughts on the Origin and Exercise of Domestic Authority* (Bath, 1841), 105–6.

[23] *Christian Lady's Magazine*, 5 (1836), 169 and 6 (1836), 115; Monica Correa Fryckstedt, 'Charlotte Elizabeth Tonna: A Forgotten Evangelical Writer', *Studia Neophilologica*, 52 (1980), 79–102, see esp. 85.

practice, and examples such as Tonna prove the point.[24] However prescriptive texts such as household manuals and educational tracts were not a discrete, hermetically sealed discursive phenomenon. Female subjectivities were formed against, in relation to, and in engagement with such perspectives—not in isolation from them. The result was that, whilst women's political influence was widely evoked, it remained a slippery, mobile concept. It had the potential to be an empowering mode of identification, but it could also be associated with excessive female input or the demarcation of a narrow political sphere for women. It also related poorly to the cut and thrust of individual relationships.

To consider these themes further, let us consider one particular feature of the contemporary conceptualization of female influence: the contribution of women to home-based political discussion. Commentators across the political spectrum commonly supposed that women had an important function to play in transmitting political positions to their offspring in this way. Tonna eschewed the sentimentalism that often typified the rhetoric of 'influence' by insisting that mothers should actively teach their children conservative political principles.[25] Sophia Chichester was a follower of the French socialist Charles Fourier, and a patron of leading British radicals. She encouraged Eliza Sharples, the freethought radical, to bring up her children as 'a little band of True Reformers, who will be in *their day*, valiant Champions for Truth and Freedom'.[26] Such attitudes were in keeping with broader cultural processes which assigned a dynamic political role to the domestic site. Many homes were perceived as political forums in their own right. The household of William Renton and his wife Agnes in Buccleuch Place, for example, was remembered as 'a centre of Liberal thought in Edinburgh'.[27] Radical and liberal families might use their homes as a political resource, allowing them to provide sanctuary for escaped slaves or political refugees from Europe. One such household was that of Jane Forster and her husband William, the Liberal MP. They altered the geography of their domestic space to reflect their commitment to intellectual

---

[24] Vickery, 'Golden Age to Separate Spheres', and Colley, *Britons*, ch. 6.

[25] See Gleadle, 'Charlotte Elizabeth Tonna'.

[26] Sophia Chichester to Richard Carlile (6 Sept. 1837), Huntington Library, California, Richard Carlile papers, RC 84. Further details on Chichester's career may be found in Jackie Latham, 'The Political and the Personal: The Radicalism of Sophia Chichester and Georgiana Fletcher Welch', *Women's History Review*, 8 (1999), 469–87.

[27] J. B. Mackie, *The Life and Work of Duncan McLaren* (London: Edinburgh and New York, 1888, 2 vols), i. 40.

and political pursuits. They had no drawing room in their Wharfeside home. Instead the library formed the hub of the household.[28]

In environments such as these parents commonly encouraged the politicization of their children through family debate. This was a habitual feature of Quaker and Dissenting families (although by no means exclusively so) who were sensitive to the active commitment required for the pursuit of heterodox causes. The campaigner against colonial abuses, Elizabeth Pease, was brought up in a Quaker household where prominent figures in the abolition movement were a routine feature of family life, accustoming her and her brother to political discussion.[29] Within families of this nature women might play an active role in explicit political education. This was an aspect of her mothering for which Elizabeth Wheler wished to be remembered, explaining in her memoirs that, 'I talked to my children, and made them interested in all that was going on at Sebastopole [sic], that they might remember the [Crimean] War, so that they were as eager for news as we were.'[30] Discussions were routinely continued in epistolary form during periods of absence. Susannah Taylor, we learn, wrote a letter to her 14-year-old daughter which was 'quite a political treatise'.[31] A clearly frustrated Elizabeth Gaskell wished her daughter to develop more deeply considered views on the issue of free trade:

> Pray *why* do you wish a Protectionist Ministry not to come in? Papa and I want terribly to know. Before you fully make up your mind, read a paper in the Quarterly on the subject of Free Trade (written by Mr George Taylor) in (I think) the year 1839; and then when you come home I will read with you Mr Cobden's speeches[.] But first I think we should read together Adam Smith on the Wealth of Nations.

Gaskell explained to Marianne that such a rigorous approach would help to dispel traditional arguments as to the inability of women to engage in political issues.[32]

The domestic space then undoubtedly had the potential to act as a stimulating environment for the expression of women's political interests. Social gatherings might operate as quasi-salons, in which the hostess took

---

[28] T. Wemyss Reid, *The Life of the Rt Hon. W. E. Forster* (London, 1888, 2 vols), i. 276.

[29] Stoddart, *Elizabeth Pease Nichol*, 16.

[30] Andrew Moilliet (ed.), *Elizabeth Anne Galton (1808–1906): A Well-Connected Gentlewoman* (Northwich, 2003), 184.

[31] Janet Ross, *Three Generations of Englishwomen: Memoirs and Correspondence of Mrs John Taylor, Mrs Sarah Austin and Lady Duff Gordon* (London, 1888, 2 vols), i. 15.

[32] Elizabeth Gaskell to Marianne Gaskell (7 Apr. 1851), in J. A. V. Chapple and Arthur Pollard (eds), *The Letters of Mrs Gaskell* (Manchester, 1966), 147–8.

a leading role in drawing out the guests. The Norwich Unitarian, Elizabeth Martineau, wrote to her acquaintance John Taylor requesting that his conversation at her supper parties be as unrestrained as possible, for 'freedom of sentiment is the great delight of our Sunday night meetings'.[33] Nonetheless, homes distinguished by intense political debate were not necessarily experienced as empowering by women. Katherine Plymley lived with her brother the Archdeacon of Shrewsbury, caring for his many children due to his wife's incapacity. Political radicals, abolitionists, and intellectuals were frequent visitors to the family home in regency Shropshire. During these encounters Plymley displayed an acute sensitivity to the gendered contours of polite conversation. Despite her own progressive Whig views Plymley noted in great detail how a visiting Irish MP had expressed radical opinions during his stay, but added approvingly that 'with women he will converse on the lighter subject of literature seemingly with great pleasure'. Whereas Plymley appears to have been comfortable to dispute with house-guests on weightier topics during informal moments— before breakfast for example, or in the drawing room before lunch—she felt more constrained on formal occasions. She attended the political dinners her brother held at his home, but she positioned herself as an onlooker and not a participant of such occasions. Plymley was involved in broader family political practices, such as electoral celebrations, but this did not fundamentally alter her muted sense of individual political identity nor her belief that she was of inferior political acumen.[34] Although the home and family might be viewed as political forums, the gendered patterns of family life complicated women's experience of them.

Whilst women frequently recorded childhoods in which they gained access to political and intellectual debate through home-centred activities of discussion and sociability, these occasions were not necessarily presented as moments of mixed-sex opportunity. Many narratives reiterated conventional gender codes by privileging the male presence. Maria Grey, the campaigner for reformed girls' schooling, noted of the intellectual education of herself and her sister, 'We gained our first experience of intimate intercourse with men of large and fine cultivation, whose conversation was a liberal education in itself, an experience to be repeated so often in our

---

[33] Elizabeth Martineau to John Taylor [n.d.], NRO, MC 257/156.

[34] Plymley Notebook, SRO, 1066/17 (1793) and 1066/122 (1820). See Kathryn Gleadle, '"Opinions Deliver'd in Conversation": Conversation, Politics, and Gender in the Late Eighteenth Century', in Jose Harris (ed.), *Civil Society in British History: Ideas, Identities, Institutions* (Oxford, 2003), 74–8.

lives.'[35] When Mary Sewell looked back to a childhood dominated by the Napoleonic Wars she recounted the tense period of the invasion crisis, noting: 'There was always a subject of interest in the atmosphere when the men met together.'[36]

It might be expected that retrospective sources such as autobiographies and family memoirs would be shaped in accordance with particular cultural conventions—in this case of gendered norms.[37] This was especially so in those families where the father was a member of parliament or a prominent campaigner. Here, daughters tended to prioritize their fathers' role in their own politicization in subsequent accounts. This led to the construction of coherent narratives which associated their political development with the status of the formal parliamentary world. The feminist reformer Josephine Butler was attentive to the progressive role model provided by her forthright aunt Margaretta Grey in her childhood, but she still assigned a central significance to the influence of her father. She recalled that her mother read aloud to them every day, but it was John Grey (a well-connected and politically active local land agent) who was remembered as the more dynamic presence. She described how he would regularly bring home parliamentary papers, and keep his children up to date on burning political issues: 'Our father's connection with great public movements of the day,—the first Reform Bill, the Abolition of the Slave Trade and Slavery, and the Free Trade movement, gave us very early an interest in public questions, and in the history of our country.'[38]

I would suggest that such representations marked not merely a retrospective desire to present a seemingly appropriate narrative. They also

---

[35] Edward V. Ellsworth, *Liberators of the Female Mind: The Shirreff Sisters, Educational Reform, and the Women's Movement* (Westport, Conn., 1979), 9.

[36] Bayly, *Life and Letters*, 19.

[37] For analyses of memory within Victorian women's autobiographies see Linda H. Peterson, *Traditions of Victorian Women's Autobiography: The Poetics and Politics of Life Writing* (Charlottesville, Va., 1999); Valerie Sanders, *The Private Lives of Victorian Women: Autobiography in Nineteenth-Century England* (London and New York: 1989); Mary Jean Corbett, *Representing Femininity: Middle-Class Subjectivity in Victorian and Edwardian Women's Autobiographies* (Oxford, 1992); Susan Pedersen, 'Eleanor Rathbone (1872–1946): The Victorian Family under the Daughter's Eye', in Susan Pedersen and Peter Mandler (eds), *After the Victorians: Private Conscience and Public Duty in Modern Britain* (London, 1994), 115. For a different perspective see Helen Rogers, 'In the Name of the Father: Political Biographies by Radical Daughters', in David Amigoni (ed.), *Life Writing and Victorian Culture* (Aldershot, 2006), 145–63.

[38] Josephine Butler, *In Memoriam: Harriet Meuricoffre* (London, 1901), 8–9, and Butler, *Memoir of John Grey of Dilston* (Edinburgh, 1869), 14–18. John Grey was first cousin to Earl Grey.

captured profound sociological processes experienced by their subjects relating to enduring modes of masculine dominance. The primacy of men in politicization processes was a recurring feature of Olive Banks's study of first-wave feminism. She found that fathers played a particularly important role in encouraging daughters to adopt heterodox political opinions.[39] As Davidoff *et al.* have recently reminded us, contemporary culture was marked by an array of material, symbolic, and cultural resources which could serve to fortify the image and experience of paternal dominance.[40] The Evangelical emphasis upon motherhood was a crucial facet of domestic ideology but, as Davidoff and Hall illustrated, it encouraged an equally important paternal role.[41] Similarly David Roberts argued from his study of elite Victorian fatherhood that the social practices of that strata produced dominant models of paternal authority. The status of these men as political and economic agents within the wider community ensured that their paternal authority spanned both the private and public spheres. This reinforced the impression of their social supremacy to their children.[42]

Therefore, despite the 'cult of motherhood', fathers continued to exert considerable influence upon the ideological development of their offspring, and the prestige with which (even absentee) fathers might be viewed by their children could intensify cultural practices which privileged the paternal role.[43] When Charlotte Hanbury was attempting to explain the motivations behind her own philanthropic interests she distinguished subtly between the influences of her Quaker parents. Although her mother assisted Elizabeth Fry in prison visiting, Hanbury assigned to her father the more dynamic persona, 'Our father's active benevolence joined with hers brought into our home the strongest influence, which we as children, and ever afterwards, deeply felt.' It was after her father took her to visit the local

---

[39] Olive Banks, *Becoming a Feminist: The Social Origins of 'First Wave' Feminism* (Brighton, 1986), ch. 3. See also Valerie Sanders, '"Fathers' Daughters": Three Victorian Anti-Feminist Women Autobiographers', in Vincent Newey and Philip Shaw (eds), *Mortal Pages, Literary Lives: Studies in Nineteenth-Century Autobiography* (Aldershot, 1996), 153–71.

[40] Davidoff *et al.*, *Family Story*, 136.

[41] Davidoff and Hall, *Family Fortunes*, ch. 7, esp. 329–35. Consider also the centrality of Mr Stanley to his daughters' education in Hannah More, *Coelebs in Search of a Wife* (London, 1808).

[42] David Roberts, 'The Paterfamilias of the Victorian Governing Classes', in A. S. Wohl (ed.), *The Victorian Family: Structure and Stresses* (London, 1978), 59–81.

[43] John Tosh, *A Man's Place: Masculinity and the Middle-Class Home in Victorian England* (New Haven and London, 1999), ch. 4. For a classic theoretical account see Nancy Chodorow, *The Reproduction of Mothering: Psychoanalysis and the Sociology of Gender* (Berkeley, Calif., 1978), esp. 94, 181.

ragged school in 1845 that she became a teacher there.[44] Samuel Blackwell, a Nonconformist Whig from Bristol provided a radical, political, and non-gendered education for all his nine children. His wife, Hannah, who came from a prosperous Episcopalian family, disapproved of her husband's efforts and attempted to persuade her daughters to pursue a more conformist path. But it was their father's lead which the girls followed, Elizabeth Blackwell becoming a pioneering female doctor and her sister, Anna, moving towards progressive Fourierite politics.[45] In the record of her early life, the Fabian social reformer Beatrice Webb explained that, despite the extensive political and intellectual interests of her mother, Lawrencina, she remained a remote figure. It was her father, and his egalitarian outlook, whose example she cherished, 'Notwithstanding frequent absence, my father was the central figure of the family life—the light and warmth of the home.'[46]

Particularly during certain phases of their development it appears that children might identify with the parent who was considered to have the greatest social cachet.[47] In some accounts it is evident that the aura of paternal political authority could be experienced by young daughters as distinctly alluring. Listen to the following account from Mary Sewell:

> As we increased in years, my father's zealous patriotism infused itself more or less into each of us. I have a sense now of the thrill which used to pass through my whole frame when any great event had happened, when my father's animated words, kindling eyes, and the manner in which he turned over the newspaper whilst giving my mother details, sent the blood through my veins with quickened speed.[48]

Girls tended to be socialized into political awareness in ways which often replicated traditional gender roles. This might sometimes provide women with the means ultimately to subvert those conventions—as in the case of those who later became feminists—yet we should not underestimate the extent to which the prestige and authority of the male political subject shaped the gendered dynamics of many families.

---

[44] Charlotte Hanbury, *An Autobiography* (London, 1901), 8–9.
[45] Ishbel Ross, *Child of Destiny: The Life Story of the First Woman Doctor* (London, 1950), 1–27.
[46] Beatrice Webb, *My Apprenticeship* (London, 1971; 1st publ. 1926), 35–9, quotation at 35.
[47] I have been helped here by the following discussions: Alfred B. Heilbrun, 'Identification with the Father and Sex-Role Development of the Daughter', *Family Co-ordinator*, 25 (1976), 411–16; C. J. Boyd, 'Mothers and Daughters: A Discussion of Theory and Research', *Journal of Marriage and Family*, 51 (1989), 291–301.
[48] Bayly, *Life and Letters*, 17.

Family identities

The identification of young girls and women with the political position of their father did have the potential to open up more empowering modes of subjectivity within the patriarchal framework, however. An individual's sense that they formed part of a cross-generational political tradition could be a powerful mode of identification. According to Pam Hirsch, Barbara Leigh Smith Bodichon believed that despite her illegitimacy she had 'earned' the name Smith for her continuation of the family tradition of radical campaigning.[49] The practices of intermarriage amongst particular kinship and religious circles facilitated this. In the dense family networks of nineteenth-century Quakers, women had a keen sense of their investment in a wider kinship identity and were often experts on the family lineage, constructing and maintaining extensive family archives.[50] Rosemary Sweet's research has established more broadly the significance of women's interest in genealogy 'as the passers on of tradition and family history'.[51] Lydia Becker, the women's suffrage campaigner, preserved a large collection of material relating to her family's genealogy.[52] Louisa Twining, the workhouse reformer, was similarly fascinated by the family annals, and included in her autobiography minute historical details of her family and family properties.[53] The perpetuation of family histories and memories could be a significant facet in the construction of an individual's identity. The mother of Scottish novelist Margaret Oliphant was a forthright politician who impressed upon her daughter the significance of her family history and traditions.[54] In accounts of family history, women often sought to record their pride in the particular traditions of their families of birth, recalling, perhaps, a lineage of public service. Sometimes this involved the construction of a particular local identity. Thus Josephine Butler dwelt upon the significance of the border community as a long-standing site of her family's local importance.[55]

---

[49] Pam Hirsch, *Barbara Leigh Smith Bodichon, 1827–1891: Feminist, Artist and Rebel* (London, 1998), 1.

[50] Sandra Stanley Holton, *Quaker Women: Personal Life, Memory and Radicalism in the Lives of Women Friends, 1780–1930* (London, 2007).

[51] Rosemary Sweet, *Antiquaries: The Discovery of the Past in Eighteenth-Century Britain* (London and New York, 2004), 73. See Ch. 6 below for further discussion.

[52] Lydia Becker papers, The Women's Library, Box FL449, 7LEB/2/01.

[53] Twining, *Recollections*, 1–8, 35.

[54] Elizabeth Jay (ed.), *The Autobiography of Margaret Oliphant: The Complete Text* (Oxford, 1990), 21; *ODNB*.

[55] Butler, *Memoir of John Grey*, 1–2.

For many women, therefore, political subjectivity was closely entwined with a collective notion of familial significance. For women who came from especially politicized families, a pride in the political heritage of their birth family had the potential to provide an independent source of political identity on their marriage. These processes, and the complicating impact of marital experiences upon the political engagement of such women, may be delineated further by considering the experiences of Priscilla McLaren. As we saw in Chapter 2, McLaren and her husband were active participants in a wide range of political issues, including women's suffrage, yet both betrayed a tendency to reinscribe a male-dominated vision of the public sphere. Similar complexities pertain to their domestic activities. Her explicit and persistent attempts to shape the political sensibilities of both her husband and their children are indicative of the possibilities of 'female influence' and how women might seek to carve out empowering identities within the home. As she herself put it, 'the social and political were so blended in our circle, that they could scarcely be separated'.[56] Nonetheless, this was a phenomenon which did not affect all family members equally, and the interdependence of family and politics was constituted within a broader cultural structure which continued to privilege the male head of household.

When Priscilla Bright married Duncan McLaren in 1848 it was in defiance of her father's wishes, as she was breaking with her Quaker back-ground.[57] Even so, her family heritage of intense political involvement proved critical to the union. Her stepchildren were keenly alert to her impact: 'There is no doubt as to the powerful influence which my present mother exerted in strengthening and refining the intellectual character of my father', wrote one.[58] Political socialization was an ongoing process within families and women of strong ideological affiliation could certainly affect the tenor of their husbands' outlook. Priscilla McLaren was instru-mental in creating an ideologically informed domestic domain, anxious as she was to rear her children and stepchildren in the principles of Quakerism and radical politics. Even the paintings on the nursery wall were chosen for their political message. Depictions of William Penn's legendary treaty with native American peoples and a painting of Charles V in Titian's studio, stooping to pick up the artist's brush, were designed to reinforce a democratic message. At meal times the McLarens developed a family

[56] Priscilla McLaren to Catherine Cobden (21 Oct. 1866), WSRO, Add MS 6027.
[57] Duncan McLaren to his son, John (15 Mar. 1848), NLS, MS 24791, fos. 9–10.
[58] Mackie, *Duncan McLaren*, i. 48.

custom of 'table talk'. It was emphasized that as parents they wished not to impose their authority but rather to appeal to their children's reason to encourage the formation of independent thinking.[59]

Priscilla's own radical heritage was thus a critical influence upon the development of the family's distinct ideological and political tenor. Her confidence and investment in this lifestyle undoubtedly owed much to a sense of her own ideological lineage and her radical Quaker upbringing. Nonetheless, despite this intensely political domestic site, the day-to-day nature of affective relationships complicated the perpetuation of the family's ideals and also compromised the extent of her own political agency. Priscilla McLaren's rapport with her stepchildren John and Agnes was strengthened by shared political sentiments, their correspondence teeming with discussion of political affairs. The same was not true of her relationship with their sister, Catharine. The letters between Catharine and Priscilla were certainly affectionate (if impeccably polite) but revolved rather around domestic issues.[60] When Catharine married, Priscilla was quick to note that she ceased to take the *Mercury*, hitherto the family's newspaper. The transmission of political principles across the generations could not be assured. 'Alas for the stability of political principle when our circumstances change — poor child!' she lamented.[61] Even heavily politicized families were not hegemonic entities but affected various family members differently.

The ongoing impact of hegemonic modes of masculinity was a further, complicating factor. Even women's rights campaigners could find it difficult to institute egalitarian personal practices. Exceptional couples of advanced feminist views might strive for genuine equality in their relationship, as in the case of John Stuart Mill and Harriet Taylor, but this was atypical.[62] The radical freethinkers Richard Carlile and Eliza Sharples had both written and lectured on the rights of women, yet she soon assumed a more traditional wifely role when they formed a family together.[63] Similarly Duncan McLaren was, as his wife put it, a 'very executive Papa'. Her own experience of living with her imperious brother John had perhaps habituated her to such behaviour.[64] Duncan's intensity and his assumption of

---

[59] Mackie, *Duncan McLaren*, i, 59–62.

[60] Letters from Catharine Oliver (McLaren) to Priscilla McLaren, NLS, MS 24786.

[61] Priscilla McLaren to Agnes McLaren (16 Dec. 1863), NLS, MS 24808, v. 54.

[62] See F.A. Hayek (ed.), *John Stuart Mill and Harriet Taylor: Their Correspondence and Subsequent Marriage* (London, 1951), 168.

[63] Rogers, *Women and the People*, 68.

[64] Priscilla McLaren to Catherine Cobden (23 Sept. 1864), WRSO, Add MS 6024; Keith Robbins, *John Bright* (London, 1979), 45, 219.

masculine authority meant that he tended to function as the emotional pivot of the family's political identities. On Sunday evenings he was accustomed to leading their reflections on pacifism. On one occasion he broke down in tears when attempting to read aloud to his family a list of those killed and wounded in the Crimea.[65] Duncan's masculine status enabled him to play a direct role in the city's electoral affairs, leading family members to privilege his investment in their outcome. As Priscilla McLaren wrote to her stepdaughters in 1847, 'this election is worse than anything else—there is not a candidate to be had . . . it would make any one ill to see how matters are . . . I am thankful you are escaping what is so heart embittering—I feel so much for Papa.'[66]

Despite his ideological commitment to encouraging independent thought in his children, and his professed support for the contemporary women's movement, Duncan frequently had recourse to the masculine identity of 'paterfamilias'. For example, he placed the family under great strain when he attempted to obstruct the marriage of his daughter, Catharine to his business partner John Scott Oliver.[67] Moreover, even though the McLarens constructed a powerful model of domestic political expression, when political meetings were held at their home it did not necessarily entail opportunities for female participation. Such occasions were viewed by family members as essentially male events. As Agnes McLaren reported to her brother John in January 1866 'last night we had a gentleman's party most of them political friends of Papa'.[68] Later that year we find Priscilla complaining to John, 'this morning the antiannuity tax deputation breakfasted with us . . . I had to spend my morning in the self denying occupation of mending clothes in my bedroom.'[69] It was the ways in which a particular space was deployed—and not the location itself— which determined the social and cultural meanings of an event. That a political meeting—to which she was not invited—was held in her home reinforced Priscilla McLaren's sense of alienation from formal political involvement. The home was not a site of undifferentiated political engagement and women might be starkly aware of the parameters of their 'influence'. On another occasion Priscilla entreated her friend Catherine

[65] Mackie, *Duncan McLaren*, i. 62.

[66] Priscilla McLaren to Grant and Agnes McLaren (18 Mar. 1857), NLS, MS 24808, v. 13.

[67] Priscilla McLaren to Catharine McLaren (27 Aug. 1862), NLS, MS 24824, f. 27; Priscilla McLaren to Catherine Cobden (23 Dec. 1862), WSRO, Add MS 6024.

[68] Agnes McLaren to John McLaren (16 Jan. 1866), NLS, MS 24797, v. 127.

[69] Priscilla McLaren to John McLaren (16 Apr. 1866), NLS, MS 24793, f. and v. 93.

Cobden (wife of the anti-Corn Law politician Richard) to attend a dinner party she was holding: 'I do sadly want a lady who is a little political and very interesting to help to make the gentlemen enjoy my dinner.'[70] Although this dinner was perceived as a forum for political socializing women were invited not because of their contribution in their own right but because they might enable men to enjoy the occasion better. She privileged male guests as the political agents, whilst also intimating that politically engaged women were rather difficult to find.

Therefore, domestic-based political activity did not necessarily erase conventionally understood boundaries of gender behaviour. Equally, whilst McLaren was fully committed to familial modes of political engagement she herself reinscribed conventional rhetoric concerning the gendered distinctions between home and politics. In a letter of condolence to Kate Cobden on Richard's death she portrayed her friend as a mere cipher of her husband who would now have to think independently for the first time: '[O]h what a *heart sinking* there is', she commiserated, 'when, the dear one, who formed the chief motive for every thought and action is taken— and the fond, loving, deserted wife has to begin the new work of thinking & acting *for herself*' (original emphasis). Remarkably, she portrayed her friend's principled refusal to accept a government pension as the voice of the deceased Richard Cobden, working through his wife: 'I felt that *he* in your refusal, still spoke in loud and *burning* words.'[71]

At times of crisis it is perhaps more likely that individuals might articulate uncontroversial tropes of gendered roles. Such language functioned as a cultural resource which could be resorted to as a 'comfortable' mode during times of stress. Here is Priscilla McLaren writing to the same correspondent in 1854, at a time when Richard Cobden was struggling unsuccessfully to oppose the Crimean War: '[P]olitical life is such that a man has much need to have the harbour of *home* to flee to, for the sake of its soothing and softening influences and to feel that truth *has* an existence here below, in the loving face of his wife and in the sincerest eyes of his children'.[72] This classic restatement of 'separate spheres' clearly does not provide a simple reflection of the lived experience of the McLaren or the Cobden families, but even progressive individuals might at times feel a cultural satisfaction in identifying with such rhetoric. The unintended consequence was the ongoing perpetuation of normative gender codes.

[70] Priscilla McLaren to Catherine Cobden (7 July [no year]), WSRO, Add MS 6029.
[71] Priscilla McLaren to Catherine Cobden (23 July 1865), WSRO, Add MS 6025.
[72] Priscilla McLaren to Catherine Cobden (1854), WSRO, Add MS 6024.

Whilst a commitment to the ideals and heritage of one's family of birth had the potential to provide a distinct source of political agency and pride (at times strikingly realized, as Chapter 6 explores), family—and especially marital interactions—often complicated their expression. Therefore, despite extensive examples of women's political agency within the home, individual subjectivities were shaped by a more intricate interplay between interiority and cultural expectations.

The family economy of political work

The critical significance of the family as a political unit could lead to the construction of expansive political identities rooted in kinship interest, as in the female electoral canvassing noted in Chapter 1. M. J. Peterson has argued that so pervasive was the assumption that women should identify with, and contribute to, the work of their male relatives that we might speak of a 'family economy' operating in the lives of the middle class.[73] This might be applied equally to political activities—fathers commonly expected daughters and wives to assist them in their labours. Girls were not simply socialized into feminine role roles and personas through the internalization or imitation of maternal behaviour. Learning to be female might involve the performance of political duties but within a frame of gendered expectation. Patty Smith was fairly typical in acting as secretary to her father, the Whig Unitarian William Smith.[74] Other daughters provided more advanced forms of assistance. Helen Colman explained that as a girl her mother assisted her father (a magistrate and poor law guardian) in his compositions.[75] Maria Edgeworth, the eldest daughter of her father's twenty-two children, was required to write 'an enquiry into the causes of poverty in Ireland' for him, which necessitated embarking upon detailed political research.[76] Lucy Toulmin Smith, the eldest daughter of Joshua, a

---

[73] Peterson, *Family, Love and Work*, ch. 6, quotation at p. 166. See also Catherine Hall, 'Strains in the "Firm of Wife, Children and Friends": Middle-Class Women and Employment in Early-Nineteenth-Century England', in Hall, *White, Male and Middle Class*, 172–202, and Davidoff and Hall, *Family Fortunes*, ch. 6.

[74] Barbara Stephen, 'Family Life' (unpublished draft of the biography of William Smith), British Library, Add MSS 72839A, f. 9.

[75] Helen Caroline Colman, *Jeremiah James Colman: A Memoir* (London, 1905), 108–11.

[76] Madeline Thompson, 'Distant Prospects and Smaller Circles: Questions of Authority in Maria Edgeworth's Irish writings', in Joan Bellamy et al. (eds), *Women, Scholarship and Criticism: Gender and Knowledge c.1790–1900* (Manchester, 2000), 49.

campaigner against state centralization, assisted her father in the editorship of the *Parliamentary Remembrancer* (1857–65).[77] For Elizabeth Fletcher, the Edinburgh radical, the clerical assistance her daughters provided for their father was part of a wider family dynamic of political engagement.[78]

However, such tasks were usually executed within conventional expectations of family interaction. After all, middle-class fathers commonly expected older daughters to provide a range of affective and practical support for them. Contributing to a father's labours might provide young women with stimulating modes of political engagement, but it did not necessarily represent a more expansive view of women's political potential. Indeed in those families where father–daughter bonds were particularly strong there was the possibility that other female family members might have comparatively little political engagement. As in many of the families cited above, fathers typically selected a particular daughter—usually the eldest—to assist in their work. The Evangelical politician Henry Thornton (1760–1815) assigned his eldest daughter Marianne as his secretary. Although he shared a life of active partnership with his wife, it was Henry and not his wife who assumed responsibility for their eldest daughter's education. He provided her with specialist training to enable her to fulfil the office of his assistant and rewarded her with politically charged treats, such as taking her to the opening of parliament.[79]

In like manner, the anti-slavery campaigner George Thompson involved his daughter, Amelia, closely in his affairs, requesting she provide secretarial assistance for his Parliamentary and Financial Reform Association, for example. On one occasion Amelia recorded in her diary that 'Papa came to tea, and I wrote for him an article on Indian matters'.[80] Thompson also depended heavily upon the political expertise of his friend Elizabeth Pease. They developed an extremely close working relationship in their protests against colonial policy and he called upon her to execute a range of literary and campaigning endeavours.[81] Despite this evident respect for the political skills of individual women, and his reliance upon the assistance of his daughter, Thompson's own household did not represent a forum of political

---

[77] *ODNB.*

[78] Eliza Fletcher, *Autobiography of Mrs Fletcher of Edinburgh* (Edinburgh, 1875), 133. Fletcher ensured that her daughters were fully cognizant of contemporary electoral politics, 345.

[79] E. M. Forster, *Marianne Thornton, 1797–1887: A Domestic Biography* (London, 2000; 1st publ. 1956), 32–3, 282–3; 'Recollections of Julia Smith', CUL, Add 7621/15, 19–20.

[80] Diary of Amelia Chesson (entry for 20 Oct. 1858), REAS/10.

[81] George Thompson to Elizabeth Pease (25 May 1837), REAS/3/6; Stoddart, *Elizabeth Pease Nichol*, 86–8.

potential for women. Anne, his wife, did not assume an active political presence in the household. In extant letters Thompson assumed an authoritative tone which included detailed instructions concerning the upbringing of their children during his absence. She was urged not to praise Amelia too much, for example, and to ensure that the girls kept up their music practice.[82] Distinct spheres of political involvement and interaction were therefore often constructed within families.

Political socialization within the home was not simply a vertical process, but also depended upon the lateral dynamics of sibling relationships. As we have seen in the case of Katherine Plymley, assisting in the political labours of a brother could have the affect of entrenching gendered codes concerning the primacy of the male subject. There were important variants, however, particularly amongst progressive circles. One radical enthusiast, Elizabeth Pickett, was effusive about her role as the 'constant companion & fellow labourer of a brother' in their joint schemes for scientific and social improvements which they presented (unsuccessfully) to Lord Morpeth, the Privy Council, and the patent office. Pickett argued that her efforts would 'effectually pave the way for the due recognition of the sex's power to do good—and of our rights'.[83] Assisting in a brother's labours might provide valuable intellectual experience and validate a woman's sense of her own abilities. Before she embarked on her career as a radical journalist, the early Victorian feminist Eliza Meteyard had helped her brother, an assistant commissioner, in the composition of tithe reports. These reports, which were essential to the implementation of the Tithe Commutation Act (1836), required technical legal expertise and specialist knowledge of landholding, valuation, and surveying.[84]

In those families which had a strong tradition of female education (as in the Quakers and Unitarians) it was not uncommon for adult sisters to play a forthright role in supporting the political ambitions of their brothers. This might be particularly the case with unmarried women. The Quaker politician Joseph Sturge appears to have held the judgement of his sister, Sophia, who assisted in his suffrage campaigns, in awe. He recounted her death-bed scene in which she pointed to many errors in his career and he

[82] e.g. George Thompson to Anne [Jenny] Thompson (29 Aug. 1843), REAS3/1/2/2, no. 46.
[83] Elizabeth Pickett to Anne Knight (8 Apr. 1850), Friends House Library, Temp MSS 725/5/38.
[84] Virginia Blain et al., The Feminist Companion to Literature in English: Women Writers from the Middle Ages to the Present (London, 1990), 734; H. M. E. Holt, 'Assistant Commissioners and Local Agents: Their Role in Tithe Commutation, 1836–54', Agricultural History Review, 32 (1984), 189–200.

was clearly relieved that 'she had no doubt of the soundness of the principle on which I had advocated the rights of the people and was quite satisfied with my having espoused their cause'.[85] Men of this denomination were perhaps aware that their sisters had the potential to achieve public prominence and respect in their own right as preachers and this may have subtly altered patterns of family interaction.[86]

If sisters and daughters were commonly involved in the political affairs of their male relatives then the same was equally true of wives. Peterson notes that contemporaries closely associated marriage with work, suggesting that 'the notion of shared work permeates every discussion of professional life'.[87] Whilst this was a phenomenon dependent upon the personalities and specificities of particular relationships (as the example of George and Anne Thompson testifies), it does appear to have been a frequent model in many political families. The common practice of acting as amanuensis and secretary to their husbands had the potential to encompass more expansive understandings of their political role. Both Harriet Grote and Mary Borrow undertook much of the correspondence for their spouses, and assumed the latitude to make their own points.[88] Mary Oastler, the wife of Tory MP Richard, played a major role in the composition of his parliamentary speeches, as well his letters and pamphlets regarding factory reform.[89] The authorial persona of a politician, as we shall see further in Chapter 7, could be conceptualized as a collaborative project.

This is a phenomenon which needs to be understood within broader practices of collective cultural production. Women so commonly contributed to the texts authored by family members that attempts at authorial attribution were often confounded. R. H. Horne intimated in his 1844 work *A New Spirit of the Age* that the works of Mary and William Howitt were 'so inextricably and so interestingly mixed up with their biographies that they can only be appropriately treated under one head'.[90] In

---

[85] Tyrrell, *Joseph Sturge*, 130. For Sophia Sturge's contribution to Joseph's work with the Chartists see William R. Hughes, *Sophia Sturge: A Memoir* (London, 1940), 15.

[86] Samuel Coltman seemed proud that his sister, Elizabeth Heyrick, might make 'an eloquent speaker'. Samuel Coltman to Mrs Coltman (10 Sept. 1820), LRO, Coltman MSS 15D57, 145. For wider discussion see Holton, *Quaker Women*, esp. 1–8.

[87] Peterson, *Family, Love and Work*, 181.

[88] George Paston [Emily Symonds], *At John Murray's: Records of a Literary Circle, 1843–92* (London, 1932), 95, 98.

[89] Colin Creighton, *Richard Oastler: Evangelicalism and the Ideology of Domesticity* (Hull, 1992), 6; *The Home*, 2 (1852), 93.

[90] Cited in Brian E. Maidment, '"Works in Unbroken Succession": The Literary Career of Mary Howitt', in Kay Boardman and Shirley Jones (eds), *Popular Victorian Women Writers*

the case of the Howitts such collaboration drew upon long traditions of collective authorship that were a component of Quaker culture.[91] Other religious communities—strikingly those most normally associated with individualism—also encouraged such sensibilities. Daniel E. White writes of the 'collaborative dynamic of the Dissenting public sphere', pointing to the collective writing practices of rational Dissenting families such as the Aikins and Barbaulds.[92] I would argue that the perpetuation of older models of familial labour was part of a much wider phenomenon. As Peter Mandler observed with reference to the publications of the Irish writer Samuel Carter Hall, the contribution of his wife, Anna Maria, was such that 'the two acted as a partnership, and it is often difficult to discern from whose pen writings under his name actually issued'.[93]

Authorial signatures were not a transparent description of the work's originators, therefore. Rather, they functioned as capacious signifiers which blurred the composite nature of a work's history and privileged the notion of an individual (male) author. When the Coventry radical Charles Bray published *The Philosophy of Necessity* it included a lengthy appendix on the theories and practice of co-operation. However, as he revealed three years later, the appendix was the work of his sister-in-law, Mary Hennell.[94] Even those works which emerged from feminist working partnerships tended to follow such a pattern. The feminist manifesto *An Appeal of One Half the Human Race* (1825) was issued under the name 'William Thompson' but had

---

(Manchester, 2004), 22–45, here at 28. Maidment insists—although the evidence is unclear—that Mary specialized in 'feminine' genres whilst William concentrated upon masculine modes of writing.

[91] Catie Gill, 'Identities in Quaker Women's Writing, 1652–60', *Women's Writing*, 9 (2002), 267–83; Michael Mascuch, *Origins of the Individualist Self: Autobiography and Self-Identity in England, 1591–1791* (Cambridge, 1997), 120, 125–6; Linda H. Peterson, 'Collaborative Life Writing as Ideology: The Auto/Biographies of Mary Howitt and her Family', *Prose Studies*, 26 (2003), 176–95.

[92] Daniel E. White, 'The "Joineriana": Anna Barbauld, the Aikin Family Circle and the Dissenting Public Sphere', *Eighteenth-Century Studies*, 32 (1999), 511–33, here at 529. See also Mary A. Waters, *British Women Writers and the Profession of Literary Criticism, 1789–1832* (Basingstoke, 2004), 141; Pamela Clemit, 'Mary Shelley and William Godwin: A Literary-Political Partnership, 1823–36', *Women's Writing*, 6 (1999), 285–95.

[93] *ODNB*. For an example from yet another ideological network see E. Jane Whately, *Life and Correspondence of Richard Whately, D. D. Late Archbishop of Dublin* (London, 1866, 2 vols), ii. 460.

[94] On Mary Hennell's death, Charles Bray issued the work separately in tribute to her, although her name still did not appear on the title-page: Mary Hennell, *An Outline of the Various Social Systems and Communities which have been Founded on the Principle of Co-operation with an Introductory Essay* (London, 1844).

been jointly composed with Anna Wheeler; and *Principles of Political Economy* (1849) which bore the name of John Stuart Mill was actually written with his wife, Harriet Taylor Mill.[95] A collective authorial identity did not necessarily imply that women's own subjectivity would remain submerged. At the micro-level such examples contributed to the mounting incidents which acknowledged women's intellectual capabilities. But at the macro-level it was a convention which reconstituted the gendered hierarchies of political culture by reinforcing a normative view as to the primacy of the male subject.

In a similar manner, a sense of investment in a husband's occupation might open up opportunities for public engagement in some spheres, yet not override profoundly gendered subjectivities in others. So women might capitalize upon a husband's position to construct greater latitude in their community roles, but this did not mean that they necessarily felt equally empowered in domestic and familial contexts. A consideration of the correspondence of Frances Smith (1758–1840) from the years of the French Revolution to the late regency, when radical debates on the family were so in flux, helps to illuminate these complicated layers of subjectivity. Smith performed administrative work for her politician husband, William, and also functioned as an energetic electoral agent in his absence. She made arrangements for the cooping (or detaining) of electors, and canvassed for votes 'where ever I think I can obtain any'.[96] In correspondence with her husband she emerges as deeply engaged in political affairs, requesting, for example that he takes 'detailed notes' on the situation in France during his stay there in the turbulent days of 1790.[97] In their loving exchanges her cultural confidence also emerges in the forthright advice she frequently gives William on his business affairs or travel arrangements.[98]

---

[95] William Thompson, *Appeal of One Half the Human Race, Women, against the Pretensions of the Other Half, Men, to Retain them in Political, and thence in Civil and Domestic Slavery* (1825), ed. Dolores Dooley (Cork, 1997); Dolores Dooley, 'Anna Doyle Wheeler (1785–c.1850)', in Mary Cullen and Maria Luddy (eds), *Women, Power and Consciousness in Nineteenth-Century Ireland: Eight Biographical Studies* (Dublin, 1995), 19–53. As Harriet Taylor Mill was aware, 'opinions carry more weight with the authority of his name alone', cited in Jo Ellen Jacobs, 'Harriet Taylor Mill's Collaboration with John Stuart Mill', in Cecile T. Tougas and Sara Ebenreck (eds), *Presenting Women Philosophers* (Philadelphia, 2000), 159.

[96] Letters from Frances Smith to William Smith [July 1802], CUL, William Smith papers, Add MSS 7621/217–18. Frances Smith also assisted the electoral aspirations of close friends. See her letter to William [1818], Add MSS 7621/257.

[97] Frances Smith to William Smith (8 July [1790]), CUL, Add MSS 7621/208.

[98] Letters from Frances Smith to William Smith, CUL, Add MSS 7621/200–75.

Her assured performances in this regard are not surprising given that the couple hailed from a radical, Dissenting, intellectual community which had a strong tradition of gender egalitarianism. (It was to Frances that the Unitarian divine, Thomas Belsham, addressed his critique of William Wilberforce's theological pamphlet in his *Letters to a Lady*.[99]) Frances Smith's notebooks confirm her intense intellectual engagement. She expressed her admiration for the work of radicals such as Thomas Paine and Joel Barlow and made clear her approval of women's contribution to the oppositional public sphere. This included praising Anna Laetitia Barbauld's theological pamphlet on public worship, and citing approvingly passages from Wollstonecraft's *Vindication of the Rights of Woman*.[100]

Nonetheless, Frances Smith's self-perceptions as a wife and a mother complicated these intellectual perceptions of female citizenship. In a letter to her husband concerning the possibility of her and her daughter giving to a female patriotic fund she asks, 'If you think it proper for us to subscribe to the two guinea subscription . . . I should be glad that you would do it for me if you think right.'[101] When acting as secretary to her husband she similarly projected a humble, female persona. Thus in a letter to William Wilberforce, with whom her husband collaborated closely on anti-slavery, she adopted the language of feminine courtesy, 'I fear you will be much disappointed at receiving a letter from me as amanuensis to my Husband, seeing I cannot equally assist you in the great Business you have so much at heart.'[102]

The perceived need to adopt such positions is not merely a strategic or cosmetic process. As Judith Spicksley explains, 'representations of identity in the public domain frequently operated *as if* identity were fixed, allocating to each individual an identity that located them securely within the socio-political framework. This in turn shaped the way individuals perceived themselves and others.'[103] The success of projecting particular aspects of the self could validate a certain identity and reinforce how that individual perceived themselves. It could make the adoption of particular personas

---

[99] Thomas Belsham, *A Review of Mr Wilberforce's Treatise Entitled 'A Practical View of the Prevailing Religious System of Professed Christians' in Letters to a Lady* (London, 1798); R. W. Davis, *Dissent in Politics, 1780–1830: The Political Life of William Smith, M. P.* (London, 1971), 9n.

[100] Abstract of the notebook of Frances Smith in Stephen, 'Family Life', appendix.

[101] Frances Smith to William Smith (22 Nov. 1803), CUL, Add MSS 7621/232.

[102] Frances Smith to William Wilberforce [n.d.], CUL, Add MSS 7621/207.

[103] Judith Spicksley, 'A Dynamic Model of Social Relations: Celibacy, Credit and the Identity of the "Spinster" in Seventeenth-Century England', in French and Barry (eds), *Identity and Agency*, 129.

more likely, or facilitate the choice of other gendered identities. Think for example of Frances's recourse to a submissive mode when she required her husband's financial sanction for a philanthropic contribution. It was the repetition of such discursive acts which perpetuated hegemonic cultural modes.

Frances Smith's identity as a mother further problematized her commitment to egalitarian citizenship. On the one hand, the confidence she had in her own views, combined with the mutual respect she enjoyed with her husband, enabled her to issue pointed instructions to William on the upbringing of their sons, 'I know you will watch over our Boys, and I form hopes that being so much with you they will form established habits of virtue and good conduct that nothing can shake.'[104] Yet it appears to have been William who attempted to inculcate progressive notions of female behaviour in their daughters, exhorting Patty to be 'governed by Reason'.[105] In contrast Frances insisted to her daughter that 'Females are born to practise Obedience, first to their Parents, and afterwards to their Husbands.'[106] As a mother, Frances Smith's desire to produce daughters who conformed to dominant understandings of appropriate female behaviour (as might befit, one supposes, the family's status as wealthy members of the local elite) undercut her intellectual commitment to more independent views of the female role. During the war with France she wrote to her husband of her views on public events and requesting his opinion of current affairs. Yet in the same letter she wrote, 'You know that I love this retirement much, and it is very salutary for the Girls, both for body and mind.'[107] Although her daughters were expected to take an active part in aspects of electioneering, such as socializing with electors and attending election balls, this appears to have been a transient phenomenon which did not represent a broader attempt to politicize them.[108] She wrote to her husband on one occasion, 'You know we do not read Newspapers, nor do I desire that the girls should read them for several reasons, but in the magazines we learn a little of what goes on in the world, without reading anything offensive.'[109]

---

[104] Frances Smith to William Smith (31 July 1812), CUL, Add MSS 7621/246.

[105] William Smith to Martha ('Patty') Smith, [n.d.], CUL, Add MSS 7621/147.

[106] Stephen, 'Family Life', 11. Her daughters appear to have had a difficult relationship with their mother, ibid. 27.

[107] Frances Smith to William Smith [n.d., c.1803/4], CUL, Add MSS 7621/240.

[108] Julia Smith to Patty Smith (20 Oct. 1812), CUL, Add MSS 7621/450.

[109] Frances Smith to William Smith [n.d., c.1809], CUL, Add MSS 7621/242.

As an independent student of modern political thought, Frances Smith could perceive of herself as part of a radical Dissenting intellectual community. Thus in her private notebooks and in epistolary exchange with her husband she had the confidence to debate and critique the ideas of her wider network as an equal participant in the enlightened public sphere. Cultural assurance as a member of an educated coterie was here a predominant factor. As a member of the local political elite it was Frances's social and economic status—and not her gender—that was most crucial in determining her acceptance as a political actor, giving her the scope to act as a canvasser and political manager. However, when her gendered role as a wife and mother was most salient, the correspondence suggests a more fragmented and fragile political identity.

A similar process is detectable in the family interactions of the Edgeworth family. The novelist Maria Edgeworth was intimately involved with the management of the family's Irish estate. When her brother, Lovell, fell into chronic financial difficulties in 1826 Edgeworth took over its proprietorship. This was a role which Edgeworth perceived to be explicitly political, noting that 'landlords must & should & ever will have influence & this is one way in which property is represented & the real balance of the B[ritish] Constitution is preserved'. Accordingly she took great pains to ensure that their tenants voted with the family, struggling through the snow in December 1835 to solicit their votes.[110] Whilst Edgeworth's identity as a member of the landowning elite was more important than her gender in these interactions, she was quick to evoke her femininity if the paternalistic relationship was challenged. When an elderly, disabled tenant of her brother's voted against him at an election, the Edgeworths' agent, Barry Fox (Edgeworth's brother-in-law) was insistent on calling for the 'hanging gale' of rent against the offender. This was a means of exerting control over a new tenant by exempting them from the first six months' rent, providing they complied with a landowner's wishes. Normally Edgeworth took full responsibility for the management of the estate in her brother's absence. On this occasion she wrote to him requesting that he take the final decision. She explained that if he wished to pursue Fox's more draconian policy, then 'as a woman', she herself could not implement it.[111] Such strategic employment

---

[110] Maria Edgeworth to Charles Sneyd Edgeworth (12 Feb. 1835), Edgeworth, c. 703, f. 229. Michael Hurst, *Maria Edgeworth and the Public Scene: Intellect, Fine Feeling and Landlordism in the Age of Reform* (London, 1969), 94.
[111] Maria Edgeworth to Charles Sneyd Edgeworth (12 Feb. 1835), Edgeworth, c. 703, f. 229. In the event Fox's view prevailed and, in a highly emotional scene, Maria Edgeworth

of a feminine identity was one of the ways in which gendered relationships within families were reiterated and upheld.

This is not to say that women could not forge autonomous political identities within their families. The interplay of particular personalities or circumstances could of course create other patterns: as in the dominant role Harriet Grote assumed in the political affairs of her husband, George; or the intellectual profile Sarah Austin cultivated to keep her family solvent during the incapacity of her husband, John. (Although we might also note that here, too, both women frequently adopted hesitant, subordinate personas when describing their labours to others.[112]) The exceptional cultural competence of these two women was evidently critical to the negotiation of family roles, but there were other factors which could also facilitate divergent models. As Clare Midgley has shown, the differing paths taken by male and female anti-slavery societies from the late 1820s (with women's organizations favouring the policy of immediate abolition, rather than the gradualist stance preferred by most male societies) could signify tensions within those families committed to abolition. She explains, 'Key members of local men's and women's societies came from the same families, and thus in espousing immediate emancipation women were not only going against the authority of the national leadership of the movement but also taking a stance in opposition to that of their fathers, husbands and brothers.'[113] It seems probable that particular constellations of factors were often at work here, however. Jane Wigham was determined to lead the Edinburgh ladies' association in a radical direction, in distinction to the policy pursued by her husband's organization. On her marriage to John, Jane was already approaching 40 years old and had an established identity as a worker in the anti-slavery cause. This encompassed a close identification with her family's politics. Her father, William Smeal, a Glasgow tea merchant, was a close friend of the radical American abolitionist, William Lloyd Garrison. Her marriage did not substantially alter this primary political identity. Her stepdaughter, Eliza, who assisted her, was a devoted Quaker who went on to become a preacher. An affiliation to the strong political heritage of her birth family, combined with the fact that Jane was

---

received the rent from Mr Dermod and his son. Marilyn Butler, *Maria Edgeworth: A Literary Biography* (London, 1972), 454. For further reference to Edgeworth's self-positioning see Hurst, *Maria Edgeworth*, 37, 49, 75 and Thompson, 'Women, Work and Politics', 59–60.

[112] *ODNB*; Elizabeth Eastlake, *Mrs Grote: A Sketch* (London, 1880), 4; L. Hamburger and J. Hamburger, *Troubled Lives: John and Sarah Austin* (Toronto, 1985), 66; Gleadle, *Early Feminists*, 31.

[113] Midgley, *Women against Slavery*, 109.

already someone of maturity on her marriage, strengthened her ability to carve out a persona independent from that of her spouse. This was enhanced by her closeness to her daughter whose Quakerism provided a further source of female public confidence.[114]

The case of Mary Sewell, a successful temperance activist and philanthropist, provides further insights into the possible combination of factors which facilitated the maintenance of a wife's autonomous political identity. The poor financial management of her husband Isaac, a struggling businessman, often affected the family and it would seem that Sewell managed to retain a degree of control over her own finances, creating further possibilities for her to execute independent interests. Publishing a children's book *Walks with Mamma* in 1824, had provided her with funds which she retained herself to purchase educational books. Her success as a writer of verse and educational works from 1858 may have helped to further alter the balance of the marital dynamics.[115] At this point the couple were living in the small Gloucestershire village of Wick. Whilst Mary flourished on their move here, establishing herself as a prominent philanthropist among local labourers, 65-year-old Isaac appears to have aged less well. In temporary retirement from his job as a bank manager, Isaac focused his energies on a Quaker congregation near Bristol, Mary having left the denomination in 1836. In addition, Sewell developed a small but intimate network of women, including her daughter Anna, who supported her work, forming alternative sources of encouragement and intimacy. By the 1860s, Sewell's local successes, combined with her cultural status as a writer, brought her national recognition amongst female temperance campaigners.[116] Although the formidable and forthright Sewell had a far more prominent public life than her husband, she chose to present a strictly gendered demarcation of her labours, writing of the 'quiet, spiritual work God has appointed for women' and that allotted to men 'who have to face the world and fight its battles'.[117] This was a common pattern. Elizabeth Fletcher cultivated a reputation as a redoubtable political figure in Georgian and Victorian

[114] Ibid. 135–7.

[115] For information on the marriage see Susan Chitty, *The Woman who Wrote* Black Beauty: *A Life of Anna Sewell* (London, 1971); Mary Sewell's *Mother's Last Words: A Ballad for Boys* (1861) was to sell over one million copies: J. L. Smith-Dampier, *East Anglican Worthies* (Oxford, 1949), 172.

[116] National Temperance League, *Woman's Work* (London, 1868), 51–5.

[117] Bayly, *Life and Letters*, 123.

Edinburgh. Nonetheless in her autobiography Fletcher portrayed her career in relation to that of her husband.[118]

A degree of financial independence, the possession of cultural confidence and success, the opportunities provided for female involvement in the parochial sphere, and the consequences of differential responses to ageing could provide women with the basis for greater autonomy. Nonetheless, these were subtleties which dominant public discourses of female activity failed to signify, and individual women found it difficult to find a language with which to articulate their independent political presence.

Conclusion

The family was an important forum for the constitution of political culture and women were sometimes fully implicated in this. It was a process which could—but did not inevitably—result in the construction of empowering female subjectivities. Whilst the bland imprecision of 'female influence' acknowledged women's potential for political input within the family, it obscured the complexities of exercising such sway within the actuality of family relations and underplayed the significance of broader cultural currents which prioritized wifely submission. It is striking that so many of the major female political figures of the day were unmarried, separated, or widowed during their time of greatest activism—as in the case of Harriet Martineau, Charlotte Tonna, Elizabeth Heyrick, Hannah More, Anne Knight, and Anna Wheeler.[119]

As we have seen, there were further social and cultural factors which could lead to the creation of more forthright political roles for women within their families. This included the status of single women in some kinship networks (particularly those from Quaker backgrounds) and the resonance of one's family of birth as a source of political confidence. Nonetheless, we should not underestimate the extent to which patriarchal assumptions might shape the experiences and identities of even seemingly

---

[118] Gleadle, 'British Women', 136; Jane Rendall, '"Women that would Plague me with Rational Conversation": Aspiring Women and Scottish Whigs, c.1790–1830', in Sarah Knott and Barbara Taylor (eds), *Women, Gender and Enlightenment* (Basingstoke, 2004), 326–47, esp. 328, 335–6.

[119] For the effect of marital status upon female anti-slavery activism see Midgley, *Women against Slavery*, 80–1.

radical families. Within the intricate scenarios of family life there were often occasions when even strong-minded, intensely political women might enact more subservient feminine identities. The assumption that the duty of wives and daughters was to prioritize the needs and aspirations of the male head of the household was deeply embedded and could problematize an individual's ideological commitment to more progressive practices. The stated legal position of married women was that their legal identity was merged into that of their husband. As Blackstone put it in his famous dictum, 'The husband and wife are one, and that one is the husband.' Women's contribution to business enterprises as well as female consumption and testatory practices are all suggestive of the inability of legal discourse to capture the day-to-day experiences of contemporary families.[120] Nonetheless, legal injunctions as to the limits to female identity did form part of the warp and weft of cultural understandings of gender relations. They contributed—if only tangentially—to a blurring of any crisply contoured notion of individualism. Similarly Anglican precepts of women's status as their husbands' 'helpmeets' further encouraged a propensity to focus upon women as 'relational beings'. It is necessary to consider therefore the many ways in which liberal understandings of the individual, rational self could be muddied and at times obscured for women.

There is a long tradition within feminist psychology which argues that normative conceptions of the self are inadequate to the understanding of women's experiences. Rather than understanding subjectivity as relating to isolated, bounded individuals, it is suggested that women develop a sense of identity through their affiliation to others, thus resulting in a relational subjectivity.[121] Similar binary constructions have been made comparing pre-modern with modern understandings of the self: the eighteenth century is often viewed as a critical moment in the emergence of 'modern',

[120] Margot Finn, 'Women, Consumption and Coverture in England, c.1760–1860', *Historical Journal*, 39 (1996), 703–22. See further Nicola Phillips, *Women in Business, 1700–1850* (Woodbridge, 2006), part I; Hannah Barker, *The Business of Women: Female Enterprise and Urban Development in Northern England, 1760–1830* (Oxford, 2006), 135–51.

[121] Chodorow, *Reproduction of Mothering*; Carol Gilligan, *In a Different Voice: Psychological Theory and Women's Development* (Cambridge, Mass., 1982); Judith V. Jordan, 'The Relational Self: A New Perspective for Understanding Women's Development', and also Hazel R. Markus and Shinobu Kitayama, 'Cultural Variation in the Self-Concept', in Jaine Strauss and George R. Geothals (eds), *The Self: Interdisciplinary Approaches* (New York, 1991), 136–49 and 18–48.

[122] For early modern notions of the fluidity of the self see Natalie Z. Davis, 'Boundaries and the Sense of Self in Sixteenth-Century France', in Thomas C. Heller *et al.* (eds), *Reconstructing Individualism: Autonomy, Individuality and the Self in Western Thought* (Stanford, Calif., 1986), 53–63.

individualistic understandings of the rational subject.[122] As we have seen here, collective understandings of identity remained critical to political agents throughout our period and were often rooted in specific cultural traditions. But the perpetual employment of relational tropes of femininity in this period, combined with processes of socialization which emphasized female duties of caring and subservience, may well have made the adoption of collective identities a particularly likely psychological resource for women.

In many of the families we have considered, it was the notion of a collective familial identity which was particularly prominent in women's engagement. This could prove an empowering and 'safe' conduit of participation, although it also had the potential to marginalize female voices which might be subsumed within a masculine political 'we'. The practices of collaboration indicated contemporaries' widespread empirical experience of women's ability to author works of serious intellectual stature. Yet there remained a critical disjuncture between such knowledge and the public discourses and practices through which women's participation in public debate were articulated.

Noticeably, it was those women who were able to develop their own local spheres of interest, whether as electoral agents or philanthropists, who were likely to have greater opportunities to exhibit more independent identities. To explore these issues further we shall therefore now turn to the involvement of women in the 'parochial realm'.

4

Community, authority, and parochial realms

Introduction

Within their communities, women could act as authoritative public figures in ways that were strikingly at odds with the highly feminized modes of action with which they were associated in the wider 'public sphere' of national campaigns. Gender was always central to individual identity and social interaction, yet in these contexts it was a less obvious predictor of public engagement. Studying the multifarious constructions of women's local personas enables us to focus upon the varying salience of gender in the experiences and representations of publicly active women. Gender did not operate as a 'pure' entity but was crucially enmeshed with other frames of identity in these encounters.[1]

This chapter will consider the various sites of the 'parochial realm'. Here the term is employed not to signal simply the historical construct of the parish. Rather, following the work of cultural geographer Lyn Lofland, it is used to denote situations characterized by daily, local interaction and personal communication.[2] On the street, in churches, the homes of the poor, shops, vestries, and farms, women played a multiplicity of roles. Probing this phenomenon necessitates synthesizing a number of developments in the historiography of middle-class women. Three themes in particular will be central: female economic agency, women's cultural activities, and female philanthropy—all of which have benefited from substantial revisionist scholarship in recent years. Combining these various themes

---

[1] See Introduction above, pp. 10–11.
[2] Lofland distinguishes between the 'public realm' and the 'parochial realm'. These two realms relate not to physical spaces (although the meanings engendered by specific locations were important) but to the nature of the relationships within a given context. The public realm includes those interactions where individuals only 'know' one another by nature of their collective or non-personal identities (as in the scenarios investigated in Ch. 2 above). Lofland, *The Public Realm*, 11–14.

enables us to imaginatively recreate the impact that women might have had upon their neighbourhoods. The aim of the chapter is to provide glimpses into the variety of ways in which contemporaries would have experienced women's political agency within their locales, and to consider how women were empowered to act in these contexts. Particular locales developed distinct patterns of elite female public behaviour which drew upon the multi-faceted authority women could establish in the parochial realm. We need to analyse, therefore, not merely widespread evidence of female public participation, but how some women were able to accrue high status. In a sense this involves a study of 'exceptional' women, rather than the rank and file. However, the ability of women to exploit certain cultural conduits to attain prominence as community figures was an important feature of early nineteenth-century parochial culture.[3]

Characterizations of women's public roles have often focused upon the urban sphere, with particular attention paid to the role of women in burgeoning centres such as Manchester and Leeds.[4] Yet for most of our period the majority of the population still lived in small, rural communities. In 1851 the census recorded that only 50.1 per cent of the population of England and Wales were residing in urban areas, with 51.8 per cent in Scotland; and it should be remembered that the definition of urban was any population greater than 2,000.[5] Paying further attention to the roles and experiences of women in smaller provincial communities enables us to construct a more nuanced picture. Yet, as we shall see, there were not strict lines of demarcation between the civic and the rural. The patterns of public engagement which typified elite women's experience of rural life were often replicated in emerging conurbations such as Leicester and Ipswich. The civic sphere, that is to say, should not be understood purely with reference to the emergence of masculinist bourgeois culture.[6] Rather, the parochial sphere provided models of authority and interaction that were often recreated in other kinds of publics.

Emphasizing the significance of the rural public sphere involves revisiting the innovative work of Leonore Davidoff and Catherine Hall, to date the only substantial consideration of women in rural England. They drew a

---

[3] A vicious literary satire on such a woman may be found in Catherine Gore, *Mrs Armytage: Or, Female Domination* (London, 1836, 3 vols), i. 144–6.

[4] e.g. Morgan, *Victorian Woman's Place*.

[5] F. M. L. Thompson, 'Town and City', in Thompson (ed.), *The Cambridge Social History of Britain, 1750–1950*, i. *Regions and Communities* (Cambridge, 1990), 2–3. For further discussion see Alun Howkins, *Reshaping Rural England: A Social History, 1850–1925* (London, 1991).

[6] See above p. 62.

bleak picture of declining opportunities for women and mounting gender stratification in English provincial life.[7] Davidoff was pessimistic concerning women's participation in cultural activities such as book clubs and reading groups, seeing this as symptomatic of the masculinization of rural public life. I will suggest that the picture was more ambivalent.[8]

Critical to the argument will be a consideration of the nature and meanings of female philanthropy. Older assessments assumed upper-class benevolence to be distinct from that of its middle-class counterpart because of the former's reliance on 'personal, localized projects' as opposed to middle-class investment in associational ventures.[9] Here it will be argued, in common with K. D. Reynolds, that in philanthropy as in other forms of local interaction it is unhelpful to assume too stark a difference between the experiences of middling, gentry, and aristocratic women. Across these strata it is important to give due weight to paternalism, rather than femininity *per se*, as a dominant mode of identification in philanthropic interactions.[10]

[7] Davidoff and Hall, *Family Fortunes,* and Leonore Davidoff, 'The Role of Gender in the 'First Industrial Nation': Farming and the Countryside in England, 1780–1850' (1st publ. 1986) in Davidoff, *Worlds Between,* 180–205.

[8] e.g. Davidoff, 'Role of Gender', 189, cites the Thaxted Book Society, noting 'there seems to have been only one woman member'. Whilst her source only mentions one female member by name, she is described as 'the first female member to be admitted'—not the only one. Many of the club's titles were explicitly aimed at a female audience (*Memoirs of a Pious Woman, A Week's Conversation between a Lady and her Nieces, Memoirs of a Female Vagrant, Interesting Conversation by a Lady, The Female Pilgrim*); and from 1830 the club's annual dinner was held in members' houses: Ethel Simcoe, *A Short History of the Parish and Ancient Borough of Thaxted* (Saffron Walden, 1934), 126–8. For another comparable example see Mary Clive (ed.), *Caroline Clive, from the Diary and Family Papers of Mrs Archer Clive (1801–1873)* (London, 1949), 124. Local women could sometimes be keen participants in the projects of local agricultural societies: *Farmers' Magazine* (Jan. 1838), 55; Canterbury Farmers' Club, *Farmers at the 'Fountain': A History of Canterbury Farmers' Club and Farmers' Meetings in Canterbury over a Period of Two Hundred Years* (Canterbury, 1997), 219–22. There was an increasing trend for the farming community to meet not in pubs, but in respectable venues such as hotels or purpose-built halls: H. S. A. Fox, 'Local Farmers' Associations and the Circulation of Agricultural Information in Nineteenth-Century England', in H. S. A. Fox and R. A. Butlin (eds), *Change in the Countryside: Essays on Rural England, 1500–1900* (London, 1979), 51; Kevin Fitzgerald, *Ahead of their Time: A Short History of the Farmers' Club, 1842–1968* (London, 1967), 8–9; William Raynbird and Hugh Raynbird, *On the Agriculture of Suffolk* (London, 1849), 264–5, 280, 286; John Player, *Sketches of Saffron Walden and its Vicinity* (Saffron Walden, 1845), 77.

[9] Jessica Gerard, 'Lady Bountiful: Women of the Landed Classes and Rural Philanthropy', *Victorian Studies,* 30 (1987), 183–210, here at 184.

[10] K. D. Reynolds, *Aristocratic Women and Political Society in Victorian Britain* (Oxford, 1998), 71–2, 111.

In addition we need to look beyond the contribution women made to charitable societies and to remember the many forms of individual patronage and philanthropy. As Mary Clare Martin has observed, despite historians' interest in female philanthropy, few studies have been undertaken from the parochial perspective. Martin's work on Walthamstow and Leyton in Essex showed that focusing upon individual women as community actors, rather than privileging institutional and associational projects, unearths very different patterns of engagement. Martin found that there was no obvious divide between 'male' and 'female' philanthropy, and that these 'lady bountifuls' represented a diverse but cohesive social stratum, many of them coming from business families and sharing a commitment to paternalistic benevolence.[11] These patterns have emerged as equally crucial in the research which underpins this chapter.

Historians are ever more alert to the cultural attainments displayed by women of these strata. Looking beyond the limitations of their experience of formal schooling, we now have a much richer sense of their often impressive levels of intellectual achievement and contributions to cultural life.[12] As Martin indicated, women were able to draw upon wider networks to establish their local authority—a theme which has resonance for this study. Here it will be further suggested that we need to extend our understanding of women's role as cultural agents by incorporating a much broader range of printed sources into our analyses. This includes the currently neglected production of ephemeral texts such as handbills and tracts, as well as the contribution women made to local print culture through poetry, local histories, and pamphlets produced specifically for a neighbourhood audience. The ability of middle-class and gentry women to capitalize upon their superior educational and literary attainments to those of their lower-class neighbours was just one of the consequences of superior financial well-being. Central to this chapter is the argument that, within local communities, women's economic standing was paramount both to the scope and nature of their activities and also to contemporaries' perceptions of them.

---

[11] Mary Clare Martin, 'Women and Philanthropy in Walthamstow and Leyton, 1740–1870', *London Journal*, 19 (1994), 119–50.

[12] e.g. Bellamy *et al.* (eds), *Women, Scholarship and Criticism*; Elizabeth Eger *et al.* (eds), *Women, Writing and the Public Sphere, 1700–1830* (Cambridge, 2001); Joanne Shattock (ed.), *Women and Literature in Britain, 1800–1900* (Cambridge, 2001); Morgan, *Victorian Woman's Place*, ch. 3.

Economic activities and local profiles

Recent scholarship has emphasized the considerable involvement of women in business activities, property holding, and investment in this period, and the widespread protection of women's assets through equitable trusts.[13] Furthermore, as we saw in Chapter 1, a substantial minority of households were headed by women, a factor which would have enabled them to act as local electors or officeholders in many communities. A popular Victorian author and clergyman, S. Baring Gould, satirized a 'Madame Grym' of 'Grimstone' in early nineteenth-century Devon whose high-handed behaviour dominated the parish vestry meetings she attended. The eponymous heroine of Charlotte Brontë's *Shirley* also revelled in the social position her economic status brought, suggesting—if with some irony—that she should be chosen as churchwarden 'the next time you elect new ones'.[14] These fictional characters tapped into local experience of powerful women who exerted considerable sway in parochial politics by dint of their social and economic status. Anne Lister, a member of the lesser gentry, was someone of cultural attainments and local political influence. She voted in local elections and also addressed meetings herself.[15] Caroline Meysey-Wigley (later Clive) was a wealthy barrister's daughter who published fiction and religious essays and also wrote for the *Quarterly Review*. In the 1830s, when she was an independent householder prior to her marriage to the local vicar, Archer Clive, she acted as one of the surveyors of highways in Solihull, and also as parish overseer. This caused local controversy not because of her gender, but due to the overbearing authority she was thought to wield over her tenants. As Archer Clive reported, 'You were re-elected but not without opposition . . . Then was raised the question of intimidation, your opponents saying that your tenants wished to vote against you but dared not, being already canvassed by you.

[13] Maxine Berg, 'Women's Property and the Industrial Revolution', *Journal of Interdisciplinary History*, 24 (1993), 233–50; R. J. Morris, *Men, Women and Property in England, 1780–1870: A Social and Economic History of Family Strategies amongst the Leeds Middle Classes* (Cambridge, 2005), ch. 6.

[14] S. Baring Gould, *Old Country Life* (London, 1890), 31–5. Baring Gould had considerable experience of rural Devonshire politics, owning an estate in Lew Trenchard: *ODNB*; Charlotte Brontë, *Shirley* (Harmondsworth, 1985; 1st publ. 1849), 213.

[15] Liddington, *Female Fortune*, 128, 132–3. See also Liddington, 'Gender, Authority and Mining in an Industrial Landscape: Anne Lister, 1791–1840', *History Workshop Journal*, 42 (1996), 59–86.

Upon which Mr Doughty in proper terms defended you, and the end is you must be Overseer again and as economical as you can.'[16]

Women's economic wealth also positioned them as critical agents within their communities in other ways—as local businesswomen or tradeswomen, for example. This sometimes led to more expansive descriptions of women than those which tended to dominate sermons or prescriptive literature. The memory of strong, individualistic women was woven into Lord Suffield's subsequent imagining of regional identity. He cited women such as Mrs Beaton, a local freemason, and Elizabeth Clayton, a shipbuilder of 'masculine' traits and pastimes, as formidable women who formed part of the Norfolk heritage.[17] Certainly the status wrought by economic capital could have wider ramifications for women's community position. Caroline Smedley ran a successful hydropathic establishment in Matlock with her husband, John. However, her involvement in the local community was also extensive: she 'presided at prayer-meetings', for example.[18] Sarah Benney, considered by contemporaries to be 'a thorough woman of business', ran a family boat firm in mid-Victorian Cornwall with 'manly independence and energy'. These qualities, combined with her economic authority and reputation for religious observance, led her to be likened to 'royalty', and a 'mother in Israel'. The latter was an expansive appellation which implied not simply feminine characteristics, but rather status, authority, and leadership.[19]

Benney was clearly an exceptional character. However, the number of women (particularly widows) who managed businesses both increased and further diversified in the 1780–1830 period. The overall numbers concerned may have remained small but the clustering of women in retail businesses meant that many areas—particular streets for example—would have had a noticeable female presence.[20] Ivy Pinchbeck demonstrated that

---

[16] Clive, *Caroline Clive*, 37; *ODNB*. For another example see Morgan, *Victorian Woman's Place*, 135–6. For the role of highway surveyors see Derek Fraser, *Urban Politics in Victorian England: The Structure of Politics in Victorian Cities* (Leicester, 1976), ch. 5.

[17] Charles Harbord, *My Memories, 1830–1913: By Lord Suffield* (London, 1913), 57.

[18] Henry Steer, *The Smedleys of Matlock Bank: Being a Review of the Religious and Philanthropic Labours of Mr and Mrs John Smedley* (London, 1897), 90.

[19] Mrs Perrin, *A Mother in Israel: The Life of Sarah Benney* (London, 1900), see Canon Mason, 'Prefatory note' and ch. 1.

[20] Barker, *Business of Women*, ch. 2; Alison C. Kay, 'Small Business, Self-Employment and Women's Work–Life Choices in Nineteenth-Century London', in David Mitch *et al.* (eds), *Origins of the Modern Career* (Aldershot, 2004), 191–206. See also Phillips, *Women in Business*; Hannah Barker and Karen Harvey, 'Women Entrepreneurs and Urban Expansion:

the pamphlet shops which studded London's streets in the late eighteenth century selling newspapers, journals, and parliamentary speeches were 'almost invariably kept by women'.[21] This was a pattern which persisted well into our period, with recent research underlining a small but persistent economic presence of female booksellers, printers, and owners of circulating libraries in the north of England.[22] Within the coteries of free-thought politics, women such as the Birmingham Owenite Frances Morrison were pivotal to the production and distribution of unstamped publications. Alice Mann was the Leeds agent for the *Ten Hours Advocate* and went to prison for the sale of unstamped newspapers in 1836. Mann also published radical pamphlets under her own press, including a memoir of William Cobbett. Equally, the soirée Glasgow rationalists held to celebrate Matilda Roalfe's release from prison for selling atheistic material is indicative of how local political cultures might develop more liberal recognition of female public engagement than was the case with national organizations.[23]

In addition a large number of provincial newspapers were managed and edited by women. This included the *Reading Mercury* (run by two generations of women); the *Inverness Courier* (edited by Christian Johnstone 1817–24); the *Bury Post* (whose proprietorship was held by Ann Gedge in the early nineteenth century); the *Coventry Mercury* (printed by Ann Rollason); Janet Harrison of the *Marylebone Mercury*; the *Shrewsbury Chronicle* (owned and printed by Mrs Wood from 1806); the *Kent Herald* (printed and edited by Elizabeth Wood from 1829); the *Nottingham Journal* (owned and edited by Mary Stretton from 1833); and the *Dunfermline News* (published by Jane Marshall in the early Victorian period).[24] In many cases

---

Manchester, 1760–1820', and Christine Wiskin, 'Urban Businesswomen in Eighteenth-Century England', in Sweet and Lane, *Women and Urban Life*, 87–129.

[21] Ivy Pinchbeck, *Women Workers and the Industrial Revolution, 1750–1850* (London, 1930), 295. See also C. J. Mitchell, 'Women in the Eighteenth-Century Book Trades', in O. M. Brack (ed.), *Writers, Books, and Trade: An Eighteenth-Century English Miscellany for William B. Todd* (New York, 1994), 25–76.

[22] e.g. female management of printing businesses averaged at just over 8% in Northumberland and Durham in 1700–1840: Hannah Barker, 'Women, Work and the Industrial Revolution: Female Involvement in the English Printing Trades, c.1700–1840', in Hannah Barker and Elaine Chalus (eds), *Gender in Eighteenth-Century England: Roles, Representations and Responsibilities* (London and New York, 1997), 89. For a specific example (Charlotte Bontoft) see Vernon, *Politics and the People*, 149, 289.

[23] Edmund Frow and Ruth Frow (eds), *Political Women, 1800–1850* (London, 1989), ch. 3; Taylor, *Eve and the New Jerusalem*, 75.

[24] This paragraph draws upon Kenneth G. Burton, *The Early Newspaper Press in Berkshire, 1723–1855* (Reading, 1954), ch. 10; Barbara Onslow, *Women of the Press in Nineteenth-Century*

these were widows of high business acumen whose control of a newspaper could result in the cultivation of a distinct political presence in the local community. Sarah Hodgson assumed management of the *Newcastle Chronicle* following her husband's death in 1800. The Unitarian minister William Turner was open about the political significance of her business when he delivered her funeral oration in September 1822. He praised her steadfast commitment to 'liberal principles' in the conduct of her newspaper and alluded to her spirited defence of 'just rights'.[25]

Other kinds of businesses could also be pitched to certain audiences. For example the hackney coach business belonging to Mrs Pugh in Birmingham in the 1820s was used primarily by liberal Dissenters.[26] The same was true of pubs and inns which often developed political reputations, not least as they frequently functioned as forums for petition-signings and meetings.[27] As Martin Hewitt points out, there were more women than men running pubs and inns in Manchester in the early 1840s.[28] The Unicorn in Manchester, described in one contemporary account as a 'Tory house', was run by a Mrs Fisher, for example.[29] The importance of female publicans to public dinners and other such events was routinely acknowledged in the local and specialist press.[30]

Women might also participate in the radical, progressive subculture through the management of vegetarian restaurants, hotels, or the sale of alternative remedies—or indeed through teaching.[31] Mary Smith, an active radical in mid-Victorian Carlisle was a school-teacher who relished the wider opportunities her role presented. One of her pupils later recalled that it 'was through her that I acquired a taste for politics'.[32] Rebecca Moore,

Britain (Basingstoke, 2000), ch. 6; Barker, 'Women, Work and the Industrial Revolution'; Denise Fowler, 'Women in Towns as Keepers of the Word: The Example of Warwickshire during the 1780s and 1830s', in Sweet and Lane, *Women and Urban Life*, 170; Charles H. Timperley, *A Dictionary of Printers and Printing, with the Progress of Literature* (London, 1839), 930; *ODNB*. My thanks to Victoria Gardner for information concerning Elizabeth Wood.

[25] William Turner, *A Sermon Preached in Hanover-Square Chapel . . . on the Occasion of the Much-Lamented Death of Mrs Sarah Hodgson* (Newcastle, 1823), 17–18.

[26] Ryland, *Reminiscences*, 42.

[27] Davidoff and Hall, *Family Fortunes*, 428.

[28] Martin Hewitt, *The Emergence of Stability in the Industrial City: Manchester, 1832–67* (Aldershot, 1996), 31, 42.

[29] Barker, *Business of Women*, 95–6. For other examples see Morgan, *Victorian Woman's Place*, 133; Cragoe, 'Jenny Rules the Roost', 161.

[30] For indicative examples see *Farmers' Journal* (11 Aug. and 29 Dec. 1845).

[31] Gleadle, 'Age of Physiological Reformers', 216–17.

[32] *Carlisle Journal*, cited in Rogers, *Women and the People,* 257.

an Irish Quaker settled in Manchester, was a woman of progressive political views who established a Froebelian school which proved attractive to local Nonconformists.[33] Politically motivated schools could bring their founders into the hub of parochial politics. The radical unitarian Caroline Hill appealed successfully to the poor law commissioners when, in 1838, a poor law guardian attempted to withhold relief from parents who sent their children to her establishment in Wisbech.[34] The paucity of alternative employment for women inevitably meant that many who turned to teaching lacked appropriate skills or education. Nonetheless, a significant constituency took seriously their role as professional educators.[35] Elizabeth Sewell, a High Church writer ran a school in the Isle of Wight, and Mary Atkinson Maurice, a conservative Anglican, established schools in Southampton and then Reading. Both adopted Pestalozzian theories to argue for the importance of inculcating obedience in pupils. Maurice, who eschewed the Unitarianism of her birth, had trained with the ultra-Evangelical Elizabeth Mayo at her school in Cheam in the 1820s. Mayo (who as noted in Chapter 3) also followed Pestalozzi, similarly prioritized the inculcation of establishment values of obedience and religion at her Home and Colonial Infant School. Maurice's desire to use education as a political tool is well exemplified in her *Patriot Warrior*, a biography of Wellington aimed at schoolchildren. It discussed the 'disgraceful' agitation of the people against the Corn Law bill and condemned the Chartists' campaigns.[36]

The burgeoning cultures of the nineteenth-century urban environment clearly provided an array of opportunities for women to exercise economic agency in politically informed ways, particularly in the fields of print, education, and service industries. Whilst recent scholarship on female businesses has focused upon the urban experience, the only sustained consideration of

---

[33] Hirsch, *Barbara Leigh Smith Bodichon*, 28.

[34] *Star in the East* (20 Jan. 1838).

[35] Christina de Bellaigue, 'The Development of Teaching as a Profession for Women before 1870', *Historical Journal*, 44 (2001), 963–88. The 1851 census recorded 67,551 women engaged in teaching, although this is likely to be a considerable underestimate. The census figures do not necessarily capture those women who contributed to educational enterprises run in the names of family members, for example. For the problems in using the census data to evaluate female employment see n. 41 below. See also pp. 95–6 above for the implications of home education.

[36] Elizabeth Missing Sewell, *Principles of Education Drawn from Nature and Revelation and Applied to Female Education in the Upper Classes* (London, 1865, 2 vols); Mary Atkinson Maurice, *Aids to Development, or Mental and Moral Instruction* (London, 1829); Atkinson Maurice, *The Patriot Warrior: An Historical Sketch of the Life of the Duke of Wellington* (London, 1853), 219–22; ODNB.

the economic contribution of middling and gentry women to rural communities in this period comes from Leonore Davidoff.[37] She rehearses the arguments of contemporary observers who lamented farmers' wives' aspirations to gentility. By the middle of the century Davidoff suggests that these sensibilities, combined with the demise of traditional female skills such as dairying, meant that it was uncommon for women to take an active role in the running of farms. Davidoff is alert to exceptions and counter-currents to this picture. However, her central argument that the gender order became increasingly sharply differentiated amongst the rural middling sort is further emphasized by her assertion that the lives of such women revolved around family and friends, shopping and visiting.[38] Subsequent scholars have dissented, noting the continuing importance of farmers' wives to the rural economy throughout the nineteenth century. This is particularly the case if one shifts attention away from the large-scale farms of the eastern counties towards the north-west and south-east. Here smaller establishments supported a rural petit bourgeoisie in which women played a highly active role.[39] A manual published in 1844 entitled *Farming for Ladies* was addressed explicitly to 'ladies in the middle ranks of life', suggesting a continuing audience for female farming advice.[40]

These were trends obscured by the census data. The 1851 census described 23,000 women as farmers in their own right—approximately 9 per cent of the total (with an additional 13,268 women classified by censors as 'landed proprietors').[41] However, studies which use alternative

[37] Dorothy Thompson was exceptional in drawing attention to women's rural activities in her 'Women, Work and Politics', 66. See also Pamela Horn, *Victorian Countrywomen* (Oxford, 1991), 184–91. In contrast, the lives of rural working-class and upper-class women have been the subject of greater scrutiny: Nicola Verdon, *Rural Women Workers in Nineteenth-Century England* (Woodbridge, 2002); Pamela Sharpe, 'The Female Labour Market in English Agriculture during the Industrial Revolution: Expansion or Contraction?', *Agricultural History Review*, 47 (1999), 161–81; Karen Sayer, *Women of the Fields: Representations of Rural Women in the Nineteenth Century* (Manchester, 1995); Reynolds, *Aristocratic Women*, ch. 1.

[38] Davidoff, 'Role of Gender', 192.

[39] Michael Winstanley, 'Industrialization and the Small Farm: Family and Household Economy in Nineteenth-Century Lancashire', *Past and Present*, 152 (1996), 157–95; Nicola Verdon, '"Subjects Deserving of the Highest Praise": Farmers' Wives and the Farm Economy in England, 1700–1850', *Agricultural History Review*, 51 (2003), 23–39.

[40] John French Burke, *Farming for Ladies: Or a Guide to the Poultry-Yard, the Dairy and Piggery* (London, 1844).

[41] Howkins, *Reshaping Rural England*, 9–10. For the inadequacies of census statistics in evaluating female experience see Edward Higgs, 'Occupational Censuses and the Agricultural Workforce in Victorian England and Wales', *Economic History Review*, 48 (1995), 700–16; Edward Higgs, 'Women, Occupation and Work in the Nineteenth-Century Censuses',

data, such as tithe commutation records, reveal a much higher female economic presence. Sylvia Seeliger's study of Hampshire found that women commonly formed up to 20 per cent of tenants on 'most manors'. Citing evidence from parishes like Penton Mewsey and South Charford she concluded that 'Women, particularly widows, were at times in control of parishes and manors.'[42] Contemporary sources were also sceptical of the census figures. John Glyde, an analyst of Suffolk society, moved in radical unitarian and Owenite circles and had a particular interest in the position of women. In an assessment of the 1851 census for Suffolk, he noted that, of the 421 individuals who described themselves as 'land proprietors', 187 were women. Puzzling over the parish of Bosmere, where he used data derived from rate books, he concluded that 'The actual number of female farmers in this union alone, is therefore greater than the census papers have returned for the whole county.'[43]

Whilst Davidoff uses Glyde's book to note his censure of (working-class) female farm labourers, she does not allude to his discussion of female farming. She contends that running a farm was 'problematic' as it was at odds with the 'model of feminine gentility'. Davidoff points to the evidence of an Essex land agent, John Oxley Parker, who urged one client to give up her attempts to run her farm following her husband's death.[44] Yet Oxley Parker's own farm in Mayland was leased from a widow, Mary Frere, and her sister. Frere firmly resisted Oxley Parker's attempts to secure a rent reduction. She lectured her tenant on his shortcomings as a farmer, arguing that were he to introduce more innovative farming methods he would realize greater profits. Frere's employment of detailed agricultural knowledge in their correspondence is indicative of her sense of authority as a farming expert.[45] Indeed, the 'lady farmer' (Louisa Cresswell) who wrote a tract on rural relations in Norfolk in 1875 assumed that relationships with land agents were dependent not upon landholders' gender, but upon the extent of their expertise and acumen.[46]

History Workshop Journal, 23 (1987), 59–80; Bridget Hill, 'Women, Work and the Census: A Problem for Historians of Women', *History Workshop Journal*, 35 (1993), 78–94.

[42] Sylvia Seeliger, 'Hampshire Women as Landholders: Common Law Mediated by Manorial Custom', *Rural History*, 7 (1996), 8, 12.

[43] John Glyde, *Suffolk in the Nineteenth Century: Physical, Social, Moral, Religious and Industrial* (London, 1856), 60, 325–6, 328–9, 333.

[44] Davidoff, 'Role of Gender', 196–7.

[45] J. Oxley Parker, *The Oxley Parker Papers: From the Letters and Diaries of an Essex Family of Land Agents in the Nineteenth Century* (Colchester, 1964), ch. 11, see also 171–2.

[46] Louisa Mary Cresswell, *Norfolk and the Squires, Clergy, Farmers and Labourers* (London, 1875), 18.

Landholding was seen to incur weighty social responsibilities on the part of owners to their tenants, labourers, and local villagers. Female proprietors were therefore critical contributors to the 'focal families' that remained so important to parish communities.[47] As such wealthy women could be exacting proprietors, supporting the dominant image of them as an imperious elite.[48] Their activities were frequently rooted in broader understandings of the duties their family position entailed, nonetheless, their consequent acts of charity were often dispensed through the medium of particular agendas. Maria Brigstocke and Fanny Saunders Davies, the owners of estates in early and mid-Victorian Wales, provided welfare services for their tenants who were expected to display deference to their benefactresses' religious and political views. Lady Llanover, a patron of Welsh language and culture, was also a wealthy landowner who saw to it that the pubs on her estate were converted to temperance inns.[49] When Elizabeth Fleming assumed responsibility for the family estate in Hampshire in the early nineteenth century she was at pains to compile leases with detailed clauses by which her tenants had to abide.[50] It was particularly common to link landownership with projects for the alleviation of poverty. Lady Vavasour, an active pioneer in agricultural science, toured the Netherlands in the early 1840s where she observed methods of husbandry and systems of poor relief. In 1842 she published an account of her visit to raise money for the cultivation of waste ground in County Wicklow. This was to provide employment and enable the establishment of an agricultural school. Her assessment of Irish poverty was fuelled both by a critique of what she felt were iniquitous English colonial policies towards Ireland and also her knowledge of land use.[51] Less ambitious programmes were also piloted by those of smaller means. Miss Wilkinson of Walsham-le-Willows in Suffolk, for example, let out small plots of land in an effort to 'destroy pauperism'.[52]

The Labourers' Friend Society (LFS), launched in the aftermath of the Swing Riots of 1830, sought to facilitate such schemes. Its aim was to promote allotments to the labouring classes, in the hope that this would

---

[47] Alan Everitt, *Landscape and Community in England* (London, 1985), 312–30.

[48] Gerard, 'Lady Bountiful', 200.

[49] Leslie Baker-Jones, *Princelings, Privilege and Power: The Tivyside Gentry in their Community* (Llandysul, 1999), 78; for Lady Augusta Hall see ODNB.

[50] Seeliger, 'Hampshire Women', 11.

[51] Anne Vavasour, *My Last Tour and First Work: Or a Visit to the Baths of Wildbad and Rippoldsau* (London, 1842). Her innovations in agricultural machinery were unsuccessful: *Farmers' Journal* (18 July 1842), supplement.

[52] Glyde, *Suffolk*, 351.

encourage industry and free the poor from dependence on poor relief. Whilst Jeremy Burchardt's recent study attempts to refine earlier assessments of the movement, which emphasized its conservative political and religious inspiration, the association's appeal to women of the middling and landed classes does accord with such an image.[53] This emerges clearly in the society's publication, the *Labourers' Friend Magazine* (which became simply the *Labourers' Friend* in June 1844). Individuals such as Mrs Danby Harcourt of Masham in North Yorkshire were prominent allotment donors. For Danby Harcourt, as for many female supporters, this was part of a much more extensive portfolio of local parochial management. Danby Harcourt, who came from a long established family in the locality, was not only responsible for the building and management of the local school, she also founded and endowed six almshouses in 1853.[54] Janet Kay-Shuttleworth was the active proprietor of a family estate and a supporter of the LFS. She took the schooling of her tenants' children so seriously that she approached a government expert, James Kay, for advice on the matter.[55] Women of less elevated status could also involve themselves in parochial activities in this way. Although the subscription lists published by the *Labourers' Friend* were predominantly male, female subscribers—sometimes considerable—were listed in every issue from July 1844. There are also reports of women attending the provincial meetings of the LFS and its associated projects, and occasional hints of women taking a more authoritative role. A Miss Yeates, for example, was the patroness of the Plaxton branch of the society.[56] As we shall explore in Chapter 6, one woman, Mary Ann Gilbert, was critical to the policies devised and printed by the organization.

An example of the porosity of the parochial and civic spheres, women's involvement in the allotment movement reflected both women's active land management at the local level and also sheds light on the ways in which ownership might be interwoven with a broader interest in parochial

---

[53] Jeremy Burchardt, *The Allotment Movement in England, 1793–1873* (Woodbridge, 2002), 82–3. Burchardt's study provides the first sustained account of the organization, but does not specifically consider female involvement. The view that the movement was essentially paternalistic is made in David Roberts, *Paternalism in Early Victorian England* (London 1979), 132–3. For further discussion see Ch. 6 below.

[54] *LFM* (April 1838), 59–60; T. Bulmer, *History, Typography and Directory of North Yorkshire* (Preston, 1890), 501–2.

[55] *LF* (Nov. 1844), 128; *ODNB*; Shuttleworth and Kay subsequently married: R. J. W. Selleck, *James Kay-Shuttleworth: Journey of an Outsider* (Ilford, 1994), 179–90.

[56] *LFM* (June 1837), 74. See also (Dec. 1836), 227; (Nov. 1846), 207; (Jan. 1847), 3; (Apr. 1846), 50–2; (Mar. 1836), 54; (Feb. 1851), 19; (Sept. 1852), 154.

and policy issues. The experience of landownership was shaped by a gendered code of property rights.[57] Yet for women who held land in their own right, either as single women or widows, or as married women with property protected under equity, the possession of land provided an economic rather than a gendered source of public authority.

Indeed, by the end of our period a recognition of women's significance as rural economic agents began to form a strand of suffrage discourse.[58] In a women's suffrage speech to the House of Commons in 1873 Jacob Bright cited census figures noting the contribution women made as the nation's farmers and graziers. He also quoted from the agricultural journal *The Field* which emphasized their contribution to rural economies.[59] Similarly the *Women's Suffrage Journal* cited George Crabbe's poetical tribute to the female farmer and her close involvement in parochial affairs: 'No parish business in the place could stir / without direction or assent from her / By turns she took each duty as it fell— / Knew all their duties and discharged them well'.[60] This could be an appealing point for conservative politicians. Percy Wyndham and Lord John Manners both claimed that they based their support for women's suffrage on their experience of the role played by female farmers within their local communities.[61] Hackneyed complaints about the shallow social aspirations of farmers' wives did not comprise the totality of viewpoints, but formed part of a richer debate about rural women.

Philanthropy, politics, and community

The example of the LFS indicates how the marginalized presence of women in the management of national philanthropic schemes might mask local cultures of forthright female activity based upon women's economic standing in their locality. Indeed, it should be remembered that female philanthropy emerged in the context of older, customary social relations, as well as in its manifestation in the emergent bourgeois culture of volun-

---

[57] See Amy Erickson, *Women and Property in Early Modern England* (London, 1993); Lee Holcombe, *Wives and Property: Reform of the Married Women's Property Law in Nineteenth-Century England* (Oxford, 1983), chs 2–3.

[58] See pp. 35–6 for the suffrage case, re women's role in parish governance.

[59] *Hansard*, 215 (30 Apr. 1873), cols 1200–1.

[60] Cited in Hollis, *Ladies Elect*, 31.

[61] Jane Rendall, 'John Stuart Mill, Liberal Politics, and the Movements for Women's Suffrage, 1865–73', in Vickery, *Women, Privilege and Power*, 197; McIlquham, *Enfranchisement of Women*, 4.

tarism. These traditional models of benevolence were particularly important in the small communities in which, as we have seen, the majority of
the population lived for most of our period. Katherine Plymley, a spinster
in late Georgian and regency Shropshire who lived with her brother, the
local archdeacon, dispensed charity on a personal basis. She viewed organized philanthropy as a male activity, writing in her diaries of her sense of
privilege when her brother permitted her to attend charity meetings held
in their home. When Plymley involved herself in collective activities they
tended to be rooted in older customs of parochial engagement, such as
organizing a village celebration for the coming of age of her nephew.[62]

The impressive number who joined anti-slavery societies[63] masks the
range of divergent attitudes which participating women might have
towards such activism in smaller, provincial communities. Many remained
more comfortable with local, paternalistic ventures. Elizabeth Wedgwood,
wife of the wealthy pottery magnate, was a firm believer in the anti-slavery
cause, but appears to have been most energized by the informal dissemina-
tion of literature amongst her networks and the male, county-led petitions
with which her husband was involved.[64] She declined to attend a local anti-
slavery lecture, because 'he is too longwinded and the seats are too high'.[65]
Whilst Wedgwood was confident about assisting in the organization of a
women-only celebration for the passage of the Reform Act in her local
parish,[66] she seemed a little at sea in the institutional world of anti-slavery.
As she reported to her sister in 1828, 'we have gone so far as to establish a
ladies society at Newcastle [under-Lyme], and our first meeting is
tomorrow, but we are a little at a loss, and the only things we have as yet
resolved upon is to buy books, and circulate them as much as we can and
to use and recommend East India sugar'.[67] Wedgwood's unmarried sister,
Frances Allen, in Pembrokeshire was similarly disposed. Despite her deeply
held anti-slavery convictions she admitted in August 1828, 'We have agreed
with regard to our Slavery Association to meet only once a quarter, it is
often enough.' Two months later she explained that their next meeting
would not be until March.[68] Allen herself appears to have been more

---

[62] Plymley Notebook, SRO, 1066/67 (1806) and 1066/78 (1809).
[63] Midgley, *Women against Slavery*, 43–56.
[64] Elizabeth Wedgwood to L. B. Allen [1826], E 57–1967, W/M; Elizabeth Wedgwood to her
daughter Elizabeth (Mar. 1824), W/M, 105.
[65] Elizabeth Wedgwood to Emma Allen (11 May 1831), W/M, 39.
[66] See below p. 178.
[67] Elizabeth Wedgwood to Frances Allen (29 May 1828), W/M, 68.
[68] Frances Allen to Sarah E. Wedgwood (30 Aug. and 7 Oct. 1828), W/M, 118.

roused by the establishment of a visiting society, which she declared she was setting about 'in good earnest'.[69]

The opportunity to reform the manners of the local populace may have been a more salient form of public engagement for women of this class. But even women of less refined status frequently viewed anti-slavery as just one facet of a much broader public persona. Hannah Hawley, a Quaker of Oakham in Leicestershire, was president of the neighbourhood ladies' anti-slavery society, but she was remembered locally as a 'mother in Israel' for her wide-ranging contribution to local life.[70] Mary Sewell was a member of a provincial anti-slavery society but insisted that individual efforts to help the local poor should take precedence over assisting 'the black populations'.[71] The emphasis on associational life in accounts of female public activity can therefore obscure other patterns of female engagement.

Charlotte Upcher, a young widow of the Norfolk gentry, whose husband, Abbot died in 1819, provides illuminating insights into these issues. She was, as her daughter put it, the 'head of her parish' of Sheringham.[72] Her visits to a local gaol in 1824 led her to establish a ladies' committee to ameliorate its desperate conditions, and she canvassed personally every household when establishing a Bible association in 1823. In addition to these associational activities she also intervened in an individual capacity to improve local amenities. She provided much of the community's infrastructure, including founding the village school in 1815, a friendly society, allotments, and a local lifeboat service in 1823. But Upcher's public profile illustrated the acute distinctions which could operate between parochial and wider axes of opportunity. A keen participant in colonial causes, Upcher was restricted to the ventilator space when she wished to hear parliamentary debates on the anti-slavery movement.[73] And, despite her status, even local meetings of the missionary society were chaired by her son. In contrast, Upcher assumed a conspicuous public pres-

---

[69] Frances Allen to Sarah E. Wedgwood (23 Feb. 1850), W/M, 118.

[70] Susannah Watts, 'On the Death of Mrs Hannah Hawley of Oakham', Scrapbook of Susannah Watts, LRO, 273; Shirley Aucott, *Susanna Watts (1768 to 1842): Author of Leicester's First Guide, Abolitionist and Bluestocking* (Leicester, 2004), 30. Other examples of women being so designated emerge in contemporary sermons: e.g. William Ogborne, *A Mother in Israel: A Funeral Sermon on the Occasion of the Sudden Death of Mrs Dexter* (St Albans, 1859).

[71] Mary Sewell, *Thy Poor Brother: Letters to a Friend on Helping the Poor* (London, 1863), 213–14.

[72] Pigott, *Memoir*, 104.

[73] Revd Abbot Upcher, 'Memorials', NRO, UPC, 156/1; 'Sherringhamia' (Journal of Abbot Upcher), NRO, UPC, 155; Pigott, *Memoir*, 118, 127, 177, 185–8.

ence in her own community. Here she presided over dedicated missionary meetings that she organized as part of her adult education project, attended by local male labourers. Furthermore, in 1834 she convened a meeting of villagers in the school house to celebrate the emancipation of slaves in the British colonies. Upcher had herself founded this school and here, confident in the public space she had created, she proceeded to deliver a lengthy lecture, giving as a local reporter put it, 'a clear and comprehensive view of the subject of emancipation'.[74]

This confident behaviour was in keeping with her sense of ownership of the local community. Little wonder that Hannah Buxton spoke of her as a 'reigning person' and local labourers referred to her as 'our Queen'.[75] Doubtless there was an element of irony in such appellations. The local gamekeeper found Upcher to be haughty and unsympathetic. He was unmoved by her anti-slavery speech noting pointedly: 'some say that they [the slaves] are better off than the men in this part'.[76] Assuming the social roles enacted in such occasions could obviously mask dissonant and dissenting personal views, but their outward conformity reinforced the dominant personas adopted by women such as Upcher. In contrast, in the memorial commissioned to honour her husband in the parish church she is depicted as a weeping, prostrate wife.[77] Prevalent stereotypes of women as relational creatures could have such cultural purchase that they could be enjoyed as an iconic image. This contributed to the construction of a dominant gender code which elided the greater complexities of experiences 'on the ground'.

As Upcher's experience illustrate, women might participate in associational activities (and indeed they could further enhance their local profile) but still feel that individual intervention was the more valuable means of effecting change. This was not a sentiment confined only to wealthy gentry such as Upcher. For example, Mary Sewell, the wife of a struggling businessman, was a member of a local visiting society, but believed individual benevolence was the most appropriate form of action.[78] If it was a mode of action with which many women were particularly comfortable, it was equally one which tended to be palatable to their communities. Collective female initiatives to gain access to institutions such as prisons and workhouses could

[74] Commonplace book of Anna Gurney and Sarah Buxton (1834), NRO, RQG; Pigott, *Memoir*, 110–11, 191–2, 195–6.
[75] Upcher, 'Memorials', 'Sherringhamia'.
[76] Norma Virgoe and Susan Yaxley (eds), *The Banville Diaries: Journals of a Norfolk Gamekeeper*, 1822–44 (London, 1986), 134; see also 112–13.
[77] http://norfolkcoast.co.uk/curiosities/cu_upcher.htm.
[78] Sewell, *Thy Poor Brother*, 213–14, see also 151, 219, 260.

often arouse controversy.[79] In contrast the approaches of individual women tended to be more successful than attempts to obtain permission for women as a group to routinely intervene. Eleanor Wigram in early nineteenth-century Walthamstow had a major effect upon parochial educational policy by persuading the vestry to merge the existing charity schools to make way for the establishment of a national school.[80] A similar pattern is discernible following the passage of the Poor Law Amendment Act in 1834, after which female philanthropists sometimes played a critical role in liaising with their boards of guardians to influence the implementation of the Act. Emma Sheppard in Frome prevailed upon local guardians to give her limited funding to allow the boarding out of paupers, against the terms of the Act. Similarly, Elizabeth Twining succeeded in reviving local almshouses in Twickenham; and Jessie Boucherett convinced Lincolnshire guardians that they should endeavour to give outdoor relief to women and children.[81]

It has been customary for historians to focus upon 'feminized' forms of women's philanthropy, such as their support for female needs, or their iden-tification as 'social mothers'.[82] However, the above examples testify to women's self-positioning as local welfare experts who prioritized status rather than gender, and who considered themselves equipped to intercede in the parochial polity. Certainly many contemporaries conceived philan-thropic women to enact a politicized role in their locale. During the political unrest of the 1810s, a 'female reformist' urged women 'in the higher walk of life' to instruct the poor in current events, claiming they might 'contribute their quota to the general good by expressing their opin-ions with spirit, and circulating them with industry'.[83] The educational reformers Maria Grey and Emily Shirreff were more explicit, insisting that the Poor Law Amendment Act would not have caused such an outcry had women used their position to explain it. '[W]omen of the educated classes', they suggested, 'might stand as interpreters of the legislature to the poor'.[84]

---

[79] For an overview see Prochaska, *Women and Philanthropy*, ch. 5.

[80] Martin, 'Women and Philanthropy', 126–7.

[81] Anne Summers, 'A Home from Home: Women's Philanthropic Work in the Nineteenth Century', in Sandra Burman (ed.), *Fit Work for Women* (London and Canberra, 1979), 49.

[82] Prochaska, *Women and Philanthropy*, 30; Yeo, *Contest for Social Science*, ch. 5 (although Morgan notes the complexities of this process in his *Victorian Woman's Place*, chs 5–6).

[83] 'Lavinia', *A Letter to Sir Francis Burdett, Bart. on the Late and Passing Events, and the Approaching Crisis* (London, 1819), 10.

[84] Maria G. Grey and Emily Shirreff, *Thoughts on Self-Culture, Addressed to Women* (London, 1850, 2 vols), i. 34. This was also the implication of Fitzjames Stephens's explication of poor law policy in his *Lectures to Ladies on Practical Subjects* (London, 1855), 150–87.

In both cases women's gender was significant not because of any innate feminine characteristics, but rather because of the roles they undertook by dint of their social status.

The fusion of politics with charity was a phenomenon to which contemporaries were well accustomed, thanks to the strategies adopted by elite women in the promotion of electoral interests.[85] This was part of a much broader phenomenon whereby philanthropic women frequently cultivated highly politicized identities within their communities. Charlotte Hanbury (1830–1900), an unmarried philanthropist from a Quaker background, lectured the local poor in Wellington on European politics;[86] whilst Mrs Scatcherd took a class of young men in Kirkstall for 'political discussions' every Sunday afternoon.[87] In the 1840s the Quaker Elizabeth Pease (1807–97), best known to-day as an anti-slavery activist, used to pay charitable visits to unemployed handloom weavers in Darlington. She wrote a series of letters to the local newspaper outlining the suffering caused by the Corn Laws, and urging for innovative projects to relieve poverty. Many local labourers would also have been aware of her status as a local political activist. Pease organized meetings to protest against slavery and other colonial issues, attended political meetings in neighbouring pubs, and liaised with Chartist leaders in the community.[88]

As these examples suggest, rather than emphasizing purely the 'feminized' aspects of female charity, it is important to incorporate into our analysis the relationships of patronage constructed between elite and middling women and lower-class men. Many women clearly felt uncomfortable socializing with lower-class men, rejecting home visiting for this reason.[89] But this was not universal, and it was perhaps less marked a problem in the small communities in which the majority lived for most of our period. Temperance women were particularly active in promoting their cause amongst working-class men. Despite Lilian Lewis Shiman's assertion that 'working with men was a job for the male reformers', she herself notes such examples as Julia Wightman, the wife of a Shrewsbury vicar, who established a temperance hall for men in the town, and Susan Theobald, a temperance campaigner amongst the Northumberland miners.[90] Activities

---

[85] See Ch. 1 n. 10 above.

[86] Hanbury, *An Autobiography*, 87–93.

[87] Jacques, *Merrie Wakefield*, 156.

[88] Stoddart, *Elizabeth Pease Nichol*, ch. 8.

[89] Prochaska, *Women and Philanthropy*, 108–9.

[90] Lilian Lewis Shiman, '"Changes are Dangerous": Women and Temperance in Victorian England', in Malmgreen, *Religion in Lives*, 195–8. Wightman's description of her work *Haste*

of this nature were not necessarily productive of an authoritative public persona, of course. Rebecca Kenrick was central to the establishment of a teetotal working men's club at Bromwich. The unmarried sister of a family of Bromwich hardware manufactures, she lived a peripatetic life assisting with her brothers' families and caring for her mother. Despite her hand in the organization's establishment she did not have the confidence to direct its public meetings, for which she turned to her male relatives.[91] Yet many such women established themselves as a prominent local presence through their efforts. The funeral of temperance activist Mrs Hawkins, of Royal Mint Street in London, was attended by thousands of local mourners.[92] Another campaigner, Miss Harford Battersby, was active in educating 'working men and lads' in her village, near Newport, and claimed that they regarded her as 'their leader'.[93] When Mary Sewell moved to the tiny mining community of Abson-cum-Wick in Gloucestershire in 1858, her temperance activities soon aroused hostility from the local vicar who was perhaps mindful of the democratic political sensibility which underpinned her work. When she was banned from using the school premises to hold meetings, she and her daughter Anna (of *Black Beauty* fame) opened a 'miniature' working men's hall and a library in nearby Wick. Here she delivered lectures and addresses and, with Anna, provided education in subjects like science, geography, and biography. When a group of men to whom she had been giving lessons formed 'a little Brotherhood of working men', they asked Mary Sewell, then in her sixties, 'to become their president'.[94] Such displays of deference, whether merely functional or not, were critical to the self-perception of philanthropic women and could further reinforce their assumption of authority.

Public identities were continually reshaped and affirmed through these social and cultural encounters. This applied equally to educational projects for the young.[95] As in the anti-slavery movement, we should be attentive to

---

to the Rescue; or, Work While it is Day (London, 1859) became a significant influence upon female temperance reformers.

[91] Kenrick Diary (1863), 107; Davidoff and Hall, *Family Fortunes*, 219.

[92] Shiman, 'Changes are Dangerous', 196.

[93] National Temperance League, *Woman's Work*, passim and 56–8.

[94] Bayly, *Life and Letters*, 155, 171; Chitty, *Woman Who Wrote* Black Beauty, ch. 6; Adrienne E. Gavin, *Dark Horse: A Life of Anna Sewell* (Thrupp, 2004), ch. 8; National Temperance League, *Woman's Work*, 51–5.

[95] For women's contribution to the voluntary education sector see K. D. M. Snell, 'The Sunday-School Movement in England and Wales: Child Labour, Denominational Control

the varying levels of commitment women demonstrated to the charity schools they established. As Rebecca Kenrick noted guiltily in her diary in 1852, 'The school has had less attention from us this year than before', a lament she repeated the following year.[96] Nonetheless, some viewed activities of this nature as a full-time occupation of quasi-professional status, employing paid assistants to administer their charities and intervening in all aspects of their pupils' lives.[97] Running a school not only allowed women to project their own ideological values to a community, but required the conscious performance of particular identities.[98] Mrs Round of Colchester, wife of the local conservative MP, visited her teenaged pupils in their factory. They responded by presenting her with a Bible on one of her visits to the factory. Philanthropic relationships required recipients to demonstrate an overt, reciprocal understanding of the status differential in this way. A wealthy proprietor, Mrs Ferguson, was publicly honoured by her tenantry in East Lothian with a portrait to thank her for her 'anxiety to promote the welfare of every individual connected with her extensive and valuable property'.[99] Interpersonal interactions of this nature enabled and reinforced the construction of empowering self-identities for elite women.

Mary Elizabeth Simpson provides a telling example of these processes. Simpson was the unmarried daughter of the vicar of Boynton and Carnaby in the East Yorkshire Wolds. From 1856 when she and her parents took up residency in the parish, Simpson established an extensive system of adult education for young male farm labourers among whom literacy rates were markedly low. Simpson's activities were not unusual. Surveys of Yorkshire in 1865 and 1868 found that 57.5 per cent of parishes had such provision, with the wives and daughters of clergy often playing a critical role.[100] However,

---

and Working-Class Culture', *Past and Present*, 164 (1999), 131; Joyce Goodman, 'Women Governors and the Management of Working-Class Schools, 1800–1861', in Joyce Goodman and Sylvia Harrop (eds), *Women, Educational Policy-Making and Administration in England* (London, 2000), 17–36.

[96] Kenrick Diary (1852), 70 and (1853), 75.

[97] Moilliet, *Elizabeth Anne Galton*, 64–5, 101–2. For interesting examples see Elizabeth Rundle Charles, *Our Seven Homes: Autobiographical Reminiscences* (London, 1896), 29; Jacques, *Merrie Wakefield*, 57.

[98] e.g. Adele Galton, a daughter of the Quaker gun-manufacturers, established a school just outside Birmingham where pupils decided upon their own punishments. It was opposed by the local clergy: Moilliet, *Elizabeth Anne Galton*, 101–2.

[99] A. F. J. Brown, *Colchester, 1815–1914* (Chelmsford, 1980), 93–4; *Farmers' Magazine* (Feb. 1838), 111.

[100] The following discussion is indebted to Clifford B. Freeman, *Mary Simpson of Boynton Vicarage: Teacher of Ploughboys and Critic of Methodism* (York, 1972). Simpson's activities are also

the extent of her schemes was striking. Simpson's ventures included not only evening classes but 'missionary fieldwork': visiting labourers at work and tirelessly pursuing those she perceived to be in spiritual danger.[101] She also appealed to the local workforce through the medium of print, issuing works such as *Short Prayers for the Hard Working* (1862) and *Scripture Lessons for the Unlearned* (1873). Whilst Simpson secured a London publisher for these efforts, she also purchased a printing press which enabled her to circulate vast quantities of ephemeral material locally. Biblical texts on various themes were printed as leaflets, letters to workers were reissued, and then edited and circulated in new forms. In addition, Simpson cultivated epistolary relationships through exploiting her clerical connections. She wrote numerous letters to clergymen on her projects and used these contacts to ensure the further circulation of her letters to farm labourers among their parishioners. Simpson prided herself on the close and reciprocal relationships she established with the farm labourers, and published many of the letters she received from them.[102]

In addition to the social position she enjoyed as the vicar's daughter, that her grandfather had been the lord of the manor in Boynton must have enhanced Simpson's sense of authority. Certainly she was a confident local actor. On one occasion she called a meeting of local labourers and proceeded to lecture them on the dangers of primitive Methodism. This was a popular denomination locally and widely feared as a seedbed for working-class radicalism. Her address was subsequently issued as a pamphlet, outlining her concerns for the mistakes made by her 'dear friends'. 'You did it in ignorance,' she chastized, 'and I doubt not the gracious God will pardon it.'[103]

Simpson came to be regarded as a respected figure on education in East Yorkshire, with her activities acknowledged by national agencies of policy reform. She wrote a paper on the education of farm labourers for a meeting of the NAPSS in York in September 1864, taking the opportunity to emphasize the paternalistic responsibilities of landowners, householders,

---

considered in J. F. C. Harrison, *Learning and Living, 1790–1960: A Study in the History of the English Adult Education Movement* (London, 1961), 188–90; M. C. F. Morris, *The British Workman Past and Present* (London, 1928), ch. 10; Alan Armstrong, *Farmworkers: A Social and Economic History, 1770–1980* (London, 1988), 106.

[101] Mary Simpson, *Ploughing and Sowing: Or, Annals of an Evening School in a Yorkshire Village* (London, 1861), p. ix.

[102] Simpson, *Ploughing and Sowing*, 30–1, 41, 105, 144–8, 221; Simpson, *Gleanings: A Sequel to Ploughing and Sowing* (London, 1876); Freeman, *Mary Simpson*, 23, 37, 39.

[103] Mary Simpson, *An Address to Farm Servants, Who had been Confirmed, Many of Whom had Soon After Joined the Primitive Methodists or Ranters* (London, 1862), 1, 6.

and employers. An organization which is often viewed as the epitome of urban, bourgeois liberalism, Simpson's contribution shows that it could also be used as a forum to uphold alternative, rural modes of engagement.[104] In 1868 Simpson was interviewed as a witness for the Royal Commission on the Employment of Children, Young Persons and Women in Agriculture. She provided an assessment of patterns of employment and education in Boynton, and her letter to the agricultural expert Edward Portman, MP, was quoted at length. Simpson cast her work within national political debates, arguing for legislation to increase agricultural wages and for the government sponsorship of adult education.[105] Her capacity to speak on local and public issues derived not from an appreciation of a feminized philanthropy, but rather from her community status and her ability to position herself as an expert in her chosen field.

Whereas historians have often emphasized the gendered lexicon of 'women's mission' in contemporary formulations of female activity, in texts such as those authored by Simpson women enacted a role which exalted the resources bestowed upon them by dint of their social class (advanced learning, for example) whilst marginalizing the significance of their sex. Simpson's interpellation of her audience as her 'friends' was a commonly used strategy. The rhetoric of friendship was suggestive of the continued salience of older modes of social interaction. Friendship in this context connoted not affective bonds nor gendered notions of emotional belonging, but rather vertical ties of patronage, obligation, and often political service. It served an 'instrumental' function that depended upon the bestowal of influence and favour.[106] Numerous, hitherto neglected, community texts, reveal the salience of this trope. Jane Louisa Willyams, a writer who specialized in works on early European Protestantism, was from an old established family in Carnaton, Cornwall. She drew upon her supposedly superior theological knowledge when she addressed 'Her Friends' in her Cornish village in a bid to deter them from Catholicism.[107] The Suffolk writer, Mrs H. Potter,

---

[104] Mary Simpson, 'The Life and Training of a Farm Boy', in F. Digby Legard (ed.), *More about Farm Lads* (London, 1865), 75–100. For the NAPSS see pp. 47–8 above.
[105] *Royal Commission on the Employment of Children, Young Persons and Women in Agriculture, First Report, Appendix* (*Evidence from Assistant Commissioners*) (London, 1867–8), pp. xxiii, 97, 381–3.
[106] Bourne, *Patronage and Society*, 79; Naomi Tadmor, *Family and Friends in Eighteenth-Century England: Household, Kinship and Patronage* (Cambridge, 2001), chs 5–6; Harold Perkin, *The Origins of Modern English Society, 1780–1880* (London, 1969), 46–52.
[107] Jane Louisa Willyams, *The Reason Rendered: A Few Words Addressed to the Inhabitants of M——, in Cornwall* (London, 1845). Willyams's most widely cited work was *A Short History of the Waldensian Church in the Valleys of Piedmont* (London, 1855).

reprimanded her 'friends' of the parish in 1851 for their low church attendance; and the trope of 'friendship' was similarly employed by Mary Bayly in her attempts to dissuade the workers in the Kensington Potteries from trade union activity. Bayly made clear the extraordinary assumption of intellectual superiority which underpinned these interventions. She could boast from her own 'acquaintance with working men' that she 'knows from themselves what their true difficulties are [and] knows that these are not such as they commonly complain of'.[108]

Women of the middling and gentry classes constructed authoritative local personas based upon their cultural and economic superiority to those of lesser status and their personal knowledge of those they sought to assist. Historians have paid much attention to the constitution of gendered space in the public sphere, but within their own vicinities philanthropic women could construct zones of opportunity based upon status, rather than gender. Sometimes this could amount to a literal space which was under their juris-diction—such as a working men's hall or school. Increasingly, these indi-vidual modes of public interaction began to intersect with wider networks of political and cultural endeavour, as local activists such as Sewell and Simpson became involved in national movements or policy debates.

Cultural authority and civic identity

As we have seen, women commonly issued tracts, letters, and pamphlets for circulation in their communities. This points to the existence of a little-explored provincial culture of letters in which middling and gentry women played a critical role. They were able to use the opportunities afforded by local publishers to contribute to debates on the themes of war, loyalism, and monarchy, often employing the medium of poetry. For example, the Newcastle poet, Mary Cockle, published such poems as 'National Triumphs' (1814) and elegies to royal family members.[109] Epistles in honour of Princess Charlotte, whose death in 1817 caused an outpouring of

---

[108] Mrs H. Potter, *An Invitation Rejected: A Few Words to the Non-Communicants of a Country Village* (London and Ipswich, 1851), 25; Bayly, *Workmen*, pp. vi, 56, 78. Other examples include Mrs Robert Hanbury, *God is Love: A Word to the Poor Man* (London, 1853), 3, and Maria Fox, *Sea-Side Thoughts: A Friendly Address to Sailors* (London, 1825).

[109] Mary Cockle, *National Triumphs* (London, 1814); Cockle, *Elegy to the Memory of her Royal Highness, the Princess Charlotte of Wales* (Newcastle-upon-Tyne, 1817); Cockle, *Elegy on the Death of his Late Majesty George the Third* (Newcastle-upon-Tyne, 1820). For women and national identity in this period see Colley, *Britons*, ch. 6.

national grief, were also common. This did not equate to a monolithic loyalism, however. Authors' profiles were comprised of complex political sensibilities: female cultural agents were clearly fully involved in the multi-faceted construction of what it meant to be a 'Briton' in the aftermath of war with France. The North Shields poet Mrs A. Sanderson wrote a lament for Princess Charlotte, but also an anti-war poem and verses in support of Queen Caroline—a cause which she linked directly to the 'rights of mankind'.[110] The Quaker poet, Isabella Lickbarrow of Kendal, cultivated a similar profile. The author of *A Lament for the Princess Charlotte of Wales*, she attracted attention for refusing the patronage of the local Tory grandee, Lord Lonsdale.[111] Some writers lamented the death of Princess Charlotte, but also penned memorials to Samuel Romilly, the radical lawyer who had opposed the continuation of war with France.[112] The common decision to use poetry, and not, say, a political tract, was presumably a gendered one. Nonetheless, it resulted in a largely forgotten genre of female civic poetry—a phenomenon which establishes that provincial women felt confident at manipulating local print culture to project political identities.

In the remaining section of this chapter we will consider how acting as a civic poet was often enmeshed with broader public roles. So far the chapter has drawn predominantly on case studies drawn from rural environments. We will now consider how, within the dynamics of early nineteenth-century towns and cities, women could replicate some of these patterns of public involvement. In particular, this involved projecting the status they accrued as cultural agents and benefactors to carve out commanding identities.

Our first example comes from the female subculture of early nineteenth-century Leicester. Here, Susannah Watts (*c.*1768–1842) was a woman of letters from an impoverished gentry family, who published in a range of genres, including poetry, hymnology, and translation. She was awarded a pension from the Royal Literary Fund in 1806, although she continued to rely upon income derived from teaching. Watts has attracted particular

[110] A. Sanderson, 'Poem on the Late Lamentable Death of her Royal Highness, the Princess Charlotte of Wales' and 'Answer to Mr Slottenberg's Question on the Life of a Soldier', in Sanderson, *Poems upon Various Subjects* (North Shields, 1819), 1–3, 54–6; Sanderson, *A Poem Most Humbly Inscribed to Her Majesty, the Queen* (North Shields, 1820).
[111] Constance Parrish (ed.), 'Introduction', *Isabella Lickbarrow: Collected Poems* (Grasmere, 2004), 16–17, 215–20.
[112] Margaret Sarah Croker, *A Monody on the Lamented Death* (London, 1817); Croker, *A Tribute to the Memory of Sir Samuel Romilly* (London, 1818); Mary Stockdale, *A Wreath for the Urn: An Elegy on the Princess Charlotte* and *A Shroud for Sir Samuel Romilly: An Elegy* (London, 1818).

attention for her contribution to the local anti-slavery movement. She canvassed door-to-door to promote the sugar boycott; edited the (short-lived) abolitionist publication *The Humming Bird*; was a founding member of the Leicester Ladies' Anti-Slavery society in 1825; and was active in collecting signatures for the ladies' petition of 1833.[113] Nonetheless her local profile was far more expansive. She was viewed not only as a civic and philanthropic figure, but also as a cultural one. Whilst Leicester itself had rather few cultural amenities in this period,[114] Watts formed part of a vibrant female coterie which included the Booth sisters (prolific contributors to periodical journalism); Miss Greatorex, an organist; the novelist Miss Hawkins; and the astronomer, Caroline Herschel. A local churchman, the Reverend Robert Throsby, referred to them testily as a 'set of Dragons' when Watts refused him entry to their women-only book society.[115] These informal networks provided a supportive environment for Watts to establish herself as a cultural figure. She published on a range of national themes with a local printer, her poetic tribute to Princess Charlotte and her poem 'Buonaparte's Fall' both urging the loyalist values of the establishment hierarchy.[116] Her civic legacy was cherished by Mary Ann Coltman with whom she had an intimate relationship. Coltman subsequently passed on her archive of Watts's work to a descendant, Clara Parkes, who was eager to uphold her great aunt's memory. Parkes's collection is suggestive of the ways in which Watts also functioned as a semi-official local laureate, writing poetic addresses for key public events. This included a prologue for the opening of the city's New Theatre, a poem published in the *Leicester Journal* to celebrate the Duke of Rutland's coming of age, an appeal in support of local infant schools, a hymn to commemorate the passage of the emancipation of slaves, a eulogy to Leicestershire's pastoral and manufacturing

---

[113] Aucott, *Susanna Watts*, provides an excellent summary of Watts's career, and the following discussion has drawn widely from it. Watts's name is often spelt 'Susanna' by modern scholars, although she herself more commonly used 'Susannah'—which is the form given here.

[114] A. Temple Patterson, *Radical Leicester: A History of Leicester, 1780–1850* (Leicester, 1954), 171.

[115] Watts was highly amused and composed a poem in response: *'Lines': To the Rev. Robert Throsby—on his Saying that a Party of Ladies Who had Established a Little Book Society . . . were a Set of Dragons Because they Refused to Admit him to their Meetings* (1800), Watts, Scrapbook, 545. See also Samuel Coltman, 'Memoirs and Letters of the Coltman Family Dictated by Samuel Coltman and Written by Mrs Coltman', LRO, Coltman MSS, 15D57, 500, vol. 3, ch. 22.

[116] Susannah Watts, *Elegy on the Death of the Princess Charlotte Augusta of Wales* (Leicester, 1817); Watts, *Buonaparte's Fall* (Leicester, n.d.) in Watts, Scrapbook, 367.

characteristics, and a historical guide-book of the city. This was just one manifestation of Watt's close involvement in city affairs. Many of Leicester's public institutions relied upon her support. This included the lunatic asylum, for which she raised funds, and the Leicester Society for the Relief of Indigent Old Age, of which she was the founder.[117] Watts was not simply a philanthropist but an active campaigner seeking to reform the quality of local welfare provision, including the delivery of scrupulously audited accounts.[118] In 1841, aged 73, she also intervened successfully in a heated political issue when she disbursed the unpaid tithes of those imprisoned for non-payment.[119]

Watts's close friend, Elizabeth Heyrick (1769–1831), the sister of Mary Ann Coltman, was also widely known in Leicester. Born to local Unitarians she suffered a troubled marriage to John Heyrick from 1789 until his death eight years later. Converting to Quakerism she went on to become a leading public figure in the city. Like Watts, Heyrick remains best known today as an anti-slavery activist, not least because of her widely circulated abolition pamphlets.[120] Her local profile was much more diverse though. She was described by the Leicester press as a 'most benevolent friend' to the poor and by Watts as a 'friend of all'.[121] She published an anti-war tract in 1805 and two educational works in the 1810s, but it was from the 1820s onwards, when, now in her fifties, she established herself as a formidable pamphleteer. She issued over twenty works, most of them dedicated to local political affairs, including Leicester elections, the corruption of the Tory corporation, and the implementation of justice in the city. In 1825 Heyrick lent support to the Leicester framework knitters' strike for higher wages (a group which had suffered terrible privations since the ending of the Napoleonic War). She

---

[117] Watts, Scrapbook, 3, 309, 486, 547; Watts, *A Walk through Leicester* (Leicester, 1967; 1st publ. 1804); Watts, 'Prologue', LRO, 15D57, 461.

[118] Coltman, 'Memoirs and Letters', vol. 3, ch. 22.

[119] Watts, *Walk through Leicester*, p. ix; Aucott, *Susanna Watts*, 37–8. See Fraser, *Urban Politics*, 53 (although he does not cite Watts by name) and, for the background, Patterson, *Radical Leicester*, ch. 13.

[120] Kenneth Corfield, 'Elizabeth Heyrick: Radical Quaker', in Malmgreen, *Religion in Lives*, 41–67; Midgley, *Women against Slavery*, 75–6, 103–15. Further, detailed biographical information may be found in Coltman, 'Memoirs and Letters'; Catherine Hutton, 'Hasty Sketch of the Coltman Family' (1802), LRO, Coltman MSS, 15D57, 387; *A Brief Sketch of the Life and Labour of Mrs Elizabeth Heyrick* (Leicester, 1862); Catherine Hutton Beale (ed.), *Catherine Hutton and her Friends* (Birmingham, 1895), 186–217.

[121] *Leicester Chronicle* (22 Oct. 1831); 'To the Memory of the Late Eliz. Heyrick of Leicester', in *Hymns and Poems of the Late Mrs Susannah Watts with a Few Recollections of her Life* (Leicester, 1842), 3–4; Corfield, 'Elizabeth Heyrick', 52–61.

issued pamphlets decrying local manufacturers and, in spirited defiance of the prevailing theories of political economy, joined the call of working-class leaders such as William Jackson for the implementation of a minimum wage.[122] In addition, she and her sister published on animal welfare and social violence and succeeded in abolishing bull-baiting in the neighbourhood through door-to-door canvassing.[123]

Despite her critical contribution to abolitionist debate Heyrick's death in 1831 went largely unnoticed in national anti-slavery publications.[124] This was in striking contrast to the way in which she and Watts were celebrated in their community. When the city marked the emancipation of slaves in the British colonies in 1834 the names of Watts and Heyrick were illuminated in large letters around the city.[125] This ritualized affirmation of their status gave public recognition to the careers of two women who had long acted as prominent civic figures. As Samuel Coltman put it when he attempted to write Watts's biography, 'my task is scarcely needed, since she was so well known and appreciated in her native town'.[126] When Watts died local journalists drew attention to the thousands of Leicester inhabitants who came to mourn at her funeral.[127] Neither Heyrick nor Watts were obvious public personalities. Both suffered from fragile emotional health and were often withdrawn. Yet they accrued their status as representatives of the community through a range of overlapping activities in the spheres of philanthropy, civic engagement, politics, and cultural endeavour. Despite dissonant voices, such as that of the Reverend Throsby, on the whole their direct intervention in civic and political affairs was not considered aberrant but was overtly championed in the city.

---

[122] Heyrick's earliest works were issued under the signature 'E. C.': *Instructive Hints in Easy Lessons for Children* (London, 1800); *The Warning* (London, 1805); *Familiar Letters Addressed to Children and Young People of the Middle Ranks* (London, 1811). Her subsequent pamphlets included *A Protest against the Spirit and Practice of Modern Legislation, as Exhibited in the New Vagrant Act* (London, 1824); *A Letter of Remonstrance from an Impartial Public to the Hosiers of Leicester* (Leicester, 1825); *Appeal to the Electors of the United Kingdom on the Choice of a New Parliament* (Leicester, 1826); *Cursory Remarks on the Evil Tendency of Unrestrained Cruelty, Particularly on that Practised in Smithfield Market* (London, 1823). See Patterson, *Radical Leicester*, chs 7–8 for the framework knitters' dispute and the controversial election of 1826.
[123] See Moira Ferguson, *Animal Advocacy and Englishwomen, 1780–1900: Patriots, Nation, Empire* (Ann Arbor, 1998), chs 2–3.
[124] Corfield, 'Elizabeth Heyrick', 48.
[125] Clara Parkes, 'Forward', in Watts, Scrapbook, 3.
[126] Coltman, 'Memoirs and Letters', vol. 3, ch. 22.
[127] *Leicester Chronicle* (19 Feb. 1842).

A comparable phenomenon is discernible in contemporary Ipswich. In the 1820s, an event of some prestige took place every year at the town's grand new Town Hall—the annual meeting of the Society for Clothing the Infant Poor. Simon Morgan has indicated that female charities of this nature could generate a sense of collective civic pride amongst participating women, but it was possible for individuals to have a 'simultaneous awareness' of themselves as having both a collective and an individual identity.[128] This certainly applied to the society's president, Elizabeth Cobbold, who dominated both the proceedings and the charity. As one contemporary pointedly observed, the charity was an example of 'the valuable results that have sprung from the energetic endeavours of one or two individuals, who have been fully impressed with the importance of their views for the benefit of society'.[129] Cobbold (1764–1824) was the daughter of Robert Knipe, a London businessman. She married John Cobbold, a prominent Ipswich brewer and banker with strong Anglican and Tory views in 1791, having been recently widowed following a brief marriage to an Ipswich portman.[130] Although early nineteenth-century Ipswich had only just over 11,000 inhabitants, it was a burgeoning industrial seaport which benefited from a number of improvements to its facilities, some of them, such as the Gas Light company, supported by the Cobbold family.[131] Cobbold's local standing emerged clearly in the charity's annual meetings, at which she delivered lengthy addresses to the mixed-sex audience assembled. As one contemporary noted, 'she was a powerful and persuasive orator', and the events were reported supportively in the local press.[132] In 1822 Cobbold's speech (which she later issued in print form) dwelt ostensibly on the charitable work of the organization, but she also considered the issues facing rural Suffolk. She noted the problems of rural unemployment and local incendiarism, observing the consequences of higher poor rates and their

---

[128] Morgan, *Victorian Woman's Place*, 108–16; Thoits and Virshup, 'Me's and We's', 127.

[129] John Glyde, *Moral, Social and Religious Condition of Ipswich in the Middle of the Nineteenth Century* (Ipswich, 1850), 169.

[130] For details of Cobbold's life see Laetitia Jermyn, 'Memoir', in Elizabeth Cobbold, *Poems, with a Memoir of the Author* (Ipswich, 1825), 3–42; ODNB.

[131] Gary Kelly, 'Clara Reeve: Provincial Bluestocking from the Old Whigs to the Modern Liberal State', *Huntington Library Quarterly*, 65 (2002), 105–25; Lilian J. Redstone, *Ipswich through the Ages* (Ipswich, 1969), 43–7, 69; Robert Malster, *250 Years of Brewing in Ipswich: The Story of Tollemache and Cobbold's Cliff Brewery, 1746–1996* (Ipswich, 1996), 4–5.

[132] G. R. Clarke, *The History and Description of the Town and Borough of Ipswich* (Ipswich, 1830), 348; *Ipswich Chronicle* (14 Apr. 1821, 27 Apr. 1822, 5, 19, and 26 Apr. 1823).

oppressive effects upon tradesmen and artisans.[133] Women's philanthropy could be carefully rooted within specific local contexts and undertaken with a shrewd eye to its political and fiscal consequences.

Cobbold's authoritative performances indicate how the associational 'public sphere' could develop in tandem with older modes of public engagement based upon female patronage and individual cultural attainment. Her capacity to act as a public figure despite numerous domestic commitments (she had fifteen stepchildren as well as seven children of her own) derived not simply from her charitable work, or from her status as the wife of a prominent businessman. Intertwined with these factors was her ability to construct herself as an important cultural figure locally. Cobbold had first published a collection of poetry in 1783,[134] but it was during her maturity as a woman in her forties that Cobbold began to position herself as a prominent force in the Ipswich arts scene. By the time Cobbold founded her charity in 1812 she had a well established reputation in this regard. The young John Constable was one of her protégés, but she specialized in promoting up-and-coming Ipswich female talent such as the singer and actress, Mary Ann Goward, and the cottage poet, Ann Chandler. Cobbold was also a patroness of local theatrical events. This gave her the opportunity to display a loyalist political profile. When the officers of the Eastern District gave a theatrical performance in 1805 she produced a patriotic address for the occasion, appealing to the city's 'Citizens in Arms, a patriot Band'.[135] Cobbold's identity as a poet was clearly important to her. A contributor to the *Ladies' Fashionable Repository*, her public addresses frequently included extracts from her poems. She presented a bound copy of her 'Ode to the Victory of Waterloo' to the Duke of Wellington, when he visited the local dignitary Lord Granville in 1818. However, Cobbold was also known for her craft work and for her wider intellectual interests, cultivating a network of epistolary relationships. She was a keen geologist, corresponding with Sir James Smith, president of the Linnean Society. In common with the Ipswich bluestocking Clara Reeve, proximity to the coast made her a keen conchologist and she assisted George Sowerby in his publications in this field.[136] Cobbold was thus able to fuse various kinds of opportunities, expertise, and cultural capital to develop a distinct and independent local persona.

---

[133] Mrs Cobbold, 'Address to the Society for Cloathing [sic] the Infant Poor' (1822), Suffolk Record Office, Ipswich branch, Elizabeth Cobbold records, HA231/3/39.

[134] Elizabeth Cobbold, *Poems on Various Subjects, by Elizabeth Knipe* (Manchester, 1783).

[135] Suffolk Record Office, HA231/3/3/4.

[136] Jermyn, 'Memoir', 28–9.

This was not an uncontested process. When a local lady of letters, Laetitia Jermyn, wrote a memoir of Cobbold in 1825 she hinted at a forthright character that could court controversy and acknowledged the great 'care and circumspection' that women needed to display when they acted 'in a public capacity'. Noting 'the world is too apt to be sarcastic and censorious, and to cast aspersions on the most laudable undertakings', Jermyn assured her readership that Cockle had 'considered her domestic claims of superior importance'.[137] The poet, Mary Cockle, was yet more circumspect in her tribute. Noting Cobbold's talents, she suggested that as a *'wife, parent and friend'* she was 'raised to a higher and better distinction', displaying 'a gentleness and sweetness of manner'. She further asserted that Cobbold's 'independence' was put to the service of 'the most extensive benevolence'.[138]

Cobbold's career was marked by a density of interaction with a number of different 'publics', including the virtual sphere of poetry publication, networks of intellectual endeavour, associational activities, and local loyalist events. Subsequent accounts of her achievements stripped her career of its diversity and, in creating an image of a publicly active woman that might be considered seemly for the town's identity, shaped it into a benign and predictable figure of the lady benefactor. The local historian, a friend of Cobbold's, presented her as a key figure in Ipswich life, noting that on her death, 'The inhabitants of Ipswich, of every sect and denomination, high and low, rich and poor, felt that they had lost their best friend, patroness, and benefactor.' A large monument in the parish church, funded by local subscription, noted her 'exalted talents' and praised her 'unwearied exertions in the cause of benevolence and charity'.[139] Acts of public memorialization therefore tended to capitulate to a vision of gendered norms which was deemed fitting for Ipswich's civic identity.

Conclusion

Davidoff and Hall's pessimistic account of gendered relations in rural England drew substantially upon late nineteenth-century memoirs. It is possible to read their sources very differently, however. The properties of

---

[137] Cobbold, *Poems*, 25, 9. Jermyn (1778–1848) was the daughter of a local bookseller and published a work on butterflies. She later married antiquarian James Ford, *ODNB*.
[138] Cobbold, *Poems*, 49–51; Mary Cockle published a number of works with Sarah Hodgson's printing business in Newcastle-upon-Tyne, see n. 109 above.
[139] Clarke, *History and Description*, 347–8.

wealthy female householders formed part of the local geography in many of these texts. John Player's description of the community of Hempstead recalled the female residents whose houses were dotted around the village,[140] and Edward Boys Ellman remembered of his Sussex boyhood, 'almost all the better class of houses in Southover were occupied by widows or unmarried ladies'.[141] George Bourne wrote of the 'little old black-dressed farm-mistresses' in his grandfather's village of Farnborough, and in particular his Aunt Susan around whom 'the whole prosperity of the farm swung'. Women were also remembered as important to their local communities in other ways. In Bourne's account this included Jane Charlton, the postmistress and his widowed great aunt, the church caretaker and pew-opener. The vicar's wife Mrs Clayton, a potter, writer, and philanthropist, was remembered for her condescending sense of superiority over the villagers, whilst the 'best school in the village' was that established by Mrs Morant, wife of the local landowner. His grandfather's second wife was described as the driving force behind the family's farming ventures, and was the instigator of a petition to the bishop on behalf of their belea-guered rector in 1839.[142] Eliza Vaughan, another of Davidoff's sources, writes of Miss Maria who ruled the village Sunday school with an iron grip, Mrs Daines, a local craftswoman of fierce Calvinist principles, Miss Mary, the village grocer and laundress who, along with her live-in female companion was 'emphatically protestant', and Mrs Bennyworth 'an intel-ligent spectator' of social change.[143] Vaughan also outlined the activities of those women who held local parish offices, such as the industrious female overseer, Mrs Whithead, and cites the example of a parish clerk whose wife undertook many of his duties.[144]

These are themes resonant with many of those considered in this chapter: the role of individual women as philanthropic agents; the impor-tance of women's economic standing as a source of local empowerment; the potential for women to exploit their position as wives of local office-holders; and the significance of female householders as political agents. In

---

[140] Player, *Sketches of Saffron Walden*, ch. 8.

[141] Edward Boys Ellman, *Recollections of a Sussex Parson* (London, 1912), 36.

[142] George Bourne, *William Smith: Potter and Farmer, 1790–1858* (London, 1920), see esp. 14–15, 24, 47–8, 108, 120–1, 132–9, 150.

[143] Eliza Vaughan, *The Stream of Time: Sketches of Village Life in Days Gone by* (Colchester, 1934, 3rd edn; 1st publ. 1926), 17–19, chs 5–6.

[144] Eliza Vaughan, *The Essex Village in Days Gone by* (Colchester, 1928), 21, see also pp. v, 44, 50, 53. Vaughan, *Stream of Time*, 84. Davidoff cites Vaughan's *The Essex Village* but not this earlier work.

contrast, when individual subjects were selected for memorialization, representations tended to reify a feminized persona which softened the more complicated facades of women's community involvement. Whereas newspapers, prescriptive literature, or acts of remembrance invariably privileged gender in their articulation of women's lives, contemporaries' day-to-day dealings with women were structured more profoundly by issues of status and authority. It is not only the high civic rituals we need to analyse if we are to comprehend the subtle enactment of gendered identities in early Victorian Britain. The hierarchies of class and status were sustained and perpetuated through more mundane processes of social interaction and in the myriad of local events and occurrences which punctuated community life, and which depended upon reciprocal demonstrations of deference. These interactions tended to be marked by a more expansive femininity (including frequent examples of public speaking) than that which was deemed appropriate at larger scale events, such as those organized by pressure-group movements.

Contemporaries' experiences of women as businesswomen, local laureates, educationists, electors, newspaper proprietors, farmers, and landowners were extensive. Single and widowed women have emerged as particularly likely actors in this regard, but not exclusively so. Married women, especially those with economic or cultural capital in their own right or those of more advanced years, were also implicated in these processes. The age difference which was so common in nineteenth-century marriages may have played to women's advantages later in life. When Cobbold assumed her active local stance, her husband, twenty years her senior, was in his sixties. Certainly age has emerged as an important leitmotif. It is interesting to note that the constitution of the Ladies' Jubilee Female Charity School in Manchester endowed the committee's oldest woman with the casting vote.[145] This is suggestive of the status which might be afforded to those of greater age, and perhaps sheds further light on the authority wielded by older women.

The parochial realm frequently provided greater scope for women to enact an empowering role by dint of their family relations (as the wives or daughters of squires, local businessmen, or clergy—the latter a particularly neglected group in the historiography) than did the domestic site or the

---

[145] This right was lost in 1856 when the male committee imposed a new bureaucratic structure. Goodman, 'Women Governors', 27. In Davidoff and Hall's census sample just under 25% of husbands were more than five years older than their wives; this rose to 37% amongst couples of independent means: *Family Fortunes*, 323.

bourgeois public sphere. This does not mean to say that identities were 'free-floating' or that women could simply adopt new personas in the various publics with which they interacted.[146] Rather, different aspects of the self might be prioritized in certain conditions. This was a constantly shifting process which had an ongoing impact upon identity formation.[147] The validation of an authoritative role could intersect with other aspects of an individual's subjectivity. Access to wider networks of cultural expertise could assist in the construction of parochial authority, and this could, in turn, lead to individuals claiming a place in wider publics of engagement. As Cobbold's career demonstrates, there was fluidity between these various sites and their functioning depended upon complex circuits of cultural exchange across the different forums. Similarly, Simpson's success in the parochial realm was recognized in reforming and government circles alike and provided her with further platforms to establish her expertise.

The impact of individual women of economic and cultural status upon their localities can sometimes be downplayed in discussions of Victorian philanthropy which tend to focus on either associational culture or major urban settings. Narratives of the growing institutionalization of charity are important, and this combined with such phenomena as the rise of organized temperance or anti-slavery movements intersected with older modes of public intervention to produce particular opportunities for elite women. Nonetheless, individual patrons remained a central feature of parochial life throughout our period. As we have seen, women's philanthropy developed by drawing upon established conduits of benevolence and patronage as much as it did upon newer forms of associational charity, with which it was intertwined. In many cases, women only established charitable societies because they already enjoyed some local status.

It is not contended here that the local sphere provided an open plain of opportunity for women. As we have seen, there were many who contested women's growing philanthropic muscle and women often had to struggle hard, and sometimes in vain, to gain access to local institutions. However, in their vicinities there were at least multiple possibilities for female authority, and the constellation of particular circumstances could produce significant opportunities for those with the talents and confidence to claim them.

---

[146] Harriet Bradley, *Fractured Identities, Changing Patterns of Inequality* (Cambridge, 1996), 212.
[147] McCall and Simmons, *Identities and Interactions*, ch. 4.

II

CASE STUDIES AND MICRO-HISTORIES

5

Women and the 1832 Reform Act

Introduction

The Reform Act of 1832 stands as one of the defining moments in British political history. Historians such as Frank O'Gorman and Norman Gash have cautioned us not to overexaggerate its significance, pointing to the many continuities in political practice.[1] Nonetheless, the introduction of a uniform £10 borough franchise, the abolition of fifty-six 'rotten' boroughs, and the redistribution of seats, including the creation of seats in industrializing cities such as Birmingham, Manchester, and Sheffield, was clearly of seminal significance to the polity. Despite this, the Act's implications for women and their involvement in its passage remain underexplored. Analyses to date have considered the ways in which it appeared to epitomize a broader cultural move towards tighter gender prescription, emphasizing the Act's stipulation that future voters should be 'male'. For James Vernon, 'The significance of this can not be over played.'[2]

It will be argued here that such an approach, which is implicitly situated within the 'watershed' narrative that long dominated discussion of the Act's consequences, is too stark an analytical tool with which to understand its complicated implications for women.[3] For a start, the reform bill pertaining to Scotland did *not* specify that the parliamentary voter should be male.[4] It

[1] Frank O' Gorman, *Voters, Patrons and Parties* (Oxford, 1989); Gash, *Politics in the Age of Peel*.
[2] Vernon, *Politics and the People,* 39. See also Catherine Hall, 'The Rule of Difference: Gender, Class and Empire in the Making of the 1832 Reform Act', in Ida Blom and Karen Hagemann (eds), *Gendered Nations: Nationalisms and Gender Order in the Long Nineteenth Century* (Oxford, 2000), 127. This was a view shared by later suffrage campaigners: Jane Marcus (ed.), *Suffrage and the Pankhursts* (London, 1987), 132.
[3] For a recent treatment of the 'watershed' theme in relation to the Act more widely see John A. Phillips and Charles Wetherell, 'The Great Reform Act of 1832 and the Political Modernization of England', *American Historical Review*, 100 (1995), 411–36, esp. 411–13.
[4] My thanks to Gordon Pentland for drawing this to my attention. In contrast, in some colonial territories, women's right to vote was explicitly banned, as in Quebec in 1849. Catherine L. Cleverdon, *The Woman Suffrage Movement in Canada* (Toronto, 1950), 216.

presumably did not occur to those drafting the Scottish legislation that such clarification was necessary; whereas the gender-specific wording of the statutes covering England, Wales, and Ireland suggests an awareness that there was a theoretical possibility that it might be otherwise open to challenge. These differences are indicative of the subtle fissures in seemingly dominant assumptions concerning female citizenship. This chapter will explore how, within the interstices of parliamentary legislation, there were many such moments of telling indeterminacy in the collective understanding of women as political subjects. That the same parliament passed the Vestries Act (1831) allowing women to continue to vote in vestry contests further underlines the point. This enables us to explore further the notion of women as 'borderline citizens'.

To date, scholars who have analysed the gendered contours of the reform debate have tended to concentrate on those political discourses which dwelt on the notion of 'manly independence'. As Earl Grey claimed of the £10 householder, they were men 'who have given a pledge to the community for their good conduct—and who for the most part are married men and the fathers of families'.[5] Certainly politicians and commentators on both sides of the debate frequently, if casually, implied that women were passive and apolitical.[6] However, the formulation of women as political dependants was but one of many, wide-ranging articulations on female political rights and privileges. These utterances illuminate a diversity of views but also the fragility of women's political claims.

In Chapter 1 some consideration was given to the vexed location of women as parliamentary constituents, and this is explored further here. The recurring disjuncture between the experiences and assumptions of women's public roles in their local communities, and the representations that were likely to be successful at Westminster, provides a telling frame of analysis for the Reform Act. This, combined with an analysis of women's varied positioning in the reform agitation and celebrations, provides the opportunity to explore in greater depth the distinctions between the 'parochial realm' and the classic 'public sphere' as outlined in Chapters 2 and 4. As authoritative community figures, female responses to the reform

---

[5] Quoted in Matthew McCormack, *The Independent Man: Citizenship and Gender Politics in Georgian England* (Manchester, 2005), 197. For the later period consult Keith McClelland, 'England's Greatness, the Working Man', in Hall *et al.*, *Defining the Victorian Nation*, 71–118. A notable recent exception to this trend is Morgan, *Victorian Woman's Place*, 127–36.

[6] e.g. Sir Vyvyan's speech concerning reform focused on the need for MPs to consider the safety of 'their wives, of their children, of their property': *The Times* (23 Apr. 1831). For further examples see *Westminster Review*, 17 (1832), 255; *Hansard*, 7 (19 Sept. 1831), col. 206.

crisis often had the effect of reaffirming their sense of superior intellectual and political acumen. Women also made critical contributions to reform debates as newspaper editors, authors of electoral ephemera, and through the exertion of their economic influence. However, there was an increasing tendency to view women's activity as part of a female collective. This usually emphasized women's political engagement in relation to their familial roles, particularly as wives who might exert their 'influence' over their husbands. In the medium term this indicated an awareness that women as well as men were implicated in the broader enfranchisement of the middle classes. Nonetheless, a consideration of women's varying experiences of 'spectatorship', including their occupation of the ventilator space, will demonstrate that dominant cultural codes of this nature impinged upon women's own articulations of the reform crisis. As we saw in Chapter 3, the family was a critical if problematic source of political identity. Here, it will be suggested that the politicization evoked by the reform debates was often intertwined with collective familial identities or anxieties concerning one's feminine profile. Although exceptional literary women were able to gain an audience as commentators on the reform issue, more generally the involvement of women throws into sharp relief the many ambiguities and tensions in their political status.

Women, parliament, and political rights, 1830–1832

Public pronouncements concerning the manly independence of the political subject were rhetorical constructs which bore little resemblance to the day-to-day political experiences of the elite. Members of Grey's cabinet such as Lords Melbourne, Holland, and Palmerston were fully accustomed to drawing upon the politicking skills of aristocratic women like Lady Holland; and the private records of Whig ministers reveal the weight they placed upon the political views of the women in their networks during the reform crisis.[7] The bill itself was the product of family collaborative practices. According to some reports, it was Lord Durham's daughter who made the copies of the scheme of the bill, the subcommittee meeting at their

[7] J. R. M. Butler, *The Passing of the Great Reform Bill* (London, 1914), 142; Roger Fulford (ed.), *The Greville Memoirs* (London, 1964), 79; Abraham D. Kriegel (ed.), *The Holland House Diaries, 1831–40: The Diary of Henry Richard Vassall Fox* (London, 1977), 38, 82, 103, 143, 179; Guy Le Strange (ed. and tr.), *Correspondence of Princess Lieven and Earl Grey*, ii. *1830–4* (London, 1890), chs 4–6; Alice Acland, *Caroline Norton* (London, 1948), 59.

house in Cleveland Row.[8] Shortly after the passage of the bill Durham (Earl Grey's son-in-law) was to seek out what proved to be a long-standing friendship with the country's most famous supporter of women's rights, Harriet Martineau.[9] In the following decade Lord John Russell, who steered the reform bill through parliament, grudgingly conceded the political skills of women such as Martineau in parliamentary speeches.[10] The diversity of elite Whigs on the woman question is further revealed through the profile of the Lord Chancellor, Lord Henry Brougham. An early advocate of female anti-slavery petitions, in 1835 he published an anonymous pamphlet *Thoughts on the Ladies of the Aristocracy* which articulated radical views on women's position.[11] The Act's identification of the electorate as male should not therefore be interpreted as a simple reflection of a homogeneous or static Whig attitude.

Equally the reform debates themselves did not operate within an exclusively masculine space. Once Lord Brougham had given his permission for high-ranking women to attend the Lords' debates on reform they came to form a visible constituency in the galleries. Charles Greville recorded that, on one occasion, 'the House of Lords was so full of ladies that the Peers could not find places'. That the animated Lady Jersey took to sitting amongst the journalists no doubt encouraged the reporting of their presence.[12] *The Times* gave an intriguing hint as to women's dynamic vocal contribution to debates. Observing their 'enthusiastic ardour' for particular political positions, it was noted that, 'whilst almost all the ancient ladies are loud in their approbation of the anti-reform speeches, the young and beautiful are, without exception for the bill, and nothing but the bill'.[13] Individual politicians would also have been cognizant of the fact that their female relatives were often listening to their speeches from the ventilator space.[14] The structures of elite political culture were clearly masculine-dominated, but women comprised a significant, if marginal strand of that sphere.

---

[8] Denis Le Marchant, *Memoir of John Charles Viscount Althorp, Third Earl Spencer* (London, 1876), 295–6.

[9] Stuart J. Reid, *Life and Letters of the First Earl of Durham, 1792–1840* (London, 1906, 2 vols), i. 257, 343–4.

[10] See above p. 32.

[11] Henry Brougham (Lydia Tomkins), *Thoughts on the Ladies of the Aristocracy* (London, 1835). Brougham was to be closely connected with the movement to reform the laws relating to women's property rights: Holcombe, *Wives and Property*, 62–4, 90–1, 123–4.

[12] E. A. Smith, *Reform or Revolution? A Diary of Reform in England, 1830–32* (Stroud, 1992), 75, 90; *The Times* (19 Dec. 1831 and 10 Apr. 1832).

[13] *The Times* (6 Oct. 1831).

[14] See below pp. 56–9.

A comparable complexity is discernible in the ideological debates on reform during which considerations of female citizenship emerged sporadically from the mid-1820s. Utilitarians and radical unitarians alike raised the issue in specialist journals such as the *Westminster Review* and the *Monthly Repository*; and republicans Richard Carlile and Eliza Sharples also protested against the bill's masculine basis.[15] Alexander Campbell, who moved in the emergent circles of co-operative politics, could be found agitating on the question in Scotland.[16] Although these examples come from the fringes of radical political culture, those advocating women's rights were not necessarily viewed as eccentric visionaries. When a Mrs Emery delivered a lecture to the Brighton Political Union on women's political rights in October 1832, journalists reported the event courteously: 'The effect of her speech was somewhat impaired by her delivering it from written notes, but she commanded much attention from the auditory.'[17] Feminist discourses were not hermetically sealed within radical coteries but could impinge upon electoral and parliamentary politics too. As we saw in Chapter 1, that Matthew Davenport Hill endorsed female suffrage during his election campaign in 1832 appears not to have damaged his reputation.[18] The government itself chose the maverick James Silk Buckingham to aid their presentation of the bill in the press. As Buckingham had made clear in his speech to his Nottingham constituents in 1831, he openly defended women's political rights, later publishing his comments and reiterating his views in parliament in 1834.[19] Two months after the passage of the Reform Act, Henry Hunt presented a woman's suffrage petition to parliament on behalf of Mary Smith from Stanmore in Yorkshire. Whilst Smith's arguments were met with bawdy humour by many MPs, Hunt took the petition seriously, insisting that it was 'deserving of consideration'.[20]

It is perhaps unsurprising therefore that leading politicians could display a shrewd awareness of the contemporary feminist case. A few months after the passage of the Reform Act, Robert Peel conceded

---

[15] e.g. *Monthly Repository*, 6 (1832), 637–42; *Westminster Review*, 21 (July 1829), 266; *The Prompter* (9 Apr. 1831); *Isis* (1832), *passim*.

[16] W. H. Marwick, *The Life of Alexander Campbell* (Glasgow, 1964), 9.

[17] *Morning Chronicle* (22 Oct. 1832).

[18] Hill and Hill, *Recorder of Birmingham*, 115.

[19] Buckingham, *Qualifications and Duties*, 12; Ralph E. Turner, *James Silk Buckingham, 1786–1855: A Social Biography* (London, 1934), 329; Butler, *Passing of the Great Reform Bill*, 151–2. Buckingham was not successful in his role for the government.

[20] *Hansard*, 14 (3 Aug. 1832), col. 1086.

> There were arguments in favour of extending the franchise to women, to
> which it was no easy matter to find any logical answer . . . women were
> allowed to hold property, to vote on many occasions in right of that prop-
> erty—nay, a woman might inherit the Throne, and perform all the functions
> of the first office of the State, why should they not vote for a Member of
> Parliament?[21]

Peel's brother Jonathan, we might note, voted in favour of female
suffrage in 1867.[22] It is supposed that Peel's purpose here was rhetorical—
to illustrate the many appeals to which parliament might be subject were
they to concede the secret ballot (the subject of the debate on this occasion).
However, that he employed the very arguments used by contemporary
feminist campaigners indicates that radical claims for female citizenship
formed part of the discursive political landscape of 'mainstream' figures.

Indeed, during the reform debates there were a number of instances
when parliament considered female citizenship. Tellingly the clause
requiring that future voters be 'male persons' was not discussed (although
later judges used it to rule against women who sought to vote in the
boroughs).[23] The practice of women voting in their own right was so rare
that this in itself did not register as important. Of far greater consequence
was the ending of freewomen's privileges. It was around this issue that a
surprisingly wide spectrum of politicians found common ground. It
provided a conduit for those sympathetic to women's political rights to
make their voice heard in parliament, as well as providing a rallying-point
for those who were opposed to the bill and/or who wished to be associated
with protecting ancient electoral privileges.

The power of freemen's daughters to confer the vote upon their
husbands in the ninety-two freemen boroughs was incompatible with the
Whig ambition to standardize franchise entitlement. The privilege was
therefore attacked under wider proposals to curtail customary freemen
rights. To date our understanding of this issue is limited to Catherine Hall's
discussion of a Commons debate of 7 February 1832. This concerned a
submission that freemen's daughters be permitted to retain their rights. Hall
dwells upon the 'hilarity' and 'ridicule' with which this suggestion was met.
According to Hall, the ribald humour exhibited by politicians, with their

---

[21] *Hansard*, 17 (25 Apr. 1833), col. 666.

[22] Rendall, 'John Stuart Mill', 178.

[23] Technically speaking, without this clause it would have been possible for those women
who held the requisite property before 1832 to continue to exert electoral influence in
burgage boroughs: *The Times* (10 Nov. 1868). Elizabeth Lawrence's use of 'pocket votes' in
the burgage borough of Ripon was challenged in 1833: *Leeds Mercury* (28 Sept. 1833).

references to the 'personal charms' and 'renowned beauty' of the women concerned, revealed their latent fears of women's political agency.[24]

Hall's analysis centres on a particular response in a single debate. In fact the matter had a more complicated history. In the summer of 1831 the Commons considered a petition presented on behalf of the metropolitan reformer, Charles Pearson. This asked the house to 'protect the right of the widows and daughters of freemen'. Pearson's argument was that the right to confer the vote was 'much valued' by the women concerned.[25] Pearson's intervention indicates the existence of a more capacious view of female citizenship than that intimated in Hall's analysis. At this time Pearson was chair of the City Board of Health which, under his chairmanship, had an active, if short-lived, ladies' committee attached to it.[26] This unusual initiative suggests that Pearson was associated with policies that sought to encourage women in public life. The politician he chose to present his petition, John Wilks, had a reputation for sponsoring independent causes in parliament, such as Dissenters' rights and anti-coercion in Ireland. Despite his reputation as a financial adventurer, he successfully mobilized popular sentiment during his election campaign in Boston, a freeman borough, making much of the support he enjoyed from his female constituents.[27]

During the debate Wilks eschewed Pearson's reference to women's political rights, tactfully employing instead a chivalric trope of protecting women's interests. The language was carefully chosen: he asserted that he had 'communicated with Government on the subject' who had shown a 'liberal disposition to meet the wishes of those who appealed at once to their gallantry and justice'. No one in the House denied that such an exchange had occurred, perhaps indicating that the government was indeed prepared to be flexible on the issue.

Two of the bill's most inveterate opponents, Sir Edward Sugden and Sir Charles Wetherell, also purported to endorse the petition. Sugden distanced his remarks from women's electoral activities, arguing that 'the right in question operated as a marriage portion, [and] he was sure the House would not be so uncourteous as to deprive the ladies of it'. On the other

[24] Hall, 'Rule of Difference', 125.
[25] *Hansard*, 6 (27 Aug. 1831), cols 698–9. See also *The Times* (29 Aug. 1831). Charles Pearson (1793–1862), a lawyer and tireless reformer, was at this time a common councilman for Bishopsgate Ward. He was to play a leading role in the development of the underground railway. *ODNB*.
[26] *The Times* (21 Dec. 1831 and 8 Feb. 1832).
[27] *A Sketch of the Boston Election, 1830* (Boston, 1830), pp. xv, xix, xx. The *ODNB* gives Wilks's career as a 'swindler'.

hand, Wetherell, the recorder of Bristol, felt happy to pose, albeit fleetingly, as the defender of women's constitutional rights. He situated this within his broader aim of maintaining 'the rights and privileges' of Bristolians where 'the ladies now had the privilege in question'. Edward Protheroe, the ardent reform member for Bristol, was furious at Wetherell's implication that the people of Bristol opposed the bill because of its threat to traditional privileges, and he insisted that they were fully behind the cause. Nonetheless, Wetherell and Sugden's cynical tactic compelled Protheroe to acknowledge the claims of the women whose city he represented. He admitted that the 'female constituency' were 'in favour of retaining the rights of widows and daughters of freemen, and granting those rights to their husbands'.[28] Whilst conservative politicians were evidently supporting women's claims for strategic reasons, that such a stance was seen as credible in itself is noteworthy. Protheroe may not have felt compelled to endorse the wishes of his female constituents, but he did feel constrained to demonstrate a respectful recognition of them. Women's 'borderline' status as citizens meant that they could be strategically evoked as respectable members of the polity and this could subtly alter the gendered dynamics of the debate.

Two days later Tory MP Edward Peel proposed an amendment to secure the rights of those freemen who derived their status from 'birth and servitude and marriage'.[29] The reform bill's proposals threatened to disenfranchise nearly a third of his constituents in Newcastle-under-Lyme and it had therefore been a central issue in the election of 1831. When local freemen laid their concerns before the borough's reforming candidate Josiah Wedgwood, he had been able to give only a lame assurance that he would bring their concerns to the attention of the House.[30] In contrast, Peel (another brother of Robert), who had lost a small fortune when he failed to win this borough in 1830, had joined forces with the elusive figure of the sitting MP, William Henry Miller.[31] Together they successfully

---

[28] *Hansard*, 6 (27 Aug. 1831), cols 698–9. Sugden (1781–1875), later Lord Chancellor, was a fierce opponent of the Infants' Custody Act (1839) which gave greater rights to mothers: *The Times* (13 June 1839). For the implications of reform in Bristol see Jeremy Caple, *The Bristol Riots of 1831 and Social Reform in Britain* (Lewiston, NY, 1990).

[29] *Hansard*, 6 (30 Aug. 1831), cols 881–3.

[30] Keele University Library (hereafter 'Keele') election broadsides (1831), E4 2984.

[31] Extraordinarily, there were rumours that Miller, who had an awkward public manner and a reputation for eccentricity, was a woman. His family connections to the Christie hat manufacturers presumably helped to seal his success in the borough, many of whose inhabitants depended upon the trade. Sir Daniel Wilson, *Memorials of Edinburgh in the Olden Time* (Edinburgh, 1892, 2 vols), ii. 122; Hannah Barker and David Vincent (eds), *Language, Print*

presented themselves as champions for the rights of freemen and their children. In electoral ephemera Peel emphasized his desire to protect 'your children's rights', and Miller was praised as the defender of 'the Rights of our Sons and our Daughters'.[32] Peel's proposal was therefore important to his local political position. Surprisingly, when his amendment was discussed in parliament a small number of pro-reform Whigs also championed the cause: this was not an issue which divided MPs simply along pro- or anti-reform lines. Captain Berkeley, the Whig member for Gloucester, was supported by fellow MP Lewis Buck, when he mounted a spirited defence of the traditional privileges of his female constituents. He observed that 'amongst the free women there was a very strong feeling against this clause of the bill', and argued that fears that they would no longer be able to take advantage of charities for the widows and children of freemen were 'well grounded'. Berkeley clearly thought it important that he should be seen to represent the interests of his female constituents, even though this conflicted with his wider pro-reform position.[33]

When Peel's amendment was lost by seventy-nine votes, Wilks immediately proposed a fresh amendment. Perhaps because of a prior commitment to Charles Pearson, he brought the question back to one of political equity, reminding the House that the effect of the existing clause would be to deprive 'females' of a long-held electoral right. Other than a feeble joke on the part of the Attorney General, the amendment prevailed with virtually no debate. This was doubtless because, despite Wilks's rhetoric of women's rights, his amendment sought only to maintain the rights of those who had married a freewoman's daughter before the passage of the Act. It did nothing to ensure the continued political influence of freewomen.[34] Therefore, during the passage of the third reform bill, the liberal reformer Thomas Barrett-Lennard (who had supported Wilks's proposal) attempted to secure these rights further. Like Pearson, Barrett-Lennard sought explicitly to protect the electoral rights of women:

> in some few boroughs, a right existed, by which the daughters of freemen conveyed the right of voting to their husbands. This privilege they would

---

and Electoral Politics, 1790–1832: Newcastle-under-Lyme Broadsides (Woodbridge and Rochester, NY, 2001), p. xxv.

[32] Keele, E4 2969 and 2968.

[33] *Hansard*, 6 (30 Aug. 1831), cols 885–6. For the wider context of Berkeley's political position see Adrian Courtenay, 'Cheltenham Spa and the Berkeleys, 1832–48: Pocket Borough and Patron?' *Midland History*, 17 (1992), 93–108.

[34] *Hansard*, 6 (30 Aug. 1831), col. 910.

lose by the Bill as it now stood, and it was the object of his Amendment to
preserve these rights. He knew they were considered as valuable, and the
right of the daughter to confer the privilege on her husband ought to be as
sacred as the right of the master to confer freedom on his apprentice.

The motion was seconded by Barrett-Lennard's fellow member for
Maldon, a conservative, Quintin Dick who defended its support of 'heredi-
tary rights'. This unlikely alliance suggests that the defence of freewomen's
rights was a significant matter in their constituency. However, the tone of
Barrett-Lennard's comments indicates that his position was not merely
political opportunism. He carefully responded to opposing arguments, noting
for example that the bill's provisions concerning the registration of voters
would serve to minimize marriages conducted fraudulently for political gain,
and he insisted that the House divide on the matter. His amendment was lost
by fifty votes, but in the process interesting positions emerged. Sir George
Clerk praised the strength of Barrett-Lennard's case, agreeing it was 'invidious
to make a distinction between the sons and daughters of freemen'. Robert
Gordon warned that, given the Lords' hostility to the amendment, there was
little point in pursuing it further. Nonetheless he endorsed both the chivalric
argument that the right was a 'kind of dowry to the ladies' which it would
be ungallant to discontinue, as well as making the case for political equity,
professing he did not understand 'upon which principle the right was to be
continued to the sons and denied to the daughters'.[35]

A final attempt to amend the proposed legislation came in May 1832
when the House of Lords received a petition from freemen's wives and
daughters in Great Grimsby who requested that 'their Rights and those of
their children and future Husbands, be preserved to them'.[36] This too was
unsuccessful. Therefore in the final Reform Act, the rights of men already
enfranchised by dint of their wives' status were upheld; and women
continued to be able to endow their husbands with freemen status in some
boroughs; but the voting rights of those made 'freemen by marriage' after
1 March 1831 were abolished.[37]

The passage of the bill through parliament indicates that in a number
of boroughs—including Grimsby, Maldon, Bristol, and Boston—the

---

[35] *Hansard*, 10 (7 Feb. 1832), cols 61–3. It is this debate which Catherine Hall discusses. See
above pp. 164–5.

[36] *Hansard*, 12 (7 May 1832), col. 669.

[37] Lord William Russell, *A Treatise on the Reform Act* (London, 1832), 42–3; Salmon, *Electoral
Reform at Work*, 203; Charles Seymour, *Electoral Reform in England and Wales: The Development
of the Parliamentary Franchise 1832–85* (Newton Abbot, 1970; originally publ. 1915), 28.

ending of freewomen's electoral rights was viewed as a significant measure by local women. In their responses, politicians in affected boroughs showed a desire to pose as representatives of their female as well as their male constituents; and there was a minority strand of opinion prepared to support the notion of female electoral rights as a matter of principle. Yet women were 'borderline citizens'. Whilst the issue raised transitory concern, women's rights were dropped, seemingly without debate, once a compromise had been secured over the broader issue of the freemen's position. Despite the explicit wish to protect the rights of both 'sons and daughters' in Newcastle-under-Lyme when, in February 1832, the Commons agreed to the clause granting rights in perpetuity to those whose status derived from birth or apprenticeship (but not marriage) Peel and his constituents represented this as a victory.[38] Moreover, knowledge of the rights and privileges which freemen's daughters had possessed in particular boroughs failed to impinge dramatically upon the national political community. When parliament debated the implications of the Municipal Corporations bill for freemen in 1835 one member seemed completely unaware of women's ability to confer the position of freemen on their husbands, protesting 'I have yet to learn that women have any rights such as the Honourable and Learned Gentleman alludes to.'[39] Older, local cultures which afforded women conduits to political status in the parochial realm were rapidly dying out in the centralized political system which emerged in the post-1832 nation.

The debates on freewomen's privileges revealed the difficulties in asserting women's local experience of political agency at the parliamentary level. This applied equally to the treatment of female-signed petitions. The Earl of Mansfield confirmed that both men and women had signed an anti-reform petition which came from Perthshire.[40] But whilst local communities might feel it appropriate for women to act as petitioners, in matters of such constitutional importance parliament was likely to call into question the validity of petitions which were not exclusively male. When the Duke of Northumberland circulated an anti-reform petition amongst his tenants he clearly felt it acceptable that women as well as men might add their names. Indeed, one MP explained that, 'wives and daughters signed for husbands and fathers'. This particular petition was given little weight because of the assumption that the tenants had been pressured by the duke,

---

[38] Barker and Vincent, *Language, Print and Electoral Politics*, 327–8.
[39] *Mirror of Parliament* (24 June 1835).
[40] *Hansard*, 9 (26 Jan. 1832), col. 830.

but the existence of women's signatures served to complete an image of its political irregularity in the eyes of parliament.[41] Local assumptions and customs as to female involvement in politics could be starkly at odds with those articulated in Westminster.

These are intricacies which were embedded in the passage of the Select Vestries Act in 1831. This legislation endorsed female voting yet this was not debated in parliament—hence Vernon's conclusion that it was an almost accidental move in a parliament preoccupied by the reform crisis.[42] However, the measure's architect, John Cam Hobhouse, was a metropolitan radical with a Unitarian background. Whilst his views on political women could be ambivalent (he scoffed at a proposal to formalize aristocratic women's access to parliamentary debates, for example) he explicitly intimated that women should play an equal role in vestry politics. In a debate on parochial politics in Marylebone he insisted that 'as householders and payers of rates' women had 'an unquestionable right to join in such a demonstration of public opinion'.[43] Hobhouse at least appears to have been clear in his views that women should have a formal voice in the local political sphere, thus problematizing Vernon's assumption.

The parliamentary debates on the reform bill were extraordinarily extensive and prolonged. Those which touched upon its implications for women formed only a minute proportion of the whole. Nonetheless, these interchanges belie the seeming simplicity and finality of the erasure of women from the national franchise and point to intriguing fault-lines within the polity. A male parliamentary electorate may have been the assumed norm, yet it could not be taken for granted. Eighteen years later the Attorney General had to intervene to quash fears that Brougham's Abbreviation Act (1850), which established that legislation using masculine pronouns should be taken to include women, had legalized female suffrage.[44] The reform crisis thus stands as a testament to the multiplicity of ways in which contemporaries might envisage, conceptualize, and experience female political agency. The myriad forms of female engagement in

---

[41] *The Times* (21 Apr. 1831).

[42] Vernon, *Politics and the People*, 20. Women were not mentioned in the many debates, see e.g. *Hansard*, 7 (30 Sept. 1831), cols 879–91; 8 (5 Oct. 1831), cols 56–7; 8 (11 Oct. 1831), cols 486–8; 8 (13 Oct. 1831), cols 697–725; 8 (15 Oct. 1831), cols 807–10.

[43] *The Times* (7 June 1828). See Robert E. Zegger, *John Cam Hobhouse: A Political Life, 1819–1852* (Columbia, Mo., 1973), ch. 6, for full details of the bill.

[44] *Hansard*, 117 (16 June 1851), cols 843–5; Sandra Petersson, 'Gender Neutral Drafting: Historical Perspective', *Statute Law Review*, 19 (1998), 106–8.

the reform question beyond the Palace of Westminster reinforces such an argument.

Women and the campaign for reform

According to scholars such as John Phillips, the two years of agitation which preceded the bill (combined with the stimulus the legislation itself gave to partisan politics) 'reshaped the political process' in constituencies across the country.[45] It is an argument which has been more forcefully restated by Philip Salmon.[46] But how were women implicated in this process? Sarah Richardson and Kim Reynolds have noted the vigorous intervention of the likes of Lady Sandwich and Elizabeth Lawrence in the elections of 1831–2; and, exceptionally, Catherine Hall has considered the involvement of middle-class women in the campaign, coming to the conclusion that women were '*spectators* and *supporters* rather than being active in their own right and on their own behalf'.[47] Nancy LoPatin-Lummis has indicated that, despite the existence of a handful of women's reform organizations, women did not play a prominent role in the reform struggle. Otherwise the issue of women's role in the agitation remains underexplored. Yet as LoPatin-Lummis's own sources suggest, some contemporaries entertained a strikingly different impression. Joseph Parkes, a leading figure in the Birmingham reform movement, reported to the metropolitan radical George Grote that 'our women [were] heroines', claiming the 'petticoats put up at Birmingham'. Here, over half the audience at one meeting of the Birmingham Political Union were reported to be women.[48] At the celebrations to mark Thomas Attwood's contribution to the movement, women were recorded as loud and enthusiastic members of the crowds and elaborate arrangements were made to accommodate them at civic celebrations.[49]

The situation in Birmingham, I suggest, was part of a broader process of female engagement in reform. An acknowledgement of female participation comprised a marginal yet persistent strand of contemporary discourse,

[45] John A. Phillips, *The Great Reform Bill in the Boroughs: English Electoral Behaviour, 1818–41* (Oxford, 1992), here at 11.

[46] Salmon, *Electoral Reform, passim*.

[47] Reynolds, *Aristocratic Women*, 135; Richardson, 'Role of Women', 133–51; Hall, 'Private Persons', 161.

[48] Nancy LoPatin-Lummis, *Political Unions, Popular Politics and the Great Reform Act of 1832* (Basingstoke, 1999), 213n., 168.

[49] C. M. Wakefield, *Life of Thomas Attwood* (London, 1885), 230–3, 236, 239, 277.

undermining assumptions that 1832 signalled the triumph of a hegemonic concept of male citizenship. One means through which women contributed to the reform debate was through the medium of print culture. Cecilia Mary Cadell's decision to entitle her 1832 novel, *The Reformer* capitalized upon the public thirst for all matters connected to the reform crisis. Set in the aftermath of the British response to the French Revolution, the novel expatiated on the dangers of raising children upon democratic principles.[50] Astute publishers realized that the reading public did not consider female authorship to be incompatible with political controversy and a small handful of women positioned themselves as authoritative commentators.

The most striking example of this phenomenon was Frances Trollope's *Domestic Manners of the Americans*. Trollope (mother of Anthony, the future novelist) had travelled to America with three of her children to escape financial problems and a difficult marriage in England, but soon became politicized by her experiences there. In the account of her travels, *Domestic Manners*, she asserted that her observation of American political culture had led to her reject her erstwhile Whiggism. Disgusted by the overfamiliarity and 'vulgarity' of those with whom she conversed, Trollope claimed that democratic principles resulted in a distasteful, disorderly society:

> the theory of equality may be very daintily discussed by English gentlemen in a London dining-room, when the servant, having placed a fresh bottle of cool wine on the table, respectfully shuts the door, and leaves them to their walnuts and their wisdom; but it will be found less palatable when it presents itself in the shape of a hard, greasy paw, and is claimed in accents that breathe less of freedom than of onions and whiskey.[51]

Trollope and her publisher, Whittaker, seized upon the opportunity of the reform debates to ensure maximum publicity. After an initial postpone-ment, the book was published on 19 March 1832 just before the final reading of the reform bill. Trollope's work included a conventional disclaimer as to her ability, as a woman, to provide an adequate political analysis, but in a new preface Trollope explicitly framed the text as a contri-bution to the public debate on reform. She claimed that her 'chief object', was 'to encourage her countrymen to hold fast by a constitution that

---

[50] Cecilia Mary Cadell, *The Reformer* (London, 1832). Cadell, a Roman Catholic, was reason-ably prolific in her own day, publishing over ten works in a variety of genres: see e.g. *A History of the Missions in Japan and Paraguay* (London, 1856) and *Summer Talks about Lourdes* (London, 1874).

[51] Frances Trollope, *The Domestic Manners of the Americans* (London, 1832, 2nd edn, 2 vols), i. 172–3.

ensures all the blessings which flow from established habits and solid principles'. In addition, Whittaker coordinated its release with a forty-page
appraisal in the *Quarterly Review* by Basil Hall, whose own work on
America had been warmly received.[52]

The tactics worked: it was an immediate bestseller.[53] It was also received
as a direct intervention in the reform debate. An extended analysis in the
Whig *Edinburgh Review* noted that the revised preface amounted to 'an
express advertisement against the Reform Bill'. It continued, 'Four-and-
thirty chapters of American scandal are dished up with the immediate
purpose of contrasting the graceful virtues of a boroughmonger with the
profligate vulgarity of a ten pound franchise.' Criticizing Trollope for
misleading reporting, fallacious logic, and weak intellectual skills, the
reviewer's distaste for Trollope's politics led him to exploit her gender as a
further source of attack. A savage assessment of her supposed lack of refinement was allied to her 'blue-stocking contempt for household cares'.[54] The
Gentleman's Magazine, which was equally hostile to the work, also
attempted to cast a slur on Trollope's femininity, casting her as vulgar and
ill-bred.[55] Yet reviewers' treatment of Trollope's gender was dependent upon
their political stance. The *Quarterly Review* claimed that as a woman she was
particularly well-suited to the minute social observations which characterized the work. In a discussion of the book's political themes Hall went on
to praise Trollope for her original and incisive treatment of the implications
of democratic principles.[56]

Gendered discourses on the female politician could, therefore, be highly
strategic. Jane Alice Sargant was a prolific contemporary pamphleteer who
produced two works on the reform crisis.[57] *An Address to the Females of
Great Britain* was intended to dissuade working-class women from participating in the agitation, claiming that 'With the merits or demerits of the

[52] Ibid., p. vi; Pamela Neville-Sington, *Fanny Trollope: The Life and Adventures of a Clever
Woman* (London, 1997), 168–9; *Quarterly Review*, 47 (1832), 39–80.
[53] Neville-Sington, *Fanny Trollope*, 170–7, for the book's reception.
[54] *Edinburgh Review* (July 1832), 479–526, here at 496, 521.
[55] *Gentleman's Magazine* (Apr. 1832), 346.
[56] *Quarterly Review*, 47 (1832), 39–80. See esp. 39–40, 67–8, 72.
[57] Jane Alice Sargant (1789–1869) wrote numerous publications for the Society for the
Promotion of Christian Knowledge and her works enjoyed an international audience. In
addition to religious tracts, at critical political junctures such as the Queen Caroline affair,
the anti-slavery agitation, and proposed reform of the marriage laws, she published grandil-
oquent pamphlets often under the pseudonym 'Sinceritas'. Little is known about her life,
although her brother, Harry Smith, wrote a popular autobiography: G. C. M. Smith (ed.),
The Autobiography of Lieutenant-General Sir Harry Smith (London, 1901).

Bill . . . we have little to do'. Sargant, like Trollope, rehearsed hackneyed pronouncements as to the limitations of female political aptitude, but she was quite prepared to expatiate herself on the constitutional implications of the bill. She emphasized the great dangers she believed the measure to represent and underlined the importance of women's political efforts within their own families where they might shield children from 'evil journals' and 'virulent discussions'.[58] In *An Honest Appeal to All Englishmen* Sargant depended upon highly stylized notions of plebeian masculinity to persuade working-class men to abandon the reforming cause.[59]

Radical women similarly employed gendered arguments strategically. Eliza Sharples hailed from a well-to-do Methodist family in Bolton. In 1832 she turned her back on her family to join Richard Carlile's radical political movement in London.[60] In her publication, *The Isis* Sharples adopted the persona of a 'leader of the people' who, in a series of letters, posed as a political tutor to Queen Adelaide. In her desire to project an image as a reliable and considered commentator Sharples also reaffirmed more restrictive modes of feminine politics. Whilst she lambasted the Queen for influencing her husband against reform, Sharples praised Adelaide for her dutiful fulfilment of the roles of wife and mother. On one occasion she insisted that politics should be severed from family concerns, yet in another issue she argued that women's greater family responsibilities meant they were more implicated than men in the public reformation which the reform bill represented.[61]

Sharples's volatile rhetoric is illustrative of the tensions inherent in projecting oneself as a radical female politician at this time. In some ways it was easier for anti-reforming women such as Trollope and Sargant to act as public spokespersons on the issue. Their political stance drew upon the maintenance of traditional social hierarchies which could diffuse anxieties as to female public activity. With the exception of Sharples, even women at the heart of radical feminist networks intervened but cautiously. Harriet Martineau and Eliza Flower chose to support the movement through the composition of reform songs. Selections of these were published in the

---

[58] Sargant, *Address to the Females*, 4–6, 13.

[59] J. A. Sargant, *An Honest Appeal to all Englishmen* (London, 1832).

[60] For Sharples's broader career see Helen Rogers '"The Prayer, the Passion and the Reason" of Eliza Sharples: Freethought, Women's Rights and Republicanism, 1832–52', in Yeo, *Radical Femininity*, 52–78.

[61] *Isis* (3 and 24 Mar., 7 Apr., 19 May 1832).

Monthly Repository, and, according to Martineau's brother, one became very popular, being 'sung by all the political unions'.[62]

Women tended not to articulate a distinctly female position on this constitutional issue as was the case with movements which could be construed as humanitarian or philanthropic. Yet contemporaries were highly aware of women's contribution, particularly at the parochial and constituency level, and tended to express this through the rhetoric of 'female influence'. Some reference has been made by historians to reformers' evocation of female influence as a malign phenomenon. This included the invidious sway Queen Adelaide and her sisters-in-law were thought to exercise over the King; the sinister female cabal with whom the Duke of Wellington was thought to be intimate; and the evocation of aristocratic women as part of a corrupt elite, profiting from iniquitous sinecures, offices, and pensions.[63] However this formed part of a broader discourse lambasting the evils of elite rule: reformers were not opposed to female influence *per se*. On the contrary. The Alderman of the Common Council wished to include women in a reform festival because, as he put it, 'the ladies, by the influence they exercised over their husbands and children, had contributed to the success of reform'.[64] Contemporaries often articulated a perception that women had an effect upon the casting of votes on this issue. One reformer claimed excitedly that at Newark (where tensions ran high due to the belligerent anti-reformism of the Duke of Newcastle) 'wives [had] implored their husbands to vote for the great and glorious cause'.[65] The failure of the Tory candidate in Maidstone in 1832 was attributed to the town's 'blue devils'—reforming women who persuaded their conservative husbands not to support Wyndham Lewis.[66]

At public meetings it was a device which could be knowingly articulated to acknowledge politely the presence of women in the audience. A speaker at a Berkshire county meeting in 1831 estimated that the bill would enfranchise half a million men: 'He hoped that some of these half million were married. He hoped that their ladies would have over them that

---

[62] Martineau, Transcribed letters, HMCO (6 June 1832); see e.g. *Monthly Repository*, 6 (1832), 371.

[63] A. W. Purdue, 'Queen Adelaide: Malign Influence or Consort Maligned?', in Clarissa Campbell Orr (ed.), *Queenship in Britain, 1660–1837: Royal Patronage, Court Culture and Dynastic Politics* (Manchester, 2002), 267–87; Smith, *Reform or Revolution*, 85, 88. For further examples see *The Times* (12, 13,18 April and 22 May 1832); *Hansard*, 8 (1831), col. 916.

[64] *The Times* (16 July 1832). His proposal was deemed too expensive.

[65] *The Times* (7 June 1831); Butler, *Passing*, 298.

[66] Phillips, *Great Reform Bill*, 58.

influence which ladies generally exercised over their lords; and sure he was, that if ladies had been sent to Parliament for the last 40 years, the country would not have been in the state in which it was at present.' Observing that the measure would also draw the sons and daughters of the newly enfranchised into the political nation he continued, 'When such increased influence was given to the middle classes, the House of Commons would exhibit the collective wisdom and the collective integrity of the nation.'[67] Rhetoric emphasizing the political significance of women could be viewed as an acceptable—indeed courteous—formula.

During the reform elections of 1830–2, the evocation of female influence sometimes formed a leitmotif in electoral ephemera, as already seen in the tactics employed by Wilks and Buckingham.[68] One election pamphlet from Northumberland appealed directly to the 'Ladies of the county', urging them to 'shew a good Example to your Sons' and support the bill which 'will benefit your Families, and the People at large'.[69] A Warwick election squib, 'An Address to the Ladies of Warwick from the Borough-Mongering Candidate' mocked the tendency to appeal to female constituents as a desperate last resort, joking that the hapless local politician had promised to bring in a bill for 'Ladies to have Votes at Elections' on his successful return to parliament.[70] That such efforts could form the subject of satire is a testament to their widespread currency. Anti-reformers adopted similar tactics. Tories in Norwich referred to a long tradition of female patriotism imploring local women to 'exert *your* persuasive influence on the minds of a father, brother, husband, or lover'.[71] A conservative ballad distributed in Halesworth during the 1832 election used the trope of the elegantly supportive female:

> The Ladies of your Country,
> The fairest in the world,
> Have smil'd upon your banner,
> Whenever 'twas unfurl'd.[72]

[67] *The Times* (17 Mar. 1831). Wahrman argues that such formulations were a common feature of the post-1832 cultural landscape: *Imagining the Middle Class*, ch. 9.

[68] See above pp. 163, 165. There were three elections (summer 1830 following the death of George IV; spring 1831 following the dissolution of parliament; and Dec. 1832–Jan. 1833, after the passage of the Act). The question of reform dominated each.

[69] *To the Ladies of the County of Northumberland* (North Shields, 1831).

[70] 'An Address to the Ladies of Warwick from the Borough-Mongering Candidate' (Oct. 1832), Warwickshire County Record Office, CR 1097/330/118.

[71] George Jacob Holyoake, *Sixty Years of an Agitator's Life* (London, 1893, 2 vols), i. 29; original emphasis.

[72] [Agnes Strickland], *Rally round your Colours* (Halesworth, 1832).

However, the gracious but passive image of female support portrayed here is complicated by the fact that it has been attributed to the historian Agnes Strickland. She was one of a number of women who contributed to the cut and thrust of local electioneering in this way. This was a trend which continued in the post-1832 years. In 1835 Mary Cockle apparently issued an anti-reform broadside 'The Banners of Blue'. Also in that year Elizabeth Adams published her *Hurrah for the Hearts of True Blue*—a Tory election song composed with William Neale which evoked local ladies as 'Angels' supporting the Tory cause.[73]

Acknowledgements of female contributions to the reform debate were thus widespread but highly formulaic. Women's participation in the controversy was recognized in a stylized manner which intimated a passive, feminized mode of political interaction. This did not map neatly onto contemporaries' experiences of actual female involvement in the parochial realm. As parliamentary constituents, parishioners, and economic agents women were often highly organized and dynamic on the issue. A proposal mooted in Chelmsford, that women should test the law by attempting to exercise the vote, appears to have been exceptional.[74] However, the ritual of gift-giving to pro-reform MPs provided a common avenue for women to position themselves as interested constituency members. In Hertford 800 local ladies honoured the unseated reformer Thomas Slingsby Duncombe with an inscribed piece of silver.[75] The ladies of Hull provided Matthew Davenport Hill with a similar tribute to his 'incorruptible patriotism' in 1832.[76] In Wakefield a number of ladies led by Mrs Marriott identified themselves as 'friendly to the Reform Act' when they made a presentation to Daniel Gaskell MP.[77]

Women could also establish their political allegiances through facilitating other kinds of meetings. During the election of 1830 in North Shields, handbills detailing a political meeting held at the Northumberland Arms drew attention to the fact that this was the house of a Mrs Sears. This is suggestive of the active service she was thought to lend to the

---

[73] [Mary Cockle], *The Banners of Blue* (Woodbridge, 1835); Elizabeth Adams, *Hurrah for the Hearts of True Blue* (Exeter, 1835).

[74] Davidoff and Hall, *Family Fortunes*, 540 n. 13. This may have been instigated by the Quaker feminist Anne Knight, who was then resident in Chelmsford.

[75] T. H. Duncombe, *The Life and Correspondence of Thomas Slingsby Duncombe* (London, 1868, 2 vols), i. 129–30.

[76] Hill and Hill, *Recorder of Birmingham*, 134.

[77] Morgan, *Victorian Woman's Place*, 182–3; Jacques, *Merrie Wakefield*, 103.

meeting.[78] Women often drew upon their local economic authority rather than their gender when acting as political agents in the parochial realm. A 'spirited landlady' in Hertford threatened to evict a tenant in 1832 if he voted against her wishes and hired 'a gang of election bullies' to pull down the election colours of her late husband.[79] Women might also make their views plain through exerting pressure upon local figures of authority. The Reverend Brontë (father of the novelists) had to defend his political position to one of his female parishioners. Admitting that he was an 'advocate for the Bill', he was careful to describe himself as a staunch supporter of 'Church and state'.[80]

Women could therefore feel fully implicated in the consequences of the reform bill. Accordingly they celebrated its passage in a variety of ways. When an elderly Scottish lady, M. M. Inglis, was unable to participate in the great Edinburgh festival in honour of Earl Grey on 15 September 1834 she penned him an enthusiastic letter of welcome and a poetic tribute instead.[81] In contrast, small-scale parochial events could provide considerable scope for women to involve themselves in reform festivities, and were perhaps more conducive to the attendance of the elderly. In one Staffordshire parish a female-only celebration was held to mark the election of their first constituency MP following reform. The occasion, aimed at older women, was overseen by women of the Wedgwood family at a venue provided by a Mrs Hardings, who lent her 'cheese room' for the occasion.[82] Such incidents are telling as to the investment women might feel in reform and their desire to mark its significance in their own way.

Parochial events of this nature were unlikely to make it into the pages of local newspapers. In contrast women's presence was frequently recorded during the larger public occasions, although more conventional gender practices applied. Public reform dinners, for example, tended to be masculine affairs, although women commonly attended the speeches given at the end of the meal.[83] This does not mean that we should dismiss women's

---

[78] *Northumberland General Election: At a Numerous and Respectable Meeting of the Freeholders and Friends of the Hon. H. T. Liddell* (1830).

[79] Gash, *Politics in the Age of Peel*, 175.

[80] Revd Patrick Brontë to Mrs Franks (28 Apr. 1831), in Margaret Smith (ed.), *The Letters of Charlotte Brontë: With a Selection of Letters by Family and Friends*, i. *1829–1847* (Oxford, 1995), 106.

[81] M. M. Inglis to Earl Grey (13 Sept. 1834), Borthwick Institute, University of York, Hickleton papers, Halifax/A1/4/67/1–2. For details of the event see E. A. Smith, *Lord Grey, 1764–1845* (Oxford, 1990), 1–3.

[82] Elizabeth Wedgwood to Emma Allen (21 Dec. 1832), W/M 39.

[83] See e.g. the practice in Kettering: *The Times* (25 Dec. 1832).

presence at reform events as merely 'spectators', as Catherine Hall has suggested.[84] For a start, the act of spectatorship was complex. It was not considered to be a uniquely female practice and it could indicate varying levels of engagement. Frances Kemble described her family's observation of the reform illuminations as 'sight-seeing'.[85] Similarly, when Wakefield hosted its first election contest after the passage of the Act, Clarkson and her mother, both suffering with heavy colds, preferred to position themselves as onlookers and not participants: 'There were hustings erected but we stood with several other ladies in the Court Yard, a little aside.'[86]

As Clarkson's comments suggests, there were different gradations of spectatorship. Clarkson's account indicates a curiosity to witness a local occasion. Those who placed themselves in the thick of the crowd, or who chose to sit on the hustings, might experience a far more active sense of participation. This was a phenomenon recognized by pro-reform journalists who had a political motive for wishing to ascribe to women an active form of spectatorship (as indicated in Chapter 2). In a typical example, at a county reform meeting held in Derby, it was noted that the 'elegantly dressed females . . . evinced the greatest interest in the absorbing topic of the day'.[87] Whilst references to 'fashionable ladies' at the windows during reform processions were commonplace, many journalists attempted to imply that this represented a deliberate engagement with the political meanings of the occasion. During the reform procession in Elgin it was noted that 'all the windows, fronting the part of the street it passed, were filled with ladies, who, if there be truth in Lavater's system of physiognomy, cordially partook of the general joy'.[88] Here, the journalist used the contemporary interest in physiognomy (the practice of using facial expression to decipher character) as a device to signify the powerful political sentiments that might be attributed to spectating women. Some correspondents discreetly alluded to women's noisy support for reform. In Newport reports referred to the 'hearty salutations' of the ladies during a reform procession.[89] As engaged audience members, women were dynamically involved in the construction and meanings of an event. In subsequent reports an imagined social order was projected which incorporated women

---

[84] Hall, 'Private Persons', 161.
[85] Frances Kemble to 'Dearest H' (c.14 May 1831), in Kemble, *Record*, iii. 13–14.
[86] Jacques, *Merrie Wakefield*, 42, 49, 98–100.
[87] *The Times* (10 Oct. 1831).
[88] *The Times* (25 May 1832). A further example may be found at *The Times* (23 May 1832).
[89] *The Times* (4 May 1831).

within images of fashionable propriety so that the respectability of the cause of reform was assured and a sense of communal unity upheld.

The complex constitution of these tropes may be illustrated by considering a lengthier example from Canterbury where a sumptuous celebration was organized on the passing of the Act.[90] The occasion was recorded in some detail in a pamphlet produced by the proprietor and editor of the *Kent Herald*. It described the extensive decoration of the city, the lavish procession, and the gun salute. Despite the rousing radicalism of the toasts which championed 'The People, the source of all legitimate power', the text highlighted the respectability and refinement of the occasion. It celebrated the 'mixture of classes' as key to the trouble-free day, praising the 'kindness and consideration' which had been shown to the labouring classes, ensuring their 'good conduct' and 'gratitude'.[91] Allusions to the gracious probity of the city's ladies played an important element in this construction, with references to the 'innumerable well-dressed females [who] promenaded the field, and were highly amused and delighted with the animated spectacle around them'. The evocation of upright females traversing the festival's terrain thus contributed to a particular imagining of cohesive, traditional social relations in the post-reform community.

However women also played a far more dynamic role in Canterbury's public sphere than this suggests. The pamphlet itself was authored by a local woman, Elizabeth Wood, who, since the death of her husband George in 1829, had assumed sole proprietorship of the *Kent Herald*. She also ran a circulating library in the city and specialized in the production of tracts on liberal political causes such as the protest against tithes and accounts of local elections.[92] Her list of the festival's subscribers revealed a significant level of female contribution, and she herself clearly had privileged knowledge of the day's planning, referring, for example, to decisions taken by its committees. The evocation of smiling, benign women in her description of the celebration was a discursive ritual. It smoothed their inclusion as political subjects whilst also contributing to the broader affirmation of a harmonious community structure.

[90] For the wider political context see Paul Hastings, 'Radical Movements and Workers' Protests to c.1850', in Frederick Lansberry (ed.), *Government and Politics in Kent, 1640–1914* (Woodbridge, 2001), 95–138.

[91] E. Wood, *A Brief Outline of the Canterbury Reform Festival, September 4 1832* (Canterbury, 1832).

[92] See her *No Tithes* (Canterbury, 1829) and *The Poll of the Electors for Members of Parliament to Represent the City of Canterbury* (Canterbury, 1830).

The narrow cultural formulas deemed acceptable for the representation of women's public presence could create tensions when women wished to express their own engagement. One angry woman wrote to *The Times* to protest at the decision of the London Guildhall to exclude women from its reform festivity. Her outrage suggests that she took participation in public events of this kind for granted. In making her case she asserted that 'the cause of Reform has derived great support from the Ladies', yet she also appealed to a vision of home-bound domesticity in her claim that women deserved attention as the cause had 'taken their husbands so many days and hours from their homes and families'. Further tensions in the text derived from the fact that women's exclusion was due to accusations of their improper behaviour on a former occasion organized by the Guildhall. Although the letter's author stoutly denied the allegation she felt constrained to make but a modest request for women's inclusion, asking only that they be permitted entrance as spectators, emphasizing that they had 'no wish to participate in the less refined part of the entertainment'.[93] Whilst this intervention was successful, the letter exemplifies the fragility of women's position within the reform agitation. It provides a rare acknowledgement that women's public behaviour could sometimes be deemed raucous and unrestrained, and the consequent importance of ensuring that a female presence could be construed as both docile and marginal. Women commonly supposed that their involvement in reform was a given, but there was ambivalence as to how this might best be conveyed.

The reform crisis and female subjectivities

The reform debate was a crisis of immense proportions. The rejection of the first two reform bills led to mass political mobilization and crisis in government. This had an intensely politicizing effect across the political nation. Contemporaries frequently wrote of their overwhelming preoccupation with the measure. As Mary Shelley declared in October 1831, 'the Reform Bill swallows up every other thought'.[94] The drama and excitement it generated could revive interest even in those who felt disengaged from the political process. As Charlotte Brontë enthused to her brother, 'the

---

[93] *The Times* (25 June 1832). A similar claim was made in a widely circulated article, 'Ladies and the Reform Bill', *The Times* (8 June 1831).
[94] Mary Shelley to Edward Trelawny (2 Oct. 1831), in H. Buxton Forman (ed.), *Letters of Edward John Trelawny* (London, 1910), 173n.

extreme pleasure I felt at the news of the Reform-bill's being thrown out "by" the House of Lords and of the expulsion or resignation of Earl Grey, &c. &c. convinced me that I have not as yet lost *all* my penchant for politics'.[95] However, the ambivalence of women's status as political subjects meant that it was a process which could have uneven outcomes. Thus, whilst the Act had the potential to open up new questions concerning female rights, identities rooted in social or economic status often proved more enduring. The Yorkshire landowner, Anne Lister, was piqued that women of property and education were denied political rights in the bill, but ultimately appears to have embraced the fresh opportunities for political influence which aspects of the legislation seemed to facilitate.[96]

One of the most common reactions to the reform agitation amongst women of the middling and gentry classes was that it reaffirmed a sense of their superior political acumen to that of the local populace. The working classes were repeatedly portrayed as child-like and naïve for their visionary hopes for the measure. Emily Shore, a Bedfordshire gentlewoman, wrote that, despite the raucous celebrations of the local 'mob' on the Act's passage, 'I do not suppose that any of them understood what they were so noisy about.'[97] Mrs Bulwer wrote to her friend Miss Greene that the 'common people' appeared to view the reform bill 'as a sort of patent steam-engine miracle-worker'.[98] The commonplace book of Susannah Watts of Leicester contains an extraordinary manuscript, 'The Assembly of Reformers' which elaborated such sentiments at length. It depicted the misguided reaction of farmyard animals to the bill's passage. They believe it will grant them liberty to feed in the richest pastures without fear of trespass. Their utopian dreams are soon dashed as they are captured on their first incursion into the squire's land. The bullock and the ass are then lectured by the plough boy, 'Why the D—l should you meddle, till you've reformed yourself?'[99] When discussing the political sensibilities of lower-class celebrants, a consciousness of their higher social status provided the most salient matrix of identity for middling and gentry women.

However, this does not mean to say that the reform crisis straightforwardly crystallized women's sense of their own political identity. It may

---

[95] Charlotte Brontë to Branwell Brontë (17 May 1832), in Smith, *Letters*, 112.

[96] Liddington, *Female Fortune*, 45, 47–8. The Chandos clause enfranchised £50 tenants in the counties, a move which was seen as shoring up the landed interest.

[97] Joyce Godber, *History of Bedfordshire, 1066–1888* (Luton, 1969), 408.

[98] Mrs Bulwer to Miss Greene (26 June 1831), in Edward Bulwer Lytton, *The Life, Letters and Literary Remains of Edward Bulwer, Lord Lytton* (London, 1883, 2 vols), ii. 309.

[99] Watts, Scrapbook, LRO, 221. For further discussion of Watts see pp. 147–50 above.

have kindled or vivified a sometimes quiescent political consciousness but this could be difficult to reconcile with self-images of appropriate female behaviour and abilities. This applied even to those women with privileged access to parliamentary politics. As we have seen, the ventilator space in the House of Commons provided a curious site where well-connected women might listen to parliamentary debates and participate in a kind of spectatorship.[100] As Elizabeth Galton later recalled, 'In March the Reform Bill came on again. We went one evening to the Ventilator in the House of Commons to hear the members speak. It was not a pleasant place, being just over the large chandelier, a sort of chimney to it, but it was the only place where ladies could go in the old House of Commons.'[101] Remembering the practice decades later Galton situated the experience within a pessimistic narrative of women's political exclusion. Contemporary accounts of the ventilator suggest more complex experiences.

For some, attending the reform debate may have been viewed as a leisure activity which had little enduring impact. Charlotte Upcher noted: 'I was present at the passing of the Bill, but do not remember about it [sic].'[102] But for others it was clearly an extraordinary experience. Frances Mackintosh, the daughter of MP Sir James Mackintosh, wrote a letter to Sarah Wedgwood from the ventilator during a critical debate. She painted a vivid description of the turbulent scenes in Palace Yard, where angry crowds were gathering. Mackintosh noted mischievously of herself and her companions, 'since we have been here we hear shouts & noise but nothing very alarming—though we all affect to be in a great fright'.[103] The drama of being cooped together within the cramped and dark confines lent an almost gothic air to the scenario and in the thrill of the hour contributed to the playful adoption of the characteristics of feminine alarm. Participants themselves might be aware that this was a strategically adopted position— but it enabled them to feel fully involved in the excitement of the reform agitation. Yet Mackintosh's letter also revealed more empowering aspects of what she referred to evocatively as 'bustling Ventilator politics'. Attendance at the debates could reinforce a woman's sense of her own political acumen. Mackintosh was highly discriminating in her attitudes towards the behaviour

---

[100] See above pp. 56–9.
[101] Moilliet, *Elizabeth Anne Galton*, 84.
[102] Pigott, *Memoir*, 194.
[103] Frances Mackintosh to Sarah Wedgwood (c.1830), W/M 167. See also Henrietta Litchfield (ed.), *Emma Darwin: A Century of Family Letters, 1792–1896* (London, 1915, 2 vols), i. 234.

of the MPs, praising the dramatic speech of the veteran Whig Lord Ebrington.[104] She provided her correspondent with details of the speeches and resolutions in favour of reform, and her predictions for the course of the discussion. Observing the debate was not a passive experience but had a marked influence on Mackintosh's own politics: 'I am turned into a much warmer reformer by this large majority.'[105] Nonetheless, women were acutely aware of their alienation from the ribald culture of the house. Mackintosh was scathing of the schoolboy humour she witnessed. Hearing a 'violent laugh', she explains: 'Mr Somebody *fell* what a set of idiots they are'. Posing as upright, superior observers was a common stance for women to adopt in the ventilator. As Emma Wedgwood joked in 1832 of her acquaintance, Miss Cardale, she 'would have been very likely to put her head through & reprove the house of commons'.[106]

Privileged access to this space enabled Mackintosh to feel closely implicated in the drama of the occasion and to develop her own views on the issues. Her experience affirmed that she was not innately inferior to the professional politicians deliberating the matter—yet the circumstances of their attendance led Mackintosh and her associates to perform a feminine sensibility that underlined their secondary status as political subjects.

The tensions created within individual subjectivities as a result of the sudden politicization wrought by the reform struggle also emerge clearly in the correspondence of the young actress, Frances Kemble. Kemble was from a famous acting dynasty, and during the time of the reform agitation she was an up-and-coming star of the London theatre. Her correspondence paints a vivid portrait of the deep divisions the bill was causing amongst social networks, 'old friendships are broken up and old intimacies cease; formal cordial acquaintances refuse to meet each other, houses are divided, and the dearest relations disturbed, if not destroyed. Society is become a sort of battle-field, for every man (and woman too) is nothing if not political.'[107] Such statements, whilst a dramatization, express a desire to amplify the ways in which national politics were impacting upon individual, affective experiences and convey a wish to write personal and family experiences into

---

[104] This may refer to Ebrington's celebrated motion for a vote of confidence in the government which would date the letter to 10 Oct. 1831 when the country was reeling from the Lords' rejection of the second reform bill. This would accord with the fevered atmosphere and outdoor unrest, although Ebrington also made significant speeches on 10 and 14 May 1832: Butler, *Passing*, 300, 385–6, 401.
[105] Frances Mackintosh to Sarah Wedgwood (*c*.1830), W/M 167.
[106] Emma Wedgwood to her sister, Sarah Elizabeth (27 Jan. 1832), W/M 168.
[107] Frances Kemble to 'Dearest H' (*c*.29 May 1831), in Kemble, *Record*, iii. 30–1.

the narrative of the reform crisis. Kemble's parenthetic inclusion of women in the last sentence is revealing as to an emergent consciousness of the politicization of women within the drama. However, this had the potential to create conflicts within an individual's self-narrative. The projection of a particular feminine image was often central to the identity of contemporary women and this might include maintaining an image of detachment from political affairs. Cultivating a normative mode of femininity was likely to be particularly important to Kemble, a budding actress. The result was an intensified assertion of a conservative female identity. Therefore, although her interest in reform progressively increased, she remained diffident as to her ability to express her views. 'You know I am no politician', she wrote to one correspondent, 'and my shallow causality and want of adequate information alike unfit me from understanding, much less discussing, public questions of great importance; but the present crisis has aroused me to intense interest and anxiety about the course events are taking.'[108] When writing to the feminist woman of letters, Anna Jameson, Kemble projected a more explicitly political character, explaining 'I write with rather a sympathetic leaning towards the Tory side of this Reform question'.[109] Yet with other correspondents she sought to forestall any impression that she might be knowledgeable or wish to discuss political affairs. 'I have other things that I care more to write to you about than politics', she protested to her favourite correspondent, despite giving a detailed and thoughtful account of the existing state of the crisis.[110] Despite her apparent disinterest in witnessing a reform procession in March 1831 (and her fear that the reading of the second bill might reduce the audience at her play), Kemble observed the extent to which political events intruded even on the supposedly reluctant, noting the 'engrossing' interest the subject had for 'almost every thinking person throughout the country'.[111] A desire to feel involved in an event of such overwhelming national importance could complicate women's self-identities and result in the articulation of fractured personas.

For many women the unstable political subjectivities evoked by the reform crisis were expressed in uneasy shifts between individual and

---

[108] Frances Kemble to 'Dearest H' (*c.*14 May 1831), ibid. iii. 13–14. My reading here is informed by David Snow, 'Collective Identity and Expressive Forms' (1 Oct. 2001), Center for the Study of Democracy, paper 01–07, http://repositories.cdlib.org/csd/01–07.

[109] Frances Kemble to Mrs Jameson (23 Dec. 1831), in Kemble, *Record*, iii. 143.

[110] Frances Kemble to 'Dearest H' (*c.*29 May 1831), ibid. iii. 30–1.

[111] Frances Kemble to 'Dearest H' (*c.*14 May 1831), in Kemble, *Record*, iii. 13–14 and (19 Mar. 1831), ii. 289. The family was facing wider financial pressures from poor revenues in the London theatre at this point: *ODNB*.

collective identities. The pressure to declare allegiance for or against the bill could crystallize family political identities and intensify individuals' investment in such positions. Many households, particularly in Birmingham and London, turned their homes into a public statement of their politics by placarding notices on their walls proclaiming that they would pay no taxes until the reform bill had been passed.[112] The home of Samuel Blackwell, a sugar refiner in Bristol, functioned as a nexus for local campaigning and it was consciously fashioned to advertise the family's reforming credentials. A huge poster hung in the parlour urging: 'A long pull! *And a strong pull!* AND A PULL ALL TOGETHER!'[113] For others a commitment to a particular family identity during the crisis was rooted within older models of kinship interest. Edward Bulwer Lytton had to obtain the permission of his mother before standing as a reform candidate.[114] Wider family networks were also important. As Davies Gilbert explained to his daughter Kitty of a family friend in 1832, Bella North's visit would be short as her sister-in-law wished to rally as much support as possible 'at the ensuing contest'.[115] Women were closely identified with the political profile of their male relatives. Thus at an event to mark the 'glorious cause of reform' at the Berkshire election, the sight of Mrs Throckmorton, who was from a long-established family in the community, apparently evoked 'loud and enthusiastic cheering and waving of hats from all parts of the hall'.[116]

As these varying modes of family political identification remind us, the family (as argued in Chapter 3) was a significant if problematic locus for the articulation of political commitment in our period. This was also reflected in the fact that in their responses to the reform crisis women employed a variety of discursive strategies which transgressed notions of individual subjectivity—often through the construction of what we might term 'we' identities. When the pottery magnate, Josiah Wedgwood II, anticipated standing for election in a constituency that was to be newly created by the Act, his wife Elizabeth pronounced, 'I fully expect that *we* shall be Members for Stoke upon Trent'.[117] On his success she conveyed her elation in the same emphatic terms to her sister, Jessie Sismondi, 'You will have heard that

[112] Butler, *Passing*, 381, 384.
[113] Samuel Blackwell was the father of Elizabeth Blackwell, the pioneering female doctor. Wilson, *Lone Woman*, 32.
[114] Lytton, *Life, Letters and Literary Remains*, 310–12.
[115] Davies Gilbert to Catherine Gilbert (Feb. 1832), CRO, Enys of Enys papers, EN 1932.
[116] *The Times* (11 May 1831).
[117] Elizabeth Wedgwood to her sister, Emma Allen (11 May 1831), W/M 39.

_we_ are come into Parliament for Stoke upon Trent.'[118] Wedgwood's striking sense of her connection with her husband's political fortunes gives weight to M. J. Peterson's insight that upper-middle-class women took seriously their role as 'help-meet' to their husbands.[119] But Wedgwood's fervour was further stimulated by the long intensity of the reform crisis which galvanized political passions and focused attention on the parliamentary process as never before. 'We are all agog', she wrote to her sister of her household's response to the change in the ministry in 1830; 'Our spirits are beginning to rise after the shock of the reform bill', she explained following the bill's defeat in the House of Lords in October 1831; 'We are all very much cast down', she lamented at the fall of the Grey administration in May 1832.

The expression of this collective political voice was facilitated by family rituals—in particular the daily, communal reading of the newspapers which validated their common responses to ongoing political issues. 'We are all interested exceedingly in public affairs just now', wrote Wedgwood, 'and the Newspapers are read with great avidity'. Within such families political identity was frequently conceived not as a question of individual sentiments or activities, but as a corporate phenomenon. As Wedgwood wrote to her sister, Emma Allen: 'I thank you very much my dear Sister for the warmth with which you have taken up _our_ cause. I am not less warm on _yours_ and if _you_ had come in at Pembroke _I_ should have been consoled for being thrown out at Newcastle'.[120]

Such positionings do not necessarily reflect fixed or permanent identities. Wedgwood sometimes wished to present more independent political thoughts, particularly in correspondence to her forthright sister, Jessie Sismondi. At the beginning of March 1831 she offered her an analysis as to whether the Lords would be 'virtuous enough to give up their close Boroughs upon public motives'. Three months later she purchased a 'frightful little bust' of Brougham 'out of my great love and admiration for him'. But Wedgwood was not a sophisticated political thinker, and the incessant debate on the reform bill could sometimes pall. She admitted to Jessie that she was wearied by the reform debates yet was anxious that the bill should succeed, 'as I suppose Jos will get a seat in Parliament if it passes'.

---

[118] Elizabeth Wedgwood to her sister, Jessie Sismondi (11 Dec. 1832), W/M 74.

[119] Peterson, _Family, Love and Work_, ch. 6. When Earl Grey was successful in his reform policy his wife received a large volume of congratulatory letters. Butler, _Passing_, 360.

[120] Letters from Elizabeth Wedgwood to Jessie Sismondi (22 Nov. 1830); to Emma Allen (16 Oct. 1831); to Eliza Roscoe (21 May 1832); to Emma Allen (27 Dec. 1830 and 11 May 1831), W/M 39, 74 and Keele, E28–19991; original emphases.

She affirmed these sentiments on Josiah's election, admitting she was 'not only gratified at seeing that Jo's character is rated as it ought by his constituents but I cannot help thinking that it will give our children a lift in point of station'.[121] Wedgwood's commitment to the national dimension of the subject may have waned, but she remained closely interested in its implications. Politics could provide the forum for women to further their family interests, as well as pursuing ideological goals.

In families who were not 'professionally' involved in politics, women's identification with the political identities of male family members could be more fragile. Dorothy Wordsworth, younger sister of the poet, William, could confidently write to their friend, one of the Unitarian literati, Henry Crabb Robinson, of 'the madness of the deluded people', but listen to the rest of her assessment:

> If it were not for the newspapers, *we* should know nothing of the turbulence of our great Towns and Cities. Yet *my poor Brother* is often heartsick and almost desponding—and no wonder—for until this point at which *we* are arrived he has been a true prophet as to the course of events . . . It remains now for *us* to hope that Parliament may meet in a different Temper from that in which they parted—and that the late dreadful events may make each *man* seek only to promote the peace and prosperity of the country.[122]

Her frequent shifts in pronouns, and the elision between her brother's sensibilities and those of her own are revealing as to the problems Wordsworth appeared to face in articulating a position as an individual political agent. Despite her evident interest and concern in the unfolding political drama she assumed that the crisis more fundamentally affected men than women, and concluded with upholding the masculine political subject.[123]

---

[121] Letters from Elizabeth Wedgwood to Jessie Sismondi (17 Mar. and 7 Oct. 1831, 11 Dec. 1832), to Frances Allen (4 June 1831), to Emma Allen (18 April 1832), W/M 74 and 68. For a comparable fictional allusion see George Eliot, *Middlemarch* (Harmondsworth, 1994, 1st publ. 1871–2), 813.

[122] Dorothy Wordsworth to Henry Crabb Robinson (1 Dec. [1831]), in Alan G. Hill (ed.), *The Letters of William and Dorothy Wordsworth: The Later Years*, part ii, *1829–1834* (Oxford, 1979), 460; emphasis added.

[123] For further discussion see Jill Ehnnen, 'Writing against, Writing through: Subjectivity, Vocation and Authorship in the Work of Dorothy Wordsworth', *South Atlantic Review*, 64 (1999), 72–90.

Conclusion

The supposition that the Reform Act signified political closure for women long dominated historical scholarship. Whilst references to women in reforming discourse were often fleeting, their continual recurrence is telling. The persistent, yet peripheral, acknowledgement of women as political subjects was symptomatic of their 'borderline' status.

Landmark events such as the Reform Act, the Queen Caroline affair, or the French Revolution were intensely politicizing experiences. During such periods individuals might feel themselves to be particularly interested or involved in politics in a manner which did not reflect their engagement in current events during less urgent times. The reform crisis does not provide a 'snapshot' of women's political engagement, for it was an exceptional moment. Rather, it provides insights both into the possible means whereby women might identify with the political process and into the strategic interpellation of women as political subjects.

Nonetheless, there were longer term implications. Judith Lewis has argued that female electoral influence was in marked decline by 1832, but contemporary perceptions were often rather different.[124] Indeed, the abolition of most rotten boroughs and the widening of the electorate meant a need for parliamentary candidates to woo a greater proportion of the local population. As noted in Chapter 1, it was from the 1830s that politicians' appeals and allusions to their female constituents became a common phenomenon. This would accord with recent suggestions that the widening of formal electoral participation enhanced opportunities for women to engage in the political process.[125] This was a phenomenon expressed in many female-authored fictional works of the immediate post-reform period. The continuing strength of female electoral influence was delineated, for example, by novelists such as Catherine Gore and Charlotte Bury, whose works continued to engage with the issues the Reform Act raised.[126]

---

[124] Lewis, *Sacred to Female Patriotism*, esp. 198–200. For a contrary impression see the sentiments expressed at a Reading reform meeting: *The Times* (1 Feb. 1831).

[125] Morgan, *Victorian Woman's Place*, 132–3; Gleadle, 'Charlotte Elizabeth Tonna'. See also Thompson, 'Women, Work and Politics', 76.

[126] Gore, *Mrs Armytage, passim*, e.g. i. 103–18. In the family drama *The Hamiltons* Gore offered her own narrative of the reform crisis to deliver an elite Whig message of considered franchise reform: *The Hamiltons: Or the New Aera* (London, 1834, 3 vols), esp. iii. chs 2 and 4. For the centrality of reform politics and debate to Gore's and Bury's novels see Edward Copeland, 'Opera and the Great Reform Act: Silver Fork Fiction, 1822–1842', *Romanticism on the Net*, 34–5 (2004).

Harriet Martin's *Canvassing*, which Maria Edgeworth claimed offered a good account of Irish elections, portrayed women as forming an intricate, if sometimes comical, part of elections—as canvassers, supporters, and spectators.[127] *A Year at Hartlebury, or the Election* published by Benjamin Disraeli and his sister, Sarah in 1834, had references to women's electoral efforts, including a chapter entitled 'The Ladies Canvass'.[128] George Eliot's *Felix Holt* similarly referenced, if ambiguously, the possibility for female interest in the electoral process;[129] whilst Elizabeth Sewell's *Katharine Ashton* alluded to the community balls organized by local political grandees in the post-reform period. As Sewell explained in her autobiography, such events often had a 'political purpose which naturally followed upon the extinction of close boroughs and the efforts of parliamentary candidates to become popular'.[130]

Even so, as we have seen, the Reform Act had uneven implications for women, and its legacy was too complicated for it to be accommodated into narratives of it as a 'watershed'. The tendency to satirize or make light of women's electoral efforts in the novels noted above betrays a continuing unease with female public activity. Meanwhile, other genres, such as electoral ephemera, increasingly referred to women as a gendered collective. This was a discursive process which had the effect of reinscribing sensitivities concerning portrayals of female public activity. The intense politicization of the reform crisis galvanized women as it did men and also provided a fresh stimulus for feminist debate; but for those who lacked self-confidence, the cachet of local authority, or close family involvement, the impact of the reform crisis could be particularly ambiguous. Women might feel the need to reassert their political ineptitude, even as their own commentaries undermined such a stance. The fractured subjectivities articulated by the likes of Elizabeth Wedgwood, Dorothy Wordsworth, and Frances Kemble suggest that women often found it hard to sustain coherent political identities in the

---

[127] Harriet Martin's novel was published in conjunction with one by John Banim under a collaborative pseudonym: 'The O'Hara Family', *The Mayor of Wind-Gap and Canvassing* (London, 1835, 3 vols), iii. 149, 179–80, 235. Maria Edgeworth to Lucy Edgeworth (6 Feb. 1835), Edgeworth, c. 714, fos. 46–9.

[128] Benjamin Disraeli and Sarah Disraeli, *A Year at Hartlebury or the Election with Appendixes by Ellen Henderson and John P. Matthews* (Toronto, 1983; 1st publ. 1834, 2 vols), i. ch. 5. See also George Brittaine, *The Election* (Dublin, 1840), esp. 6, 14.

[129] George Eliot, *Felix Holt* (Harmondsworth, 1997; 1st publ. 1866), e.g. 266, 282, 288.

[130] Elizabeth M. Sewell, *Katharine Ashton* (London, 1854, 2 vols), i. 58–9; Sewell, *Autobiography*, 142.

face of these cultural pressures. Moreover, for many contemporaries politics continued to be viewed as a matter of familial, rather than individual concern. The Reform Act may have enshrined the principles of political independence but a study of women's responses to it suggests a more complex legacy.

6

Land and dynastic subjectivity: the public spheres of Mary Ann Gilbert[1]

Introduction

Restoring women to the political record can result in an emphasis upon exceptional cases. In the course of previous chapters this study has tried to include the experience of the less confident or less engaged women whose voices are nonetheless important in constructing the warp and weft of contemporary political culture. Even so, I would maintain that the phenomenon of exceptionality is an important issue which should also be examined in its own right. Understanding the conditions which enabled particular women to act as influential political agents enables us to analyse the complexities and fissures within the gender order which could be exploited by certain individuals. This chapter considers the public career of one very extraordinary woman, Mary Ann Gilbert (1776–1845). Gilbert was a landed proprietor in Eastbourne in East Sussex. Here and in the neighbouring parishes, she established herself as a leading agricultural expert and poor law reformer. Her activities had a substantial impact on local parochial politics and her work was cited and discussed in parliamentary reports and government commissions.

Whilst the reach of Gilbert's influence may be unusual, she may be situated within the much broader phenomenon of female parochial activity delineated in Part I. Gilbert personifies the overlapping themes of landownership, local influence, and personal authority. Her ability to construct herself as a female expert through cultural confidence and specialized knowledge; her employment of the varying modes of epistolary exchange; her use of ephemeral print culture; and her relationship with parochial

---

[1] In contemporary publications the subject of this chapter was often cited as 'Mrs Davies Gilbert'. Here her husband will be referred to as 'Davies Gilbert', but she will be referred to as 'Mary Ann Gilbert', which is how she usually signed her name.

government all emerge as particularly important themes.[2] In addition, Gilbert's investment in a collective family identity rooted in a pride in her lineage enables us to explore further the salience of dynastic subjectivity, as discussed in Chapter 3.

Excavating Gilbert's career reveals further the hidden history of provincial women whose political landscapes were very different to the imperatives of pressure-group campaigning and liberal causes which have tended to dominate considerations of women's activism. Whilst we know much about women's support for the anti-Corn Law movement, their contribution to the protectionist movement is rarely considered. It will be shown here that for many women of the gentry and middling classes it was land— its management and protection—which was most critical to their politics. Judith S. Lewis has written of the 'political agronomy' of the late Georgian period, noting that, 'it was . . . because of this emphasis on property that politics could become a part of the family economy of the landed classes'.[3] Here I will contend that the ownership of land provided women with more expansive modes of authority than purely that of electoral influence. Assuming responsibility for its careful husbandry could structure an individual's sense of self and be critical to their capacity for authoritative action. The ownership of land might be implicated in a sense of regional or even national identity—drawing variously upon specific or more fluid notions of place. It had the potential to provide an imagined identification with those of lower status, who might be believed to share in a broad understanding of patriotism that depended upon a physical, visceral knowledge of the country's land. Furthermore an individual's relationship to the land, whether as agriculturists, improvers, or proprietors, could be imbricated with an emotional identity to the heritage of one's family. As Klein remarks, 'land was pictured as an inheritance, it was firmly situated in time as well as in place'.[4]

Save for a minor article published in 1956, a biography of her husband Davies Gilbert, and brief allusions to her work in specialist monographs on agricultural reform, Gilbert has been virtually forgotten by historians.[5] She

---

[2] See Chs 1 and 4 above

[3] Lewis, *Sacred to Female Patriotism*, 11.

[4] Lawrence Klein, 'Property and Politeness in the Early Eighteenth-Century Whig Moralists: The Case of the *Spectator*', in John Brewer and Susan Staves (eds), *Early Modern Conceptions of Property* (London, 1995), 223.

[5] A. C. Todd, 'An Answer to Poverty in Sussex', *Agricultural History Review*, 4 (1956), 45–51; Todd, *Beyond the Blaze: A Biography of Davies Gilbert* (Truro, 1967); Burchardt, *Allotment Movement*, 70, 157.

was born in Lewes in 1776 to Thomas and Ann Gilbert and was their only child. Thomas Gilbert, the owner of a grocery business, was the younger son of a wealthy and long-established Eastbourne family; his wife Ann, whom he married in 1771, came from the Cossum family in nearby Hastings. Despite her father's comparatively modest circumstances (caused in part by poor financial management and alcoholism), Gilbert's rich relatives ensured a stimulating upbringing, introducing her to famous politicians and intellectuals.[6] A year after her mother's death in 1807, Gilbert married Davies Giddy (1767–1839), bringing £12,000 to the marriage settlement. In 1816, on the death of her bachelor uncle Charles, Gilbert inherited the family's considerable estates. At this point Davies Giddy assumed the name of Gilbert—a condition stipulated in their marriage settlement—and the couple took up residence in Eastbourne.[7] In Gilbert's day Eastbourne was a quiet town with a population of just under 3,000, and enjoying only modest facilities.[8] Here they proved active in enlarging the family estate, although Davies Gilbert remained MP for Bodmin until 1832. During their marriage, Gilbert gave birth to eight children, four of whom (John, Catherine, Anna, and Hester) survived to adulthood. Their eldest daughter, Mary, suffered from profound disabilities, requiring constant nursing care until her premature death in 1826.[9]

Davies Gilbert had wide-ranging political and scientific interests.[10] He was closely acquainted with the distinguished network of Enlightenment figures who comprised the Lunar Circle, and was intimate with the radical physician Thomas Beddoes. Davies Gilbert dissented from Beddoes's revolutionary enthusiasm, however.[11] Classified as a typical paternalist by historians, he staunchly supported the electoral influence of the landed classes.[12] An MP for Helston (1804–6) and then for Bodmin (1806–32), in 1808 he was appointed to the Board of Agriculture. He also worked with Humphry Davy, to whom he acted as a patron, in the field of agricultural chemistry.

[6] See Mary Ann Gilbert, 'Autobiographical Notes' and also her journal (1803–4), CRO, Enys of Enys papers, EN/1915 and 1917; 'Notes compiled by Mary Ann Gilbert', East Sussex Record Office (ESRO), Davies Gilbert papers, GIL 4/313.

[7] Will of Charles Gilbert (24 Nov. 1815), CRO, Davies Gilbert papers, DD/DG/50.

[8] David Cannadine, *Lords and Landlords: The Aristocracy and the Towns, 1774–1967* (Leicester, 1980), 234–74; A. G. S. Enser, *A Brief History of Eastbourne* (Eastbourne, 1976); Graham Neville, *Religion and Society in Eastbourne, 1735–1920* (Eastbourne, 1982).

[9] For details of the couple's children see the family tree at CRO, DG/116.

[10] See Todd, *Beyond the Blaze.*

[11] Thomas Beddoes to Davies Giddy (18 July 1792), CRO, DG 41/14 and see also DG 41/35.

[12] Bourne, *Patronage and Society*, 57.

In 1817 Gilbert, who was sceptical as to the merits of poor relief, was appointed to a committee to investigate the costs of the poor laws. Ten years later he was elected President of the Royal Society. Davies Gilbert's political interest in poor law reform, his paternalist politics, and involvement in agricultural and scientific advance were subjects that his wife also developed as fields of expertise. What is particularly striking about the work of Mary Ann Gilbert is that it was seen as significant in its own right, quite independent from the career of her husband.

Responding to distress: agricultural reform and the allotment movement

Sussex had experienced chronic unemployment since the cessation of the Napoleonic Wars and rural unrest was sporadic throughout the 1820s.[13] By 1830 the county was once again suffering from desperate levels of unemployment.[14] Sussex was one of the counties worst hit by the Swing riots, with disturbances lasting from October to September for which over fifty were tried.[15] The riots themselves consisted of arson, attacks on machinery and farms, and the spread of anonymous, threatening letters. Appalling economic distress was clearly at the heart of the disorder, but the perception of those involved was that their suffering was exacerbated by insensitive and provocative policies on the part of local elites. This included unfeeling workforce policies (such as the introduction of threshing machines which were thought to contribute to rural unemployment) and a belief that the welfare systems of the parish were failing. The provision of poor relief was a particularly contentious issue in East Sussex. Overseers in Ringmer, for example, were said to be threatened by a group of men demanding 'money or blood'.[16] Needless to say, the poor law commissioners appointed in 1832 saw matters rather differently. Sussex spent more on poor relief than any other county. Commissioners blamed this on overindulgent magistrates who

---

[13] Pamela Horn, *The Rural World 1780–1850: Social Change in the English Countryside* (London, 1980), 85; Roger Wells, 'Social Conflict and Protest in the English Countryside in the Early Nineteenth Century: A Rejoinder', *Journal of Peasant Studies*, 8 (1980–1), 514–30.

[14] J. P. D. Dunbabin, 'The Rise and Fall of Agricultural Trades Unionism in England', in Dunbabin, *Rural Discontent in Nineteenth-Century Britain* (London, 1974), 65.

[15] Eric Hobsbawm and George Rudé, *Captain Swing* (London, 2001; 1st publ. 1969), 170, 308–9.

[16] J. P. Huzel, 'The Labourer and the Poor Law, 1750–1850', in G. E. Mingay (ed.), *The Agrarian History of England and Wales*, vi. *1750–1850* (Cambridge, 1989).

supposedly allowed soaring poor rates and a spirit of idleness to afflict the
entire region.[17]

These problems appear to have been particularly acute in Gilbert's
parish of Eastbourne. Here commissioners asserted that an organized class
of labourers attempted to set their own wage levels and intimidated local
officials into providing higher poor relief. The assistant poor law commissioner for the south-east referred wearily to 'Eastbourne, to the condition
of which we have had so often to refer'.[18] Eastbourne's escalating levels of
poor relief (commissioners claimed able-bodied paupers received more
money from the parish per week than was earned by the average labourer),
and the existence of a forthright and partially organized labouring class
prepared to agitate for greater assistance, fitted perfectly the commissioners'
narrative as to the iniquities of the existing system. But it was not only the
seemingly feckless nature of local labourers and costly poor relief that interested the commissioners in Eastbourne. They were perplexed that local
initiatives to reform local welfare systems had been met with intransigence
by local farmers. The commissioners cited at length an interview with an
Eastbourne farmer, John Mann, who was asked to explain why proposals to
secure employment for paupers and reduce the rates had been rejected. To
the evident frustration of the interviewer Mann insisted that farmers did
not concede the need to lower the poor rates, explaining 'The farmers like
that their men should be paid from the poor-book'.[19]

The schemes to which the commissioner referred were those of Mary
Ann Gilbert.[20] Gilbert had experimented with schemes to reform local
poor relief from the late 1820s but it was the rural disturbances that hit
agricultural England in 1830 which prompted her to more concerted
efforts.[21] She was one of many landed proprietors to have been affected by

---

[17] *Royal Commission of Inquiry into the Administration and Practical Operation of the Poor Laws*
(1834), part 1, ii(4). See also D. A. Baugh, 'The Cost of Poor Relief in South-East England,
1790–1834', *Economic History Review*, 28 (1975), 52.

[18] *Royal Commission*, 65. For helpful background on the emergence of the rural proletariat
see Andrew Charlesworth, 'The Development of the English Rural Proletariat and Social
Protest, 1700–1850: A Comment', *Journal of Peasant Studies*, 8 (1980), 101–11; Roger Wells,
'Mr William Cobbett, Captain Swing and King William IV', *Agricultural History Review*, 45
(1997), 34–48; Roger Wells, 'Rural Rebels in Southern England in the 1830s', in Clive
Elmsley and James Walvin (eds), *Artisans, Peasants and Proletarians, 1760–1860: Essays Presented
to Gwyn A. Williams* (London, 1985), 128.

[19] *Royal Commission*, 63–4; see also 22–3.

[20] Gilbert's many efforts were described in some detail by the poor law commissioners who
cited verbatim from some of her publications: *Royal Commission*, 1490–3.

[21] William Page (ed.), *The Victoria History of the Counties of England: A History of Sussex*, ii
(London, 1907), 208.

the incendiarism during the autumn of 1830, later referring to her 'unremitted endeavours to discover the cause and remedy of the fires by which I was nightly surrounded at Eastbourne for a month in 1830'.[22] In common with many of those affected, she issued a public declaration offering £100 for information.[23] This was the start of a series of ambitious projects to reform the landscape of local welfare provision.

At the heart of Mary Ann Gilbert's schemes lay a preoccupation with agricultural improvement. As we saw in Chapter 4, female landowners might pride themselves on their agricultural expertise and believe it a duty to pass this knowledge on to their tenants. Like other local women such as Mary Frewen and Janet Shuttleworth, with whom she was acquainted, Gilbert took her position as the owner of an estate extremely seriously.[24] She sought to utilize the latest methods in agricultural techniques to bring into cultivation unused tracts of land, such as local shingle to the east of Beachy Head. She proposed to hire the local poor to work on these projects with the aim of negating the need for parish relief. Gilbert's researches into agricultural productivity and land drainage were extensive, earning her a silver medal from the Society for the Encouragement of Arts, Manufacture, and Commerce in 1833. The society awarded a number of prizes to female innovators in the fields of agricultural production, crops, and rural industries; and it was an organization whose 'protectionist and paternalistic aims' accorded well with her own agendas.[25]

The apex of Gilbert's endeavours was the provision of allotments to the local poor. This, she believed, would enable labouring families to provide for themselves even during periods of unemployment. In 1830 she secured 50 allotment tenants, a figure that had risen to 213 five years later. She was eventually to let over 400 plots. Gilbert's work formed part of a broader trend. Such schemes were modestly facilitated by the Select Vestries Act of 1819, which was extended in 1831–2 with some success, and it was at this

---

[22] Printed letter to the SICLC (1 May 1844) in the scrapbook compiled for Mary Ann Gilbert's grandson, Carew Davies Gilbert, CRO, DD/DG/35 (hereafter 'C. D. Gilbert, Scrapbook'), 76.

[23] C. D. Gilbert, Scrapbook, 53.

[24] There is a rich archive relating to Mary Frewen at ESRO, FRE 2780 ff. For Janet Shuttleworth, who was living in nearby Hastings at this time, see Selleck, *James Kay-Shuttleworth*, 176 and *passim*. Her half-sister, Marianne North, refers to the friendship with the Davies Gilberts, see n. 132 below.

[25] Charles Taylor to Mary Ann Gilbert (13 May 1833), CRO, DN/127, 3. For the society itself see Phillips, *Women in Business*, 196–201.

point that the LFS was formed which sought to promote allotments for the poor.[26]

Historians disagree as to the social and cultural significance of the allotment movement. John E. Archer, David Roberts, Roger Wells, and Pamela Horn situate such schemes within the revived paternalism of the early 1830s. Wells, for example, writes that it was part of the 'rapid intensification of paternalism' that accompanied the loss of working people's rights to welfare in 1834. Noting the prizes given for agricultural produce and the award of allotments to those who displayed the values of industry, cleanliness, and thrift, he asserts: 'Many of the benefits paid as a right under the old Poor Law were now bountifully bestowed by the affluent as rewards under the new.'[27] Similarly Archer views the allotment movement as a device for reinforcing gentry authority in the face of growing independence on the part of contemporary farmers.[28] The most recent scholar of the movement, Jeremy Burchardt, dissents, pointing to the radicalism of the movement's founding members. For Benjamin Wills, a key promoter of the movement in its early days, allotments were part of a wider vision of reformed social and economic relationships, which included demands for a minimum wage and the abolition of capitalist monopolies. The movement's core values such as thrift, economy, and land reform further presaged, observes Burchardt, those of mid-Victorian liberalism.[29]

Gilbert's involvement in allotment schemes accords with the argument for a revived paternalism, however. Like other agricultural innovators, such as Thomas Coke, she distributed printed cards to her tenants detailing her requirements. This included the production of manure and compost, and their tenancies could be forfeit if there was evidence of waste in the use of resources.[30] Her measures were designed not only to improve productivity but also to shape the morals and habits of the poor. The pamphlet 'Useful Hints for the Labourer', of which she disseminated over 100 copies

---

[26] For full details see Burchardt, *Allotment Movement*, ch. 3. The poor law commission collated significant amounts of data concerning allotment schemes but further legislation was not forthcoming until 1845 when a General Enclosure Act stipulated (rather unsuccessfully) that allotments had to be provided on waste ground unless there were extenuating circumstances. See also Todd, 'Answer to Poverty'; and pp. 134–6 above.

[27] Wells, 'Rural Rebels', 148–9; Horn, *Rural World*, 142–3; Roberts, *Paternalism*, 118, 132–3.

[28] John E. Archer, 'The Nineteenth-Century Allotment: Half an Acre and a Row', *Economic History Review*, 50 (1997), 21–36, esp. 25–7.

[29] Burchardt, *Allotment Movement*, 74–83.

[30] There are examples of such cards in the scrapbook compiled for Mary Ann Gilbert's grandson, John Sancroft Holmes, CRO, DD.DG/36 (hereafter 'J. S. Holmes, Scrapbook'), 109; Todd, 'Answer to Poverty', 48. For Coke see Horn, *Rural World*, 82.

amongst her allotment tenants, concerned the upbringing of children (including the importance of child labour), bodily hygiene, and money management.[31] This was a paternalism that was increasingly informed by middle-class discourses of missionary activism. As the Lord Bishop of Norwich put it in his speech to the annual meeting of the Society for the Improvement of the Condition of the Labouring Classes (the SICLC, the body which succeeded the LFS in 1844), 'We are in fact, a missionary society.'[32] Although she did not advertise her involvement, Gilbert had close connections with the LFS. She frequently submitted material to their publication, the *Labourers' Friend Magazine*. In addition her work was repeatedly cited and applauded in its publications, and material that she authored was incorporated into the society's clauses and literature.[33] In addition to sharing its views concerning the potential of allotments for resolving the problems of rural poverty and poor law expenditure, Mary Ann Gilbert may also have felt an accord with the premillenarian Evangelicalism which typified many of its supporters.[34] Gilbert appears to have been a staunch ultra-Evangelical: she was opposed to the granting of political rights to non-Protestants and could be extremely hostile to the Roman Catholic faith.[35]

Gilbert's endeavours, as Chapter 4 has argued, were part of a wider phenomenon of female engagement in the politics of land reform and parochial intervention. Neither Gilbert nor those who promoted her work presented it in terms of a feminized philanthropy. Rather, in common with

---

[31] C. D. Gilbert, Scrapbook, p. 25. For Gilbert's authorship of the pamphlets see John Lee to Mary Ann Gilbert (25 Jan. 1840), J. S. Holmes, Scrapbook, 103. Such desires to discipline the local workforce had long been a feature of welfare programmes in the county: Wells, 'Social Conflict'.

[32] *LF* (Aug. 1845), 280.

[33] For examples of Gilbert's contributions to the *LFM* see (no month, 1833), 423; (Dec. 1835), 192; (June 1841), 81–2. References to Gilbert's work in the *LFM* include: (Sept. 1840), 121–5; (May 1841), 67; (July 1841), 91–3; (Aug. 1842), 114–16; (May 1843), 67–9; (July 1843), 93–4; (Oct. 1843), 149–50; (June 1844), 81–2; (Feb. 1847), 28; (Aug. 1850), 137. For Gilbert's contribution to the organization's official literature see: London Metropolitan Archives, SICLC minutes (6 June 1833), ACC/3445/SIC/01/04, 297; J. S. Holmes, Scrapbook, 33.

[34] Other premillenarians associated with the organization included Lord Ashley, Hugh McNeile, and Revd Edward Bickersteth: *LF* (June 1844), 3, 32. According to her husband, Charlotte Elizabeth Tonna, another premillenarian, was extremely influential in the establishment of the SICLC: See his 'Concluding Remarks' in Charlotte Elizabeth Tonna, *Personal Recollections* (London, 1847, 3rd edn), 409–10.

[35] For Gilbert's religious stance see Mary Frewen to John Frewen (19 Apr. 1808), ESRO, FRE 2193 and ESRO, GIL/4/299; *Extracts from Two Letters on the Poor Laws* (1817) in F. G. Enys, Scrapbook, CRO, EN/1924 (hereafter 'F.G. Enys, Scrapbook').

those cited in the earlier chapter, Gilbert considered her projects as part of a broader agenda to intervene in poor law policy. This was a subject she had been researching for many years.[36] Gilbert's hope, as one report explained, was that the allotment schemes would enable the able-bodied man 'who is now merely a pauper, and a consumer only', to be become 'a producer of wealth, and a benefactor too, instead of a burden upon his country'.[37] This was keenly appreciated by her supporters who cited detailed statistics as to the salutary effect of her allotment schemes upon local poor law expenditure.[38]

The public spheres of Mary Ann Gilbert

The nature and execution of Gilbert's projects led her to intervene in a variety of different, sometimes overlapping, publics. This included the local, parochial realm; the virtual public of printed literature and epistolary networks; associational activities; and national policy debates. Within these modes of engagement the significance of gender was often muted or tangential. Nonetheless it formed an integral part of the broader cultural framework which underpinned Gilbert's experiences. On one level she was often successful in suspending or ignoring its implications. Yet as the rest of this chapter will also indicate, Gilbert was simultaneously operating in environments in which her gender was deemed highly relevant. A woman such as Gilbert could negotiate across these conflicting expectations to assume influential roles. This could create tensions however—not least within her family.

Allotment schemes, such as Gilbert's, were the source of friction in many rural communities.[39] Such tensions were acute in Sussex. There was a strong regional tradition of paternalism amongst local landowners which

---

[36] Gilbert collected material relating to the poor law and poor rates from 1803 onwards: CRO, DD/EN/1917. The ESRO attributes *Two Letters on the Poor Laws* (1817) to Gilbert: GIL/4/322.

[37] See newspaper cutting (9 Apr. 1844), C. D. Gilbert, Scrapbook, 77.

[38] When Dr Mackenzie sought to establish a Scottish wing of the SICLC he used Gilbert's schemes as evidence, although his figures ignored the impact of the 1834 legislation upon poor rate expenditure in Sussex. *LF* (Apr. 1847), 54n.

[39] Jeremy Burchardt, 'Rural Social Relations, 1830–50: Opposition to Allotments for Labourers', *Agricultural History Review*, 45 (1997), 165–75; Archer, 'Nineteenth Century Allotment', and Boaz Moselle, 'Allotments, Enclosure, and Proletarianization in Early Nineteenth-Century Southern England', *Economic History Review*, 48 (1995), 494–9.

often conflicted with the agendas of tenant farmers.[40] Gilbert herself was furious that wealthy farmers had monopolized the local select vestry, believing they sanctioned mounting poor law rates to ensure a supply of low-paid labour.[41] As a consequence, by 1830–1 Gilbert was actively intervening in parochial poor law debates. Through meetings, petitions, and the endless circulation of tracts, pamphlets, and handbills, she sought to influence local discussion and rally supporters.

The Davies Gilbert family had set up their own domestic printing press in 1825. This was put to constant use. Gilbert's daughter, Catherine, appears to have been designated the role of principal typesetter (occasionally her sister, Ann contributed) and publications were edited, rewritten, reissued, combined with other contemporary extracts, and recirculated in a dizzying whirl of letters. Prior to vestry meetings efforts would reach a crescendo with a fresh supply of printed matter distributed to encourage ratepayers to use their vote at the forthcoming meeting; and direct appeals were made to parish overseers. Her works were often issued as anonymous handbills or pamphlets, or printed under the names of the estate's agents and bailiffs. The local press was employed too.[42] Gilbert sent anonymous letters to numerous publications, including the *Sussex Advertiser* and the *Brighton Gazette*, lamenting the policies of the select vestry, or offering prizes for readers' ideas concerning the points she raised. An article which appeared in the latter, 'What has been the Effect of Laws for the Relief of the Poor in your Neighbourhood?' discussed Gilbert's Eastbourne schemes and invited readers to direct further inquiries to Mr Starr, her bailiff.[43] Gilbert often used Starr as an intermediary in correspondence relating to her projects,

---

[40] Roberts, *Paternalism*, ch. 4, esp. 122–4.

[41] For the troubled relationship between tenant farmers, landowners, and the vestry see Bryan Keith-Lucas, *The English Local Government Franchise: A Short History* (Oxford, 1952), 13–14. Gilbert launched a particularly scathing attack on the tenant farmers who controlled select vestries in an anonymous letter to the *Brighton Gazette* (6 Mar. 1834).

[42] The Gilbert archive, which is divided between the East Sussex Record Office and the Cornwall Record Office, contains numerous copies and annotated drafts of her many handbills, tracts, pamphlets, letters to the vestry, and newspaper articles (some of which appeared under the pseudonym 'Clericus') as well as other material whose sentiments she supported. Much of this material is pasted into the three substantial scrapbooks assembled for her grandsons: Carew Davies Gilbert, John Sancroft Holmes, and Francis Gilbert Enys. Gilbert used specialist agricultural printers such as C. Putt for some of her work, see J. S. Holmes, Scrapbook, 103. Catherine Gilbert also printed a variety of other kinds of material, mostly of local or family interest. See the family scrapbook in CRO, DG/116. Some pamphlets have pencilled notes at the top indicating the numbers printed and circulated, see e.g. J. S. Holmes, Scrapbook, 95, and C. D. Gilbert scrapbook, 25, 40.

[43] Extract from *Brighton Gazette*, in J. S. Holmes, Scrapbook, 35.

occasionally specifying that material should be directed to 'MG' in the care of Mr Starr.[44]

Gilbert's publications were fluid texts which, in common with the ephemera authored by women such as Mary Simpson,[45] were continuously reworked and recycled, with some texts and phrases (or versions of them) repeatedly reused. She borrowed freely from the work of others, just as she was happy for them to use her content in their publications.[46] Gilbert also participated in complex projects of composite publication. One pamphlet, *Poor Rates Reduced by Self-Supporting Reading, Writing and Agricultural Schools*, a detailed description of Gilbert's Eastbourne projects, bears the name of B. King but Gilbert was clearly intimately involved with its composition. Benjamin King was a local gardener who acted as her agent.[47] The pamphlet articulates Gilbert's views and is dedicated to the Right Reverend A. T. Gilbert, Lord Bishop of Chichester, presumably a relative of hers. A revised version of the text (there were multiple variants of it) was later published in the *Farmers' Almanac* in which certain passages were now attributed to Gilbert.[48] A version of the pamphlet was subsequently bound with a number of other short treatises on the efficacy and potential of the allotment scheme. This appeared under the name of John Nowell, a staunch supporter of Gilbert's work from Huddersfield. Nowell contributed the project's primary work—a paper he had read to a local scientific society which praised her schemes. Extant letters between Nowell and Gilbert reveal that he deferred to Gilbert's views as to the pamphlets that should be included in the collec-

---

[44] C. D. Gilbert, Scrapbook, 53. The editor of the *Mark Lane Express* initially corresponded with John Starr over Gilbert's pamphlet on Malthusianism, evidently believing him to be the author; although his subsequent correspondence was addressed to Gilbert. Cuthbert Johnson to John Starr (Feb. 1838) and enclosures, J. S. Holmes, Scrapbook, 85. Johnson indicates his subsequent awareness of Gilbert's authorship in a letter pasted into J. S. Holmes, Scrapbook, 109.

[45] See above p. 144.

[46] e.g. in one pamphlet she borrowed freely (with his blessing) from an address given by Mr Shaw Lefevre to his tenants. Mary Ann Gilbert to Kitty Gilbert [1837], CRO, EN/1932. Gilbert frequently made use of arguments concerning the superiority of the Scottish poor law system which concur closely with material used in a pamphlet written by the assistant commissioner for the inquiry into the Irish poor, James O'Flynn, *The Present State of the Irish Poor, with the Outlines of a Plan of General Employment* (London, 1835). In 1836 she printed extracts from it, along with her own additional comments on the employment of the poor, C. D. Gilbert, Scrapbook, 32.

[47] J. S. Holmes, Scrapbook, 131. The 1841 census lists a Benjamin King, a gardener and his family, living next to Gilbert. Eastbourne Local History Society, *The 1841 Census for the Parish of Eastbourne, Sussex* (Eastbourne, 1990), 47–8.

[48] *Farmers' Almanac* (1844), 121–6; (1845); 121–9; (1846), 226–7.

tion. Their correspondence also reveals that Gilbert contributed (at the least) particular phrases to his text, although Gilbert declined to have the material attributed to her.[49]

Gilbert's wish to obscure her identity was not necessarily because of her gender. Many of her husband's publications were also anonymous.[50] As Robert J. Griffin argues, 'Anonymity during this period . . . was at least as much a norm as signed authorship'.[51] Whilst recent scholarship has focused upon women's contribution to the emergent republic of letters, Gilbert's œuvre points to the continuing importance of older, traditional practices of collaborative and anonymous authorship. This was in keeping with the literary dynamics of the rural public sphere: anonymous letters, handbills, and advertisements, not to mention the avalanche of ephemera circulated during election times, were a common feature of provincial print culture.[52] Individuals might feel empowered to intervene in local politics not because of the emergence of a classic Habermasian public sphere facilitating the expression of liberal individualism, but through the more amorphous authorial identities practised in rural publicity.

Gilbert's employment of the modes of the rural public sphere did secure some successes. In March 1832 she informed the select vestry that she had hired all surplus labourers in the parish to cultivate a piece of marsh land using local shingle. She proposed, apparently unsuccessfully, to provide these labourers with small plots of land and also offered to continue to hire surplus labour in this way, providing the parish furnished her with the materials to erect gates for the allotments. In April 1832 she was successful in persuading the vestry to adopt a proposal that underemployed labourers should be provided with seeds and hired to cultivate land. The labourers

---

[49] John Nowell to Mary Ann Gilbert (18 Jan. 1844), J. S. Holmes, Scrapbook, 131. Compare John Nowell, *On Self-Supporting Schools of Industry and Mental Discipline* (Huddersfield, 1844) [pamphlet bound into Nowell, *An Essay*], 29–30, with Nowell, *Manual of Field Gardening, or Belgian Agriculture Explained* (Huddersfield, 1846), 119, and Nowell, *Manual of Field Gardening* (Huddersfield, 1845), 106–7.

[50] e.g. *A Cornish Dialogue between Tom. Pengersick and Dic. Trengurtha* (Eastbourne, 1830) and *Cursory Observations on the Act for Ascertaining the Bounties and for Regulating the Exportation and Importation of Corn* (London, 1804).

[51] Robert J. Griffin, 'Introduction', in Griffin (ed.), *The Faces of Anonymity: Anonymous and Pseudonymous Publication from the Sixteenth Century to the Twentieth Century* (Basingstoke, 2003), 6.

[52] This remains an under-researched field, but see Edward P. Thompson, 'The Crime of Anonymity', in Douglas Hay *et al.* (eds), *Albion's Fatal Tree: Crime and Society in Eighteenth-Century England* (Harmondsworth, 1975), 255–308, and the editors' introduction in Barker and Vincent, *Language, Print and Electoral Politics*.

were required to repay their start-up costs but were permitted to keep any subsequent profits. In September that year seven paupers did enter into an agreement with the Eastbourne vestry to forego part of their poor relief in exchange for hiring small plots of land. It would appear that the scheme was aborted when the labourers concerned failed to fulfil all of Gilbert's stringent conditions, however.[53]

Gilbert articulated her motives explicitly in an address she published the following year, 'To the Tenants of Chough Brook Marsh'. Here she explained that she had purchased this land with the express purpose of addressing the issue of poor relief. It would enable her to provide local labourers with gardens and she explained that, in lieu of rent, she would accept shingle.[54] In November that year she published a letter to the parish overseers criticizing what she perceived to be their indiscriminate provision of poor relief to the able-bodied. In January 1834 Gilbert managed to persuade a reluctant vestry to levy a labour rate. But she had to fight hard for every measure and victory could never be assured. Later that year the tenants of the local earl voted en masse against a proposal she publicized for the hiring of surplus labour.[55]

As this complicated history indicates, the relationship between Gilbert, the vestry, and local farmers was not one of unabated hostility. In November 1834 she came to an amicable agreement with the parish concerning the upkeep of the local fire engine; and a number of local farmers took up her ideas for the installation of specially designed tanks to store liquid manure after one poor law guardian circulated her pamphlet on the matter. Equally, some of the agricultural awards she organized were supported by local farmers.[56] All the same, her relationship with both constituencies remained tense. In 1838 she issued a fresh batch of pamphlets as to the short-sightedness of parochial policy when the vestry voted to institute a rural police: 'To Proprietors is submitted the consideration whether many men employed in profitable labour by day, would not be more likely to prevent depredation than a few men patrolling the parish by

[53] Mary Ann Gilbert to Richard Whately (1832), J. S. Holmes, Scrapbook, 11. See also printed ephemera, ibid. 19, 35; ESRO, DE/B28/4 and F. G. Enys, Scrapbook.

[54] C. D. Gilbert scrapbook, 9. See also the printed pamphlets, ibid. 5.

[55] Parish of Eastbourne vestry papers, ESRO, DE/B/29/34, J. S. Holmes, Scrapbook. Todd, 'Answer to Poverty'. Vestries lost the right to levy labour rates under the new poor law. See Anthony Brundage, *The English Poor Laws, 1700–1930* (Basingstoke, 2002), 57.

[56] Vestry minutes (25 Oct. and 15 Nov. 1838, 11 Apr. 1839), ESRO, DE/A1/4; DE/B/29/40; letters from Mary Ann Gilbert to 'Kitty' (her daughter, Catherine) (7 July 1835 and Jan. 1836), CRO, EN/1932; R. Joanes to Mary Ann Gilbert (10 Feb. 1840), ESRO, GIL/3/27.

night'.[57] Local sensitivities concerning Gilbert's interventions emerged plainly in the evidence given to the poor law commissioners. John Mann explained that Eastbourne farmers were staunchly opposed to landed proprietors attending the vestry meetings.[58] Whilst local women were free to participate in the Eastbourne vestry (some women of lesser social standing did attend and vote) Gilbert herself appeared to appreciate the need to keep some distance and was often represented at meetings by her bailiff, John Starr.[59]

However, in her response to the Poor Law Amendment Act, Gilbert revealed that as a local paternalist she could make political alliances with the local poor which could enable her to have a dramatic impact upon parochial policy. Sussex was one of the first counties to be divided into unions, and Eastbourne was incorporated into the Eastbourne Union along with a number of neighbouring parishes on 25 March 1835. The new system quickly aroused heated opposition in Eastbourne. The Eastbourne Union was highly unusual in the south-east for the level of organization attained by the anti-Poor Law agitation, with an Agricultural Labourers' Benefit Society established in 1835. In addition, a series of mass meetings were organized in Eastbourne and its neighbouring parishes against the provisions of the Act. The separation of families within the workhouse was particularly contentious and dissatisfaction reached a climax with a 'near riot' in the Eastbourne workhouse in 1835. It was not only the labourers who were exerting pressure. Gilbert arranged a parish meeting attended by the poor law guardians of the fourteen parishes of the union to protest against the separation of spouses. The poor law commissioners were clearly unnerved by the level of hostility the policy of spousal separation aroused in Eastbourne and recommended a climb-down. Their response amounted to a deferral to Gilbert's ideas, suggesting that rather than admitting married paupers to the workhouse they should initially be given relief 'in return for work performed for the parish'—a proposal that was immediately acted upon.[60]

---

[57] 'Rural Police' (4 Jan. 1838), F. G. Enys, Scrapbook, and C. D. Gilbert, Scrapbook, 46. For parochial debates on the merits of a rural constabulary, see Eastwood, *Governing Rural England*, ch. 9.

[58] *Royal Commission*, 63.

[59] Eastbourne vestry minutes, Dec. 1837, ESRO, DE/A1/4. For evidence of female participation in the Eastbourne vestry: ESRO, DE/B/29/34.

[60] C. D. Gilbert, Scrapbook, 25; Todd, 'Answer to Poverty', 48; Hobsbawm and Rudé, *Captain Swing*, 284; Nicholas Edsall, *The Anti-Poor Law Movement, 1834–44* (Manchester, 1971), 31–2. There were cases of assaults on relieving officers in Eastbourne in 1835: Philip Harling, 'The

As Gilbert's intervention in this issue establishes, her efforts were not simply based upon local concerns, but were rooted in a wider knowledge of national policy debates. The poor law commissioners had ensured a 'barrage of publicity' for their findings by releasing, a year before the publication of its report, a 400-page volume of extracts from the assistant commissioners' preliminary report.[61] The ensuing pamphlet debate was a process in which Gilbert herself played a part, now experimenting with a variety of methods for the wider circulation of her publications.[62] As the multiple handbill drafts, letters, and pamphlets in the Gilbert archives demonstrate, Gilbert was highly critical of the centralizing nature of the bill. She believed the establishment of a poor law commission to be an iniquitous departure from parochial autonomy.[63] In circulating these concerns Gilbert did not draw upon any distinctly feminized public identity. Whilst most of her works were anonymous, those that she did issue in her own name (usually those designed for a local readership) were typically signed 'M. A. Gilbert', rather than, say, 'Mrs Gilbert'. It was the Gilbert name she wished to foreground and not her gender.[64]

Gilbert also drew upon her access to elite networks of specialist expertise and her privileged position as a landed proprietor. Correspondents reacted to her accordingly. In 1833 Gilbert sent Edwin Chadwick, the poor law commissioner, a copy of one of her agricultural reports. His reply, which Gilbert heavily annotated, shows that he responded to her primarily as an owner of landed property. For example, he sent her documents which outlined the ways in which the proposed legislation would increase the

---

Power of Persuasion. Central Authority, Local Bureaucracy and the New Poor Law', *English Historical Review*, 107 (1992), 40n.

[61] Gertrude Himmelfarb, *The Idea of Poverty: England in the Early Industrial Age* (London, 1984), 155.

[62] A pamphlet on the employment of the poor is annotated to the effect that 'a copy was sent to every Dean and Chapter under cover to the Bishop of their Diocese': J. S. Holmes, Scrapbook, 95. A pamphlet entitled 'Justification of Magistrates' was circulated to all Lord Lieutenants and London newspapers in July 1844. She also used the LFS to circulate her literature: C. D. Gilbert, Scrapbook, 19, 62–3, 70. Gilbert appears to have been involved in lobbying local parliamentarians too: J. S. Holmes, Scrapbook, 49.

[63] For full details on the Act and debate on its consequences consult Peter Dunkley, 'Whigs and Paupers: The Reform of the English Poor Laws, 1830–1834', *Journal of British Studies*, 20 (1981), 124–49; Anthony Brundage, 'The Landed Interest and the New Poor Law: A Reappraisal of the Revolution in Government', *English Historical Review*, 87 (1972), 27–48; Peter Mandler, 'The Making of the New Poor Law *Redivivus*', *Past and Present*, 117 (1987), 131–57.

[64] e.g. C. D. Gilbert, Scrapbook, 9.

value of her property and provided her with material for local circulation.[65] Richard Whately, Archbishop of Dublin (and former professor of political economy at Oxford), who chaired the royal commission on the condition of the Irish poor 1833–6 was another of her correspondents.[66] Whately similarly responded to Gilbert in her capacity as a local landowner. Evidently alert to Gilbert's status within the local community, he recommended that she organize a labourers' petition concerning the ill-effects of high poor rates.[67] In addition to providing information concerning the forthcoming report of the commissioners, he encouraged her to publicize her schemes in the press and proposed that the two of them continue to exchange ideas. Gilbert's husband had parliamentary expertise in this field, but neither Whately nor Chadwick mentioned his interest in these matters and Gilbert was treated by both as an independent political agent. Whilst Whately sometimes adopted the role of adviser, cautioning against her proposal to distribute prizes to her tenants for example, he also relied upon her expertise.[68] Whately has been associated with a misogynistic stance, but his letters reveal the extent to which his work drew upon an epistolary network of intellectual women.[69]

Gilbert seems to have concurred with Whately's advice to mobilize local people. At least three petitions from Eastbourne were directly organized by her. In February 1834 she was responsible for a petition to parliament requesting that it extend the term of the Labour Rate Act, evidently issued to coincide with the publication of Chadwick's bill. In 1841 she appears to have instigated two further petitions, one of which she herself

---

[65] Edwin Chadwick to Mary Ann Gilbert (9 Dec. 1833), J. S. Holmes, Scrapbook, 37; C. D. Gilbert, Scrapbook, 15.

[66] Whately was responsible for first alerting Gilbert to the possibility of cultivating coastal land in 1831: *LFM* (Feb. 1835), 34. Whately was a fierce opponent of outdoor relief to the able-bodied. A full study of Whately's career is provided in Donald Harman Akenson, *A Protestant in Purgatory: Richard Whately, Archbishop of Dublin* (Hamden, Conn., 1981).

[67] Richard Whately (who often signed himself as 'Dublin') to Mary Ann Gilbert (12 May 1833), J. S. Holmes, Scrapbook, 13.

[68] Letters from Richard Whately to Mary Ann Gilbert (11 and 24 Mar., 28 Nov. 1832, 22 July and 27 Apr. 1833, 18 Sept. 1835). He also assisted her when the assistant commissioners' investigations into Gilbert's schemes suggested lower rates of success to those which she claimed. Richard Whately to Mary Ann Gilbert (14 July 1838). All letters at J. S. Holmes, Scrapbook, 11, 13. The Gilbert archive also contains numerous references to the schemes of Whately's brother, Thomas, in Cookham, Berks.

[69] William John Fitzpatrick, *Memoirs of Richard Whately, Archbishop of Dublin: With a Glance at his Contemporaries and Time* (London, 1864, 2 vols), see esp. i. 96, 102, 376, 379; Whately, *Life and Correspondence*, see esp. his correspondence with Miss Crabtree, Anna Gurney, Mrs Arnold, and Mrs Hill. See the entries listed in the index under 'Letters', and also ii. 170–1.

signed, using the non-gendered signature 'M. A. Gilbert'. The latter, presented to the Lords, was from the 'principal rate payers of Eastbourne', asking for a revision in the poor law—particularly with regard to the assessment of rates so as to augment proprietors' influence. She also drafted another petition, addressed to the 'clergy of England', proposing that proprietors should be responsible for poor law rates.[70] In addition in April 1834 Gilbert was behind an open letter to Lord Althorp (a member of the cabinet committee which drafted the poor law amendment bill) ostensibly from 'John Starr' and issued to protest against the proposal's centralizing measures. She further lobbied for change to the proposed legislation through incessant pamphlets and tracts. Again, these were often designed to appear just before readings of the new poor law bill. Gilbert appears to have been closely involved with the production of two very similar pamphlets in 1834 entitled, *A Clue to the Cause of Falling Rents* and *A Clue to the Cause of Dear Bread and Fallen Rents*. They appeared under the pseudonym 'a landed proprietor', which was in keeping with Gilbert's strategy of privileging her landed identity as the basis for public intervention. They repeated points and examples frequently used by her (such as the benefits of stall feeding and spade husbandry). The pamphlets were indicative of the contemporary concern that England was distinct from its sister kingdoms in charging ratepayers for the relief of the locally settled poor. This particularly exercised Gilbert, who frequently adverted to the superiority of the Scottish poor laws.[71]

After the bill's passage she continued to lobby for its repeal, insisting that the role of the landed gentry should be reinstated in local poor law decisions. In July 1835 she printed a proposal that landowners should be allowed to pay the poor rates levied on their tenants, and appoint their own guardians and relieving officers.[72] As well as publishing material in specialist

---

[70] Petition from the Parishioners of East Bourne (7 Feb. 1834), J. S. Holmes, Scrapbook, 45; F. G. Enys, Scrapbook, contains further details of the petitions.

[71] Goldsmith's Library, University of London, attributes both these pamphlets to 'Arch Scott'. Gilbert was a patron of an Archibald Scott, an agricultural reformer from East Lothian. The two corresponded closely on the issues raised in the pamphlets and information was clearly circulated and reproduced between them. F. G. Enys, Scrapbook. See also Archibald Scott to Mary Ann Gilbert (6 June 1836 and 6 May 1837), in J. S. Holmes, Scrapbook, 77, 83. Gilbert's pamphlet 'Justification of Magistrates', which she circulated widely, also used the identity of 'a proprietor', C. D. Gilbert, Scrapbook, 19. For debate on the contrasts between Scottish and English poor laws see Joanna Innes, 'The Distinctiveness of the English Poor Laws, 1750–1850', in Donald Winch and Patrick K. O'Brien (eds), *The Political Economy of British Historical Experience* (Oxford, 2002), 381–408.

[72] C. D. Gilbert, Scrapbook, 29.

agricultural journals, Gilbert used her membership of the SICLC to push the point home. In 1844 she issued an open letter to the organization which she circulated to the national press.[73] This reiterated her commitment to the society's projects but stated that a wider reform of poor law policy was also required. Gilbert argued for a strengthening of traditional local hierarchies, insisting that the clergy should be made *ex officio* guardians. She also demanded that the pecuniary qualification for parochial guardians be abolished. Instead, Gilbert wanted 'those authorised to vote [to] appoint the persons they believe to be the most trustworthy'. She favoured greater openness and accountability, arguing that the boards of guardians and their accounts should be open to scrutiny by all ratepayers. By this period Gilbert herself was acting as one of the seventeen guardians for the Eastbourne Union, presumably deciding that this was a pragmatic means to ensure that her views were felt.[74]

In the mean time, Gilbert had been further refining her expertise in agricultural science. By the mid-century the genre of agricultural literature was well-established and many echelons of the farming community were active in disseminating and promoting such material.[75] Women such as Gilbert could be closely involved in these processes. Contemporary farming journals had no compunction about advertising the experiments of female farmers.[76] Mary Wedlake, for example, ran a highly successful engineering business specializing in reduced-weight farm tools. The enterprise had an office close to Mark Lane, the focal point of farming journalism and associational life. The Royal Agricultural Society distributed her catalogue of farm implements along with their journal.[77] Gilbert similarly established contacts at the heart of such ventures, contributing articles and letters to specialist publications such as the farming newspaper *Mark Lane Express*.[78] In common with many contemporary agriculturists she was particularly interested in Belgian methods of husbandry. Like Anne Vavasour she undertook a tour of that country in the late 1830s to better familiarize herself with its agrarian techniques. Her visit convinced

---

[73] *The Times* (2 May 1844), *Church and State Gazette* (10 May 1844), *Ecclesiastical Gazette* (14 May 1844), C. D. Gilbert, Scrapbook, 76.

[74] C. D. Gilbert, Scrapbook, 67.

[75] Nicholas Goddard, 'Agricultural Literature and Societies', in Mingay, *Agrarian History*, 370.

[76] See e.g. the case of Mrs Deman: *Farmers' Journal* (22 Jan. 1844).

[77] G. E. Fussell, 'Review', *Technology and Culture*, 12 (1971), 350–1.

[78] Cuthbert Johnson to Mary Ann Gilbert [n.d.], J. S. Holmes, Scrapbook, 109; the *Farmers' Magazine* also has articles written from Eastbourne concerning the agricultural innovations with which Gilbert was associated: (Mar. 1838), 182–3.

her of the utility of stall-feeding cattle. She believed it facilitated the efficient collection of manure, allowed more effective use to be made of pasture, and for more stringent feeding practices to be introduced for the welfare of stock. On her return Gilbert established the Willingdon School. This was a largely self-supporting venture which applied Belgian methods of husbandry and was conceived as a development to the allotment scheme. The salaries of school teachers were saved by allowing them to rent land. The schoolboys were taught literacy, accounting, husbandry, and stall feeding in the mornings; and after lunch assisted the teacher in cultivating a small farm of five acres. An associated girls' school was later to provide female instruction in household economy and domestic management. The success of the Willingdon School prompted Gilbert to establish two further institutions in East Dean and Pevesney. Gilbert made much of the fact that the schools she established were run by men who had formerly been workhouse inmates. They thus contributed to her broader argument of the need for imaginative and constructive approaches to poor law relief.[79]

The local public sphere therefore provided a testing and dynamic environment in which Gilbert sought to exert the influence of landed authority and agricultural expertise. Utilizing a whole variety of techniques she intervened rigorously in the cut and thrust of parochial politics; but her agenda was also framed as a response to the ongoing national debate concerning poor law policy. To date historical attention upon elite female responses to the Poor Law Amendment Act has inevitably focused upon the work of Harriet Martineau, who was employed as a propagandist for the measure by the Whig government. As a result little consideration has been given to those women who campaigned against the new law, both on its passage and in subsequent years. In novels (such as Elizabeth Sewell's *Katharine Ashton* (1854) and Charlotte Elizabeth Tonna's *Helen Fleetwood* (1841)) but also in dedicated pamphlets and prose publications, women contributed to the rich public discussion of poor law policy. Melesina Trench used her review of the Irish writer, Mary Leadbeater's *Cottage Comforts* as a platform for the consideration of wider poor law principles.[80] As we have seen in Chapters 1 and 4, it was common for philanthropists such as Mary Barber, Mary Bayly, Margaret Fison, Frances Power Cobbe,

---

[79] Nowell, *On Self-Supporting Schools*. For Anne Vavasour see p. 134 above.

[80] Mary Leadbeater, *Cottage Dialogues among the Irish Peasantry* (London, 1811). Melesina Trench (1768–1827) also wrote poetry and works on education. Her extant archive includes copies of the reviews she wrote of Leadbeater's work. I have not to date traced where the review was published. Hampshire Record Office, Austen-Leigh papers, 23M93/4/1.

Ellen Barlee, and Elizabeth Pease to critique poor law policy, both at the national and parochial level in their printed interventions. The belief of the Birmingham campaigner Mrs Toll that the press had proved the most affective medium for agitating on such issues as the poor law also points towards a hitherto unexplored vein of anonymous female local journalism on these themes.[81] Whilst these interventions represent the high point of Victorian women's philanthropy they should also be situated within the specific chronology of local female authority which Gilbert's career so well exemplifies.

Gilbert's authority derived not only from her status as a local landowner: her expertise in the fields of agricultural science and poor law policy were critical to her capacity for authoritative action. As in the case of other female experts, the construction of an epistolary network of specialist correspondents was critical in establishing such a persona.[82] This included not only Whately and Chadwick, but a much wider circle of correspondents. Some of these, such as Brailsford Henry Beedham, a member of the Royal Geographical Society, and the American reformer, Henry Coleman, themselves approached Gilbert.[83] Others, like Edward Sabine, secretary of the Royal Society 1827–9, whom she persuaded to disseminate her work, she presumably knew through her husband's contacts.[84] However she established most of her epistolary relationships independently, being assiduous in approaching politicians, scientists, clerics, political economists, and philanthropists with information about her schemes. Some (including Harriet Martineau, Jane Marcet, the Earl of Chichester, and Lord Morpeth) politely declined her invitations to visit the estate.[85] Even so, those whom she contacted clearly felt obliged to respond within the code of genteel politeness and her initiatives often led to important collaborations. Of particular significance was her association with William Blacker, the land agent for the Earl of Gosford and Colonel Close on their estates in North Armagh. He was an authoritative figure in the networks of land reform. Blacker was

---

[81] Mrs Toll to M. W. Chapman (7 Jan. 1844), Boston Public Library, MS A.9.2.20, 7.

[82] See above pp. 49–50, 54–5, 152.

[83] B. H. Beedham to Mary Ann Gilbert (8 Mar. 1845), Henry Coleman to Mary Ann Gilbert (10 Mar. 1845), J. S. Holmes, Scrapbook, 139.

[84] Edward Sabine (12 Oct. 1844) to Mary Ann Gilbert, J. S. Holmes, Scrapbook, 133.

[85] Letters to Mary Ann Gilbert from Jane Marcet (24 Apr. 1833), Harriet Martineau [n.d.], Sydney Smith (5 Feb. 1841), Lord Morpeth (9 Jan. 1843), J. S. Holmes, Scrapbook, 31, 35, 96, 109, 123. Whilst dissenting from her conclusions, Gilbert approved of Martineau's wish to openly discuss the moral implications of political economy: Mary Ann Gilbert to Richard Whately (1832), ibid. 11.

often cited by such publications as the *Farmers' Journal* and appeared as an expert witness before the House of Commons select committee inquiry into the state of agriculture in 1836. He liaised with other female proprietors such as Lady Frances Basset of Cornwall, but collaborated particularly closely with Gilbert. They promoted the same agricultural techniques and there is evidence to suggest they coordinated their publicity.[86] Gilbert also cultivated the support of prominent protectionists like George Law, the Bishop of Bath and Wells; Charles Shaw Lefevre, chair of the Commons' committee on agricultural distress; agricultural journalists like Cuthbert Johnstone; and experts in husbandry such as the Reverend W. Rham, whose knowledge of Flemish husbandry greatly influenced her.[87]

For Gilbert the letter was in keeping with the mode of personal influence that was important to her identity as a landed proprietor. It also provided her with an acceptable avenue to other kinds of publics. Thus she composed letters for wider consumption to be read aloud at agricultural meetings. These letters often flaunted the 'no politics' rule of agricultural societies by their overt support for the protectionist cause. Earl Fitzwilliam's decision to read one of Gilbert's letters to a York meeting was reported to have caused considerable discomfort to the anti-Corn Law members present.[88] George Webb Hall, a Bristolian active in agricultural associations and the protectionist cause, read a similar communication by Gilbert to a meeting of the British Association in Manchester; as did Alexander Dunlop,

[86] William Blacker, *Review of Charles Shaw Lefevre, Esq.'s Letter to his Constituents* (London 1837); Blacker, *Prize Essay, Addressed to the Agricultural Committee of the Royal Dublin Society* (Dublin, 1834); Blacker, *An Essay on the Improvement to be Made in the Cultivation of Small Farms* (Dublin, 1837); *Farmers' Journal* (14 Nov. 1842); William Blacker to Mary Ann Gilbert (20 Apr. 1845), J. S. Holmes, Scrapbook, 141. Gilbert also circulated extracts from Blacker's work in pamphlet form, ESRO, GIL/4/324.

[87] Cuthbert Johnson to Mary Ann Gilbert [1841], George Law to Mary Ann Gilbert (14 Aug. 1834), J. S. Holmes, Scrapbook, 109, 55. Law's own allotment schemes were alluded to in a pamphlet which clearly emanates from the Gilbert camp, bearing the authorial signature of B. King (Gilbert's agent): *A Poor Man's Mite towards the Relief of the Distressed Classes, Addressed to Members of Parliament* (1842). William Lewis Rham founded a school of industry very similar to those established by Gilbert in Winfield, Berks. He was active in the Royal Society of Agriculture and enjoyed a Europe-wide reputation as a scientific agriculturist: e.g. William Lewis Rham, *The Dictionary of the Farm* (London, 1844). Gilbert put other interested parties in touch with Rham, Joseph Yorke to Mary Ann Gilbert (22 June 1842), J. S. Holmes, Scrapbook, 117.

[88] John Nowell to Mary Ann Gilbert (18 Jan. 1844), J. S. Holmes, Scrapbook, 131. Fox, 'Local Farmers' Associations', 59 n. 32.

the Scottish poor law reformer, at a meeting of the Highland Agricultural Society.[89] Gilbert was not exceptional in having her views aired in this way. In one year alone (1847–8) the following women had letters read out to the SICLC: Mrs Dumaresq, Miss Marriott, Lady Caroline Murray, Miss Hawkins, Mrs Leycester, Mrs Bartlett, Miss Alexander, Miss Winter, Miss Frazor, Miss Portal, Miss Newcombe, Lady Falmouth, and Lady Emily Foley.[90] Men also commonly composed letters for public readings, but there was an obvious gender asymmetry—they also had the option to read their texts aloud at meetings themselves. I have found no examples of women acting in such a capacity. Women's epistolary exchanges could position them as authoritative experts within the virtual sphere of correspondence or the interpersonal dynamics of the parochial realm. Once translated to the wider public sphere these interventions assumed a gendered profile. Whilst Gilbert's gender was not an important factor in either the discussion or promotion of her work, her own interaction with the public sphere was nonetheless structured through normative gendered codes.

Responses to Mary Ann Gilbert's work

Gilbert's estate came to be viewed as a model scheme by a wide range of reforming journalists, landowners, and clerics who viewed her projects in the late 1830s and 1840s.[91] The Earl of Dartmouth instituted an allotment system in his Yorkshire estates after his tour.[92] A group of Herefordshire clergy followed suit, adopting a scheme in their area and advertising Gilbert's influence in their local newspaper. Gilbert's schemes were presented as the inspiration behind similar projects in Huddersfield and Surrey, as a report in *The Times* noted in 1844, and her work was cited in

---

[89] *LFM* (Aug. 1842), 114; Alexander Dunlop to Mary Ann Gilbert (31 Jan. 1844), J. S. Holmes, Scrapbook, 131. For further examples see *LF* (June 1844), 81–2; John Nowell, *An Essay on Cottage Allotments, or Field Garden Cultivation* (Huddersfield, 1844), 6.

[90] *LF* (1847–8).

[91] Note that there were some dissenting voices, as her daughter admitted: Hester Gilbert to Ann Dorothea Gilbert (30 Nov. 1867), ESRO, GIL/4/365/5; *Sussex Advertiser* (6 May 1845). Robert Peel hinted that her schemes might only suit particular parishes: Robert Peel to Mary Ann Gilbert (11 Feb. 1841), J. S. Holmes, Scrapbook, 109. By 1845 however, Peel was recommending the allotment system in parliament: C. D. Gilbert, Scrapbook, 17. The visitors' book which Gilbert kept at her school reveals an impressive list of visitors: C. D. Gilbert, Scrapbook, 3 and *passim*.

[92] Nowell, *An Essay on Cottage Allotments*, 9.

provincial farmers' clubs by sympathetic supporters.[93] MP Edward D. Davenport similarly alluded to the importance of Gilbert's schemes in his essay, 'How to Improve the Condition of the Labouring Classes' for the *Farmers' Almanac*.[94]

Gilbert's work was also seen as valuable by agents in the emerging professionalization of government policy. Her industrial schools received a generally favourable report from the Committee of the Council on Education following a visit by Seymour Tremenheere, an inspector of schools in 1842. When Tremenheere was appointed as a poor law commissioner he liaised with another commissioner, Edward Carleton Tufnell (who was very familiar with Gilbert and her work), to arrange a return visit, explaining that her scheme made an important contribution to debates on political economy. The resultant visit produced a lively exchange of views between Tremenheere and Gilbert as to the merits of the government's poor law policies.[95] Other educationists such as Professor Daubeney, another visitor to Eastbourne, also wrote positively of the project.[96] In addition a number of those associated with Gilbert's work were called as witnesses before the parliamentary committee into allotments. This included the Reverend J. M. Maxfield, chair of the Huddersfield board of guardians and a keen promoter of her schemes, and Mr Thynne, who was enthusiastically following Gilbert's schemes in Yorkshire. Mr Cruttenden, one of Gilbert's allotment tenants and conductor of the Willingdon School, provided written evidence.[97] When William Blacker submitted a report to parliament in 1845 he reprinted a letter of Gilbert's in the appendix, and her work was similarly lauded by John Mackenzie in his evidence to the 1844 inquiry into the Scottish poor law.[98] Gilbert's name carried sufficient capital that campaigners might wish to identify themselves with her work even after her death. At a public meeting held in 1847 to establish the

---

[93] Nowell, *On Self-Supporting Schools*, 26, 30; Nowell, *An Essay on Farms of Industry* (1844), 7; *The Times* (25 Nov. 1844); Stewponey Farmers' Club, *Essays on Various Subjects by Members of the Stewponey Farmers' Club during the Year, 1844* (Stourbridge, 1845), 76.

[94] *Farmers' Almanac* (1846), 226–7.

[95] Seymour Tremenheere to Mary Ann Gilbert (10 and 12 Sept. 1842); poor law commissioners also corresponded with Gilbert concerning the report on the sanitary condition of the labouring poor: J. S. Holmes, Scrapbook, 119; Minutes of the Committee of the Council on Education (1842–3), CRO, DD.DG.153/2.

[96] Nowell, *On Self-Supporting Schools*, 24.

[97] Nowell, *Manual of Field Gardening*, 119; Nowell, *On Self-Supporting Schools*, 27, 30; *Report of the Select Committee to Inquire into the Allotment System* (1843), pp. viii, 40–7, 70–80, 146.

[98] Willim Blacker to Mary Ann Gilbert (8 Mar. 1845), J. S. Holmes, Scrapbook, 139; *Poor Law Inquiry (Scotland)* (1844), appendix, part 2, 130; see also *The Times* (4 Mar. 1845).

Scottish arm of the LFS, Mackenzie noted that he had 'inspected the small tenantry of the late Mrs Davies Gilbert, at Eastbourne'.[99]

Those who described or portrayed Gilbert's efforts rarely did so within a gendered discourse. The reports cited above emphasized rather her social and economic status through telling references to 'her village', and 'tenantry'. The subtle undertones of deference are similarly apparent in the report of Gilbert's work published in *Chambers' Edinburgh Journal* which was confident that 'the public is already partly aware of the benevolent proceedings of Mrs Davies Gilbert upon her estate in Sussex'. This publication quoted a report from the *Norwich Mercury*, which, whilst noting that the achievements at Eastbourne had been effected by an 'elderly lady', affirmed that Gilbert's exertions 'are prompted entirely by a sense of justice to those who have not land, and expediency to those who have'.[100] As this matter of fact explanation suggests, to describe Gilbert's activities as 'benevolent' was not to associate them with a feminized philanthropy. 'Benevolence' was the term most commonly used by male-dominated organizations such as the LFS to promote their work.[101]

If the concept of benevolence was frequently employed to convey the nature of Gilbert's work, then so too was that of patriotism. One archdeacon wrote approvingly of the 'success of your benevolent & truly patriotic efforts to promote industry & good conduct amongst our agricultural population';[102] and the *Sussex Advertiser* hoped 'she may live to reap her reward in the wide adoption of views as firmly founded in truth as they are prompted by a warm and true patriotism'.[103] The allotment movement was imbued with the discourse of patriotism, the LFS often dwelling upon images of the British labourer's 'heart of oak'.[104] Gilbert's pamphlets similarly drew upon an emotional identification of 'Englishmen's' relationship with the 'native soil' as a factor which united both proprietor and labourer.[105] Hers was a patriotism which drew not upon gendered associations of women's functions as mothers or auxiliaries to national causes. It was predicated upon a profound attachment to the country's physical landscape and rooted in a detailed knowledge of how to manage its resources

---

[99] *LF* (Apr. 1847), 54.
[100] Cited in *Chambers' Edinburgh Journal* (13 July 1844).
[101] *LF* (June 1844), 3–32.
[102] Archdeacon of Ely to Mary Ann Gilbert (25 Dec. 1839), J .S. Holmes, Scrapbook, 85.
[103] *Sussex Advertiser* (9 Apr. 1844).
[104] Burchardt, *Allotment Movement*, 92.
[105] C. D. Gilbert, Scrapbook, 21.

through specialized practices of husbandry. As such it was a patriotism which prided itself upon sensitivity to regional variation and local specificities.

Marriage and dynastic identities

Mary Ann Gilbert's enthusiasm for poor law policy predated her marriage, although doubtless her husband's professional activities provided Gilbert with a rich fund of resources—particularly during her child-bearing years when independent research may have been more difficult. Yet despite her husband's status in the fields of poor law policy and agricultural science, it was clearly understood that the schemes in Eastbourne were Gilbert's sole responsibility. Davies Gilbert appears to have been involved in some projects to provide employment in Eastbourne and improve local drainage, and there are handbills from 1831 which were issued in their joint names, but it is apparent that he quickly came to view the Eastbourne endeavours as entirely her concern.[106] The poor law commissioners' report stated explicitly that the schemes were the work of Gilbert alone.[107] The extant correspondence of Davies Gilbert (who died in 1839) confirms his abiding involvement in scientific circles—nonetheless his intellectual energies appear to have been increasingly channelled into pursuing his antiquarian interest in Cornish folklore and history.[108] One is left with the impression that the couple's separate regional identities and particular interests were extremely important to them, leading them to pursue independent projects from the 1820s.

Gilbert performed, and was treated as, an agent with the authority to act independently of her husband in public enterprises. Her forthright, somewhat dogmatic personality clearly facilitated this, but a number of overlapping social and cultural features also structured this dynamic. As delineated in previous chapters, women who enjoyed a greater empowerment in their marriage often shared one or more of the following characteristics: financial independence; the assumption of public activities later in life; opportunities to construct a distinct local identity based upon personal

---

[106] ESRO, ACC 7526/3; DE/B/28/1.

[107] *Royal Commission*, 1490. For an exceptional reference to the work of her husband see Nowell, *An Essay on Farms of Industry*, 6.

[108] e.g. Davies Gilbert, *A Cornish Cantata* (Eastbourne, 1826); *A Cornish Dialogue; Collections and Translations Respecting St Neot and the Former State of his Church in Cornwall* (London, 1830). For Davies Gilbert's correspondence see http://www.nra.nationalarchives.gov.uk/nra/searches/pidocs.asp?P=P11247 (accessed 25 Oct. 2005).

interests; and the cultural skills and confidence to establish wider (often epistolary) networks in appropriate fields of expertise. All these applied to Gilbert. However, there was one further feature which crystallized Gilbert's self-identity as a public actor: her sense of family lineage. Whilst family was central to Gilbert's conception of herself as a political actor, this was deeply rooted not in her sense of allegiance to her husband, but in a consciousness of her own heritage.

As Naomi Tadmor has persuasively illustrated, the cultural resonance of lineage remained powerfully embedded in the mental landscapes of Georgian Britons who were finely sensitized to the authority it bestowed. This applied particularly at the local level where individual properties and houses could be invested with the identity of a particular family.[109] Given the huge interest evoked by the publication of John Burke's famous books on the genealogy of the British gentry from the late 1830s, it is perhaps surprising that historians of the nineteenth century have yet to develop the analysis for this later period. However, in one of the few scholarly assessments of the issue, Jill Liddington has demonstrated that dynastic concerns could be central to the property arrangements undertaken by women of the lesser gentry. Equally as we saw in Chapter 3, women's subjectivities were often closely invested in the genealogical identities of their birth families.[110]

The case of Mary Ann Gilbert well exemplifies the centrality of dynastic concerns to middling and gentry women. That Gilbert's husband had to change his name on her heritage and that they moved to her Sussex estates meant that Gilbert's family, heritage, and wealth were central to the very fabric of her marriage. As Amanda Capern discerned in her study of early modern female landholding, land 'established and defined their relationships within the family and was the means by which the balance of power within those relationships was measured'.[111] Gilbert's marriage settlement had been devised with a careful eye to upholding her interests and to ensuring that the Gilbert line continued to exert influence in the Eastbourne area. She and her husband were jointly named as owners of many parts of the Eastbourne estate, for example. However, Gilbert's

[109] Tadmor, *Family and Friends*, ch. 3.
[110] Jill Liddington, 'Beating the Inheritance Bounds: Anne Lister (1791–1840) and her Dynastic Identity', *Gender and History*, 7 (1995), 260–74.
[111] Amanda Capern, 'Women, Family and Land in Early-Modern Yorkshire', conference paper, Economic History Society, University of Reading, Apr. 2006. My thanks to Amanda Capern for allowing me to cite this unpublished paper.

identity as a landed proprietor, and her confidence in leading local affairs, drew not only upon her financial status, but upon a long family tradition of local influence. Her uncle, Charles, had provided garden allotments to his cottage tenants at the end of the eighteenth century.[112] More broadly the Gilberts were one of the oldest established families in the county, descending from both the Gildredge and Gilbert lines whose connections with the county and to Eastbourne Manor stretched back to the sixteenth century.[113]

It was not merely her family's long lineage which inspired her. A peculiar aspect to the family's history was the ending of the male line in 1668 and the prominent role played by subsequent female heirs. When, in 1816, Gilbert became the family heiress she also inherited the title of Lord of the Manor, as had her grandmother and great-grandmother before her.[114] In the beautifully elaborate pedigree of the Gildredge family, Gilbert made tiny pencil amendments which emphasized the importance of the female line.[115] In the local church, the inscriptions Gilbert chose for her husband and her aunt invested herself with unique responsibility for perpetuating the traditions of the Gilbert dynasty. The memorial tablet for her aunt's death in 1816 refers to Gilbert as the 'sole representative of their family'. Similarly in the memorial to her husband she could not resist a reference to herself as 'heiress of her family'.[116] Through inscribing her dynastic significance on the very public site of the church wall, Gilbert was not only commemorating her family lineage, she was pronouncing her authority and status to the local community. Family memory could thus serve to uphold hierarchical social relationships within the parish. Gilbert's desire to perpetuate the family memory motivated her to execute a huge array of pictures of the family property. The family seats of both near and distant relatives were sketched by Gilbert and annotated with personal details of their owners, family anecdotes, and the like; and she was careful to preserve portraits of her mother and grandmother for her children.[117]

As noted in Chapter 3, middle-class women such as Louisa Twining, were also fascinated by family ancestry and property in this way. Rosemary Sweet has carefully delineated the importance which Georgian gentry

[112] MS note in Mary Ann Gilbert's hand on a pamphlet by Burnet Grieve of Berwick relating to agricultural experiments: F. G. Enys, Scrapbook.
[113] Walter Budgen, *Old Eastbourne: Its Church, its Clergy, its People* (London, 1913), 239–45.
[114] Ibid. Gilbert-Gildredge family tree inserted between pp. 238–9.
[115] ESRO, GIL/4/311.
[116] Budgen, *Old Eastbourne*, 243–4.
[117] Gilbert, 'Autobiographical Notes'; Mary Ann Gilbert, Sketchbook, CRO, EN/1918.

ascribed to their local histories, observing that 'identities operated at a local, regional and national level and were constructed through a sense of history, tradition and continuity'.[118] The significance of lineage, and a recognition of women's important role within the family's ancestry, clearly formed part of the structuring myths and memories which comprised Gilbert's sense of dynastic identity.

The intersection of kinship and place further reinforced Gilbert's investment in these values.[119] Eastbourne Manor and its estate functioned not merely as a visible signifier of the family's elite status within the community, it was also woven into the family's own narrative of their cultural heritage. Gilbert kept detailed records as to the family's care in maintaining the fabric of the estate's buildings.[120] The manor was 'a socially imagined place' which could form a locus for the family's sense of their significance and contribution to the local community.[121] As Jon Lawrence observes, 'more local forms of identity . . . remained integral to competing notions of what "Britishness" meant'.[122] The family narrative Gilbert constructed was frequently interlaced with references to the significance of their locality and its landscape. She dwelt upon its vulnerability as a coastal area—noting the importance of the local volunteer force during the war with France. In poetry she referred back to the Battle of Hastings and the implications of the 'Norman tyrant', noting the site of William's landing in sketches of the family's estate.[123] The patriotism with which Gilbert was associated was thus interwoven with a strong sense of her own regional heritage.

Remembering Mary Ann Gilbert

The importance which Gilbert attached to her family legacy is apparent in the enormous family archive assembled by her and her (more methodical)

---

[118] Sweet, *Antiquaries*, 42.

[119] This idea is explored in Elizabeth V. Chew's suggestive study, '"Repaired by Me to My Exceeding Great Cost and Charges": Anne Clifford and the Uses of Architecture', in Hills, *Architecture and the Politics of Gender*, 99–114.

[120] ESRO, GIL/4/36/4–5.

[121] This reading has been informed by Lindsay Proudfoot, 'Hybrid Space? Self and Other in Narratives of Landownership in Nineteenth-Century Ireland', *Journal of Historical Geography*, 26 (2000), 203–31.

[122] Jon Lawrence, 'The Politics of Place and the Politics of Nation', *Twentieth Century British History*, 11 (2000), 83.

[123] Mary Ann Gilbert, volume of MS poetry (1823), ESRO, AMS 6515/1; Mary Ann Gilbert, Sketchbook.

husband. Together they amassed a huge corpus of material relating to the
family's lineages dating back to the late middle ages.[124] Gilbert also sought
to shape future generations' knowledge of her own work through compiling
an archive of her activities. Many documents are marked 'to be kept by my
heirs and their descendants'.[125] Her will contained explicit instructions that
each of her children should have 'a copy of everything printed by me, to
be bound in purple leather and gilt lettered with their names, mine and the
date of my decease on it'.[126] In common with Clara Parkes, who wished to
uphold the memory of her aunt Susannah Watts, Gilbert's loyal daughter
Hester was keen to perpetuate her mother's legacy. Having inherited her
mother's manuscripts and papers Hester compiled volumes of material for
the benefit of the next generation.[127] Yet Gilbert's male descendants were
less supportive. Despite her best efforts (she often sent him autographed
copies of her pamphlets) Gilbert's son and heir, John, appears to have
endorsed the broader aims of the movement but was somewhat hostile to
his mother's local activism and he based himself at the family seat in
Trelissick.[128] Gilbert's grandson, Carew, a Tory MP, barely mentioned
Gilbert's activities in his chronicle of the family, privileging instead the

[124] Detailed evidence for her husband's assistance in collecting relevant legal documents may
be found at ESRO, GIL/4/281; GIL/4/288–9; A7526/3; GIL/3/18; GIL/3/21/1;
GIL/4/12/1. He hinted that his researches were in fulfilment of strictures laid down by
Charles Gilbert (ESRO, GIL/4/288–9), although his and his wife's joint pride that the
Gilbert family may have originated in Cornwall also suggests a personal investment in the
history. For Mary Ann Gilbert's researches and her desire to compile her memoirs for her
children see GIL/4/313.

[125] Letters to Mary Ann Gilbert from the Archdeacon of Ely (Christmas Day, 1839), John
Lee (25 Jan. 1840), and from the English Agricultural Society to John Starr (11 Oct. 1839),
J. S. Holmes, Scrapbook, 85, 98, 103. Lee (1783–66) was a founder member of the
Astronomical Society and Geographical Society. He was actively involved in philanthropic
projects in Buckinghamshire, including allotment schemes; his work was cited in Nowell,
On Self-Supporting Schools, 22. For Lee's support of female suffrage see p. 31 above.

[126] ESRO, AMS 6073.

[127] Letters from Hester Gilbert to Ann Dorothea Gilbert (14 Oct. and 30 Nov. 1867), ESRO,
GIL /4/365/3, 365/5; ESRO, AMS 6073. Rather pointedly she bequeathed the two medals
she was awarded by the Society of Arts to her sceptical son. Gilbert's interventionist
approach towards local issues was carried on by her daughter-in-law, Ann Dorothea Gilbert,
who managed the estate during her son's minority following the death of John Gilbert in
1851. See ESRO, GIL/3/38/7. For Clara Parkes see p. 148 above.

[128] For pamphlets inscribed to John Gilbert see ESRO, GIL/4/324–5. Hester Gilbert refers
to her brother's antagonism in a letter to Ann Dorothea Gilbert (30 Nov. 1867), ESRO,
GIL/4/365/5. The obituary of John Davies Gilbert in the *Royal Cornwall Gazette* (21 Apr.
1854) paid considerable attention to his mother's work.

career of Gilbert's husband.[129] It is possible that Gilbert disrupted their normative assumptions of appropriate female behaviour. Sensitivities concerning how the family wished Gilbert to be remembered in the Eastbourne community are also evident in the memorial tablet they commissioned for the local church which reads,

> Having faithfully and affectionately discharged the duties of a daughter, wife and mother, she devoted the latter years of her life to improving the condition of the labouring classes and with the view of facilitating their education established several agricultural schools in this neighbourhood and zealously promoted every measure which appeared to her likely to advance their true interest.[130]

The wording reflected an important literal fact: it was not until the death of her chronically disabled daughter that she began to assume an active public life. However, the allusion to the discharge of her female duties also served to forestall any intimation that Gilbert's public work had been undertaken at the expense of her womanly duties. The use of the adverb 'zealously' is the only hint that Gilbert's activities amongst the labouring classes were exceptional. But by coupling this to a reference to her family responsibilities the epitaph enables a conventional reading of the 'meaning' of Gilbert's life. It would be possible for observers to interpret her activities through the filter of culturally dominant images of genteel womanhood. The process of memorializing Gilbert smoothed away the jagged contours of a biography that could not—during her lifetime—be readily accommodated within any public discourse of female endeavour.

In the wider public sphere the act of remembering Mary Ann Gilbert was also shaped with reference to culturally available models of conventional womanhood. Gilbert's obituary in the local newspaper, noting that some of her agricultural experiments had failed, attributed this to 'the great ambition of her aims, as well as her sex and age'.[131] In fact there is little evidence to support the notion that Gilbert's advanced years (she was 69 years old on her death) limited her capacities during the final period of her life. The reference to her 'great ambition' provided the reader with an oblique hint that Gilbert's dogmatic approach fitted uneasily within contemporary formulations of a womanly philanthropist. No other printed or written sources hint that Gilbert was inhibited because of her gender. To attribute her failings in part to her 'sex' may have been a 'common-sense'

---

[129] Carew Davies Gilbert, MS notes on Davies Gilbert family, ESRO, GIL/4/497.
[130] Budgen, *Old Eastbourne*, 244.
[131] *Sussex Advertiser* (6 May 1845).

or hackneyed response, a piece of journalistic rhetoric which prevented the need for a more penetrating analysis of the obstacles Gilbert faced. The effect was to sidestep the biting class tensions her schemes laid bare, and to imply that the issues raised were simply those of an ambitious and slightly misguided individual. This shaping of Gilbert's image reiterated and affirmed a culturally dominant view of womanhood.

In contrast, anecdotal and personal memories hint at Gilbert's eccentricity, indicating the problems individual writers could face when trying to find an appropriate language with which to convey her labours. When recalling her early Victorian Hastings childhood, Marianne North referred to Gilbert as a 'clever wife a most inveterate talker, full of philanthropic schemes for improving the condition of the labouring classes . . . She used to carry models of ploughs, draining-tiles, and other machines in her huge pockets, and the slightest gap in the conversation brought them out, with all her arguments for and against them.'[132] Here, as on the memorial tablet, Gilbert's life was conveyed within the narrative of the conjugal family. In fact, Gilbert's own testimony reveals that it was her consanguineal family which was most important to her in structuring her sense of political subjectivity. This discursive shift had the effect of casting Gilbert within a less empowering gender order, but one which was becoming an increasingly ascendant mode of conveying female publicity.[133]

Conclusion

Gilbert was a leading member of her community whose status and expertise in farming, local land use, and the poor law enabled her to make striking interventions in parochial policy. Her sense of dynastic attachment to Eastbourne was critical to her political identity. As Anthony Brundage has observed, a 'durable component of paternalism was a sense of identity with, and domination of, a particular locality'.[134] Gilbert's career exemplified a revived paternalism. She believed the landed gentry had the necessary local knowledge, cultural expertise, and authority to shape local decision-

---

[132] Mrs Addington Symonds (ed.), *Recollections of a Happy Life: Being the Autobiography of Marianne North* (London, 1892, 2 vols), i. 10. See also Ellman, *Recollections of a Sussex Parson* (London, 1912), 60.
[133] Ruth Perry, *Novel Relations: The Transformation of Kinship in English Literature and Culture, 1748–1818* (Cambridge, 2004), 51.
[134] Anthony Brundage, 'The Making of the New Poor Law *Redivivus*', *Past and Present*, 127 (1990), 185.

making. Women's involvement in such parochial politics has not yet been adequately explored by historians. The case of Mary Ann Gilbert supports the notion that 'the politics of the poor rate' had the potential to function as a site for female political agency well into the nineteenth century.[135]

The landed elite have played a prominent role in recent discussions of the 1834 Poor Law. Peter Mandler argued they largely embraced the new Poor Law because it accorded with a 'modernized gentry ethos'. He notes that those who opposed the Act were 'the atypical landlords who were able to play a day-to-day role on their local Boards of Guardians: in other words, *successful* local reformers'.[136] Gilbert would certainly fit with this model of an active local reformer who protested against the Act's centralizing agenda. In many areas the gentry found the measure a disincentive for local parish involvement, looking upon the circumscribed role of relief guardians as somewhat distasteful.[137] In contrast, Gilbert campaigned ceaselessly against it, believing it threatened the traditional influence of the landed gentry.

However, her story is evidence that such landowners could also be inspired by 'modernizing' agendas. In addition to applying the latest theories in agricultural science, Gilbert used new technology wherever possible to facilitate her projects. Printed schedules of the Eastbourne allotment system were regularly telegraphed to a committee in Slaithwaite which was attempting to introduce the method.[138] Indeed, she situated her schemes within a narrative of industrial progress, arguing that England's mechanical expertise should be matched by innovation in the field of agriculture.[139] This was a paternalism ready to appropriate the methods of middle-class activism, with its associational philanthropy and educational strategies. Gilbert utilized the increasingly prevalent middle-class agendas of civilizing the lower orders; but, in their translation to the countryside, such discourses do not appear to have been as sharply gendered as they were in either the urban or colonial contexts.

Gilbert drew upon traditional structures of political and social authority, and her methods of publication are testament to the continuing salience of pre-modern authorial practices. In addition, she provides ample evidence that the shift from a 'consanguineal to a conjugal system', whereby

---

[135] This phrase comes from Steve Hindle, 'Power, Poor Relief, and Social Relations in Holland Fen, c.1600–1800', *Historical Journal*, 41 (1998), 96. Hindle is pessimistic concerning the opportunities available to women.

[136] Mandler, 'Making of the New Poor Law *Redivivus*', 133, 155.

[137] Dunkley, 'Whigs and Paupers'; Anne Digby, *Pauper Palaces* (London, 1978), 214.

[138] Nowell, *An Essay on Farms of Industry*, 9–10.

[139] Nowell, *On Self-Supporting Schools*, 30–1.

women derived their status as wives and mothers, rather than as daughters and sisters, was by no means as stark as recent scholars have supposed.[140] In certain contexts women could continue to derive their primary identity from their family of birth.

John Brewer and Susan Staves asked in 1995, 'how does the construction of self depend upon the possession of a certain quantum of property?'[141] The case of Mary Ann Gilbert indicates that the possession of agricultural land could facilitate the construction of particular subjectivities, including: dynastic identity, local loyalties, and paternalist assumptions of status, not to mention the potential to amass cultural capital as agricultural experts. Gender does not appear to have been a prominent consideration in Gilbert's understanding of, or promotion of, her activities and contemporaries largely disregarded Gilbert's gender in their references to her work. Gendered constraints operated to exclude her from making an equal contribution to the public sphere of pressure-group campaigning, but the opportunities available to her in other spheres meant that knowledge of these limitations could be suspended in her day-to-day activities. Gilbert was able to fuse various sources of authority into a powerful public persona. However, this did have implications for family dynamics, and the sensitivities her endeavours aroused are suggested in the way in which family and friends chose to represent her labours after her death.

---

[140] Perry, *Novel Relations*, 51.
[141] Brewer and Staves, 'Introduction', in their *Early Modern Conceptions of Property*, 7.

7

'Doing good by wholesale': women, gender, and politics in the family network of Thomas Fowell Buxton

Introduction

In the last chapter we focused upon a single woman to consider the ways in which the parochial sphere provided a forum for female public engagement. It was argued that the nature of that woman's engagement also highlights subtle patterns in family identification as well as a fractured experience of the 'public sphere'. In this final chapter we will pursue a family network, rather than an individual. The aim is to consider how the various sites of political engagement delineated in Part I—the 'public' sphere, the parochial realm, and the family—functioned together in the construction of subjectivities and political experience. We shall pursue many of the themes delineated in the first half of the book, particularly concerning the conceptualization of female influence; the gendered complexities of collaborative authorship; the construction of corporate family identities; the problematic position of women within the civic, as compared to the parochial, sphere; and the significance of gendered space for the constitution of female political subjectivity.

Since the publication of Clare Midgley's acclaimed study of female anti-slavery activism, the involvement of women in the campaign to liberate slaves in Britain's colonial territories has become a firmly established feature of our understanding of nineteenth-century political culture.[1] Here I would like to narrow our focus to analyse the family network involved in one particular anti-slavery organization: the Society for the Extinction of the Slave Trade and the Civilization of Africa (hereafter African Civilization

---

[1] Midgley, *Women against Slavery*. Before the publication of Midgley's work two excellent essays had also focused upon female anti-slavery activism: Corfield, 'Elizabeth Heyrick'; Billington and Billington, 'A Burning Zeal for Righteousness'.

Society). It was the founder and leading light of this society, Thomas Fowell Buxton, who presented the famous ladies' anti-slavery petition to parliament in 1833. Yet strikingly the African Civilization Society did not itself promote female involvement in the campaign. On the other hand both this project and the other anti-slavery work with which Buxton was involved depended heavily upon the labours of his family network, particularly the contribution of Priscilla Johnston (his daughter), Anna Gurney (his cousin), and Sarah Buxton (his sister).

Therefore, whilst the public sphere of pressure-group campaigning did not provide a significant outlet of political activity for women in this circle, the family and the domestic site most clearly did. As Zoë Laidlaw has made clear, the home of Anna Gurney and Sarah Buxton at Northrepps Cottage in Overstrand, near Cromer, where they were close to the Buxton family home at Northrepps Hall, formed one of two family political spaces. The cottage was the site where the masses of evidence collected by the family was studied, filed, digested, and collated. Meanwhile the family's rented London home in Devonshire Street, shared by Thomas and his wife Hannah with Priscilla and her MP husband, Andrew, provided a forum for parliamentary lobbying and planning. Laidlaw's assessment expertly illustrates the intersection of public and private histories in the political process.[2]

My purpose here is not to critique Laidlaw's excellent study but rather to push her insights yet further. The rich family archive illuminates the ways in which different, sometimes competing, political identities might coexist and overlap within the subjective landscape of the individuals involved. Gendered notions of the self played a critical, but sometimes unpredictable role within this process. An enduring attachment to collective models of public identity and the primacy of religious sensibilities problematized notions of the individual political actor. At the same time, whilst family political collaboration provided multiple avenues for female engagement, this could often reinforce patriarchal family structures. In contrast, within their own neighbourhoods the women of the Buxton family circle played forthright and distinctive roles in their own right.

---

[2] Zoë Laidlaw, '"Aunt Anna's Report": The Buxton Women and the Aborigines Select Committee, 1835–7', *Journal of Imperial and Commonwealth History*, 32 (2004), 1–28. See also Laidlaw, *Colonial Connections, 1815–45: Patronage, the Information Revolution and Colonial Government* (Manchester, 2005), 146–54.

'All doing good by wholesale': the Buxton family circle and political work

Thomas Fowell Buxon (1786–1845) was MP for Weymouth from 1818 to 1837. Strongly influenced by his Quaker mother (his father, an Anglican squire, had died when he was a young boy) Buxton became friendly with the Gurneys of Earlham in his teens and, in 1807, he married Hannah Gurney (sister of Elizabeth Fry and of Buxton's great friend Joseph John Gurney). The following year Buxton joined a family brewery business of which he was later to assume sole ownership. Sharing with Fry and Gurney a passion for the cause of penal reform, in 1823 Buxton's focus shifted to anti-slavery when he took up Wilberforce's Evangelical mantle in the House of Commons. From this point onwards Buxton was principally associated with colonial reform, for which he was awarded a baronetcy in 1840. He was a founding member of both the Aborigines Protection Society and the African Civilization Society. The latter sought to eradicate slavery through promoting 'Christianity and civilization' in Africa. This led to the disastrous Niger expedition: a failed attempt to promote trade in West Africa which culminated in the deaths of 143 members of the British crew. The African Civilization Society was disbanded three years later.[3]

Buxton's status as the parliamentary leader of the anti-slavery movement was often controversial. He was seen by many grass-roots campaigners as too close to elite Whig politics and he was criticized for compromising on the issue of apprenticeship, whereby 'liberated' slaves were initially bound as labourers to their former owners. This brought him into tension with the provincial Nonconformist activism which was the seedbed for much female anti-slavery mobilization. Equally, Buxton's strategy of marshalling data and detailed evidence to support his case, rather than dwelling upon moral and religious imperatives, also distinguished him from the strategies so often adopted by women anti-slavery campaigners.[4] Nonetheless, despite his public political profile as an elite male politician, Buxton himself often referred to the critical 'influence' his female relatives had had upon his career. In addition to the model provided by his sister Anna, who refused to eat slave-produced sugar in their childhood, Thomas

---

[3] For Buxton's career consult Charles Buxton, *Memoirs of Sir Thomas Fowell Buxton* (London, 1848); Howard Temperley, *British Antislavery, 1833–1870* (London, 1972), ch. 3. The Niger expedition is considered in John A. Gallagher, 'Fowell Buxton and the New African Policy, 1838–1842', *Cambridge Historical Journal*, 10 (1950), 36–58.

[4] David Turley, *The Culture of English Anti-Slavery, 1780–1860* (London, 1991), 42, 70–4.

pointed to the effect of his mother, wife, and sisters-in-law in his political development. It was Providence, he explained to his wife, that led his mother to 'sow the seeds of abhorrence of slavery in my mind', and that induced his wife's sister, Priscilla Gurney, to exhort him to take up the cause on her deathbed. Equally it was the 'goodness of Providence' that had provided him with a wife such as Hannah whose many affective, nursing, and intellectual gifts ensured his recovery from illness. In addition, Thomas acknowledged the influence of his most famous sister-in-law, Elizabeth Fry, upon him.[5] Although an Anglican throughout his life, the Evangelical Quakerism of the family into which he married accustomed him to expansive models of female public activity. During the preparations for the ill-fated Niger expedition Elizabeth Fry acted as something of a family figurehead. Best known for her work as a prison reformer, Fry was also accustomed to public speaking as a Quaker preacher. Two parties held during March 1841, one at the family brewery and the other at Ham House (the home of Fry's brother, Samuel Gurney) and attended by Ashanti princes and expedition leaders, both concluded with addresses from Fry.[6] 'Female influence' was a trope which held clear meaning for Buxton—it was not simply an empty rhetorical gesture.

Even so, an acceptance and celebration of the exceptional profile accrued by such a woman as Elizabeth Fry did not equate with a fundamental revision of traditional gender relations. The family shared a perception of themselves as individual actors working as the humble instruments of divine providence. This encouraged a sense of the subordination of the self and the promotion of larger, divinely inspired aims.[7] Whilst gender might not be central to this process, that those projects were enacted within the contours of a patriarchal family relationship meant that conventional formulations of masculine and feminine identity were closely interwoven in their execution. As we shall see, an extraordinary degree of female participation in family political projects did not necessarily result in the cultiva-

---

[5] Reid, *W. E. Forster*, i. 21; Thomas Fowell to Hannah Buxton (3 Apr. 1836), Brit. Emp. S. 444* (1), 425; Thomas Fowell Buxton to Priscilla Johnston and Catherine Buxton (1 Apr. 1840), ibid. (19), 244–5; Thomas Fowell Buxton to Elizabeth Fry (7 Mar. 1839), ibid. (17), 366.

[6] Catherine Buxton to Richenda Buxton (9 Mar. 1841), ibid. (20), 181–2; [Catherine Buxton to Anna Gurney?] (23 Mar. 1841), ibid. 192–3; Catherine Buxton to Anna Gurney [?] (29 Mar. 1841), ibid. (20), 200–1.

[7] For further discussion on the relationship between religion and the subordination of the self see Phyllis Mack, 'Religion, Feminism and the Problem of Agency: Reflections on Eighteenth Century Quakerism', *Signs*, 29 (2003), 149–77.

tion of robust female political identities. The 'rules of engagement' which shaped women's experience of politics across the different zones of family, the public, and the parochial remained firmly in place.

It was Priscilla Johnston, Anna Gurney, and to a lesser extent Sarah Buxton who were particularly implicated in Buxton's parliamentary endeavours. Prior to her marriage in 1834 to Andrew Johnston (an Evangelical MP who was also closely involved in Buxton's work) Priscilla acted as her father's chief assistant and secretary. After her wedding the role of Buxton's leading coadjutor was taken up for six months by Anna (his cousin), while Priscilla and Andrew spent time on their estate in Scotland. On their return to London in the spring of 1835 both Andrew and Priscilla resumed their labours for Buxton, along with Anna, Buxton's sister Sarah, and to a lesser extent Buxton's other children, Richenda, Edward, and Charles.[8]

Anna and Priscilla often laboured for twelve-hour days, sometimes to the detriment of their health. They undertook extensive research and composed synopses of documents to facilitate Thomas's political performances. The following request to Anna was typical: 'Will you oblige me by looking over the enclosed papers, & giving me your opinion as to what I shall do? and telling me the substance of what is in them?'[9] They were not merely playing an auxiliary role. His speeches, for example, were routinely composed by Anna or Priscilla. As Thomas reported to Anna in May 1838, 'Your speech [on abolition], as delivered at Exeter Hall yesterday was very good'.[10] Or, as Priscilla wrote to Anna, 'My father spoke for an hour "out of Miss Gurney" he says'.[11] Thomas Fowell Buxton's signature on reports and letters did not signify an autonomous, individual identity. 'Thomas Fowell Buxton' functioned almost as a 'brand name' that could be utilized by other family members.[12] For example, Priscilla did not merely act as her

---

[8] There was also a third son, Fowell. Contrary to the *ODNB*, it is clear from family records that Thomas and Hannah had ten, not eight children. Four died in a whooping cough outbreak in 1820, a further son, Harry, died in 1830. This is also the finding of Laidlaw, 'Aunt Anna's Report', 7. Family members will be referred to largely by their first names to avoid confusion.

[9] Thomas Fowell Buxton to Anna Gurney (15 July 1841), Brit. Emp. S. 444 (20), 285.

[10] Thomas Fowell Buxton to Anna Gurney and Sarah Buxton (17 May 1838), ibid. (17), 147g.

[11] Priscilla Johnston to Anna Gurney (17 May 1838), ibid. (17), 148. For other examples see Thomas Fowell Buxton to Anna Gurney (15 Feb. 1834), ibid. (13), 9; Thomas Fowell to Hannah Buxton (5 Feb. 1836), ibid. (15), 9; Thomas Fowell Buxton to Anna Gurney (28 April 1838), ibid. (17), 138–40.

[12] See Mark Rose, *Authors and Owners: The Invention of Copyright* (Cambridge, Mass., and London, 1993), 1.

father's amanuensis, she undertook correspondence in his name. She noted with amusement Thomas's confusion when William Lloyd Garrison, the American abolitionist, thanked him for a letter which he had sent to *The Liberator*. Thomas was unable to recall the letter as it was she who had written it.[13] This appears to have been a common practice within the family.[14] It was the cause which mattered, and individual identities were subordinated to it.

Priscilla and Anna's confidence in writing under Thomas's name (and his acquiescence in this process) suggests that it was perceived by the family not to signify simply his own individuality, but to be rather representative of a corporate political project. As we noted in Chapter 3, just as the franchise might be regarded as a piece of family property, so too might the career of a politician be viewed as a channel for the furtherance of family political objectives. The Buxtons' assumption of a collective familial identity was integral to this process. As Priscilla put it, '*we* are *all* doing good by wholesale'.[15] The subtleties of this phenomenon may be discerned by exploring two particular instances of Buxton family collaboration: the Select Committee on Aborigines (1835–7) and the composition of an extensive monograph on the slave trade, *The Remedy* (1840).

A key political objective of the Buxton family was to secure the humanitarian treatment of the Xhosa peoples on the Cape coast. The Xhosa had long suffered from aggressive territorial policies on the part of white settlers. Tensions resulted in renewed fighting on the frontier from 1834 during which the Governor, Benjamin D'Urban, stood accused by local missionaries of excessively punitive actions. The Buxtons' contacts with missionary personnel, in particular John Philip, the director of the London Missionary Society in South Africa, had galvanized the family to act and Thomas pledged himself to effecting a change in government policy. He relied extensively upon the researches of Anna and Sarah who supplied him with huge amounts of data, including detailed statistics concerning the social and economic condition of native peoples.[16] This provided Thomas with the material to influence the Evangelical Secretary

---

[13] Priscilla Buxton to Sarah Buxton (29 June 1833), Brit. Emp. S. 444*, suppl. vol. 1, pp. 178–82. See further Laidlaw, 'Aunt Anna's Report', 25 n. 68.
[14] e.g. Thomas Fowell Buxton to Hannah Buxton (7 Nov. 1832), Brit. Emp. S. 444, suppl. vol. 1, p. 46. Thomas Fowell Buxton to Anna Gurney (24 Nov. 1835), ibid. (2), 81–3; Laidlaw, 'Aunt Anna's Report', 13.
[15] Priscilla Johnston to Richenda Buxton, Sarah Buxton, and Anna Gurney (27 Feb. 1837), Brit. Emp. S. 444 (15), 195.
[16] See Laidlaw, 'Aunt Anna's Report' for a full account.

of State for the Colonies in the new Melbourne administration, Lord Glenelg, and to call successfully for a committee of inquiry into the treatment of colonial subjects in all British settlements. As Thomas wrote to Anna and Sarah, '[O]wing exclusively to you the committee was formed, & that saved a nation'.[17] Thomas acted as the chair of the committee and his son-in-law Andrew was also a member.

The committee's subsequent report urged for greater colonial intervention based upon the propagation of Christianity and commerce in the subject territories.[18] The report was officially authored by Thomas Fowell Buxton—but in fact it was written collaboratively at Northrepps Cottage. Here the whole family participated in mammoth working sessions, joined by John Philip. Whilst Buxton referred to the ceaseless efforts of the 'whole party', he particularly singled out the role played by Anna Gurney. She had, he told his son, Edward, 'done her part superbly'.[19] Hannah also referred to the document as 'dearest Aunt Anna's report'.[20] As the report proceeded through the committee Buxton wrote to Gurney of 'your report', admitting: 'I hardly know how to look when they commend me—knowing as I do how little a portion justly belongs to me.'[21] When the report achieved one of its objectives in securing the withdrawal of British troops from the Xhosa territories Buxton was fulsome in Anna's praise: 'the hand of the proud Oppressor in Africa has been under Providence, arrested by Miss Gurney of Northrepps Cottage'.[22]

Clearly the home was a critical site for political action amongst the Buxton network, but within the family there were differentiated levels of engagement. Family-based political activities did not necessarily empower

---

[17] Thomas Fowell Buxton to Anna Gurney and Sarah Buxton (2 June 1836), Brit. Emp. S. 444 (15), 54. See also Thomas Fowell to Hannah Buxton (21 Aug. 1835), ibid. (14), 83b.

[18] Elizabeth Elbourne, 'The Sin of the Settler: The 1835–36 Select Committee on Aborigines and Debates over Virtue and Conquest in the Early Nineteenth-Century British White Settler Empire', *Journal of Colonialism and Colonial History*, 4 (2003); Alan Lester, *Imperial Networks: Creating Identities in Nineteenth-Century South Africa and Britain* (London, 2001), 105–23. The committee also considered the position of Australian peoples: for debate see David Philips, 'Evangelicals, Aborigines and "Land Rights": A Critique of Henry Reynolds on the Select Committee on Aborigines', *Australian Studies*, 17 (2002), 147–65.

[19] Thomas Fowell to Edward Buxton (17 Jan. 1837), Brit. Emp S. 444 (15), 171.

[20] Hannah Buxton to Fowell and Charles Buxton (23 Feb. 1837), ibid. (15), 189.

[21] Thomas Fowell Buxton to Anna Gurney and Sarah Buxton (6 June 1837), ibid. (15), 307, a.

[22] Thomas Fowell Buxton to Anna Gurney and Sarah Buxton (18 Mar. 1837), ibid. (15), 225. See also the congratulations bestowed upon Gurney by Joseph John Gurney in his letter to Anna Gurney and Sarah Buxton (11 Apr. 1837), Brit. Emp. S. 444 (15), 231c–d. More generally the impact of the report was limited however, as Laidlaw discusses.

all members in the same way. When referring to the report Hannah and Thomas, as we have seen, particularly singled out the contribution of Anna, but Priscilla's interpretation was more inclusive. She reported that the whole family was involved in the writing sessions, even the children. Surrounded by papers and blue books, Priscilla noted fondly that even 'Charlie's little clear voice now pops in an observation; in short, we all help.'[23] In her diary Priscilla presented her own role as rather passive, noting that John Philip, her father, husband, and Anna formed the core group whilst, 'We all sit round, I say, like the ostrich's eggs scattered outside the nest, to look on and give our valuable assistance from time to time.'[24] But Sarah Buxton intimated that Priscilla was a more active contributor than this suggests, explaining to her nephew Edward, 'We often met twice a day . . . My Brother, Dr P, Andrew Johnston & my partner [i.e. Anna Gurney] around the table. Priscilla taking part with them, & my sister, Richenda & I listening.'[25] In making a distinction between participants and audience in this way, Sarah's description indicated varying levels of involvement. The corporate political project of the Buxton kinship network was not a mono-lithic entity but was comprised of multiple viewpoints, shaped by the personal dynamics and perceptions of those involved. Equally, Priscilla's desire to downplay her own contribution to the report in her personal journal is indicative of the fact that family political labours did not neces-sarily facilitate the construction of forthright, independent, political identi-ties. Indeed Hannah, Thomas's wife, cultivated a non-political persona as a materfamilias, providing emotional and practical support for other family members. She wrote 'it is no business of mine to write about the [committee] Report' which so preoccupied her family.[26]

The complex implications of the family's collaboration are further demonstrated in the composition of *The Remedy*. Published in 1840 and bearing the authorial signature of 'Thomas Fowell Buxton' it was a sequel to *The African Slave Trade* (1839). The work insisted on the need to augment the British naval presence and for diplomatic initiatives to be undertaken with African chiefs to ensure the cessation of the slave trade. It was an auda-cious, expansionist vision of imperial rule which included extensive plans for agricultural and commercial development. Although it represented a

[23] Hannah Buxton, *Memorials of Hannah, Lady Buxton* (London, 1883), 152–3.
[24] E. MacInnes (ed.), *Extracts from Priscilla Johnston's Journal and Letters* (Carlisle, 1862), 113.
[25] Note by Sarah Buxton in a letter from Thomas Fowell Buxton to Edward Buxton (17 Jan. 1837), Brit. Emp. S. 444 (15), 171.
[26] Hannah Buxton to Anna Gurney (10 June 1837), ibid. (15), 312.

reversal of many strands of existing colonial policy, remarkably, many of its arguments were to be accepted.[27]

Whilst Thomas appears to have been responsible for the general scheme of the work and an initial draft, Sarah Buxton and Anna Gurney were both closely involved in its composition. A letter to them from Thomas finds him very pleased with the sections they have sent and especially that on cruelty: 'what an argument it is for Missionaries'.[28] It was Priscilla, however, who bore the brunt of the work. In the winter of 1839 she wearily explained to her sister Richenda that she had been working 'night & day' on the publication, going through the proofs and making extensive alterations so as to render it more accessible. Although she felt a responsibility to adhere to the substance of her father's plans for the work, Priscilla clearly felt she had the authority to substantially rewrite much of it, confessing: 'my only fear & doubt is whether my father & you all knowing it so well, will not feel it strange'.[29]

The authorial signature of 'Thomas Fowell Buxton' thus silenced the fact that this was a work with an intricate history of collaborative composition. This does not mean to say that it was a process devoid of conflict. Thomas charged Priscilla with finishing the work when he was in Italy unwell, yet he found it difficult to relinquish control. He acknowledged that Priscilla's revisions, which had overturned 'the whole existing arrangement of my book', had greatly improved it—although characteristically he claimed he too would have made similar changes.[30] Priscilla wrote to Anna in desperation at her father's refusal to resign command of the project.[31] Her father mocked her anxiety, writing to Edward that she should 'trot along a little more soberly'.[32] Priscilla's frustration is understandable. Whilst her father reassured her that she should not have paid any attention to his 'nonsensical' suggestions for alteration he nonetheless requested that his 'brilliant' passage on racial prejudice be reinstated.[33] Her faith in providential destiny provided her with a means of justifying her exasperation. Observing that her father was duty-bound to be in Rome because of her mother's health, she noted: 'I feel for myself the truest faith that all this mighty work is under the closest care of Providence—it seems to me that we are bound to trust the

---

[27] Gallagher, 'Fowell Buxton'.
[28] Thomas Fowell Buxton to Anna Gurney and Sarah Buxton (10 June 1839), Brit. Emp. S. 444 (18), 126.
[29] Priscilla Johnston to Richenda Buxton (19 Dec. 1839), ibid. (19), 24–5.
[30] Thomas Fowell Buxton to Priscilla Johnston (26 Dec. 1839), ibid. (19), 36–42.
[31] Priscilla Johnston to Anna Gurney (20 Jan. 1840), ibid. (19), 86.
[32] Thomas Fowell Buxton to Edward Buxton (30 Jan. 1840), ibid. (19), 108.
[33] Thomas Fowell Buxton to Priscilla Johnston (31 Jan. 1840), ibid. (19), 115.

Master & Doer. If servants are dismissed for a time (which I firmly believe my Father is providentially) they must bear to be passive—such is the required service.'[34]

The family's firm belief in providential destiny helped to abate somewhat the emotional demands of working with the often imperious Thomas. He could be considered not as a dominant political agent for whom they offered services—but rather as another humble servant working in God's name. Even so, Thomas's gendered self-positioning as paterfamilias was interwoven into the family's identity as a collective political unit.

'The chief': Thomas Fowell Buxton and family dynamics

Whilst the family articulated a collective contribution to colonial causes, Thomas was accepted as the dominant force within this dynamic. In many ways he exemplified the modes of domineering masculinity which could often typify males of the ruling elite.[35] He was a demanding and occasionally inconsiderate task master. For example, on 9 April 1838 he jovially admonished Anna over reports that 'you are so inveterately industrious, that you are working yourself to the death', joking that, 'If I hear that you continue to deny yourself all exercise & recreation I shall dismiss you from my service without a character.'[36] This did not restrain him from requiring, less than three weeks later on 28 April, that she 'make me a good speech out of our Report on the Aborigines, & let me have it by the 7th May, or within a day or two. I trust to you for this & dismiss it from my mind'.[37] Buxton behaved in this high-handed manner to male and female assistants alike, taking their acquiescence equally for granted. Andrew and Anna referred to him privately as 'The Chief', and made telling allusions to his exacting manner.[38] Occasionally these complaints became a little more pointed. In 1839 Andrew wryly noted to Hannah that her husband was becoming as 'mysterious as Lord Glenelg'. Anna Gurney would have none of this, adding ironically, 'We *Independent* Slaves won't stand these affectations'.[39]

---

[34] Priscilla Johnston to Anna Gurney (20 Jan. 1840), ibid. (19), 86.

[35] Roberts, 'Paterfamilias'.

[36] Thomas Fowell Buxton to Anna Gurney and Sarah Buxton (9 Apr. 1838), Brit. Emp. S. 444 (17), 129.

[37] Thomas Fowell Buxton to Anna Gurney (28 Apr. 1838), ibid. (17), 138–9.

[38] Andrew Johnston to Anna Gurney (10 May 1838), ibid. (17), 144.

[39] Notes from Andrew Johnston and Anna Gurney to Hannah Buxton enclosed in a letter from Thomas Fowell Buxton (4–5 Jan. 1839), ibid. (17), 326.

Given the scale of commitment, hours of work, and expert knowledge that Buxton demanded of his assistants, it is perhaps not surprising that Richenda was somewhat apprehensive at taking up the post of her father's secretary.[40] Younger female members of the family were often recruited to perform more routine tasks,[41] but the post of secretary was viewed as a skilled and full-time role that could be undertaken by men or women in the Buxton network. Occasionally it was undertaken by male employees for remuneration. Equally, Priscilla's responsibilities over Thomas's work were such that she occasionally required a secretary of her own.[42]

Thus, within the Buxton network, many aspects of political work were conceived in what we might consider 'gender neutral' ways.[43] Thomas's instructions to those who assisted him made no distinction between 'male' or 'female' activities. In 1838 he wrote to Anna Gurney, explaining that he and Andrew Johnston were about to send down a large consignment of anti-slavery material to Northrepps Cottage where 'you have a good force ... viz: yourself, Wm Forster, Christiana [the children's governess] & Richards [his sons' tutor], my purpose is to send these books down to you to be threshed'.[44] A fortnight later he reported that Anna's parcel on commerce had arrived safely, and that he was about to return it with three volumes of statistics for herself, Richards, or William Forster to work on.[45] On another occasion he wrote requesting that either Anna or Andrew should collate evidence on the climate in the African interior.[46]

Thomas's overbearing attitude towards his political assistants was symptomatic of a broader pattern of behaviour. He expected family members to be at his personal disposal. Characteristically, during an illness in 1840 he confided to Priscilla and Catherine (his daughter-in-law) that 'I enjoy to have Hannah fidgetting [sic] about me all day & all night'.[47] Little wonder

---

[40] Richenda Buxton to Hannah Buxton (9 May 1839), ibid. (18), 98.

[41] e.g. Thomas Fowell Buxton to Joseph John Gurney (18 Aug. 1838), ibid. 199a. He also relied upon the family's wider network, including Charlotte Upcher and Mrs Trotter, for research assistance: Thomas Fowell Buxton to Mrs Trotter (9 Nov. 1840), ibid. (20), 29–30; 'Mrs Upcher's Extracts', (1838–40), ibid. (37).

[42] Catherine Buxton to Priscilla Johnston (10 Nov. 1839), ibid. (18), 431; Priscilla Johnston to Richenda Buxton (19 Dec. 1839), ibid. (19), 25.

[43] When Elizabeth Fry undertook tours of Europe her husband and their friend, Josiah Forster, acted as her companions and assistants: Elizabeth Fry to her sisters (7 Feb. 1838), ibid. (17), 43.

[44] Thomas Fowell Buxton to Anna Gurney (30 Apr. 1838), ibid. (17), 141.

[45] Thomas Fowell Buxton to Anna Gurney (19 May 1838), ibid. (17), 151.

[46] Thomas Fowell Buxton to Hannah Buxton (23 Apr. 1839), ibid. (18), 63–4.

[47] Thomas Fowell Buxton to Priscilla Johnston and Catherine Buxton (1 Apr. 1840), ibid. (19), 244.

that when he accompanied his son and daughter-in-law on a trip to Italy in 1840 his wife issued them with strict instructions for his 'good management': they should be insistent on keeping separate apartments, he should have his own secretaries and servants, and Catherine should refuse to take on any of his work.[48] Even so, Catherine later worried that this inhibited Buxton from requesting the assistance he required from her.[49] Whilst Buxton had every respect for the intellect and abilities of Priscilla and Anna, he had a tendency to assume that these were abilities which might be brought forward to instruct or amuse him whenever he so desired. 'Anna Gurney', he wrote to Priscilla and Catherine, 'is my glass of champagne— I send for her when I want to be brightened up a little.'[50] In similar fashion he wrote to his sons in April 1835 of Priscilla that, 'Whenever I want to clear & brighten up my mind—I find nothing so effectual, as an interchange of thoughts with her'.[51] He was equally demanding of the men in his family. Whilst travelling in Italy he expected his son, Fowell, to read to him at night when he was unable to sleep.[52]

Thomas therefore was acutely conscious of his position as the head of the family. His self-positioning as a paterfamilias combined with the prestige of his political career afforded him the key role within the family's political imaginary. Whilst the family articulated a collective political identity, this tended to be construed through the figure of Thomas. Despite occasionally protesting to her husband that she feared for their children should they take up his political mantle,[53] Hannah was nonetheless concerned that they should perpetuate the family political legacy, and this was viewed in traditional, masculinist terms. Writing to her sons in 1826, she stressed her hopes that they might follow in their father's footsteps. When the eldest son, Edward, took his seat in the House, both Priscilla and Hannah sought to instil in him a consciousness that he was now responsible for continuing the work of his father.[54]

Families who cooperated in political labour did not necessarily empower all members equally, nor did they provide unproblematic spaces

[48] Hannah Buxton to Catherine and Edward Buxton (26 Feb. 1840), ibid. (21), 39–42.

[49] Catherine Buxton to Priscilla Johnston (23 May 1840), ibid. (19), 282.

[50] Thomas Fowell Buxton to Priscilla Johnston and Catherine Buxton (1 Apr. 1840), ibid. (19), 245.

[51] Thomas Fowell Buxton to his sons (3 Apr. 1835), ibid. (2), 190–1.

[52] Thomas Fowell Buxton to Hannah Buxton (2 Dec. 1839), ibid. (18), 458k.

[53] Thomas Fowell Buxton to Anna Gurney and Priscilla Johnston (29 Jan. 1842), ibid. (20a), 3.

[54] Hannah Buxton to Edward and Harry Buxton (10 May 1826) and to Edward Buxton (6 Aug. 1847), ibid. (2), 239–43; Laidlaw, 'Aunt Anna's Report', 19.

for the exercise of female agency. To be involved in political work within this context could have complicated implications for the construction of female identity. To probe these issues further let us consider in greater depth the experience of Priscilla Johnston. Perhaps the most intellectually gifted and politically astute of Hannah and Thomas's children, Laidlaw has remarked upon her 'forceful use of the first person' in her correspondence. Priscilla contributed many unsigned pieces to contemporary publications such as the *Edinburgh Review* and *The Record* on colonial affairs. In addition to her work for her father she was engaged in associational activities, acting as co-secretary of the London Female Anti-Slavery Society.[55] However, it was she who most frequently and explicitly conceptualized her political endeavours as part of a collective familial enterprise. This included electoral as well as anti-slavery activities. Note her use of pronoun in the following letter written during her father's unsuccessful election campaign in 1837, 'there is a brisk Tory Canvass going on, so we have been writing an Address'.[56] Yet Priscilla was differently empowered than her sister, Richenda, who tended to portray elections as essentially male concerns. When many members of the Buxton family were involving themselves in the general election of 1841, Richenda appeared to feel somewhat aloof from the cut and thrust of the electoral theatre. She wrote to Anna Gurney in July 1841, 'our Gentlemen, that is, the three brothers are *devoted* to the Elections'.[57] Whilst Priscilla always felt fully implicated in the electoral contests of her male kin and thrived on political discussion, such activities were viewed rather differently by her sister. In 1837 a somewhat bewildered Richenda wrote to her brother Charles of the political whirlwind currently being experienced in the Devonshire Street household as it buzzed with avid discussion on the church question.[58] Similarly Hannah's political contributions tended to be of an ancillary nature, and she protested ignorance of detailed political matters. As she wrote to Priscilla in 1826, 'all the variations of electioneering concerns would interest you were you here; but the state of things is like a web of tangled silk to me'.[59] These opposing attitudes suggests that there were 'micro-climates' of political engagement operating within the family.

---

[55] Laidlaw, 'Aunt Anna's Report', 10; Midgley, *Women against Slavery*, 66, 121–2.
[56] Priscilla Johnston to her brothers (11 Mar. 1837), Brit. Emp. S. 444 (15), 218.
[57] Richenda Buxton to Anna Gurney (1 July 1841), ibid. (20), 280.
[58] Richenda Buxton to Charles Buxton (23 May 1837), ibid. (15), 296–9.
[59] Buxton, *Memorials*, 100.

These divergent propensities were not simply the result of differing temperaments. As in many political families, Thomas had singled out his oldest daughter as a political apprentice from an early age. In her account of her daughter's childhood Hannah described how from infancy Thomas had set about 'cultivating her mind, exercising her powers, and pleasing her by entering into her pursuits'.[60] He groomed her carefully as his political assistant, not only through her domestic education but enabling her to listen to debates on slavery in the House of Commons and setting her demanding essays on colonial history.[61] In addition he sought to inspire her with models of other father–daughter relationships. As the 14-year-old Priscilla wrote excitedly at the end of January 1823,

> How I shall enjoy it if I become useful to him in his objects! He told me yesterday that Mr Cobbett's second daughter writes almost all his papers for him, and that he should make me Miss Cobbett the second. I have not heard anything that delighted me so much for a long time. To be his companion in any way is the highest object of my ambition.[62]

Central to her approach to politics and the family, therefore, was her relationship with her father. Although Priscilla wrote warmly of her intense love and emotional dependence upon her mother, it was her father whom she idolized.[63] Despite their closeness this was a most hierarchical relationship. Her mother recalled that Thomas secured his obedience over his daughter during a dramatic incident in her early childhood when he struck her hard when she attempted to defy him.[64] This combination of strict discipline and emotional intensity was symptomatic of the texture of their relationship: Priscilla held her father in awe, yet felt intricately involved in his political and emotional life.

Whilst the family's involvement in elite anti-slavery politics necessitated considerable investment in social politics, with breakfasts and dinners often devoted to networking and campaigning, this does not mean that such occasions were necessarily viewed as empowering opportunities by female family members. When Thomas arranged a 'large Anti-Slavery party' at his Devonshire Street home in February 1831, Hannah chose not to attend and Elizabeth Fry pulled out at the last minute. Priscilla, then aged 22, clearly felt somewhat daunted by the 'twenty gentlemen, lords, M.P.s' assembled,

[60] MacInnes, *Priscilla Johnston's Journal*, p. vi.
[61] Ibid. 11–12.
[62] Ibid. 9.
[63] e.g. ibid. 33.
[64] Ibid., p. iv.

but was commanded to appear by her father and uncles. Whilst she went on to find the occasion extremely stimulating, it nonetheless further ingrained the experience of masculine political privilege as an awesome, sometimes intimidating quality. Reporting the party to her friend she felt the need to reiterate her marginal feminine status, emphasizing how she 'sheltered myself in a corner of the sofa' and 'begged' to be allowed to sit near the door 'that I might make my escape'. She positioned herself as an onlooker, rather than as an active participant, observing that 'Their conversation and debate were well worth hearing'.[65] Indeed, Priscilla persistently presented female spectatorship of male politics as a highly privileged practice. This applied to witnessing parliamentary debates from the ventilator space, as well as the 'very great treat' of surreptitiously watching male anti-slavery dinners, 'from a little morsel of an invisible gallery'.[66] On the other hand, attendance at public anti-slavery meetings could often be more uplifting and less ambivalent than social or domestic sites as political spaces for women. Thus at a meeting at Exeter Hall in 1831 she described to her brother, Edward, how 'We roared with pleasure', 'We cheered immensely', and 'made a fine noise' at her father's speech.[67]

Yet the allure of a powerful father could be a complicated emotion, intensified by the aura of his public status. Listen to this rhapsody upon her father's speech at an anti-slavery meeting in 1832:

> my beloved father's speech the best I ever heard. May I never lose the vivid picture of him as I saw him yesterday, the beauty and majesty of his appearance, the perfect grace of his manner, the energy and force of every movement and gesture. He stood like a living colossus, and I looked at him till I could bear it no longer.[68]

As her marriage approached Priscilla found these feelings difficult to reconcile. She confided to Anna Gurney of her decision to stand down as Thomas's secretary, 'I *dare not* be alone with him, my heart is so touched with my old and precious place and he is so overinteresting to me'.[69] For Priscilla the political cause of the anti-slavery campaign was inextricably

---

[65] Priscilla Buxton to Catherine Hankinson (17 Feb. 1831), ibid. 46.

[66] Priscilla Johnston to Sarah Buxton (12 May 1835), Brit. Emp. S. 444 (14), 33; MacInnes, *Priscilla Johnston's Journal*, 58.

[67] Priscilla Buxton to Edward Buxton (26 Mar. 1831), in MacInnes, *Priscilla Johnston's Journal*, 47.

[68] Ibid. 52. For other examples, ibid. 27, 32 and Priscilla Buxton to Zachary Macaulay (1 Aug. 1833), Brit. Emp. S. 444 (12), 34–5.

[69] Priscilla Buxton to Anna Gurney (25 July 1834), Brit. Emp. S. 444 (13), 98: original emphasis. For the complicated dynamics of their relationship see also Laidlaw, 'Aunt Anna's Report', 9, 12, 16.

linked to the figure of the father, such that she seemed unable to distinguish between them. As she wrote of the cause in May 1833, 'To us personally it is of such immense importance . . . My dearest father's health and comfort are so involved in it that I feel it one of the most important turns in our lives.'[70] The slippage in pronouns here is symptomatic of the centrality of her father to her sense of the family as a political collective. The work she executed for Thomas may not have been viewed in gendered terms by their circle, but it was enacted within a hierarchical father–daughter relationship. The dynamics of their interaction, and the attraction of her father's ascendancy, created perilous emotional terrain.[71]

Priscilla's intimate identification with her family's public persona, but also the privileging of the masculine subject within it, is further illustrated in the arrangements for her marriage to Andrew Johnston. The day chosen for the wedding was 1 August 1834—the date of the emancipation of the slaves in British colonies. The dual purposes of this event were intertwined throughout the day. The date was punctuated by the gentlemen (only) of the party leaving to attend a 'Grand public dinner' held to commemorate the termination of slavery. Later, during an elaborate presentation ceremony, Thomas was bestowed with a number of celebratory gifts. Hannah and Priscilla were then offered souvenirs from Hannah's siblings—gifts which positioned them in relation to Thomas. Louisa Hoare presented Hannah with a silver cup with the inscription, 'To Hannah Buxton, the Partner of her Husband's Labours Sorrows and Joys in the Abolition of Slavery'. The engraving on Priscilla's memento described her as 'the able and devoted assistant of her Father'. Thus, the marriage of the young couple was accorded secondary place to the need to celebrate and affirm the self-perception of Thomas Fowell Buxton and his wider family as primary movers in the political struggle for abolition.[72]

---

[70] MacInnes, *Priscilla Johnston's Journal*, 43, 59.

[71] The theoretical framework of this book draws upon social and cultural psychology. However, Priscilla's relationship with her father might fruitfully be interpreted within the framework of psychoanalyatical approaches. (For another comparable example see above Ch. 3 n. 49.) For a succinct reference to the use of psychoanalytical (particularly Lacanian) theories in the exploration of female political subjectivities see Rogers, *Women and the People*, 42–3 n. 62.

[72] Extract from Anna Gurney's journal, Brit. Emp. S. 444(13), 112–14. Priscilla's honeymoon was similarly shaped by the public concerns of her kin. Her aunt Elizabeth Fry accompanied them on a visit to the Dumbarton area where, to the alarm of local officials, Fry carried out a stately inspection of the local prison, taking the opportunity to recommend many reforms. Commonplace book of Anna Gurney and Sarah Buxton (1834) [n.p.] NRO, RQG, 407.

Following her marriage Priscilla's developing relationship with her husband appears to have tempered the adulation she previously exhibited towards her father. She found herself siding with Andrew, rather than with Thomas, on contentious political issues such as the Irish Church, although she clearly found this painful.[73] In letters to Anna Gurney she began to join in the affectionate jokes concerning Thomas's imperious and egotistical behaviour.[74] Whilst Priscilla's attitude towards her father thus shifted as she matured, the political role she assumed continued to be performed through a cultural framework of masculine political privilege. Involvement in her father's parliamentary work had uneasy implications for Priscilla's own political subjectivity throughout his career, often creating harmful psychological landscapes.

The parochial realms of the Buxton network

By contrast, in her community Priscilla's confidence as a public agent was far less ambivalent. Here, she was assured in her role as a philanthropist and leader and comfortable as a public speaker. For example, in 1830 she claimed that a speech she delivered to the recipients of her clothing charity in the servants' hall had 'brought many of my audience to tears'. The following year she confessed herself pleased with the relationship she had established with the local poor, noting that 'The women are all to come here to eat a dinner and hear a speech from me next Thursday on the subjects of a clothing-charity, the school, punctuality, cleanliness, bible subscription and vaccination!'[75] It was in the parochial realm, rather than the family or civic sphere, that Priscilla appears to have enjoyed the most unequivocal sense of herself as a public figure. Whilst their contribution to colonial politics was subsumed within the wider Buxton identity, in their own community spheres the women of this network were confident public actors in their own right. They would never have delivered a speech at mixed-sex anti-slavery meetings, but they were at ease with public speaking in the parochial realm of kinship networks and neighbourhood relations. The stark differences in women's opportunities and identities across the

---

[73] Priscilla Johnston to her brothers (28 Mar. and 4 Apr. 1835), Brit. Emp. S. 444 (13), 418–20, 430–1.
[74] Priscilla Johnston to Anna Gurney (31 Mar. 1835), ibid. (13), 422; Priscilla Johnston to Anna Gurney and Sarah Buxton (28 Dec. 1838), ibid. (17), 302.
[75] Priscilla Johnston to C. E. Hoare (23 Oct. 1831), MacInnes, *Priscilla Johnston's Journal*, 48.

various zones of their engagement can be illustrated more fully in the career of Anna Gurney.

Anna Gurney (1795–1857) was born at Keswick Hall, near Norwich, to Richard and Rachel Gurney. Despite being born to a prominent Quaker family she herself was to be baptized as an Anglican in adulthood. Possessed of a prodigious intellect, in 1819 she published the first modern translation of the Anglo-Saxon Chronicle. She provided advanced tuition in Anglo-Saxon studies to young male students, one friend referring to her affectionately as 'Dr Gurney'.[76] As the catalogues compiled by her assistant Sarah Rushmore establish, she also carried out extensive research into the Norse sagas, Icelandic languages, and ancient northern history. She later mastered many modern northern European and African languages.[77] In addition to her campaigns in the field of animal welfare,[78] she shared with her partner (and first cousin) Sarah Buxton, a love of zoology, natural history, and fossils. In 1845 her status as a scholar of national repute was recognized when she became the first woman to be made an associate of the British Archaeological Association, to whose publication *Archaelogia* she was also a contributor.

As well as her scholarly activities and collective campaigning with the wider Buxton family Anna Gurney was a formidable presence in her local community. Overstrand was perched on a dangerous stretch of the Norfolk coast which frequently claimed the lives of the local fishing community. Gurney took it upon herself to establish and maintain lifeboat services and implemented a new method of sea rescue—the 'Manby Gun'—which used mortar shells to send life lines to sinking ships. She regularly supervised extensive drills in the use of this equipment and during storms would call upon servants to take her to the sea front where she would direct rescue operations. She also leant on her political contacts to effect change—putting pressure upon Thomas to raise the subject of lifeguard stations

---

[76] Anna Gurney, *A Literal Translation of the Saxon Chronicle* (Norwich, 1819); letter from Amelia Opie [?] to Sarah Buxton and Anna Gurney (2 Aug. 1834) in Gurney and Buxton, Commonplace book. For Gurney's biography consult *ODNB* and Richard Lane, *Anna Gurney 1795–1857* (Dereham, 2001).

[77] Lists of Anna Gurney's MSS, compiled by Sarah [Lucy] Rushmore (1857) NRO, RQG, 412/2–5; Anna Gurney to Priscilla Johnston (Mar. 1843), Brit. Emp. S. 444 (20a), 383.

[78] A paper Gurney authored on animal cruelty was presented to the pope and apparently secured some measure of reform. Thomas Fowell Buxton to Edward Buxton (9 Mar. 1840), Brit. Emp S. 444 (19), 217–18; Augusto Garofilini to Anna Gurney (8 Mar. 1841), ibid. 177e–h. Female members of the Cobden family also attempted to intercede with the pope on the issue of animal rights: Frances Allen to Sarah Wedgwood (2 Nov. 1847), W/M 118.

before the House of Commons. Through lobbying Trinity House she established the 'Gurney Light' which was affixed to a small lifeboat on the most dangerous stretch of sand.[79]

Gurney's efforts regarding the coastal rescue services were part of a much larger project of local improvement. In addition to financing the upkeep of the lifeboats she undertook the construction of a new road through the village. Indeed she and her partner, Sarah, provided much of the community's infrastructure.[80] This included establishing, running, and funding the local Belfrey school which enabled the women to experiment with innovative educational ideas. The punishment of pupils, for example, was replaced by a method of positive discipline. The two women ran many of the local charities, including clothing and Bible clubs. When Gurney died the local vicar Paul Johnson maintained that the community's elderly poor were her 'pensioners' and almost entirely supported by her. Anna Gurney's influence extended to the operation of the local church. At the time of her death she had been making plans for a major restoration and extension of the church building. She was also behind a proposal to enable the church to run two services by paying for the salary of a curate. In 1839, when her beloved Sarah died, she insisted that she herself should give the funeral oration in their local parish church.[81]

Gurney's assumption of local authority was rooted in her financial capacities as a local benefactor, her association with the famed Gurney and Buxton network, and her wider confidence as a highly regarded cultural agent. She constructed herself as an accomplished intellectual figure to the local poor (she provided evening classes to the village's labouring men). According to her obituary in the *Gentleman's Magazine*, they 'justly regarded [her] as a superior being'.[82] In addition, Gurney's colonial politics provided her with a clear sense of her own ethnic superiority. She was extremely progressive in inviting an African preacher to deliver sermons in her local parish church. However this was an interchange which strengthened her investment in a particular racial identity. She appeared fascinated with her

---

[79] Thomas Fowell Buxton to Anna Gurney (15 Apr. 1823), Brit. Emp. S. 444 (2), 53; Verily Anderson, *The Northrepps Grandchildren* (London, 1968), 172.

[80] A summary (probably written by the local vicar, Paul Johnson) of Anna Gurney's contributions to the local community may be found at: NRO, RQG, 412/30. Anna Gurney mentions her new road in a letter to Priscilla Johnston (10–12 Oct. 1843), Brit. Emp. S. 444★ (20a), 468.

[81] Anderson, *Northrepps Grandchildren*, 143–4, 184; letter from Paul Johnson (25 June 1857), NRO, RQG, 412/41 and NRO, RQG, 412/37.

[82] *Gentleman's Magazine* (Sept. 1857), 342.

visitor's physical appearance and the choice of language she used to describe him is disturbing for a modern audience, writing to Priscilla that 'It was *refreshing* to see a woolly head in Overstrand pulpit'. Later that year when she entertained the Reverend Samuel Crowther, a former slave, she joked: 'I am growing *half* a Nigger myself', noting that her guest was '*perfectly* black'.[83] The Buxton circle was infused with a profound sense of their cultural and racial difference from those they wished to assist.

Despite the silencing of Gurney's contribution to colonial policy in the official record, her extensive cultural achievements and extraordinary contribution to coastal safety meant that she did accrue some eminence amongst the reading public. When travelling in Frankfurt in 1836, Anna Gurney and Sarah Buxton had achieved sufficient notice for them to be invited for an audience with the Princess Elizabeth.[84] The writer George Borrow was determined to visit Anna Gurney as 'one of the three celebrities of the world he desired to see'.[85] The nature of her representation in contemporary texts is revealing, however. It was frequently refracted through the nature of her relationship with Sarah. The two women were ubiquitously referred to, both within family circles and also to a wider public, as 'the cottage ladies'. Associating them metonymically with their home feminized their image whilst also implying modest perimeters to their lives and influence. On delivering his funeral oration to Gurney, Edward Hoare declared to his audience that 'Northrepps Cottage is without its tenant'.[86] Associating Gurney with the cottage was a rhetorical device which shifted the potentially disruptive meanings of Gurney's life to the neutral signifier of a physical location.

Representing Sarah and Anna in relation to their abode was a means of obliquely hinting at, yet also containing, their unusual domestic arrangements. The relationship between Sarah and Anna was one of deep emotional attachment. They lived together in Northrepps Cottage from 1823 until Sarah's death and referred to each other as 'partners'. As those close to them appreciated, this signalled an arrangement akin to marriage.

---

[83] Anna Gurney to Priscilla Johnston (Mar. and 10–12 Oct. 1843), Brit. Emp. S. 444 (20a), 383, 462.

[84] Diary of Sarah Ann Nichols (Apr.–Sept. 1836), NRO, FX 38 /1. Nichols was a paid travelling companion of Buxton and Gurney.

[85] In the event Borrow found himself overwhelmed by Anna Gurney's exuberant conversation whilst trying to elucidate a point of Arabic grammar and claims he fled the room. Herbert Jenkins, *The Life of George Borrow* (London, 1912), 423–4.

[86] Edward Hoare, *The Coming Night: A Sermon Preached in Cromer Church on Occasion of the Death of Miss Anna Gurney of Northrepps Cottage* (London, 1857), 4.

Following Sarah's death Thomas wrote sorrowfully to his brother-in-law, John Joseph Gurney, 'Poor Anna . . . the affection she bore her partner was indeed remarkable, it is more than widowhood.'[87] Their relationship was memorialized as such in their local church, the commemorative tablet referring to them as 'partners and chosen sisters'.[88] As this suggests, locals did not convey their relationship as necessarily aberrant. Indeed, at the village school the initials of the two women were featured in pink pebbles at the front of the building.[89] This is in keeping with scholarship on women's same-sex relationships which suggests that, prior to the creation of the discourse of 'the lesbian', there was greater latitude in contemporary opinions on this question.[90] Nonetheless associating Gurney so closely with her home served to limit and circumscribe impressions of her sphere of influence (in the same way that Lady Eleanor Butler and Sarah Ponsonby, who attracted renown as 'the ladies of Llangollen', were discursively tied to the geographical site of their relationship.[91])

In fact, of course, Northrepps Cottage did not function as a site of simple domesticity. When the Buxton family embarked upon the select committee report it was taken for granted by the family that Northrepps Cottage would form the locus for this massive undertaking.[92] It was at Northrepps Cottage that Gurney amassed an extensive library as well as accumulating an impressive archaeological collection. (As Amelia Opie wrote fondly to a friend from Northrepps Cottage in 1834, 'Anna Gurney abounds in mammoth remains'.[93]) It was also at Northrepps Cottage that the two women provided adult education classes, and where they entertained visiting African dignitaries. For the young William Forster, the future Liberal MP, Northrepps

[87] Thomas Fowell Buxton to Joseph John Gurney (6 Jan. 1840), Brit. Emp. S. 444 (19), 76. For further references to Anna's response to her partner's death see Anna Gurney (later Backhouse) to Joseph John Gurney (21 Dec. 1829) and Amelia Opie to Anna Gurney, Friends House Library, London, Gurney papers 3/92 and 4/43.

[88] Memorial tablet, Overstrand Church. My thanks to Rowan Gleadle for locating this.

[89] Anderson, *Northrepps Grandchildren*, 149. The building now forms part of the local primary school where these initials are still clearly visible.

[90] See Lillian Faderman, *Surpassing the Love of Men: Romantic Friendship and Love between Women from the Renaissance to the Present* (New York, 1981); although for further debate on this point consult Alison Oram, 'Telling Stories about the Ladies of Llangollen: The Construction of Lesbian and Feminist Histories', in Ann-Marie Gallagher *et al.* (eds), *Re-presenting the Past: Women and History* (Harlow, 201), 44–62.

[91] Elizabeth Mavor, *The Ladies of Llangollen: A Study in Romantic Friendship* (Harmondsworth, 1971).

[92] Priscilla Johnston to Sarah Buxton (28 June 1836), Brit. Emp. S. 444 (15), 64.

[93] Amelia Opie to Charles Sneyd Edgeworth (7 Mar. 1834), Edgeworth, c.741, 171v. See also the inventory of Northrepps Cottage (15 June 1857), NRO, RQG, 412/21.

Cottage was a centre of political advice and learning, where he relied upon Gurney to tutor him in his early political career.[94] The 'cottage ladies' was a cosy image of domesticity that depoliticized their endeavours.

Those discussions of Gurney's achievement which did not utilize the trope of the 'cottage ladies' tended to focus upon her physical status. Childhood poliomyelitis and its mistreatment made it difficult for her to walk unaided.[95] Despite bouts of ill health and considerable mobility problems, family letters indicate that, save for the last years of her life, Gurney was fairly vigorous and physically flexible—with references to her dancing with Sarah, or playing skittles with the African visitors to her home. Moreover having the financial resources for sophisticated mechanical apparatus and attentive personal staff meant that the impact of her disabilities was less than might otherwise have been the case. Yet portrayals of Gurney overstated her physical difficulties, seemingly fascinated by the apparent incongruity of a woman with disabilities playing such an active part in coastal rescue service. Joanna Baillie's 'Night Scene by the Sea' referred to her awkwardly as:

> One with limbs nerve-bound,
> Whose feet have never touched the ground,
> Who loves in tomes of Runic lore
> To scan the curious tales of yore.

Reprinting the poem in her *Book of Golden Deeds*, Charlotte Yonge similarly marvelled at Gurney's physical achievements:

> Surely there can be no more noble picture than this infirm woman, constantly in pain, whose right it would have seemed to be shielded from a rough blast or the very knowledge of suffering, coming forth in the dead of night, amid the howling storm, beating spray, and drenching rain, to direct and inspirit its rugged seafaring men, and send them on errands of life or death.

For Yonge, Gurney's physical strength was something of an enigma, but she suggested that her extraordinary personal activity was the 'strangest thing of all'. Attempting to convey the breadth of Gurney's community involvement, Yonge's descriptions became more overtly gendered, referring to her 'grace', 'kindness and helpfulness'. Gurney's atypical body and intellect disrupted such an image though. Describing her as an 'invalid' and 'scholar',

---

[94] Reid, *W. E. Forster*, i. 47–50, 85.
[95] 'Account of Anna Gurney by her Cousin', Gurney papers, 2/23.

Yonge concluded that, 'The cripple gave what she had—her vigorous mind, her means, and her spirit.'[96]

Anna Gurney was not presented as an exemplar of a wider phenomenon, therefore, but rather as an atypical case for whom the normal expectations of feminine conduct need not apply. Invalidism could be a source of empowerment for female intellectuals in this sense.[97] However, presenting Gurney's parochial activities to a wider public in this way obscured any acknowledgement of the breadth and potential of female publicity more broadly.

Gurney herself displayed similar complexity in the articulation of her activities. On the one hand she was concerned to emphasize not affective qualities but rather her economic responsibilities as the rationale for community involvement. For example, she insisted that intervention in rescue provision was incumbent upon coastal property owners: 'It is particularly desirable that all persons possessing property on the coast should feel it their imperious duty to provide beforehand for the safety of those unfortunate men, who may be cast away on their own estates, or in their immediate neighbourhood.'[98] That wealth brought with it local public responsibilities was often expressed in her circles. As the family friend who delivered her funeral sermon put it, 'She was intrusted with property, and you all know what use she made of it.'[99] However, this could have a gendered dimension. In a letter to Hudson Gurney in 1854, Anna Gurney explained that their brother, Richard, had made Hudson and not Anna his heir. This is hardly surprising, given the financial conventions of the day, but Richard clearly wished to make a point in arranging his affairs thus. According to Anna Gurney, he told her that his reason was that 'I do not approve of women having large responsibilities'. 'In this', she continued, 'I _honestly_ acquiesced & concurred with him'. Insisting that she was very grateful for the financial terms under which she was permitted to live at Northrepps Cottage, she further observed that she would not want a 'larger sphere'. She expressed fears that she would not

---

[96] Charlotte Mary Yonge, *A Book of Golden Deeds of All Times and All Lands* (London, 1864), 431–3. Elizabeth Wheler evoked Gurney as 'a very remarkable woman' who, during fierce storms, 'would be wheeled to the cliff, [where she] gave all directions, and saved many lives'. Moilliet, *Elizabeth Anne Galton*, 186. It was a theme which was to be much laboured by Gurney's obituarists. See e.g. *Gentleman's Magazine* (Sept. 1857), 342–3.

[97] For a similar argument with reference to Harriet Martineau see Alison Winter, 'Harriet Martineau and the Reform of the Invalid in Victorian England', *Historical Journal*, 38 (1995), 599–600.

[98] Anna Gurney, *On the Means of Assistance in Cases of Shipwreck* (Norwich, 1825), 1.

[99] Hoare, *Coming Night*, 13.

'properly fulfil its *dictates*' and thus would not desire 'any greater material responsibilities'.[100]

As a woman nearing the end of her life, and who already had such a wealth of philanthropic, community, political, and scholarly commitments, it is perhaps not surprising that Gurney might be reluctant to increase her responsibilities. Yet Gurney's apparent compliance with the notion that women should not, in any case, have weighty public obligations suggests how individuals might feel constrained to adopt discrete aspects of a female identity at specific moments. The delicate family circumstances of the letter's composition led Anna to assure her brother that she was untroubled that she had not benefited from Richard's will. That she underlined 'honestly' twice is an indication that she assumed her brother to entertain some doubts as to her real acquiescence in such views. Positioning herself with more conventional views as to the female role may have formed part of a tactful recognition that her personal circumstances and lifestyle could sometimes have been difficult for all family members to view with equanimity. Gurney often tended to present an unfeminine identity in her immediate personal relations, adopting what were read by her family as masculine hairstyles, for example, and having a series of 'intimate friends' who stayed in the cottage with her following the death of her partner.[101] This is not to say that womanliness could be simply assumed as a 'masquerade', rather that in social interaction individuals might modify their self-presentation according to situational factors. This in itself had the potential to gradually reorientate the ways in which an individual desired to act and perceive themselves. It formed part of a deeper process of the ongoing construction of identity. In Anna Gurney's case, the deferential role she assumed in correspondence with her more conservative brother was part of a broader process of self-presentation and performance. This perhaps contributed to the facilitation of other behaviours, such as the adoption of a subordinate role in relation to Thomas Fowell, comparative to the dominant, authoritative tone she so often assumed in other social interactions.[102]

---

[100] Anna Gurney to Hudson Gurney (5 Jan. 1854), NRO, RQG, 412/42.

[101] 'Account of Anna Gurney'.

[102] Joan Riviere, 'Womanliness as a Masquerade' (1929), repr. in Athol Hughes (ed.), *The Inner World and Joan Riviere: Collected Papers, 1920–1958* (London and New York, 1991), 94–6. Feminist critiques of social identity theory posit the need for fluid understandings of the working of gender within social interaction: Thoits and Virshup, 'Me's and We's', 110. An overview of social identity approaches is provided in Dominic Abrams and Michael A. Hogg (eds), *Social Identity Theory: Constructive and Critical Advances* (Hemel Hempstead, 1990). For the implications for feminist scholarship see Baker and Skevington, *Social Identity of Women*.

The 'public sphere' of anti-slavery

So far we have considered the varying gendered dynamics which shaped the experience of this network of women in their domestic and parochial settings. In this final section we will examine, through a detailed reading of a single event, how the gendered contours of the public sphere were implicated in the construction of female subjectivity.

On 18 November 1840 a meeting was held in Norwich to establish an auxiliary body of Thomas Fowell Buxton's African Civilization Society. Instrumental in the organization of this event was Buxton's brother-in-law and close friend, Joseph John Gurney. As a Quaker J. J. Gurney was uneasy with the fact that the Niger expedition—a primary objective of the society—was to request military support. (Buxton's plans for the development of the Niger region incorporated the establishment of permanent military squadrons along the coast.) Yet, fresh from his anti-slavery tour of the United States of America, Gurney was keen to galvanize the citizens of Norwich.[103] The meeting took place in St Andrew's Hall. T. F. Buxton and J. J Gurney were both on the platform, along with local dignitaries such as the high sheriff and the Bishop. They were joined by a number of women—including members of the Bishop's family and other high-status locals such as Lady Suffield and Lady Acheson. Present too on the platform were Amelia Opie, Priscilla Johnston, and Katharine Fry (the daughter of Elizabeth Fry and thus Priscilla's cousin). The front rows of the hall were also filled with women, leading a reporter to refer to the 'numerous and brilliant assemblage of the *elite* of the ladies of the city and county'.[104]

However, the meeting quickly turned into a contentious and dramatic event thanks to the attendance of some 200 local Chartists. Buxton and Gurney's known hostility to democratic politics and the society's appeal to Tory politicians no doubt made them obvious targets for Chartist protest.[105] Thus when the Bishop of Norwich moved a resolution calling for a 'strenuous' exertion against the evils of slavery, the Chartists attempted to move a competing resolution through the agency of two Chartist speakers. The

---

[103] David E. Swift, *Joseph John Gurney: Banker, Reformer and Quaker* (Middletown, Conn., 1962), 236–7.

[104] *The Times* (20 Nov. 1840).

[105] Turley, *Culture of English Antislavery*, 100–1, 183–5. For the tense relationship between anti-slavery and Chartism see Betty Fladeland, '"Our Cause Being One and the Same": Abolitionists and Chartism', in James Walvin (ed.), *Slavery and British Society, 1776–1846* (London, 1982), 69–99. For background see J. K. Edwards, 'Chartism in Norwich', *Yorkshire Bulletin of Economic and Social Research*, 19 (1967), 85–100.

business of the meeting eventually had to be abandoned due to the noise and confusion this occasioned. The incident had a deep impact upon those present. Priscilla Johnston claimed it to be 'one of the most painful scenes I ever saw'.[106]

In a detailed account of the affair composed in a letter to a friend, Priscilla's cousin Katharine Fry placed the Chartists' failure to conform to the niceties and rituals of public oratory at the foremost of her narrative.[107] Displaying a heightened awareness of the codes and etiquette of public deportment, she dwelt upon the physiognomical differences between the two parties. The composure of her uncles' expressions during the disturbances 'so patient and so sad' was compared to the 'savage' '*prison* countenances' of the Chartists.

The apparent peculiarity of being addressed by someone wearing working men's fustian garments also shocked her, as did their failure to comply with the subtle, internalized rituals of bodily conduct that typified the bearing of the bourgeois male in the civic sphere. That one Chartist chose to deliver his speech, 'standing on one bench with one foot, & the other on the back of another' grated against her sensibilities, as did the 'sort of swaggering insolent fun in his manner'. She observed their ignorance of the usual codes of public speaking, disapproving of their interruption of speeches. The Chartist speakers' reliance upon written notes was also commented upon by Fry—as was their apparently halting delivery— leading her to the conclusion, 'I infer their speeches were made for them by some higher than themselves'. The strong local dialect of the two Chartist orators further confirmed to Fry their illegitimate claims to speak. '[T]he accent & pronunciation was the broadest Norfolk', Fry wrote of the first speaker. The incongruity of someone with such a dialect laying claim to public attention and the supposed naivety of his words was such that Fry and many of the other anti-slavery supporters found it, 'impossible not to laugh'. '[H]is broad Norfolk was so very droll', she added, 'that no one could resist it'. Tensions in the meeting then reached new heights as the high sheriff attempted to take a vote on the competing amendments proposed by the Chartist leader, John Dover, and Archdeacon Bathurst. As the noise and confusion mounted, in Fry's account the Chartists were likened to animals, 'leaping along like wild beasts, shouting, yelling & bellowing'. Similarly Charlotte Upcher, who was also at the meeting, referred to the 'groans, or more correctly the wolf-like howl' of the

---

[106] Priscilla Johnston to Anna Gurney (19 Nov. 1840), Brit. Emp. S. 444 (20), 43e–f.
[107] Katharine Fry to Louisa Pelly (19 Nov. 1840), ibid. (20), 37–43.

Chartists.[108] As Madeline Hurd has observed, 'The public sphere . . . created its own out-groups. Those who were rational, capable of disinterested argument, whose mental processes were autonomous and free, belonged. Others did not.' This included an acute sensitivity to normative modes of speech, deportment, and mien—the transgression of which could lead to the 'mental invocation of disqualifying stereotypes'.[109]

Fry's experience and representation of the event was also shaped by the ritualized use of space at the meeting. Her physical elevation on the platform, she explained to her correspondent, meant that she had been able to observe everything most clearly. The vantage point enjoyed by means of her privileged status as a member of the platform party gave Fry a sense of political authority to read and interpret the event. She consequently composed a highly didactic account of its significance: 'I thought much of the scenes of the first French Revolution . . . I saw how a few wicked & determined men excited & led on the others . . . I plainly saw how mobs are led on to desperation'. For Fry the depravity of the Chartists was additionally symbolized by the influence exerted by their womenfolk: 'I also saw some women who excited the men, & whose shill voices outscreamed the roar of the men. I heard they were three well known Socialist sisters, the vilest of the vile.' In contrast to the unrestrained behaviour of the working-class women, Fry notes that the middle-class women were sheltered and protected by the 'gentlemen' who, on the advice of the police, began to evacuate them from the hall. Fry's account articulates a highly gendered version of the public sphere. The presence of middle-class women is conveyed as being managed and overseen by their male peers who rightfully control the meeting.

There is, though, a curious anomaly in Fry's narrative. She portrays the Chartists as dangerous, violent, and potentially revolutionary. Charles Buxton gave a similar impression in his account, maintaining that 'a large body of Chartists broke into the hall'.[110] Yet there is no indication that Fry was herself frightened and, as noted above, she records the expressions of her uncles as 'sombre' rather than concerned. This dissonance is readily explained. What Fry omitted to explain in her narrative was that the Chartists' interventions were, in fact, perfectly in accordance with the custom of the meeting. The event had originally been conceived as a county

[108] Pigott, *Memoir*, 283.
[109] Madeline Hurd, 'Class, Masculinity, Manners and Mores: Public Space and Public Sphere in Nineteenth-Century Europe', *Social Science History*, 24 (2000), 75–110, quotes at 77, 93.
[110] Buxton, *Memoirs*, 522.

meeting. These were a long established tradition in English shires, called when it could be proven that a majority of (elite) opinion in the county was in favour of convening to discuss a pressing political issue. J. J. Gurney had accordingly canvassed prominent and notable figures in Norwich and Norfolk obtaining a petition with over 200 signatures for presentation to the high sheriff. On receiving a deputation bearing this petition the high sheriff had announced that he was to 'appoint a meeting of the freeholders and inhabitants of the county of Norfolk, to be holden in the Shire-Hall, Norwich'.[111] This anti-slavery occasion was therefore qualitatively different from many of those organized by the networks of provincial, middle-class Nonconformist activism. It was a county event, drawing upon long traditions of local identity and regional pride. The sheriff, Mr Villebois, made the decision that the event should be convened initially in the Shire-Hall—the proper site for a county meeting. However, perhaps sensitive to the fact that Gurney's family network included many women who had been central to the anti-slavery movement, or cognizant of the widely publicized female interest in the cause, he proclaimed that it would then move to St Andrew's Hall, where 'seats would be provided for the ladies'. This decision confused the boundaries of the meeting. A county event had now been transposed to a specifically civic location—a site where freemen were permitted to participate, and to affirm addresses and petitions from the city. Local Chartist weavers were quick to seize upon this meeting as an opportunity to make their political voice heard. As an astute reporter for *The Times* explained, 'had the business of the day been proceeded with in the Shire-Hall, where legitimately a county court could be held, instead of in St Andrew's-Hall, which being the property of the freemen of the city they could not be excluded, all would have been regular, and the programme of the day not disturbed by the ebullitions of Chartist freemen'.[112]

The local Chartists were quick to organize themselves in response to the high sheriff's announcement. Dover, their leader, took particular advantage of the notice concerning the provision of seats for ladies. He issued handbills calling upon Chartists to ensure that their wives and daughters

---

[111] *The Times* (20 Nov. 1840). See also the Gurney papers, 3/792–801 and 3/805–13. For useful background on contemporary Norwich see Penelope Corfield, 'From Second City to Regional Capital', in Carole Rawcliffe and Richard Wilson (eds), *Norwich since 1550* (London and New York, 2004), 139–66.

[112] *The Times* (20 Nov. 1840). For the significance of 'space' for political utterance see James Epstein, *In Practice: Studies in the Language and Culture of Popular Politics in Modern Britain* (Stanford, Calif., 2003), ch. 5.

would take advantage of the move.[113] Once at the meeting Dover was challenged by the high sheriff when he rose to speak. However, on explaining that he was 'a freeholder of the county, and a freeman of the city of Norwich', he was given permission to address the meeting. When the seconder of his amendment, Robert Paine, was forced to admit that he did not qualify as a freeholder or a freeman, another Chartist, Thomas Hewitt, was found who did. The actions of the Chartists may have been 'noisy and turbulent beyond description', as J. J. Gurney recorded in his journal, but they were acting within the conventions of the meeting, as dictated by the choice of venue.[114] This explains why the atmosphere of the meeting may have been hostile and uncomfortable, but does not appear to have been experienced as frightening.

Fry's portrayal of the Chartists' behaviour as an anarchic act of rebellion thus erased the fact that, in delivering his speech, Dover acted in perfect accord with the conventions of a freemen's hall. Dover was not, as Fry represented, a wild proto-revolutionary, but was a recognized working-class representative with whom the elites had previously worked. J. J. Gurney himself had enjoyed a 'long and friendly discussion over an ample meal' with Dover and others in 1829 when they met to discuss the situation of the city's unemployed weavers. In 1841 Dover was to be a parliamentary candidate.[115] Furthermore whilst Fry implied a strict division between the Chartists and the anti-slavery supporters, there was not in fact a consensus even amongst those on the platform as to the Chartists' behaviour. Archdeacon Bathurst had risen to profess his sympathy with the Chartist argument that it was the ills of English labourers which should be prioritized. The Chartist speakers had made many references to the iniquities of the new Poor Law and Bathurst admitted that he shared their opposition to it. Strikingly, Bathurst next openly criticized the meeting's organizers and in particular the policy of affording accommodation to ladies. To 'great applause' from the Chartists, Bathurst pronounced that,

> With all respect to the sheriff and to the fair sex, by whom it was delightful to be surrounded, he must say, that at this, a county meeting, to the ladies ought not to have been allotted the front seats, delightful as it was to have

---

[113] *Norfolk Chronicle* (21 Nov. 1840); Revd Francis Cunningham to Revd Robert E. Hankinson (19 Nov. 1840), Brit. Emp. S. 444 (20), 43.
[114] Cited in Swift, *Joseph John Gurney*, 237.
[115] Ibid. 108–9. Dover's candidature ended dismally with accusations of electoral corruption: Barry Doyle, 'Politics, 1833–1945', in Rawcliffe and Wilson, *Norwich*, 350.

them present; still it was to men the arguments of such a meeting were to be addressed, and by men those arguments ought to be adjudicated upon.[116]

It is particularly significant that Fry censored from her account these criticisms of the women's presence that evening. Her need to edit this vital detail is illustrative of the cultural work which could underscore the maintenance of individual identity.[117]

The contested organization of public space is central to these competing accounts of the anti-slavery meeting. Katharine Fry's reading of the episode constructed a simple morality tale that depended upon a dichotomous representation of the unruly Chartists and the upright anti-slavery supporters. In so doing she drew upon a web of cultural associations as to appropriate public behaviour. This validated her own presence at the meeting as a (literally) elevated member of the local elite, casting the Chartists as intemperate transgressors of the public space. She silenced the fact that the Chartist leaders acted in accordance with the conventions of a civic meeting, and failed to acknowledge that it was the presence of women, rather than the actions of the Chartists, that was seen as transgressive and ill-judged by many at the meeting. Women's presence within the civic public sphere—even on such an issue as anti-slavery—could be the source of considerable tension. Women might be present at meetings but their attendance was seen as secondary and liable to be revoked. Indeed, at an earlier anti-slavery meeting in Norwich, women had been 'ordered to leave the room' when the debate became acrimonious.[118] Yet despite women's marginalization, they were not simply passive spectators at occasions of this nature. Their ongoing interpretations of, and reactions to, events were critical to the construction of the social and political conflicts occurring. As privileged, elite women they could be construed both as important, yet simultaneously ancillary to the meeting. Fry's account therefore speaks of the paradoxical location of platform women, being concurrently in a position of centrality (due to their social status) and marginality (due to their gender).[119]

Gender operated in highly complex ways in the public sphere with unpredictable consequences for individual subjectivity. Katharine Fry wished to construct a narrative of the event which repressed the outright hostility demonstrated towards women's presence, a phenomenon at odds

---

[116] *The Times* (20 Nov. 1840).

[117] Similarly, the meeting's organizers published an account of the resolutions passed which made no reference to the Chartists' interventions: Brit. Emp. S. 444 (20) 43j.

[118] Pigott, *Memoir*, 119.

[119] Rose, *Feminism and Geography*, 151–2.

with her habituation to her mother's publicity and the wider family's identity of female collaboration in the anti-slavery cause. Female subjectivities in the public sphere, and consequent reflections upon their experience, could necessitate silencing aspects of their gendered dimension—a process illustrative of the frequently conflictual nature of women's political identity.

Conclusion

The apparent masculinity of the official public sphere emerges in these sources as a fractured and unstable entity. Whilst the family's public memorialization of Thomas Fowell Buxton's career, written by his son, Charles, is reticent on the role played by female relatives, the unpublished family archive compiled by the women family members amounts to an extensive, unofficial history of collective family endeavour.[120] Nonetheless, as we have seen, despite the opportunities family political work afforded for women to engage in the parliamentary process, their own identities (and that of other subaltern males within the network) could be subsumed beneath the weight accorded to the head of the family. The construction of a 'we' identity in this context sometimes amounted to an elision of individual identities into the persona of Thomas Fowell Buxton, rather than the construction of a more expansively empowering collective identity.

Across the various scenarios we have considered it is clear that gender did not always construct notions of citizenship in obvious or predictable ways. Its functioning was complicated by the hierarchies of age, birth order, marital and sexual status, and location. Buxton's wife constructed herself as a supportive but apolitical matriarch, but gendered roles were less clear cut in the case of Sarah Buxton and Anna Gurney whose relationship defied conventional sexual norms. In the younger generation men and women were treated interchangeably as political labourers for the cause, although the emotional texture of their relationship with Thomas Fowell Buxton varied according to both gender and their place in the family order. Individuals invested in particular identities to varying degrees, with group identities achieving their greatest salience when they reaffirmed existing self-perceptions. Contrast Priscilla's ready absorption in the collective

---

[120] Buxton, *Memoirs*, is more explicit about the assistance lent by Andrew Johnston, e.g. 431, 433; Laidlaw, 'Aunt Anna's Report', 24 n. 58. The role of Anna Gurney and Sarah Buxton in constructing the archive is given in Patricia M. Pugh, *Calendar of the Papers of Sir Thomas Fowell Buxton, 1786–1845* (London, 1980), p. i.

familial identity with the more hesitant response of the less confident Richenda. That is to say, 'within-gender variability' might be as significant as gender difference *per se*.[121]

In addition, as we have seen, the significance of gender as a cultural variable operated very differently in the public sphere of the anti-slavery meeting than it did in the parochial realm of the Buxtons' neighbouring community. Personal accounts of women's experiences on the platform of the meeting of the African Civilization Society in Norwich were highly revealing as to the ways in which subjectivity was shaped and formed in accordance with the gendered spaces of the public sphere. In contrast, far less problematic was the experience of the Buxton women in their 'parochial realms'. Here, the intricate enmeshing of social, cultural, political, and ethnic status enabled the construction of authoritative identities, even if they might wish to sometimes represent their role in more restrictive, gendered terms. However, whilst gender could be performed by individuals as a means of self-construction, this was not a free-floating phenomenon. Rather, it was enacted within the context of coherent (if at times subconscious) personal strategies and patterns of behaviour.

[121] This term is taken from Lott, 'Dual Natures', 72–6.

Conclusions

When the painter Benjamin Haydon executed his ambitious study of the world anti-slavery convention which met in London 1840, he was at pains to include women in his portrayal. However, they were situated as—literally—borderline figures. The dramatic centerpiece of the work focused upon the veteran campaigner, Thomas Clarkson, who is surrounded by a host of male anti-slavery crusaders. Women are positioned around the edges of the great painting. Whilst some famous female activists are clearly visible, such as Anne Knight and Elizabeth Pease, the woman who was given the greatest prominence in the work, just to the left of Thomas Clarkson, was Mary Clarkson. Tellingly, she had not achieved prominence due to her grass-roots campaigning. Rather, her status derived from the fact that she was Clarkson's daughter.[1] Haydon's image encapsulates many of the themes of this book. Women occupied an enduring but peripheral location within the contemporary political imagination. Their status within the world of public politics remained problematic throughout this period—even in campaigns apparently deemed suitable for female activism, such as anti-slavery. Family identities, moreover, remained crucial to the positioning of women as political subjects. In the years between the ending of the war with France in 1815 and the second Reform Act in 1867 there were gathering opportunities for female political engagement. But, as we have seen, these shifts occurred in complex ways.

New opportunities occasioned by the gradual acceptability of some aspects of women's public interventions (such as petitioning and public speaking) were not straightforwardly assimilated into female identities. Engaging in such work often went hand-in-hand with the reactive or

---

[1] Benjamin Robert Haydon, *The Great Meeting of Delegates, Held at the Freemasons Tavern, June 1840, for the Abolition of Slavery and the Slave Trade throughout the World* (1841). The painting may be viewed at the National Portrait Gallery. The Gallery's website provides a helpful key to the work: http://www.npg.org.uk/live/search/portrait.asp?LinkID=mp00069&rNo=0&role=sit

tactical assertion of heightened gender difference. Articulations that emphasized women's inferior political understanding, or insisted that their political role should be enacted through domestic or affective relationships, were commonplace. However, the circumstances of these utterances were always intricate and dependent upon a complex constellation of factors, including family sensitivities, political tactics, and civic identities. Whilst there could be a multitude of reasons for succumbing to such representations at the micro-level, at the macro-level these repeated articulations contributed to the perpetuation of a hegemonic gendered code.[2]

Yet if gendered hegemonies were upheld through the constant, repeated action of individuals, this also provided the potential for gradual adjustments as subtle shifts in inflections, or alternative appropriations of these tropes, could open up the possibility for heterodox readings. Therefore, although there were many 'losses' for women in this period— such as the ending of freewomen's rights, the decline in parochial authority, and the decreasing significance of patronage networks—we have also seen how the seeds of change emerged. The enthusiastic electoral candidate mooting the possibility of female suffrage; the female constituents who subverted electoral customs of gift-giving to deliver addresses to their MP, the women who braved male-dominated meetings—in all these cases there was the possibility to exploit the points of tension or ambiguity in the cultural and political order to presage greater opportunities for women. This occurred in tandem with broader social processes. For example, the growth of pressure-group politics, the accession of a female monarch, and the increasing political strength of the middle classes all served to habituate contemporaries to fresh models of female political activity.

Within these contexts the ways in which subjectivity could be expressed and conceptualized was historically specific. As Mary Jean Corbett observes, 'Subjectivities themselves have histories'.[3] The grand narratives of liberal individualism through which the nineteenth century are often read are deeply flawed as a means of understanding female subjectivity.[4] Liberal individualism was a powerful discourse, but its development was not a simple linear process. Perceptions of the autonomous self emerged within,

---

[2] Judith Butler's work is apposite here: *Gender Trouble: Feminism and the Subversion of Identity* (London and New York, 1999).

[3] Corbett, *Representing Femininity*, 5.

[4] See also Rendall, 'Introduction', in her *Equal or Different*, 4. Other scholars have also indicated the need to include notions of community and collectivity in our narratives of the 19th cent. See Eugenio F. Biagini (ed.), *Citizenship and Community: Liberals, Radicals and Collective Identities in the British Isles, 1865–1931* (Cambridge, 1996).

and continued to be held in tension with, older paradigms which privileged mutuality and drew upon shared modes of expression and labour.
Equally, a profound commitment to certain understandings of the religious
self as the instruments of God's will shaped the consciousness of both men
and women and further nuanced any simple understanding of rational
individualism.

Women's allegiance to family identities has emerged as central in
tracing the long trajectories of early modern selfhood. As Patrick Joyce
discovered in his study of John Bright, 'Within the household, the collectivity of the family took precedence over individual actions, another curb
on the supposed "individualism" of a bourgeoisie'.[5] The home was conceptualized as a political site across our period (whether for networking and
socializing, the ideological rearing of children, the transmission of female
influence, or the practice of politically informed lifestyle choices). Yet, as we
have seen, this did not mean that it was an unproblematic locus for the
articulation of female political identity. The collaborative conceptualization
of family endeavours meant that in their capacity as wives, sisters, and
daughters numerous middle-class women made contributions to state
governance through their contributions to the official and quasi-official
public literature of their male kin. Yet this was within a framework which
privileged the masculine political subject. This deeply rooted identification
of politics with masculine status had multiple, at times potentially insidious,
implications. It has been suggested that during particular phases of female
adolescent development this might result in complex patterns of gender
identification, during which politically engaged young women valorized
their male, rather than their female kin (with, as we saw in Chapter 7,
sometimes troubling consequences).

Moreover, family politics were not a static phenomenon: sensibilities
shifted in accordance with broader political developments, and women
might be differently empowered in their families at different moments.
Generational factors further complicated the ebb and flow of political
engagement within individual families. The persistence of patriarchal
assumptions in cultural and legal texts, as well as in individual psycholo-
gies, further complicated women's experience of home-based politics. This
is not to argue that the family lacked significance for women's political
engagement. However women's position as family members was often
more significant for the way in which it empowered them in their

---

[5] Patrick Joyce, *Democratic Subjects: The Self and the Social in Nineteenth-Century Cambridge*
(Cambridge, 1994), 124.

communities than it was in their own homes. Women's support for their husband's ambitions in constituency politics could enable them to exploit their status as wives to carve out local authority and influence. This applied to other kinds of occupations also. Vicars' wives and daughters, for example, commonly cultivated an active interest in local affairs and institutions in a manner which could broaden the usual scope of female public involvement. Acting as a dominant local figure might foreground one's individuality but this could still be held in tandem with an investment in a collective family identity.

Prescriptive literature and political rhetoric tended to emphasize women's roles as wives and mothers. In contrast, family archives and auto-biographical texts often reveal a different axis of female identification: the investment many daughters had in the identities of their birth family. Most strikingly illustrated in the case of Mary Ann Gilbert, dynastic subjectivity could be felt as keenly by women as by men. However, this was another example where political modernization led to a diminution in the sources of agency available to women. The blow to the electoral privileges of freemen's daughters in 1832 ended a significant, alternative means of imag-ining female political roles (one which parliamentarians were happy to champion when it suited their cause). There are other respects in which the discursive emphasis upon wives and mothers can be misleading: married women were actually a demographic minority in our period, most were widowed or single. Certainly it has been single women, widows, those in same-sex relationships, and older married women who have emerged as the most striking political actors in this study. An intriguing leitmotif has been the more active public role often assumed by mature women. The older and more experienced may have felt more able to exert authority than their younger peers. The relative freedom brought by the later stage of the life cycle, when most were less constrained by the ties of motherhood, is striking (although the prominence of older women in this study also included the childless). The phenomenon of mature female activism, which cut against the grain of dominant discourses stressing women's public engagement as mothers or wives, further underlines the discursive lacunae in the representation of female politics, pointing again to the lack of an acceptable language in which the generality of independent women might claim their citizenship.

One 'sphere' in which some women did appear able to perform a more overt public role was in their communities. Whereas in the public sphere of national societies, associations, and large-scale meetings women were conveyed as a marginal presence, with emphasis being placed upon their decorous femininity, contemporaries' day-to-day experiences were more diverse. A rich literature has established the importance of community to the public activities of plebeian women, yet to date little has been done to conceptualize its significance for middling and gentry females.[6] As we have seen, local environments were critical to the public identities of women of this class. Local communities were continually in the process of defining and asserting their attitude towards such practices as female voting, officeholding, and petitioning. Even so, there was much greater latitude for forthright female political activity in the parochial realm than was the case in national forums.

Women's work as cultural agents has also emerged as a recurring theme in this respect. It is striking that those who were most dominant in their localities were so frequently engaged in a variety of intellectual networks. Understanding the cultivation and display of female local authority involves rescuing the many ephemeral works women produced for their communities. This includes election ballads and broadsides, handbills, civic poetry, religious exhortation, and publicly circulated letters to local labourers or the vestry. It amounts to a rich, but hitherto neglected corpus of female literature which owed as much to early modern patterns of the anonymous, rural public sphere as it did to women's investment in a bourgeois public sphere.

Examining female activity at the parish level, rather than from the perspective of associational ventures, has unearthed neglected patterns of philanthropic engagement. For example, projects such as the allotment movement drew upon specialized knowledge of husbandry and upon customary paternalistic expectations, rather than upon formulations of gendered roles. Unlike their male counterparts the ownership of significant amounts of land did not entitle women to vote (although it could provide them with other forms of electoral influence). Yet for vast numbers of women, their sense of agency—particularly within their own communities—depended not upon any discursive construction of their qualities as mothers, wives, or daughters, nor upon any sense of the particular feminine attributes women might bring to the public sphere. Rather, it drew primarily upon the authority bestowed by land and money.

---

[6] e.g. John Bohstedt, 'Gender, Household and Community Politics: Women in English Riots, 1790–1810', *Past and Present*, 120 (1988), 88–122; Ellen Ross, 'Survival Networks: Women's Neighbourhood Sharing in London before World War One', *History Workshop*, 15 (1983), 4–27.

Shifting our attention to the salience of women's economic resources as a basis for political intervention reveals further neglected aspects of female political engagement. This includes the complex constitution of female national identities. For active landowners this depended not simply on an investment in an 'imagined community', but could be rooted in more visceral ties of belonging to the land—a process in which local knowledge and loyalties were critically enmeshed. Equally, women's sense of involvement in an imperial nation did not necessarily draw upon feminized notions of the imperial mission, but could be rooted in their confidence as economic agents (as shareholders of the East India Company, for example). A sense of involvement in parochial modes of governance—often viewed as the country's Anglo-Saxon heritage—could also form part of the tapestry of national identity.

More broadly, significant adjustments to women's public roles were only possible once the disparity between women's opportunities at the local level and their marginalization in national politics began to be articulated in mainstream discourses. Whilst women's local authority declined over our period, it nonetheless provided the basis for new imaginings of their potential as citizens. By the 1850s female philanthropists of national standing were seeking to uphold the local authority of community ladies in the face of growing state involvement in parochial welfare issues. This involved a tactical emphasis upon women's particular, feminine contribution to social welfare, although these writers insisted that it was not simply women *per se* whose activities they sought to safeguard, but rather those of 'superior social position'.[7] Equally, claims for citizenship did not necessarily emerge within liberal discussions of individual rights, but could be rooted in an appreciation for women's customary roles in rural communities, either as farmers and proprietors, or as parochial officeholders. For example, from the 1850s a desire to synthesize knowledge of women's seemingly sporadic local electoral rights was emerging in wider circles. The *Law Times* reminded its readership that women 'are not merely eligible to serve the office of overseer, but may be compelled to serve it, and in many parishes do really serve it. But more than all, the law has actually enfranchised them for parochial voting.'[8] *Notes and Queries* also hosted debates over the incidence and nature of such cases in the mid and late

---

[7] e. g. Hill, *Children of the State*, 239; Twining, *Workhouses*, 12n.
[8] Cited in Williams, 'Public Law', 97.

1850s, with contributors reporting their own experiences of female voting and officeholding.[9]

Thus one dynamic which was to eventually drive broader public discussion of women's political roles was the disjuncture between women's local political profile compared with the more narrow vision of acceptable female behaviour delineated in wider, formal, and national contexts. A further significant distinction was the contrast between the activities contemporaries were prepared to accept from exceptional, individual women, compared to the narrower conceptualization of broader female mobilization. William Wilberforce, for example, was happy to ask individual women of his acquaintance to 'stir up a petition' on the subject of Indian missions, whereas he was opposed to rank-and-file female campaigners going 'from house to house stirring up petitions'.[10] As governments' preparedness to utilize the skills of female policy experts indicated, personal knowledge of astute women and a readiness to call upon their political services did not necessarily translate to a broader willingness to facilitate wider female political participation. This is indicative of the fluid and contingent nature of gendered proscriptions. Contemporary ideas of gender were sufficiently flexible that contemporaries might not feel threatened or unnerved by the display of political acumen in individual women they encountered.

It has been suggested here that the phenomenon of female exceptionalism, represented in many of these examples, should not be dismissed as simply aberrant or atypical. It enables us to explore the fissures within the gender order which could be exploited by individual women. Secondly, the growing incidence of dominant individual women on the public scene—whether as writers, experts, parish overseers, preachers, or lecturers—gradually became a significant 'critical mass' in its own right, accustoming contemporaries to alternative models of female public behaviour, and providing inspiration and precedence for those seeking to challenge women's political exclusion. As we saw in Chapter 2, gendered conventions of female public behaviour were upheld and enacted by knowing individuals. Change was dependent upon the agency of independent, individual women who had the courage and daring to, say, address a gathering of the NAPSS for the first time. Such decisions were

---

[9] *Notes and Queries* (12 Nov. 1853, 15 July and 30 Sept. 1854, 26 Jan. and 8 Mar. 1856, 31 Jan., 30 May, 20 June and 17 Oct. 1857, 2 Oct. 1880).

[10] Anne Stott, 'Patriotism and Providence: The Politics of Hannah More', in Gleadle and Richardson, *Women in British Politics*, 40–1; Midgley, *Women against Slavery*, 48.

vital to the gathering, if uneven, momentum for change across broader social structures.[11]

This was a process which occurred in tandem with an ever more stylized reporting of women as a political collective. As we have seen, evocations of women as politicized blocks of constituency opinion were a more regular feature of electoral rhetoric in the post-reform world. Electoral communities had to acknowledge their quotidian experience of female involvement yet also project an identity which would signal their probity through conformity to dominant cultural codes. The same applies to the increasingly ubiquitous (and fleeting) references to 'well dressed ladies' at public events. The homogeneous style of reporting which emerged marginalized and complicated any cognizance of a female public presence. Despite the growing opportunities available to women, it remained very difficult for the rank and file to claim an unequivocal public voice, or to articulate an assured political identity.

Identity was constructed not merely from discursive resources but through social practice, of course. Simon Morgan observes that there was the potential for the gendered nature of the public sphere to lead to empowering female public sensibilities. Thus, the custom whereby male committees oversaw female philanthropic societies could lead to conflicts in which women insisted that they be more fully consulted.[12] It has been suggested here that probing some of the subtleties of newspaper reports conveying women as a decorative presence also enables us to see how they could be actively, and sometimes noisily, engaged in these events. Women, like men, could manage and experience multiple identities, and a sense of one's passion for a particular cause cut across the gendered subjectivity in which they were represented. Yet the fixing of female identity in discursive representations involved a repression, a silencing of other aspects of women's engagement.[13] As noted in Chapter 7, this could lead to the construction of highly selective narratives of their public experiences which are testament to the unconscious pressures women might feel to enact particular identities. Similarly, as illustrated in Chapter 2, even progressive women could be compliant in the replication of an exclusionary masculine public sphere.

---

[11] For theoretical reflections see Randall Collins, 'Historical Change and the Ritual Production of Gender', in Joan Huber (ed.), Macro–Micro Linkages in Sociology (London, 1991), 109–20, esp. 111.

[12] Morgan, Victorian Woman's Place, ch. 6.

[13] Jerry Tew, Social Theory: Power and Practice (Basingstoke, 2002), ch. 6.

This compromised women's ability to develop lucid and unambiguous imaginings of their public role.

During the course of this study we have seen that participation in public affairs was not necessarily empowering or inspiring for women, and it could be undertaken from a sense of reluctant duty. Some women, like men, were bored or uninterested in the opportunities the public might seem to afford. Some professed anti-slavery campaigners could be decidedly apathetic; whilst interest in political affairs, such as elections, might derive from the opportunities they afforded for socializing, or the excitement they brought, rather than a genuine interest in parliamentary issues. The 'public' did not represent a golden vista of opportunities to which women necessarily yearned for access. Equally, an engagement in political affairs could be fleeting or sporadic, prompted by isolated issues. If we are to understand the full complexities of women's positioning within contemporary political culture it is important to incorporate these experiences. The uninterested or disengaged women formed a significant constituency against which other contemporaries would judge those who did intervene more actively. Whilst the study has argued for the critical significance of 'exceptionality', focusing only on the exceptional is equally misleading. We need a narrative which incorporates the reactions of the less motivated who were also a constitutive element of political culture and its gendered contours.

The structure of the book has encouraged a consideration of the different public and political forums available to women. Nonetheless, the various spheres of a woman's life did not act in isolation from each other, but were continually evolving and mutually informing. As we saw in the case of Mary Sewell, a woman's mounting experience in the parochial realm, as a philanthropist, employer, or campaigner, could bring greater self-confidence. This had the potential to subtly affect the balance of power within individual family relationships. And it was the confidence and authority which women could bring to the parochial realm by dint of their access to wider kinship and intellectual networks which often assisted in the successful performance of local authority. Within this process, gender played no simple, obvious, or predictable role, but could form a 'varied and changing' aspect of the self. Gender identification could consist of many, sometimes contradictory elements, and gender in itself frequently functioned in a 'chameleon-like' capacity—being so differently invoked in particular contexts.[14] In the 'public sphere' the dynamic between the

[14] Deborah Baker, 'Social Identity in the Transition to Motherhood', in Baker and Skevington, *Social Identity of Women*, 102–3; Moi, 'Appropriating Bourdieu', 288.

fluctuating components of subjectivity had the potential to lead to the eventual assertion of more forthright, feminist profiles. This applied to Lydia Becker, for example, whose female consciousness began to override her identification with the cause of Mancunian pacifism. For others, though, the greater salience of gendered identities could result in less confident personas. Whilst Dorothy Wordsworth could position herself as a superior member of the local gentry in contrast to local labourers, she articulated a far more humble persona when interacting with her brother.

But whilst gender was experienced differently as it was reproduced across social and cultural locations, this does not mean to say that identities were reproduced 'fresh' in each context. Individuals retained their personal coherence. Subjectivity may well be better conceived as a process rather than an entity in many respects but this does mean that it could be simply re-enacted and invented according to circumstances. The widespread difficulties women experienced in explicitly articulating their political roles and interests, as outlined in the Introduction, exemplifies the cultural and psychological limitations women faced and the consequent impact upon the shaping of their psyches. These different manifestations of subjectivity intertwined to produce the complex, sometimes contradictory, but coherent personas which are recognizable to us.

Even the public life of Mary Ann Gilbert, surely one of the most 'empowered' women in this study, was structured by a profound gender asymmetry. Her contribution to the protectionist cause never extended to an involvement in its public associational life. Instead she confined herself to extensive, persistent (almost obsessive?) attempts to circulate her agendas through anonymous texts and local exertions. This in turn created tensions within her own family, particularly for her seemingly embarrassed sons and grandsons. Anna Gurney exerted formidable authority at the parochial level and within academic networks. Yet her contributions to colonial reform were enacted only through the paterfamilias, Thomas Fowell Buxton, and she felt constrained to perform a modest feminine sensibility in correspondence with her brother. Frances Smith was a confident electoral agent in her constituency, but reaffirmed models of female obedience in her family relationships. It is tempting to wonder whether the domineering mien many such women exhibited in their locales may have functioned to give vent to these tensions. In situations where their position depended primarily upon their status rather than their gender they tended to exploit the available opportunities to the full.

Women's political subjectivity was always in the making. Their status as political subjects was continually in the process of construction and depended upon the myriad layers of decisions ceaselessly made by individual actors. Within this process there was the possibility for new directions and practices to be tested and to sometimes gain wider currency. This simultaneously involved the gradual demise of some of the older customs and discourses which had facilitated female political engagement in other (often more direct and less problematic) ways. The impact of this upon the constitution of female political subjectivity was profound but uneven. Whilst these years may superficially represent 'progress' in terms of the increased numbers engaging in widespread political activity, and the emergence of a well-organized feminist movement, the costs were high. Women remained borderline citizens whose ability to imagine themselves unambiguously as forthright political actors was continually compromised by the pull of conflicting discursive currents and the instability of their ambivalent political status.

Bibliography

Manuscript sources

Birmingham City Archives, Birmingham
  Galton papers, MS 3101
  Catherine Hutton papers, MS 168
  Diary of Rebecca Kenrick, MS 2024/1/1
Bodleian Library, University of Oxford
  Dep. Lovelace Byron 1–460
  Edgeworth MSS. Eng. lett. c. 696–747
Borthwick Institute, University of York
  Hickleton papers, Halifax/A1/4
Boston Public Library, Boston
  Anti-slavery collection
British Library, London
  Clarkson papers, Add MS 41,267
  William Lovett papers, Add 78161
  Robert Peel papers, Add MS 40, 524–6
  Barbara Stephen, 'Family Life', Add MSS 72839 A
Cambridge University Library, Cambridge
  Maria Grey letters, Add 7218
  Smith family papers, Add 7621
  Marianne Thornton papers, Add 7674
Centre for Buckinghamshire Studies, Buckingham
  Robert Gibbs papers, D 15/10
Cornwall Record Office, Truro
  Davies Gilbert papers, DG
  Enys of Enys papers, EN
East Sussex Record Office, Lewes
  Davies Gilbert papers, GIL, Add MSS AMS6073, AMS6515, A7526
  Frewen family archive, FRE
  Vestry papers, DE/B/28–9, DE/A1/4
Friends House Library, London
  Gurney papers, MSS section II
  Anne Knight papers, MS Box, W2; Temp MSS 725/5
Hampshire Record Office, Winchester
  Austen-Leigh family papers, 23M93

Harris Manchester College, University of Oxford
    Harriet Martineau and James Martineau papers
Hertfordshire Archives and Local Studies, Hertford
    Edward Bulwer Lytton papers, D/EK
Huntington Library, Art Collections and Botanical Gardens, San Marino
    Richard Carlile papers, RC/84
John Rylands Library, University of Manchester
    Raymond English Anti-Slavery collection (REAS)
Keele University Library, Keele
    Wedgwood manuscripts
Leicestershire, Leicester, and Rutland Record Office, Leicester
    Coltman family papers, 15D57
    Susannah Watts scrapbook
London Metropolitan Archives
    Minutes of the Society for Improving the Condition of the Labouring Classes,
    ACC/3445
National Library of Scotland, Edinburgh
    McLaren family papers, F. Scott Oliver, MSS 24781–24815
National Library of Wales, Aberystwyth
    Sir George Cornewall Lewis papers, Harpton Court collection, C/817–24
Norfolk Record Office, Norwich
    Gurney papers, RQG; MC 234
    Amelia Opie letters, MS 5252, MS 6181, Boi 63/5–6
    Taylor family, MS 257
    Upchers of Sheringham, UPC
Oxfordshire Health Archives, Oxford
    Radcliffe Infirmary records, RI/II/99 (6)
Private hands
    Papers of Sophia Dobson Collet
Rhodes House Library, University of Oxford
    Thomas Fowell Buxton papers, Brit Emp S. 444
Shropshire Archives, Shrewsbury
    Katherine Plymley notebooks, 1066/1–148
Suffolk Record Office, Ipswich branch
    Elizabeth Cobbold papers, HA231
Warwickshire County Record Office, Warwick
    Election handbills, CR1097
Wellcome Library for the History and Understanding of Medicine, London
    Thomas Hodgkin papers, PP/HO
West Sussex Record Office, Chichester
    Catherine Cobden letters, MS 6024–9
West Yorkshire Archives, Leeds
    Edward Baines papers
Women's Library, London Metropolitan University, London
    Lydia Becker papers, 7/LEB
    Louisa Twining papers, 7/LOT

Newspapers and periodicals

Belfast Newsletter
Birmingham Journal
Brighton Gazette
Bulwark; or Reformation Journal
Carlisle Journal
Chambers' Edinburgh Journal
Christian Lady's Magazine
Church and State Gazette
Dietetic Reformer
Durham Chronicle
Ecclesiastical Gazette
Edinburgh Review
Englishwoman's Journal
Englishwoman's Magazine
Farmers' Almanac
Farmers' Journal
Farmers' Magazine
Gentleman's Magazine
Howitt's Journal
Ipswich Chronicle
Isis
Journal of the Workhouse Visiting Society
Labourers' Friend Magazine
Leeds Intelligencer
Leeds Mercury
Leicester Chronicle
Liverpool Mercury
Manchester Guardian
Manchester Times
Metropolitan Magazine
Mirror of Parliament
Monthly Repository
Morning Chronicle
National Association Gazette
Norfolk Chronicle
Norwich Mercury
Notes and Queries
People's Journal
Protestant Magazine
Quarterly Review
Royal Cornwall Gazette
Star in the East
Sussex Advertiser
Sussex Chronicle
The Home

The Prompter
The Reasoner
The Times
Tocsin or the Sheffield Protestant Alarm Bell
Truth Tester
Vegetarian Advocate
Vegetarian Messenger
Westminster Review
Women's Suffrage Journal

Parliamentary papers

Hansard 1815–70
Reports of the Select Committee of the House of Commons on Public Petitions (1833, 1839).
Report of the Select Committee to Inquire into the Allotment System (1843).
Royal Commission for Inquiring into the Administration and Practical Operation of Poor Laws in Scotland (1844).
Royal Commission of Inquiry into the Administration and Practical Operation of the Poor Laws (1834).
Royal Commission on the Employment of Children, Young Persons and Women in Agriculture, First Report, Appendix (Evidence from Assistant Commissioners) (1867–8).

Printed sources: pre-1920 publications

Adams, Elizabeth, Lady, *Hurrah for the Hearts of True Blue* (Exeter, 1835).
An Authentic Account of the Whole Proceedings of the Saint Mary-le Bone Meeting of the Married Ladies, and Inhabitant Householders of the Parish (London, 1820).
Archer, Hannah, *A Scheme for Befriending Orphan Pauper Girls* (London: Longman & Co., 1861).
Balfour, Clara Lucas, *The Women of Scripture* (London: Houlston & Stoneman, 1847).
Barber, Mary Ann Serrett, *Earning a Living: Or, from Hand to Mouth, Scenes from the Homes of Working People* (London: J. Nisbet & Co., 1861).
Barlee, Ellen, *Our Homeless Poor; and What we can Do to Help Them* (London: James Nisbet, 1860).
—— *Friendless and Helpless* (London: Emily Faithfull, 1863).
—— *A Visit to Lancashire in December, 1862* (London: Seeley & Co., 1863).
Bayly, Mary, *Ragged Homes and How to Mend Them* (London: J. Nisbet, 1859).
—— *Workmen and their Difficulties* (London: J. Nisbet & Co., 1861).
—— (ed.), *The Life and Letters of Mrs Sewell* (London: J. Nisbet & Co., 1889).
Beale, Catherine Hutton (ed.), *Catherine Hutton and her Friends* (Birmingham: Cornish Brothers, 1895).
Becker, Lydia, *The Rights and Duties of Women in Local Government: A Paper Read at the Conference on Behalf of Extending the Parliamentary Franchise to Women* (Manchester: A. Ireland & Co., 1879).

Belsham, Thomas, *A Review of Mr Wilberforce's Treatise Entitled 'A Practical View of the Prevailing Religious System of Professed Christians', in Letters to a Lady* (London: J. Johnson, 1798).

Berkeley, Grantley F., *My Life and Recollections*, 2 vols (London: Hurst & Blackett, (1865–6).

Blacker, William, *Prize Essay, Addressed to the Agricultural Committee of the Royal Dublin Society on the Management of Landed Property in Ireland* (Dublin: William Curry, Jun. & Co., 1834).

—— *An Essay on the Improvement to be Made in the Cultivation of Small Farms by the Introduction of Green Crops, and Housefeeding the Stock Thereon; Originally Published in an Address to the Small Farmers on the Estates of the Earl of Gosford and Colonel Close, in the County of Armagh* (Dublin: W. Curry, 1837).

—— *Review of Charles Shaw Lefevre, Esq.'s Letter to his Constituents, as Chairman of the Select Committee Appointed to Inquire into the Present State of Agriculture* (London: R. Groombridge, 1837).

Bodichon, Barbara, *A Brief Summary in Plain Language of the Most Important Laws Concerning Women; Together with a Few Observations Thereon* (London: John Chapman, 1854).

Bourne, George, *William Smith: Potter and Farmer, 1790–1858* (London: Chatto & Windus, 1920).

Bright, John, and James E. Thorold Rogers (eds), *Speeches on Questions of Public Policy by Richard Cobden M.P.*, 2 vols (London: Macmillan & Co., 1870).

Brittaine, George, *The Election* (Dublin: Richard Moore Tims, 1840).

Brontë, Charlotte, *Shirley* (Harmondsworth: Penguin, 1985; 1st publ. 1849).

Brougham, Henry [Lydia Tomkins], *Thoughts on the Ladies of the Aristocracy*, 2nd edn (London: Hodgsons, 1835).

Buckingham, James Silk, *Qualifications and Duties of Members of Parliament, Being the Substance of an Address, Delivered to the Inhabitants of Sheffield in the Music Hall* (Nottingham: R. Sutton, 1831).

Budgen, Walter, *Old Eastbourne: Its Church, its Clergy, its People* (London: Frederick Sherlock, 1913).

Bulmer, T., *History, Topography and Directory of North Yorkshire* (Preston: T. Bulmer & Co., 1890).

Burke, John French, *Farming for Ladies: Or, a Guide to the Poultry-Yard, the Dairy and Piggery* (London: J. Murray, 1844).

Burney, Frances, *Brief Reflections Relative to the Emigrant French Clergy: Earnestly Submitted to the Humane Consideration of the Ladies of Great Britain* (London: Thomas Cadell, 1793).

Butler, James Ramsay Montagu, *The Passing of the Great Reform Bill* (London: Longmans, 1914).

Butler, Josephine, E., *In Memoriam: Harriet Meuricoffre* (London: Marshall & Son, 1901).

—— *Memoir of John Grey of Dilston* (London: H. S. King & Co., 1869).

Buxton, Charles, *Memoirs of Sir Thomas Fowell Buxton: With Selections from his Correspondence* (London: John Murray, 1848).

Buxton, Hannah, *Memorials of Hannah, Lady Buxton* (London: Bickers & Son, 1883).

Cadell, Cecilia Mary, *The Reformer*, 3 vols (London: Effingham Wilson, 1832).

—— *A History of the Missions in Japan and Paraguay* (London: Burns & Lambert, 1856).

—— *Summer Talks about Lourdes* (London: Burns & Oates, 1874).

Canning, George, *The Speeches and Public Addresses of the Right Hon. George Canning during the Election in Liverpool* (Liverpool: T. Kaye, 1818).

Cappe, Catharine, *Thoughts on Various Charitable and Other Important Institutions and on the Best Mode of Conducting Them* (York: Longman, 1814).

—— *On the Desirableness and Utility of Ladies Visiting the Female Wards of Hospitals and Lunatic Asylums* (York: Thomas Wilson & Sons, 1817).

Carpenter, J. Estlin, *The Life and Work of Mary Carpenter* (London: Macmillan & Co., 1879).

Carpenter, Mary, *Reformatory Schools, for the Children of the Perishing and Dangerous Classes, and for Juvenile Offenders* (London: C. Gilpin, 1851).

—— *The Claims of Ragged Schools to Pecuniary Educational Aid from the Annual Parliamentary Grant* (London: Partridge & Co., 1859).

Charles, Elizabeth Rundle, *Our Seven Homes: Autobiographical Reminiscences* (London: J. Murray, 1896).

Charlesworth, Maria Louisa, *The Ministry of Life* (London: Seeley, Jackson, & Halliday, 1858).

'A Churchman', *A Letter to the Church Members of the Auxiliary Bible Society, Liverpool* (Liverpool: F. B. Wright, 1819).

Clarke, G. R., *The History and Description of the Town and Borough of Ipswich, Including the Villages and Country Seats in its Vicinity* (Ipswich: S. Piper, 1830).

Cobbe, Frances Power, *The Sick in Workhouses: Who they are, and How they should be Treated* (London: J. Nisbet & Co., 1861).

Cobbold, Elizabeth, *Poems, with a Memoir of the Author by L. Jermyn* (Ipswich: J. Raw, 1825).

—— *Poems on Various Subjects, by Elizabeth Knipe* (Manchester: C. Wheeler, 1783).

Cockle, Mary, *National Triumphs* (London: C. Chapple, 1814).

—— *Elegy to the Memory of Her Royal Highness, the Princess Charlotte of Wales* (Newcastle-upon-Tyne: S. Hodgson, 1817).

—— *Elegy on the Death of his Late Majesty, George the Third* (Newcastle-upon-Tyne: S. Hodgson, 1820)

—— *The Banners of Blue* (Woodbridge: G. Loder, 1835).

Coleridge, Sara, *Memoir and Letters of Sara Coleridge*, ed. Edith Coleridge, 4th edn (London: Henry King, 1875).

Colman, Helen Caroline, *Jeremiah James Colman: A Memoir* (London: Chiswick Press, 1905).

Cresswell, Louisa Mary, *Norfolk and the Squires, Clergy, Farmers and Labourers* (London: Simpkin, Marshall, & Co., 1875).

Croker, Margaret Sarah, *A Monody on the Lamented Death of Her Royal Highness the Princess Charlotte-Augusta of Wales and of Saxe Cobourg Saalfield* (London: Edmund Lloyd; J. Booth, 1817).

—— *A Tribute to the Memory of Sir Samuel Romilly* (London: John Souter, 1818).

Dickens, Charles, *Sketches by Boz: Illustrative of Every-Day Life and Every-Day People*, 2 vols (London: Chapman & Hall, 1836).

Disraeli, Benjamin, and Sarah Disraeli, *A Year at Hartlebury: Or, the Election*, with Appendixes by Ellen Henderson and John P. Matthews (London: Murray, 1983; 1st publ. 1834).

Dorchester, Lady (ed.), *Recollections of a Long Life by Lord Broughton (John Cam Hobhouse)*, 6 vols (London: John Murray, 1909).

Dowden, Edward (ed.), *The Correspondence of Robert Southey with Caroline Bowles* (Dublin: Hodges, Figgis & Co., 1881).

Duncombe, Thomas H., *The Life and Correspondence of Thomas Slingsby Duncombe*, 2 vols (London: Hurst & Blackett, 1868).

Eastlake, Elizabeth, *Mrs Grote: A Sketch* (London: John Murray, 1880).

Eliot, George, *Felix Holt* (Harmondsworth: Penguin, 1997; 1st publ. 1866).

—— *Middlemarch* (Harmondsworth: Penguin, 1994; 1st publ. 1871–2).

Elliot, Miss, and Frances Power Cobbe, *Destitute Incurables in Workhouses* (London: James Nisbet & Co., 1861).

Ellis, Sarah, *The Women of England: Their Social Duties, and Domestic Habits* (London: Fisher, Son, & Co., 1839).

—— *The Daughters of England: Their Position in Society, Character and Responsibilities* (London: Fisher, Son & Co. 1842).

—— *The Mothers of England: Their Influence and Responsibility* (London: Fisher, Son, & Co., 1843).

—— *The Wives of England: Their Relative Duties, Domestic Influence and Social Obligations* (London: Fisher, Son, & Co., 1843).

—— *The Home Life and Letters of Mrs Ellis: Compiled by her Nieces* (London: J. Nisbet & Co., 1893).

Ellman, Edward Boys, *Recollections of a Sussex Parson, Rev. Edward Boys Ellman 1815–1906, Rector of Berwick, East Sussex with a Memoir by his Daughter, Maude Walker* (London: Skeffington, 1912).

Evangelical Alliance British Organization, *Report of the Proceedings of the Conference of British Members Held at Manchester, 4–9 November 1846* (London: Partridge & Oakey, 1847).

Fison, Margaret, *Handbook of the National Association for the Promotion of Social Science* (London: Longman, Green, Longman, & Roberts, 1859).

Fitzpatrick, William John, *Memoirs of Richard Whately, Archbishop of Dublin: With a Glance at his Contemporaries and Time*, 2 vols (London: Richard Bentley, 1864).

Fletcher, Eliza, *Autobiography of Mrs Fletcher of Edinburgh: With Letters and Other Family Memorials, Edited by the Survivor of her Family*, 2nd edn (Edinburgh: Edmonston & Douglas, 1875).

Forman, H. Buxton (ed.), *Letters of Edward John Trelawny* (London: Henry Frowde, 1910).

Fox, Maria, *Thoughts by the Sea-Side: Or a Friendly Address to Sailors* (London: Tract Association of the Society of Friends, 1825).

Gilbert, Davies, *Cursory Observations on the Act for Ascertaining the Bounties and for Regulating the Exportation and Importation of Corn* (London: J. Brettell, 1804).

—— *A Cornish Cantata: Names of Places of Cornwall Arranged in Verse* (Privately printed, 1826).

Gilbert, Davies, *A Cornish Dialogue between Tom. Pengersick and Dic. Trengurtha* (Privately printed, 1830).

—— *Collections and Translations Respecting St Neot and the Former State of his Church in Cornwall* (London, 1830).

Gilbert, Josiah (ed.), *Autobiography and Other Memorials of Mrs Gilbert*, 2 vols (London: H. S. King & Co., 1874).

Glasgow Emancipation Society Sixth Annual Report (Glasgow, 1840).

Glyde, John, *The Moral, Social, and Religious Condition of Ipswich in the Middle of the Nineteenth Century, with a Sketch of its History, Rise and Progress* (Ipswich: J. M. Burton, 1850).

—— *Suffolk in the Nineteenth Century: Physical, Social, Moral, Religious and Industrial* (London: Simpkin, Marshall & Co, 1856).

Gore, Catherine, *The Hamiltons: Or the New Aera*, 3 vols (London: Saunders & Otley, 1834).

—— *Mrs Armytage: Or, Female Domination*, 3 vols (London: Henry Colburn, 1836).

Gould, S. Baring, *Old Country Life* (London, Methuen & Co., 1890).

Greenwell, Dora, *On the Education of the Imbecile* (London: Strahan & Co., 1869).

Grey, Maria G., and Emily Shirreff, *Thoughts on Self-Culture, Addressed to Women*, 2 vols (London: E. Moxon, 1850).

Gurney, Anna, *A Literal Translation of the Saxon Chronicle* (Norwich: Stevenson, Machett, & Stevenson, 1819).

—— *On the Means of Assistance in Cases of Shipwreck* (Norwich: S. Wilkin, 1825).

Hanbury, Charlotte, *An Autobiography: Ed., by her Niece Mrs Albert Head* (London: Marshall Bros., 1901).

Hanbury, Mrs Robert, *God is Love: A Word to the Poor Man* (London: James Nisbet & Co., 1853).

Hankin, C. C. (ed.), *Life of Mary Anne Schimmelpenninck* (London: Longman, Brown, Green, Longmans, & Roberts, 1858).

Harbord, Charles, *My Memories, 1830–1913: by Lord Suffield*, ed. Alys Lowth (London: Herbert Jenkins, 1913).

Hatfield, Sibella, *Letters on the Importance of the Female Sex: With Observations on their Manners, and on Education* (London: J. Adlard, 1803).

Hennell, Mary, *An Outline of the Various Social Systems and Communities Which have been Founded on the Principle of Co-operation with an Introductory Essay* (London: Longman, Brown, Green, & Longmans, 1844).

Heyrick, Elizabeth, *Instructive Hints in Easy Lessons for Children* (London: Harvey & Darton, 1800).

—— *The Warning: Recommended to the Serious Attention of All Christians, and Lovers of their Country* (London: Darton & Harvey, 1805).

—— *Familiar Letters Addressed to Children and Young People of the Middle Ranks* (London, 1811).

—— *Cursory Remarks on the Evil Tendency of Unrestrained Cruelty, Particularly on that Practised in Smithfield Market* (London: Darton & Harvey, 1823).

—— *Immediate, Not Gradual Abolition: Or, an Inquiry into the Shortest Safest, and Most Effectual Means of Getting Rid of West Indian Slavery* (London: J. Hatchard & Son, 1824).

—— *A Protest against the Spirit and Practice of Modern Legislation, as Exhibited in the New Vagrant Act* (London: Harvey & Dalton, 1824).

—— *A Letter of Remonstrance from an Impartial Public to the Hosiers of Leicester* (Leicester: A. Cockshaw, 1825).

—— *Appeal to the Electors of the United Kingdom on the Choice of a New Parliament* (Leicester: A. Cockshaw, 1826).

—— *Observations on the Offensive and Injurious Effect of Corporal Punishment on the Unequal Administration of Penal Justice and on the Pre-eminent Advantages of the Mild and Reformatory over the Vindictive System of Punishment* (London: Hatchard & Son, 1827).

—— *Appeal to the Hearts and Consciences of British Women* (Leicester: A. Cockshaw, 1828).

—— *A Brief Sketch of the Life and Labour of Mrs Elizabeth Heyrick* (Leicester: Crossley & Clarke, 1862).

Hill, Florence Davenport, *Children of the State: The Training of Juvenile Paupers* (London: Ayr, 1868).

Hill, Georgiana, *Women in English Life from Mediaeval to Modern Times*, 2 vols (London: R. Bentley & Son, 1896).

Hill, Rosamond Davenport, and Florence Davenport Hill, *The Recorder of Birmingham: A Memoir of Matthew Davenport Hill* (London: Macmillan, 1878).

Hoare, Edward, *The Coming Night: A Sermon Preached in Cromer Church on Friday June 12, 1857 on Occasion of the Death of Miss Anna Gurney of Northrepps Cottage* (London: Thomas Hatchard, 1857).

Holyoake, George Jacob, *Sixty Years of an Agitator's Life*, 2 vols (1893; London: Fisher Unwin, 1906).

—— *Bygones Worth Remembering*, 2 vols (London: Fisher Unwin, 1905).

Hyde, Mary A., *How to Win our Workers: A Short Account of the Leeds Sewing School for Factory Girls* (Cambridge: Macmillan & Co., 1862).

Ireland, Annie E. (ed.), *Selections from the Letters of Geraldine Endsor Jewsbury to Jane Welsh Carlyle* (London: Longmans & Co., 1892).

Jameson, Anna, *Sisters of Charity: Catholic and Protestant, Abroad and at Home* (London: Longman, Brown, Green, & Longmans, 1855).

—— *The Communion of Labour: A Second Lecture on the Social Employments of Women* (London: Longman, Brown, Green, Longmans, & Roberts, 1856).

Jenkins, Herbert, *The Life of George Borrow* (London: John Murray, 1912).

Kemble, Frances Ann, *Record of a Girlhood*, 3 vols (London: Richard Bentley, 1878).

Kenyon, Frederic G. (ed.), *The Letters of Elizabeth Barrett Browning*, 2 vols (London: Smith, Elder, & Co., 1897).

Kilvert, Adelaide Sophia, *Home Discipline, or Thoughts on the Origin and Exercise of Domestic Authority* (Bath: W. Pocock, 1841).

King, Benjamin, *A Poor Man's Mite towards the Relief of the Distressed Classes, Addressed to Members of Parliament* (London: J. Ridgway, 1842).

—— *Poor Rates Reduced by Self-Supporting Reading, Writing and Agricultural Schools* (London, 1844).

'Lavinia', *A Letter to Sir Francis Burdett, Bart. on the Late and Passing Events, and the Approaching Crisis: By a Female Reformist of the 'Higher Order'* (London: R. Carlile, 1819).

Leadbeater, Mary, *Cottage Dialogues among the Irish Peasantry* (London: J. Johnson & Co., 1811).

Leader, Robert E. (ed.), *Life and Letters of John Arthur Roebuck, with Chapters of Autobiography* (London and New York: E. Arnold, 1897).

Lee, Rachel, *An Essay on Government* (London, 1808).

Lewis, Sarah, *Woman's Mission*, 2nd edn (London: John W. Parker, 1839).

Litchfield, Henrietta (ed.), *Emma Darwin: A Century of Family Letters, 1792–1896*, 2 vols (London: John Murrray, 1915).

Liverpool Protestant Association, *The Third (Fourth, Seventh) Annual Report of the Liverpool Protestant Association, Presented to the Subscribers at their Annual Meeting, October, 1838 (1839, 1842)* (Liverpool: Henry Perris, 1838–42).

Lumley, William G., *The Poor Law Election Manual, Comprising the General Order of the Poor Law Commissioners Respecting the Election of Guardians; With a Summary of the Law Applicable Thereto, and of the Opinions Published by the Commissioners on their Former Election Orders: Arranged under Distinct Heads; for the Use of Clerks and Others Engaged in the Conduct of Such Elections* (London: Shaw & Sons, edns publ. in 1845, 1855, 1877).

Lytton, Edward Bulwer, *The Life, Letters and Literary Remains of Sir Edward Bulwer Lytton*, 2 vols (London: Kegan Paul Trench & Co., 1883).

McIlquham, Harriet, *The Enfranchisement of Women: An Ancient Right, a Modern Need* (Congleton: Women's Emancipation Union, 1891).

MacInnes, E., *Extracts from Priscilla Johnston's Journal; and Letters* (Carlisle: Charles Thurnam & Sons, 1862).

Mackie, John B., *The Life and Work of Duncan McLaren*, 2 vols (London: Thomas Nelson & Co., 1888).

Marchant, Denis Le, *Memoir of John Charles Viscount Althorp, Third Earl Spencer* (London: Bentley, 1876).

Martin, Harriet, and John Banim, *The Mayor of Wind-Gap and Canvassing*, 3 vols (London: Saunders & Otley, 1835).

Massie, J. W., *The Evangelical Alliance: Its Origin and Development* (London: J. Snow, 1847).

Masson, David, *Memories of London in the 'Forties* (Edinburgh and London: William Blackwood & Sons, 1908).

Maurice, Mary, *Aids to Development, or Mental and Moral Instruction Exemplified in Conversation between a Mother and her Children*, 2 vols (London: R. B. Seeley & W. Burnside, 1829).

—— *The Patriot Warrior: An Historical Sketch of the Life of the Duke of Wellington* (London: John Farquhar, 1853).

Maurice, Priscilla, *Help and Comfort for the Sick Poor* (London: Rivingtons, 1853).

Mayo, Charles, and Elizabeth Mayo, *Practical Remarks on Infant Education: For the Use of Schools and Private Families* (London: R. B. Seeley & W. Burnside, 1837).

Miles, Sibella, *An Essay on the Factory Question, Occasioned by the Recent Votes in the House of Commons: Addressed to the Ladies of England* (London: R. Hastings, 1844).

More, Hannah, *Coelebs in Search of a Wife*, 2 vols (London: T. Cadell & W. Davies, 1808).

National Temperance League, *Woman's Work in the Temperance Reformation: Being Papers Prepared for a Ladies' Conference Held in London, May 26 1868, Introduction by Mrs S. C. Hall* (London: W. Tweedie, 1868).

Northumberland General Election: At a Numerous and Respectable Meeting of the Freeholders and Friends of the Hon H. T. Liddell Resident in North Shields and Vicinity, Held at the House of Mrs Sears, Northumberland (North Shields: Henderson, 1830).

Nowell, John, *An Essay on Farms of Industry, and an Essay on Cottage Allotments, or Field Garden Cultivation* (Huddersfield: T. Kemp, 1844).

—— *On Self-Supporting Schools of Industry and Mental Discipline: Where Reading, Writing and Arithmetic are Taught and United with the Healthy Exercise of Garden Farm Culture, as Practised at Eastbourne in Sussex* (Huddersfield: T. Kemp, 1844).

—— *Manual of Field Gardening: Or, Belgian Agriculture Made Easy*, 2nd edn (Huddersfield: T. Kemp, 1846).

O'Flynn, James, *The Present State of the Irish Poor, with the Outlines of a Plan of General Employment* (London: W. Clowes & Sons, 1835).

Ogborne, William, *A Mother in Israel: A Funeral Sermon on the Occasion of the Sudden Death of the late Mrs Dexter* (St Albans: R. Gibbs, 1859).

O'Rorke, L. E., *The Life and Friendships of Catherine Marsh* (London: Longmans & Co., 1917).

Ostrogorski, M., 'Woman Suffrage in Local Self-Government', *Political Science Quarterly*, 6 (1891), 677–710.

Page, William (ed.), *The Victoria History of the Counties of England: A History of Sussex*, ii (London: Archibald Constable & Co., 1907).

Parsons, Benjamin, *The Mental and Moral Dignity of Woman* (London: John Snow, 1842).

Perrin, Mrs, *A Mother in Israel: The Life of Sarah Benney, with an Introduction by Canon Mason* (London: Wells, Gardner, Darton, & Co., 1900).

Phillipps, Lucy F. March, *Strong and Free: Or First Steps towards Social Science* (London: Longmans, Green, & Co., 1869).

Pigott, Emma, *Memoir of the Honourable Mrs Upcher of Sheringham* (London: Harrison & Sons, 1860).

Player, John, *Sketches of Saffron Walden and its Vicinity* (Saffron Walden: Youngman, 1845).

Porritt, Edward, and Annie G. Porritt, *The Unreformed House of Commons: Parliamentary Representation before 1832*, 2 vols (Cambridge: Cambridge University Press, 1903).

Potter, Mrs H., *An Invitation Rejected: A Few Words to the Non-Communicants of a Country Village* (Ipswich: Pawsey, 1851).

Pryme, George, *Autobiographic Recollections of George Pryme*, ed. Alicia Pryme (Cambridge: Deighton, Bell, 1879).

Rathbone, Emily A. (ed.), *Records of the Rathbone Family* (Edinburgh: R. and R. Clark, 1913).

Raynbird, William, and Hugh Raynbird, *On the Agriculture of Suffolk* (London: Longman & Co., 1849).

Reid, Marion, *A Plea for Woman: Being a Vindication of the Importance and Extent of her Natural Sphere of Action* (Edinburgh: W. Tait, 1843).

Reid, Stuart J., *Life and Letters of the First Earl of Durham, 1792–1840*, 2 vols (London: Longmans & Co., 1906).

Reid, T. Wemyss, *The Life of the Right Hon. W. E. Forster* (London: Chapman & Hall, 1888).

Rham, William L., *The Dictionary of the Farm* (London: C. Knight & Co., 1844).

Richardson, R. J., *The Rights of Woman* (Edinburgh: J. Duncan, 1840).

Roberton, John, *Suggestions for the Improvement of Municipal Government* (Manchester: Transactions of the Manchester Statistical Society, 1854).

Ross, Janet, *Three Generations of Englishwomen: Memoirs and Correspondence of Mrs John Taylor, Mrs Sarah Austin and Lady Duff Gordon*, 2 vols (London: John Murray, 1888).

Russell, William Lord, *A Treatise on the Reform Act* (London: Saunders & Benning, 1832).

Ryland, Thomas Henry, *Reminiscences of Thomas Henry Ryland*, ed. William Henry Ryland (Birmingham: The Midland Counties Herald Ltd, 1904).

Sanderson, A., *Poems on Various Subjects* (North Shields: W. Barnes, 1819).

—— *A Poem Most Humbly Inscribed to Her Majesty, the Queen* (North Shields: J. K. Pollock, 1820).

Sargant, Jane Alice, *An Englishwoman's Letter to Mrs Hannah More, on the Present Crisis*, 2nd edn (London: John Hatchard & Son, 1820).

—— *An Honest Appeal to All Englishmen* (London: J. G. and F. Rivington, 1832).

—— *An Address to the Females of Great Britain on the Propriety of their Petitioning Parliament for the Abolition of Negro Slavery by an Englishwoman* (London: J. G. and F. Rivington, 1833).

Sewell, Eleanor L. (ed.), *The Autobiography of Elizabeth Missing Sewell* (London: Longmans, Green, & Co., 1907).

Sewell, Elizabeth Missing, *Katharine Ashton*, 2 vols (London: Longman & Co., 1854).

—— *Principles of Education Drawn from Nature and Revelation and Applied to Female Education in the Upper Classes*, 2 vols (London: Longman, Green, Longman, Roberts, & Green, 1865).

Sewell, Mary, *Mother's Last Words: A Ballad for Boys*, 2nd edn (London: Jarrold & Sons, 1861).

—— *Thy Poor Brother: Letters to a Friend on Helping the Poor* (London: Jarrold & Sons, 1863).

Shaw, George, *Old Grimsby* (Grimsby: George Shaw, and London: W. Andrews & Co., 1897).

Sheppard, Emma, *Sunshine in the Workhouse*, 2nd edn (London: James Nisbet, 1860).

Simpson, Mary, *Ploughing and Sowing: Or, Annals of an Evening School in a Yorkshire Village, and the Work that Grew out of it by a Clergyman's Daughter*, ed. F. Digby Legard (London: J. and C. Mozley, 1861).

—— *An Address to Farm Servants, Who had been Confirmed, Many of Whom had Soon After Joined the Primitive Methodists or Ranters* (London: J. and C. Mozley, 1862).

—— 'The Life and Training of a Farm Boy', in F. Digby Legard (ed.), *More about Farm Lads* (London: Hamilton, Adams & Co., 1865), 75–100.

—— *Gleanings: A Sequel to Ploughing and Sowing by a Clergyman's Daughter*, ed. F. Digby Legard (London: W. Skeffington & Son, 1876).

A Sketch of the Boston Election; Comprising the Speeches of the Candidates, and Copies of the Printed Addresses, Songs, and Other Pieces Issued during the Contest (Boston: John Noble, 1830).

Smith, Henry George W. (ed.), *The Autobiography of Lieutenant-General Sir Harry Smith*, 2 vols (London: John Murray, 1901).

Smith, Sidney, *The Enfranchisement of Women the Law of the Land* (London: Trübner, and Manchester: A. Ireland & Co., 1879).

Solly, Henry, *These Eighty Years: Or, the Story of an Unfinished Life*, 2 vols (London: Simpkin, Marshall, 1893).

Somerville, Mary, *Personal Recollections: From Early Life to Old Age* (London: John Murray, 1874).

Southey, Robert, *Letters from England*, 3 vols (London: Longman & Co., 1807).

Spurr, Mrs Thomas, *Course of Lectures on the Physical, Intellectual, and Religious Education of Infant Children: Delivered Before the Ladies of Sheffield* (Sheffield: George Ridge, 1836).

Steer, Henry, *The Smedleys of Matlock Bank: Being a Review of the Religious and Philanthropic Labours of Mr and Mrs John Smedley* (London: E. Stock, 1897).

Stephens, Fitzjames, *Lectures to Ladies on Practical Subjects* (London: Macmillan & Co., 1855).

Stewponey Farmers' Club, *Essays on Various Subjects by Members of the Stewponey Farmers' Club during the Year, 1844* (Stourbridge, 1845).

Stockdale, Mary, *A Shroud for Sir Samuel Romilly: An Elegy* (London: Mary Stockdale, 1818).

—— *A Wreath for the Urn: An Elegy on the Princess Charlotte* (London: Mary Stockdale, 1818).

Stodart, Mary Ann, *Every Day Duties: In Letters to a Young Lady* (London: R. B. Seeley, & W. Burnside, 1840),

—— *Principles of Education Practically Considered, with an Especial Reference to the Present State of Female Education in England* (London: Seeley, Burnside, & Seeley, 1844).

Stoddart, Anna M., *Elizabeth Pease Nichol* (London: J. M. Dent & Co., 1899).

Stopes, Charlotte Carmichael, *British Freewomen: Their Historical Privilege* (London: Swan Sonnenschein & Co., 1907).

Strange, Guy Le (ed. and tr.), *Correspondence of Princess Lieven and Earl Grey*, ii. *1830–4* (London: Richard Bentley & Son, 1890).

Strickland, Agnes, *Rally round your Colours* (Halesworth: Tipple, 1832).

Symonds, Mrs John Addington (ed.), *Recollections of a Happy Life: Being the Autobiography of Marianne North*, 2 vols (London: Macmillan & Co., 1892).

Thompson, William, *Appeal of One Half the Human Race, Women, against the Pretensions of the Other Half, Men, to Retain them in Political, and Thence in Civil and Domestic Slavery* (1825), ed. Dolores Dooley (Cork: Cork University Press, 1997).

Timperley, Charles H., *A Dictionary of Printers and Printing, with the Progress of Literature* (London: H. Johnson, 1839).

To the Ladies of the County of Northumberland (North Shields: G. Walker, 1831).

Tonna, Charlotte Elizabeth, *Helen Fleetwood* (London: R. B. Seeley & W. Burnside, 1841).

Tonna, Charlotte Elizabeth, *Personal Recollections*, 3rd edn (London: Seeley, Burnside, & Seeley, 1847).

Tough, Margaret H., *A Plain Practical Address to the Ladies of Scotland, Concerning their Church* (Edinburgh: J. Johnstone, 1840).

—— *The Offering: A Selection from the Poems, Published and Unpublished of a Minister's Daughter* (Edinburgh: W. P. Kennedy, 1851).

Trollope, Frances, *The Domestic Manners of the Americans*, 2 vols (London: Whittaker, Treacher & Co., 1832).

—— *Jessie Phillips: A Tale of the Present Day* (London: Henry Colburn, 1844).

Turner, William, *A Sermon Preached in Hanover-Square Chapel, Newcastle-upon-Tyne, Sept. 15 1822, on the Occasion of the Much-Lamented Death of Mrs Sarah Hodgson, on Sept 10 1822, in the Sixty-Third Year of her Age* (Newcastle: T. and J. Hodgson, 1823).

Twining, Louisa, *Metropolitan Workhouses and their Inmates* (London: Longman & Roberts, 1857).

—— *Workhouses and Women's Work* (London: Longman, 1858).

—— *A Letter to the President of the Poor Law Board on Workhouse Infirmaries* (London: W. Hunt, 1866).

—— *Recollections of Life and Work, Being the Autobiography of Louisa Twining* (London: Arnold, 1893).

Vavasour, Lady Anne, *My Last Tour and First Work: Or a Visit to the Baths of Wildbad and Rippoldsau* (London: H. Cunningham, 1842).

Verney, Frances Parthenhope, *Memoirs of the Verney Family during the Civil War*, 2 vols (London: Longmans, 1892).

Walker, Alexander, *Woman Physiologically Considered as to Mind, Morals, Marriage, Matrimonial Slavery, Infidelity and Divorce* (London: A. H. Bailey, 1840).

Wakefield, C. M., *Life of Thomas Attwood* (London: Harrison & Sons, 1885).

Ward, Charlotte, *Lending a Hand: Or, Help for the Working Classes* (London: Seeley, Jackson, & Halliday, 1866).

Watts, Susannah, *A Walk through Leicester: Being a Guide Containing a Description of the Town and its Environs, with Remarks upon its History and Antiquities* (Leicester: T. Combe, 1804).

—— *Elegy on the Death of the Princess Charlotte Augusta of Wales* (Leicester: I. Cockshaw, 1817).

—— *Hymns and Poems of the Late Mrs Susannah Watts with a Few Recollections of her Life* (Leicester: J. Waddington, 1842).

Webb, Sidney and Beatrice, *English Local Government from the Revolution to the Municipal Corporations Act* (London: Longmans, Green & Co., 1906).

West, Jane, *Letters to a Young Lady, in which the Duties and Character of Women are Considered*, 3 vols (London: William Pickering, 1996; 1st publ. 1811).

Whately, E. Jane, *Life and Correspondence of Richard Whately, D. D. Late Archbishop of Dublin*, 2 vols (London: Longmans, 1866).

Wightman, Julia, *Haste to the Rescue* (London: James Nisbet & Co., 1860).

Willyams, Jane Louisa, *The Reason Rendered: A Few Words Addressed to the Inhabitants of M——, in Cornwall. By an Old Friend*, 2nd edn (London: Hamilton, Adams & Co., 1845).

—— *A Short History of the Waldensian Church in the Valleys of Piedmont* (London: Nisbet, 1855).

Wilson, Sir Daniel, *Memorials of Edinburgh in the Olden Time*, 2 vols, 2nd edn (Edinburgh: A and C. Black, 1892).

Wood, Elizabeth, *No Tithes!* (Canterbury: Elizabeth Wood, 1829).

—— *The Poll of the Electors for Members of Parliament to Represent the City of Canterbury* (Canterbury: E. Wood, 1830).

—— *A Brief Outline of the Canterbury Reform Festival September 4, 1832* (Canterbury: Elizabeth Wood, 1832).

Wright, John C., *Bygone Eastbourne* (London: Spottiswoode & Co., 1902).

Yonge, Charlotte Mary, *A Book of Golden Deeds of All Times and All Lands* (London: Macmillan & Co., 1864).

Printed sources post-1920

Abrams, Dominic, and Michael A. Hogg (eds), *Social Identity Theory: Constructive and Critical Advances* (London: Harvester Wheatsheaf, 1990).

Acland, Alice, *Caroline Norton* (London: Constable, 1948).

Adkins, Lisa, and Beverley Skeggs (eds), *Feminism After Bourdieu* (Oxford: Blackwell, 2005).

Akenson, Donald Harman, *A Protestant in Purgatory: Richard Whately, Archbishop of Dublin* (Hamden, Conn.: Archon Books, 1981).

Alcoff, Linda, 'Cultural Feminism versus Post-Structuralism: The Identity Crisis in Feminist Theory', in Nicholas B. Dirks, Geoff Eley, and Sherry B. Ortner (eds), *Culture/Power/History: A Reader in Contemporary Social Theory* (Princeton: Princeton University Press, 1994), 96–122.

Alexander, Sally, *Becoming a Woman: And Other Essays in Nineteenth and Twentieth Century Feminist History* (London: Virago, 1994).

Aminzade, Ronald, and Doug McAdam, 'Emotions and Contentious Politics', in Ronald Aminzade and J. A. Goldstone (eds), *Silence and Voice in the Study of Contentious Politics* (Cambridge: Cambridge University Press, 2001), 14–50.

Anderson, Michael, 'The Social Position of Spinsters in Mid-Victorian Britain', *Journal of Family History*, 9 (1984), 377–93.

Anderson, Olive, 'Women Preachers in Mid-Victorian Britain: Some Reflexions on Feminism, Popular Religion and Social Change', *Historical Journal*, 12 (1969), 467–84.

Anderson, Verily, *The Northrepps Grandchildren* (London: Hodder & Stoughton, 1968).

Archer, John E., 'The Nineteenth-Century Allotment: Half an Acre and a Row', *Economic History Review*, 50 (1997), 21–36.

Armstrong, Alan, *Farmworkers: A Social and Economic History, 1770–1980* (London: Batsford, 1988).

Ashton, Owen R., and Paul A. Pickering (eds), *Friends of the People: Uneasy Radicals in the Age of the Chartists* (London: Merlin, 2002).

Aucott, Shirley, *Susanna Watts (1768 to 1842): Author of Leicester's First Guide, Abolitionist and Bluestocking* (Leicester: Shirley Aucott, 2004).

Bailey, Peter, *Popular Culture and Performance in the Victorian City* (Cambridge: Cambridge University Press, 1998).

Baker, Deborah, 'Social Identity in the Transition to Motherhood', in Deborah Baker and Suzanne Skevington (eds), *The Social Identity of Women* (London: Sage, 1989).

Baker-Jones, Leslie, *Princelings, Privilege and Power: The Tivyside Gentry in their Community* (Llandysul: Gwasg Gomer, 1999).

Banks, Olive, *Becoming a Feminist: The Social Origins of 'First Wave' Feminism* (Brighton: Wheatsheaf, 1986).

Barker, Hannah, 'Women, Work and the Industrial Revolution: Female Involvement in the English Printing Trades, c.1700–1840', in Hannah Barker and Elaine Chalus (eds), *Gender in Eighteenth-Century England: Roles, Representations and Responsibilities* (London and New York: Addison Wesley Longman, 1997), 81–100.

—— *The Business of Women: Female Enterprise and Urban Development in Northern England, 1760–1830* (Oxford: Oxford University Press, 2006).

—— and David Vincent (eds), *Language, Print and Electoral Politics, 1790–1832: Newcastle-under-Lyme Broadsides* (Woodbridge: Boydell, 2001).

—— and Karen Harvey, 'Women Entrepreneurs and Urban Expansion: Manchester, 1760–1820', in Rosemary Sweet and Penelope Lane (eds), *Women and Urban Life in Eighteenth-Century England: 'On the Town'* (Aldershot: Ashgate, 2003), 111–30.

Baugh, D. A., 'The Cost of Poor Relief in South-East England, 1790–1834', *Economic History Review*, 28 (1975), 50–68.

Behrman, Cynthia F., 'The Annual Blister: A Sidelight on Victorian Social and Parliamentary History', *Victorian Studies*, 11 (1968), 483–502.

Bellaigue, Christina de, *Educating Women: Schooling and Identity in England and France, 1800–1867* (Oxford: Oxford University Press, 2007).

—— 'The Development of Teaching as a Profession for Women before 1870', *Historical Journal*, 44 (2001), 963–88.

Bellamy, Joan, Anne Laurence, and Gill Perry (eds), *Women, Scholarship and Criticism: Gender and Knowledge, c.1790–1900* (Manchester: Manchester University Press, 2000).

Bennett, Bruce S., 'Banister v Thompson and Afterwards: The Church of England and the Deceased Wife's Sister's Marriage Act', *Journal of Ecclesiastical History*, 49 (1998), 668–82.

Berg, Maxine, 'Women's Property and the Industrial Revolution', *Journal of Interdisciplinary History*, 24 (1993), 233–50.

Bevis, Matthew, 'Volumes of Noise', *Victorian Literature and Culture*, 31 (2003), 577–91.

Biagini, Eugenio F. (ed.), *Citizenship and Community: Liberals, Radicals and Collective Identities in the British Isles, 1865–1931* (Cambridge: Cambridge University Press, 1996).

Billington, Louis, and Rosamund Billington, '"A Burning Zeal for Righteousness": Women in the British Anti-Slavery Movement, 1820–1860', in Jane Rendall (ed.), *Equal or Different: Women's Politics, 1800–1914* (Oxford: Basil Blackwell, 1987), 82–111.

Blain, Virginia, Patricia Clements, and Isobel Grundy (eds), *The Feminist Companion to Literature in English: Women Writers from the Middle Ages to the Present* (London: Batsford, 1990).

Bohstedt, John, 'Gender, Household and Community Politics: Women in English Riots, 1790–1810', *Past and Present*, 120 (1988), 88–122.

Bordo, Susan, 'Feminism, Postmodernism and Gender-Scepticism', in Linda J. Nicholson (ed.), *Feminism/Postmodernism* (London and New York: Routledge, 1990), 133–56.

Bourdieu, Pierre, *Outline of a Theory of Practice*, tr. Richard Nice (Cambridge: Cambridge University Press, 1977).

—— *Masculine Domination*, tr. Richard Nice (Cambridge: Polity Press, 2001).

Bourne, John M., *Patronage and Society in Nineteenth-Century England* (London: Edward Arnold, 1986).

Bowen, Huw V., *The Business of Empire: The East India Company and Imperial Britain, 1756–1833* (Cambridge: Cambridge University Press, 2006).

Boyd, C. J., 'Mothers and Daughters: A Discussion of Theory and Research', *Journal of Marriage and Family*, 51 (1989), 291–301.

Braddick, Michael J., and John Walter (eds), *Negotiating Power in Early Modern Society: Order, Hierarchy and Subordination in Britain and Ireland* (Cambridge: Cambridge University Press, 2001).

Bradley, Harriet, *Fractured Identities, Changing Patterns of Inequality* (Cambridge: Polity Press, 1996).

Braidotti, Rosi, *Nomadic Subjects: Embodiment and Sexual Difference in Contemporary Feminist Theory* (New York: Columbia University Press, 1994).

Brett, Peter, 'Political Dinners in Early Nineteenth-Century Britain: Platform, Meeting Place and Battleground', *History*, 81 (1996), 527–52.

Brewer, John, and Susan Staves (eds), *Early Modern Conceptions of Property* (London: Routledge, 1995), 1–18.

Briggs, Asa, 'Middle-Class Consciousness in English Politics, 1780–1846', *Past and Present*, 9 (1956), 65–74.

Brown, A. F. J., *Colchester, 1815–1915* (Chelmsford: Essex County Council, 1980).

Brown, Heloise, *'The Truest Form of Patriotism': Pacifist Feminism in Britain, 1870–1902* (Manchester: Manchester University Press, 2003).

Brundage, Anthony, 'The Landed Interest and the New Poor Law: A Reappraisal of the Revolution in Government', *English Historical Review*, 87 (1972), 27–48.

—— 'Debate: The Making of the New Poor Law *Redivivus*', *Past and Present*, 127 (1990), 183–6.

Brundage, Anthony, *The English Poor Laws, 1700–1930* (Basingstoke: Palgrave, 2002).

Burchardt, Jeremy, 'Rural Social Relations, 1830–50: Opposition to Allotments for Labourers', *Agricultural History Review*, 45 (1997), 165–75.

—— *The Allotment Movement in England, 1793–1873* (Woodbridge: Boydell, 2002).

Burman, Barbara, and Carole Turbin (eds), *Gender and History*, special edn, 14 (2002).

Burton, Kenneth G., *The Early Newspaper Press in Berkshire, 1723–1855* (Reading: K. G. Burton, 1954).

Butler, Judith, *Gender Trouble: Feminism and the Subversion of Identity* (London: Routledge, 1999).

Butler, Marilyn, *Maria Edgeworth: A Literary Biography* (Oxford: Clarendon Press, 1972).

Calhoun, Craig (ed.), *Habermas and the Public Sphere* (Cambridge, Mass.: MIT Press, 1992).

Cannadine, David, *Lords and Landlords: The Aristocracy and the Towns, 1774–1967* (Leicester: Leicester University Press, 1980).

Canning, Kathleen, 'Feminist History After the Linguistic Turn: Historicizing Discourse and Experience', *Signs*, 19 (1994), 368–404.

—— and Sonya O. Rose, 'Gender, Citizenship and Subjectivity: Some Historical and Theoretical Considerations', *Gender and History*, 13 (2001), 427–43.

Caple, Jeremy, *The Bristol Riots of 1831 and Social Reform in Britain* (Lewiston, NY: E. Mellen Press, 1990).

Ceadel, Martin, 'Cobden and Peace', in Anthony Howe and Simon Morgan (eds), *Rethinking Nineteenth-Century Liberalism: Richard Cobden Bicentenary Essays* (Aldershot: Ashgate, 2006), 189–207.

Cerulo, Karen A., 'Identity Construction: New Issues, New Directions', *Annual Review of Sociology*, 23 (1997), 385–409.

Chalus, Elaine, *Elite Women in English Political Life, 1754–1790* (Oxford: Clarendon Press, 2005).

Chapple, J. A.V., and Arthur Pollard (eds), *The Letters of Mrs Gaskell* (Manchester: Manchester University Press, 1966).

—— and Anita Wilson, *Private Voices: The Diaries of Elizabeth Gaskell and Sophia Holland* (Keele: Keele University Press, 1996).

Charlesworth, Andrew, 'The Development of the English Rural Proletariat and Social Protest, 1700–1850: A Comment', *Journal of Peasant Studies*, 8 (1980), 101–11.

Chew, Elizabeth,V. '"Repaired by Me to My Exceeding Great Cost and Charges": Anne Clifford and the Uses of Architecture', in Helen Hills (ed.), *Architecture and the Politics of Gender in Early Modern Europe* (Aldershot: Ashgate, 2003), 99–114.

Chitty, Susan, *The Woman who Wrote* Black Beauty: *A Life of Anna Sewell* (London: Hodder & Stoughton, 1971).

Chodorow, Nancy, *The Reproduction of Mothering: Psychoanalysis and the Sociology of Gender* (Berkeley, Calif.: University of California Press: 1978).

Clark, Anna, 'The Rhetoric of Chartist Domesticity: Gender, Language and Class in the 1830s and 1840s', *Journal of British Studies*, 31 (1992), 62–88.

—— *Struggle for the Breeches: Gender and the Making of the British Working Class* (London: Rivers Oram Press, 1995).

—— 'Gender, Class, and the Constitution: Franchise Reform in England, 1832–1928', in James Vernon (ed.), *Re-reading the Constitution: New Narratives in the Political History of England's Long Nineteenth Century* (Cambridge: Cambridge University Press, 1996), 230–53.

Clemit, Pamela, 'Mary Shelley and William Godwin: A Literary-Political Partnership, 1823–36', *Women's Writing*, 6 (1999), 285–95.

Cleverdon, Catherine L., *The Woman Suffrage Movement in Canada* (Toronto: University of Toronto Press, 1950).

Clive, Mary (ed.), *Caroline Clive, from the Diary and Family Papers of Mrs Archer Clive, 1801–1873* (London: Bodley Head, 1949).

Cohen, A. P. (ed.), *Symbolising Boundaries: Identity and Diversity in British Cultures* (Manchester: Manchester University Press, 1986).

Cohen, Michèle, 'Gender and the Private/Public Debate on Education in the Long Eighteenth Century', in R. Aldrich (ed.), *Public or Private Education? Lessons from History* (London: Woburn Press, 2004), 15–35.

Colley, Linda, *Britons: Forging the Nation, 1707–1837* (New Haven and London: Yale University Press, 1992).

Collins, Randall, 'Historical Change and the Ritual Production of Gender', in Joan Huber (ed.), *Macro-Micro Linkages in Sociology* (London: Sage, 1991), 109–20.

Corbett, Mary Jean, *Representing Femininity: Middle-Class Subjectivity in Victorian and Edwardian Women's Autobiographies* (Oxford: Oxford University Press, 1992).

Corfield, Kenneth, 'Elizabeth Heyrick: Radical Quaker', in Gail Malmgreen (ed.), *Religion in the Lives of English Women* (London: Croom Helm, 1986), 41–67.

Corfield, Penelope, 'From Second City to Regional Capital', in Carole Rawcliffe and Richard Wilson (eds), *Norwich since 1550* (London and New York: Hambledon, 2004), 139–66.

Courtenay, Adrian, 'Cheltenham Spa and the Berkeleys, 1832–48: Pocket Borough and Patron?', *Midland History*, 17 (1992), 93–108.

Cragoe, Matthew, '"Jenny Rules the Roost": Women and Electoral Politics, 1832–68', in Kathryn Gleadle and Sarah Richardson (eds), *Women in British Politics: The Power of the Petticoat, 1760–1860* (Basingstoke: Macmillan Press, 2000), 153–68.

Crawford, Elizabeth, *The Women's Suffrage Movement: A Reference Guide, 1866–1928* (London: UCL Press, 1999).

Creighton, Colin, *Richard Oastler: Evangelicalism and the Ideology of Domesticity* (Hull: University of Hull, 1992).

Daniels, Elizabeth Adams, *Jessie White Mario: Risorgimento Revolutionary* (Athens, Ohio: Ohio University Press, 1972).

Davidoff, Leonore, *Worlds Between: Historical Perspectives on Gender and Class* (Cambridge: Polity, 1995).

—— 'Gender and the "Great Divide": Public and Private in British Gender History', *Journal of Women's History*, 15 (2003), 11–27.

—— M. Doolittle, J. Fink, and K. Holden, *The Family Story: Blood, Contract and Intimacy, 1830–1960* (London: Longman, 1990).

—— and Catherine Hall, *Family Fortunes: Men and Women of the English Middle Class, 1780–1850* (London: Hutchinson, 1987).

Davis, Natalie Zemon, 'Boundaries and the Sense of Self in Sixteenth-Century France', in Thomas C. Heller, Sosna Morton, and David E. Wellbery (eds), *Reconstructing Individualism: Autonomy, Individuality and the Self in Western Thought* (Stanford, Calif.: Stanford University Press, 1986), 53–63.

Davis, Richard W., *Dissent in Politics, 1780–1830: The Political Life of William Smith, M.P.* (London: Epworth Press, 1971).

Deane, Theresa, 'Late Nineteenth-Century Philanthropy: The Case of Louisa Twining', in Ann Digby and John Stewart (eds), *Gender, Health and Welfare* (London: Routledge, 1996), 122–42.

Deaux, Kay, and Brenda Major, 'A Social-Psychological Model of Gender', in Deborah Rhode (ed.), *Theoretical Perspectives on Sexual Difference* (New Haven and London: Yale University Press, 1990), 89–99.

Dickey, Brian, '"Going about and Doing Good": Evangelicals and Poverty, c. 1815–1870', in John Wolffe (ed.), *Evangelical Faith and Public Zeal: Evangelicals and Society in Britain, 1780–1980* (London: SPCK, 1995), 38–58.

Digby, Anne, *Pauper Palaces* (London: Routledge & Kegan Paul, 1978).

Doern, Kristin G., 'Equal Questions: The "Woman Question" and the "Drink Question" in the Writings of Clara Lucas Balfour, 1808–78', in Sue Morgan (ed.), *Women, Religion and Feminism in Britain, 1750–1900* (Basingstoke: Palgrave Macmillan, 2002), 159–75.

Dooley, Dolores, 'Anna Doyle Wheeler (1785–c.1850)', in Mary Cullen and Maria Luddy (eds), *Women, Power and Consciousness in Nineteenth-Century Ireland: Eight Biographical Studies* (Dublin: Attic Press, 1995), 19–53.

Doyle, Barry, 'Politics, 1833–1945', in Carole Rawcliffe and Richard Wilson (eds), *Norwich since 1550* (London and New York: Hambledon, 2004), 343–60.

Dunbabin, J. P. D., *Rural Discontent in Nineteenth-Century Britain* (London: Faber & Faber, 1974).

Dunkley, Peter, 'Whigs and Paupers: The Reform of the English Poor Laws, 1830–1834', *Journal of British Studies*, 20 (1981), 124–49.

Eastbourne Local History Society, *The 1841 Census for the Parish of Eastbourne, Sussex* (Polegate: Eastbourne Local History Society, 1990).

Eastwood, David, *Governing Rural England: Tradition and Transformation in Local Government, 1780–1840* (Oxford: Clarendon Press, 1994).

Edsall, Nicholas, C. *The Anti-Poor Law Movement, 1834–44* (Manchester: Manchester University Press, 1971).

—— *Richard Cobden: Independent Radical* (Cambridge, Mass., and London: Harvard University Press, 1986).

Edwards, J. K., 'Chartism in Norwich', *Yorkshire Bulletin of Economic and Social Research*, 19 (1967), 85–100.

Eger, Elizabeth, Charlotte Grant, Cliona O' Gallchoir, and Penny Warburton (eds), *Women, Writing and the Public Sphere, 1700–1830* (Cambridge: Cambridge University Press, 2001).

Ehnnen, Jill, 'Writing Against, Writing Through· Subjectivity, Vocation and Authorship in the Work of Dorothy Wordsworth', *South Atlantic Review*, 64 (1999), 72–90.

Elbourne, Elizabeth, 'The Sin of the Settler: The 1835–36 Select Committee on Aborigines and Debates over Virtue and Conquest in the Early Nineteenth-Century British White Settler Empire', *Journal of Colonialism and Colonial History*, 4 (2003).

Ellens, J. P., *Religious Routes to Gladstonian Liberalism: The Church Rate Conflict in England and Wales, 1832–68* (University Park, Pa.: Pennsylvania State University Press, 1994).

Ellsworth, Edward V., *Liberators of The Female Mind: The Shirreff Sisters, Educational Reform, and the Women's Movement* (Westport, Conn.: Greenwood Press, 1979).

Enser, A. G. S., *A Brief History of Eastbourne* (Eastbourne: Eastbourne Local History Society, 1976).

Epstein, James, 'Rituals of Solidarity: Radical Dining, Toasting and Symbolic Expression', in Epstein, *Radical Expression: Political Language, Ritual and Symbol in England, 1790–1850* (New York and Oxford: Oxford University Press, 1994), 147–66.

—— In Practice: Studies in the Language and Culture of Popular Politics in Modern Britain (Stanford, Calif.: Stanford University Press, 2003).

Erickson, Amy, Women and Property in Early Modern England (London: Routledge, 1993).

Eustance, Claire, 'Protests from Behind the Grille: Gender and the Transformation of Parliament, 1867–1918', Parliamentary History, 16 (1997), 107–26.

Everitt, Alan, Landscape and Community in England (London: Hambledon Press, 1985).

Faderman, Lillian, Surpassing the Love of Men: Romantic Friendship and Love between Women from the Renaissance to the Present (London: Women's Press, 1981).

Felski, Rita, Beyond Feminist Aesthetics: Feminist Literature and Social Change (London: Hutchinson Radius, 1989).

Ferguson, Moira, Animal Advocacy and Englishwomen, 1780–1900: Patriots, Nation, Empire (Ann Arbor, Mich.: University of Michigan Press, 1998).

Finlayson, Geoffrey, Citizen, State and Social Welfare in Britain, 1830–1990 (Oxford: Clarendon Press, 1994).

Finn, Margot, 'Women, Consumption and Coverture in England, c. 1760–1860', Historical Journal, 39 (1996), 703–22.

Fitzgerald, Kevin, Ahead of their Time: A Short History of the Farmers' Club, 1842–1968 (London: Heinemann, 1968).

Fladeland, Betty, '"Our Cause Being One and the Same": Abolitionists and Chartism', in James Walvin (ed.), Slavery and British Society, 1776–1846 (Basingstoke: Macmillan, 1982), 69–99.

Forster, E. M., Marianne Thornton, 1797–1887: A Domestic Biography (London: André Deutsch, 2000; 1st publ. 1956).

Fowler, Denise, 'Women in Towns as Keepers of the Word: The Example of Warwickshire during the 1780s and 1830s', in Rosemary Sweet and Penelope Lane (eds), Women and Urban Life in Eighteenth-Century England: 'On the Town' (Aldershot: Ashgate, 2003), 157–72.

Fox, H. S. A., 'Local Farmers' Associations and the Circulation of Agricultural Information in Nineteenth-Century England', in H. A. S. Fox and Robin A. Butlin (eds), Change in the Countryside: Essays on Rural England, 1500–1900 (London: Institute of British Geographers, 1979), 43–63.

Fraser, Derek, Urban Politics in Victorian England: The Structure of Politics in Victorian Cities (Leicester: Leicester University Press, 1976).

Fraser, Nancy, 'The Uses and Abuses of French Discourse Theories for Feminist Politics', boundary 2, 17 (1990), 82–101.

—— and Linda J. Nicholson, 'Social Criticism without Philosophy: An Encounter between Feminism and Postmodernism', in Linda J. Nicholson (ed.), Feminism/Postmodernism (London and New York: Routledge, 1990), 19–38.

Fraser, Peter, 'Public Petitioning and Parliament before 1832', History, 46 (1961), 195–211.

Freeman, Clifford B., Mary Simpson of Boynton Vicarage: Teacher of Ploughboys and Critic of Methodism (York: East Yorkshire Local History Society, 1972).

Frow, Edmund, and Ruth Frow, Political Women, 1800–1850 (London: Pluto Press, 1989).

Fryckstedt, Monica Correa, 'Charlotte Elizabeth Tonna: A Forgotten Evangelical Writer', *Studia Neophilologica*, 52 (1980), 79–102.

Fulcher, Jonathan, 'Gender, Politics and Class in the Early Nineteenth-Century English Reform Movement', *Historical Research*, 67 (1994), 57–74.

Fulford, Roger (ed.), *The Greville Memoirs* (London: Longman & Co., 1964).

Fuller, Richard Mackney, *Farmers at the 'Fountain': A History of Canterbury Farmers' Club and Farmers' Meetings in Canterbury over a Period of Two Hundred Years, 1793–1993* (Sutton-by-Dover: Cornilo Partners, 1997).

Fussell, G. E., 'Review', *Technology and Culture*, 12 (1971), 350–1.

Gallagher, John A., 'Fowell Buxton and the New African Policy, 1838–1842', *Cambridge Historical Journal*, 10 (1950), 36–58.

Gash, Norman, *Politics in the Age of Peel: A Study in the Technique of Parliamentary Representation, 1830–1850* (London: Longman & Co., 1953).

Gavin, Adrienne E., *Dark Horse: A Life of Anna Sewell* (Stroud: Sutton, 2004).

Gerard, Jessica, 'Lady Bountiful: Women of the Landed Classes and Rural Philanthropy', *Victorian Studies*, 30 (1987), 183–210.

—— *Country House Life: Family and Servants, 1815–1914* (Oxford: Blackwell Press, 1994).

Gibbs-Smith, Charles H., *The Fashionable Lady in the Nineteenth Century* (London: HMSO, 1960).

Giddens, Anthony, A., *The Constitution of Society: Outline of the Theory of Structuration* (Cambridge: Polity Press, 1984).

—— *Modernity and Self-Identity: Self and Society in the Late Modern Age* (Cambridge: Polity Press, 1991).

Gill, Catie, 'Identities in Quaker Women's Writing, 1652–60', *Women's Writing*, 9 (2002), 267–83.

Gilligan, Carol, *In a Different Voice: Psychological Theory and Women's Development* (Cambridge, Mass., and London: Harvard University Press, 1982).

Gleadle, Kathryn, *The Early Feminists: Radical Unitarians and the Emergence of the Women's Rights Movement, c. 1831–51* (Basingstoke: Macmillan, 1995).

—— '"Our Several Spheres': Middle-Class Women and the Feminisms of Early Victorian Radical Politics', in Kathryn Gleadle and Sarah Richardson (eds), *Women in British Politics, 1760–1860: The Power of the Petticoat* (Basingstoke: Macmillan, 2000), 115–52.

—— 'British Women and Radical Politics in the Late Nonconformist Enlightenment, c. 1780–1830', in Amanda Vickery (ed.), *Women, Privilege and Power: British Politics 1750 to the Present* (Stanford, Calif.: Stanford University Press, 2001), 123–51.

—— *Radical Writing on Women, 1800–1850: An Anthology* (Basingstoke: Palgrave Macmillan, 2002).

—— '"Opinions Deliver'd in Conversation": Conversation, Politics, and Gender in the Late Eighteenth Century', in Jose Harris (ed.), *Civil Society in British History: Ideas, Identities, Institutions* (Oxford: Oxford University Press, 2003), 61–78.

—— '"The Age of Physiological Reformers": Rethinking Gender and Domesticity in the Age of Reform', in Arthur Burns and Joanna Innes (eds), *Rethinking the Age of Reform* (Cambridge: Cambridge University Press, 2003), 200–19.

—— 'Charlotte Elizabeth Tonna and the Mobilization of Tory Women in Early Victorian England', *Historical Journal*, 50 (2007), 97–117.

—— 'Revisiting *Family Fortunes: Men and Women of the English Middle Class, 1780–1850*', *Women's History Review*, 16 (2007), 773–82.

—— and Sarah Richardson (eds), *Women in British Politics, 1760–1860: The Power of the Petticoat* (Basingstoke: Macmillan, 2000).

Godber, Joyce, *History of Bedfordshire, 1066–1888* (Bedford: Bedfordshire County Council, 1969).

Goddard, Nicholas, *Harvests of Change: The Royal Agricultural Society of England 1838–1988* (London: Quiller Press, 1988).

—— 'Agricultural Literature and Societies', in G. E. Mingay (ed.), *The Agrarian History of England and Wales*, vi. *1750–1850* (Cambridge: Cambridge University Press, 1989), 361–83.

Goldman, Lawrence, *Science, Reform and Politics in Victorian Britain: The Social Science Association, 1857–1886* (Cambridge: Cambridge University Press, 2002).

—— 'A Peculiarity of the English? The Social Science Association and the Absence of Sociology in Nineteenth-Century Britain', *Past and Present*, 114 (1987), 133–71.

Goodman, Joyce, 'Women School Board Members and the Management of Working-Class Schools, 1800–1861', in Joyce Goodman and Sylvia Harrop (eds), *Women, Educational Policy-Making and Administration in England: Authoritative Women since 1800* (London: Routledge, 2000), 50–77.

Gordon, Eleanor, and Gwyneth Nair, *Public Lives: Women, Family and Society in Victorian Britain* (New Haven: Yale University Press, 2003).

Graves, C. Pamela, 'Civic Ritual, Townscape and Social Identity in Seventeenth and Eighteenth Century Newcastle upon Tyne', in Susan Lawrence (ed.), *Archaeologies of the British: Explorations of Identity in Great Britain and its Colonies, 1600–1945* (London: Routledge, 2003), 31–54.

Grayson, Ruth, 'Who was Master? Class Relationships in Nineteenth-Century Sheffield', in Alan Kidd and David Nicholls (eds), *The Making of the British Middle Class? Studies of Regional and Cultural Diversity since the Eighteenth Century* (Stroud: Sutton, 1998), 42–57.

Green, D. R., and A. Owens, 'Gentlewomanly Capitalism? Spinsters, Widows, and Wealth Holding in England and Wales, c. 1800–1860', *Economic History Review*, 56 (2003), 510–36.

Griffin, Christine, ' "I'm Not a Women's Libber, But . . .": Feminism, Consciousness and Identity', in Suzanne Skevington and Deborah Baker (eds), *The Social Identity of Women* (London: Sage, 1989), 173–93.

Griffin, Robert J. (ed.), *The Faces of Anonymity: Anonymous and Pseudonymous Publication from the Sixteenth Century to the Twentieth Century* (Basingstoke: Palgrave Macmillan, 2003).

Griffiths, Paul, Adam Fox, and Steve Hindle (eds), *The Experience of Authority in Early Modern England* (Basingstoke: Macmillan, 1996).

Gunn, Simon, *The Public Culture of the Victorian Middle Class: Ritual and Authority and the English Industrial City, 1840–1914* (Manchester: Manchester University Press, 2000).

Habermas, Jürgen, *The Structural Transformation of The Public Sphere* (1989), tr. Thomas Burger (Cambridge: Polity Press, 1992).

Haight, Gordon S., *The George Eliot Letters*, ii. *1852–1858* (London: Oxford University Press, 1954).

Hall, Catherine, *White, Male and Middle Class: Explorations in Feminism and History* (Cambridge: Polity, 1992).

—— 'The Rule of Difference: Gender, Class and Empire in the Making of the 1832 Reform Act', in Ida Blom and Karen Hagemann (eds), *Gendered Nations: Nationalisms and Gender Order in the Long Nineteenth Century* (Oxford: Berg, 2000), 107–35.

—— Keith McClelland, and Jane Rendall, *Defining the Victorian Nation: Class, Race, Gender and the British Reform Act of 1867* (Cambridge: Cambridge University Press, 2000).

Hamburger, L., and J. Hamburger, *Troubled Lives: John and Sarah Austin* (Toronto: University of Toronto Press, 1985).

Hardy, Sheila, *The Diary of a Suffolk Farmer's Wife, 1854–69: A Woman of her Time* (Basingstoke: Macmillan, 1992).

Harling, Philip, 'Rethinking "Old Corruption"', *Past and Present*, 147 (1995), 127–58.

—— 'The Power of Persuasion: Central Authority, Local Bureaucracy and the New Poor Law', *English Historical Review*, 107 (1992), 30–53.

Harrison, John F. C., *Learning and Living, 1790–1960: A Study in the History of the English Adult Education Movement* (London: Routledge & Kegan Paul, 1961).

Hastings, Paul, 'Radical Movements and Workers' Protests to c. 1850', in Frederick Lansberry (ed.), *Government and Politics in Kent, 1640–1914* (Woodbridge: Boydell and Kent County Council, 2001), 95–138.

Hayek, F. A. (ed.), *John Stuart Mill and Harriet Taylor: Their Correspondence and Subsequent Marriage* (London: Routledge & Kegan Paul, 1951).

Heilbrun, Alfred B., 'Identification with the Father and Sex-Role Development of the Daughter', *Family Co-ordinator*, 25 (1976), 411–16.

Heineman, Helen, *Restless Angels: The Friendship of Six Victorian Women. Frances Wright, Camilla Wright, Harriet Wright, Frances Garnett, Julia Garnett Pertz, Frances Trollope* (Athens, Ohio: Ohio University Press, 1983).

Hempton, D. N., 'Evangelicalism and Eschatology', *Journal of Ecclesiastical History*, 31 (1980), 179–94.

Hewitt, Martin, *The Emergence of Stability in the Industrial City: Manchester, 1832–67* (Aldershot: Scolar Press, 1996).

Higgs, Edward, 'Occupational Censuses and the Agricultural Workforce in Victorian England and Wales', *Economic History Review*, 48 (1995), 700–16.

—— 'Women, Occupation and Work in the Nineteenth-Century Censuses', *History Workshop Journal*, 23 (1987), 59–80.

Hill, Alan G. (ed.), *The Letters of William and Dorothy Wordsworth: The Later Years*, part 2. *1829–1834* (Oxford: Clarendon Press, 1979).

Hill, Bridget, 'Women, Work and the Census: A Problem for Historians of Women', *History Workshop Journal*, 35 (1993), 78–94.

Hills, Helen, 'Theorising the Relationship between Architecture and Gender in Early Modern Europe', in Helen Hills (ed.), *Architecture and the Politics of Gender in Early Modern Europe* (Aldershot: Ashgate, 2003), 3–22.

Hilton, Boyd, *The Age of Atonement: The Influence of Evangelicalism on Social and Economic Thought, 1785–1865* (Oxford: Clarendon Press, 1988).

Himmelfarb, Gertrude, *The Idea of Poverty: England in the Early Industrial Age* (London: Faber, 1984).

Hinde, Wendy, *Catholic Emancipation: A Shake to Men's Minds* (Oxford: Blackwell, 1992).

Hindle, Steve, 'Power, Poor Relief, and Social Relations in Holland Fen, c. 1600–1800', *Historical Journal,* 41 (1998), 67–96.

Hirsch, Pam, *Barbara Leigh Smith Bodichon, 1827–1891: Feminist, Artist and Rebel* (London: Chatto & Windus, 1998).

Hobsbawm, Eric, and George Rudé, *Captain Swing* (London: Phoenix, 1969).

Holcombe, Lee, *Wives and Property: Reform of the Married Women's Property Law in Nineteenth-Century England* (Oxford: Martin Robertson, 1983).

Hollis, Patricia, *Ladies Elect: Women in English Local Government, 1865–1914* (Oxford: Clarendon Press, 1987).

Holt, H. M. E., 'Assistant Commissioners and Local Agents: Their Role in Tithe Commutation, 1836–1854', *Agricultural History Review,* 32 (1984), 189–200.

Holton, Sandra Stanley, *Quaker Women: Personal Life, Memory and Radicalism in the Lives of Women Friends, 1780–1930* (London: Routledge, 2007).

Horn, Pamela, *The Rural World, 1780–1850: Social Change in the English Countryside* (London: Hutchinson, 1980).

—— *Victorian Countrywomen* (Oxford: Basil Blackwell, 1991).

Howkins, Alun, *Reshaping Rural England: A Social History, 1850–1925* (London: Harper Collins, 1991).

Huzel, J. P., 'The Labourer and the Poor Law, 1750–1850', in G. E. Mingay (ed.), *The Agrarian History of England and Wales,* vi. *1750–1850* (Cambridge: Cambridge University Press, 1989), 755–810.

Hughes, William R., *Sophia Sturge: A Memoir* (London: G. Allen & Unwin, 1940).

Hurd, Madeline, 'Class, Masculinity, Manners and Mores: Public Space and Public Sphere in Nineteenth-Century Europe', *Social Science History,* 24 (2000), 75–110.

Hurst, Michael, *Maria Edgeworth and the Public Scene: Intellect, Fine Feeling and Landlordism in the Age of Reform* (London: Macmillan, 1969).

Innes, Joanna, 'The Distinctiveness of the English Poor Laws, 1750–1850', in Donald Winch and Patrick K. O'Brien (eds), *The Political Economy of British Historical Experience, 1688–1914* (Oxford: Oxford University Press, 2002), 381–407.

—— 'Legislation and Public Participation, 1760–1830', in David Lemmings (ed.), *The British and their Laws in the Eighteenth Century* (Woodbridge: Boydell Press, 2005), 102–32.

Jacobs, Jo Ellen, 'Harriet Taylor Mill's Collaboration with John Stuart Mill', in Cecile T. Tougas and Sara Ebenreck (eds), *Presenting Women Philosophers* (Philadelphia: Temple University Press, 2000), 155–66.

Jacques, Ann K., *Merrie Wakefield Based on Some of the Diaries of Clara Clarkson, 1811–89, of Alverthorpe Hall, Wakefield* (Wakefield: West Yorkshire Printing Co., 1971).

Jay, Elizabeth (ed.), *The Autobiography of Margaret Oliphant: The Complete Text* (Oxford: Oxford University Press, 1990).

Johnson, Richard, 'Educational Policy and Social Control in Early Victorian England', *Past and Present*, 49 (1970), 96–119.

—— 'Administrators in Education before 1870: Patronage, Social Position and Role', in G. Sutherland (ed.), *Studies in the Growth of Government* (London: Routledge & Kegan Paul, 1972), 110–38.

Jopling, David A., 'A Self of Selves?', in Ulric Neisser and David A. Jopling (eds), *The Conceptual Self in Context: Culture, Experience, Self-Understanding* (Cambridge: Cambridge University Press, 1997), 249–67.

Jordan, Judith V., 'The Relational Self: A New Perspective for Understanding Women's Development', in Jaine Strauss and George R. Geothals (eds), *The Self: Interdisciplinary Approaches* (New York: Springer-Verlag, 1991), 136–49.

Joyce, Patrick, *Democratic Subjects: The Self and the Social in Nineteenth-Century Cambridge* (Cambridge: Cambridge University Press, 1994).

Kay, Alison C., 'Small Business, Self-Employment and Women's Work–Life Choices in Nineteenth-Century London', in David Mitch, John Brown, and Marco H. D. van Leeuwen (eds), *Origins of the Modern Career* (Aldershot: Ashgate, 2004), 191–206.

Keast, John, *A History of East and West Looe* (Chichester: Phillimore & Co., 1987).

Keith-Lucas, Bryan, *The English Local Government Franchise: A Short History* (Oxford: Basil Blackwell, 1952).

Kelly, Audrey, *Lydia Becker and the Cause* (Lancaster: University of Lancaster, 1992).

Kelly, Gary, 'Clara Reeve: Provincial Bluestocking from the Old Whigs to the Modern Liberal State', *Huntington Library Quarterly*, 65 (2002), 105–25.

Kennedy, Catriona '"Womanish Epistles?": Martha McTier, Female Epistolarity and Late Eighteenth-Century Irish Radicalism', *Women's History Review*, 13 (2004), 649–67.

Klein, Lawrence, 'Gender and the Public/Private Distinction in the Eighteenth Century: Some Questions about Evidence and Analytic Procedure', *Eighteenth-Century Studies*, 29 (1995), 97–109.

—— 'Property and Politeness in the Early Eighteenth-Century Whig Moralists: The Case of the Spectator', in John Brewer and Susan Staves (eds), *Early Modern Conceptions of Property* (London: Routledge, 1995), 221–33.

Kriegel, Abraham D. (ed.), *The Holland House Diaries, 1831–40: The Diary of Henry Richard Vassall Fox, Third Lord Holland, with Extracts from the Diary of Dr John Allen* (London: Routledge & Kegan Paul, 1977).

Kroska, Amy, 'Does Gender Ideology Matter? Examining the Relationship between Gender Ideology and Self- and Partner-Meanings', *Social Psychology Quarterly*, 65 (2002), 248–65.

Laidlaw, Zoë, '"Aunt Anna's Report": The Buxton Women and the Aborigines Select Committee, 1835–37', *Journal of Imperial and Commonwealth History*, 32 (2004), 1–28.

—— *Colonial Connections, 1815–45: Patronage, the Information Revolution and Colonial Government* (Manchester: Manchester University Press, 2005).

Lane, Richard, *Anna Gurney, 1795–1857* (Dereham, Norfolk: Larks Press, 2001).

Laqueur, Thomas, 'The Queen Caroline Affair: Politics as Art in the Reign of George IV', *Journal of Modern History*, 54 (1982), 417–66.

Larrabeiti, Michelle de, 'Conspicuous before the World: The Political Rhetoric of the Chartist Women', in Eileen J. Yeo (ed.), *Radical Femininity: Women's Self-Representation in the Public Sphere* (Manchester: Manchester University Press, 1998), 106–26.

Latham, Jackie, 'The Political and the Personal: The Radicalism of Sophia Chichester and Georgiana Fletcher Welch', *Women's History Review*, 8 (1999), 469–87.

Lawrence, Jon, 'The Politics of Place and the Politics of Nation', *Twentieth Century British History*, 11 (2000), 83–94.

Lester, Alan, *Imperial Networks: Creating Identities in Nineteenth-Century South Africa and Britain* (London: Routledge, 2001).

Levi, Giovanni, 'On Microhistory', in P. Burke (ed.), *New Perspectives on Historical Writing*, 2nd edn (University Park, Pa.: Pennsylvania State University Press, 2001), 93–113.

Lewis, Brian, '"A Republic of Quakers" : The Radical Bourgeoisie, the State and Stability in Lancashire, 1789–1851', in Alan Kidd and David Nicholls (eds), *The Making of the British Middle Class? Studies of Regional and Cultural Diversity since the Eighteenth Century* (Stroud: Sutton, 1998), 72–91.

Lewis, Judith Schneid, *Sacred to Female Patriotism: Gender, Class and Politics in Late Georgian Britain* (London: Routledge, 2003).

Leys, Colin, 'Petitioning in the Nineteenth and Twentieth Centuries', *Political Studies*, 3 (1955), 45–64.

Liddington, Jill, *The Long Road to Greenham: Feminism and Anti-Militarism in Britain since 1820* (London: Virago, 1989).

—— 'Beating the Inheritance Bounds: Anne Lister (1791–1840) and her Dynastic Identity', *Gender and History*, 7 (1995), 260–74.

—— 'Gender, Authority and Mining in an Industrial Landscape: Anne Lister 1791–1840', *History Workshop Journal*, 42 (1996), 59–86.

—— *Female Fortune: Land, Gender and Authority. The Anne Lister Diaries and Other Writings, 1833–1836* (London: Rivers Oram Press, 1998).

Lofland, Lyn H., *The Public Realm: Exploring the City's Quintessential Social Territory* (New York: Aldine de Gruyter, 1998).

Lopatin-Lummis, Nancy D., *Political Unions, Popular Politics and the Great Reform Act of 1832* (Basingstoke: Macmillan, 1999).

Lott, Bernice, 'Dual Natures or Learned Behaviour: The Challenge to Feminist Psychology', in Rachel T. Hare-Mustin and Jeanne Marecek (eds), *Making a Difference: Psychology and the Construction of Gender* (London and New Haven: Yale University Press, 1990), 65–101.

Lovell, Terry, 'Thinking Feminism with and against Bourdieu', in Bridget Fowler (ed.), *Reading Bourdieu on Society and Culture* (Oxford: Blackwell, 2000), 27–48.

Lubenow, William C., *The Politics of Government Growth: Early Victorian Attitudes toward State Intervention, 1833–1848* (Newton Abbot: David & Charles, 1971).

Lynch, Katherine A., 'The Family and the History of Public Life', *Journal of Interdisciplinary History*, 24 (1994), 665–84.

McAdams, Dan P., 'The Case for Unity in the (Post)Modern Self: A Modest Proposal', in Richard D. Ashmore and Lee Jussim (eds), *Self and Identity: Fundamental Issues* (Oxford and New York: Oxford University Press, 1997), 46–78.

McCall, George J., and J. L. Simmons, *Identities and Interactions* (London: Collier-Macmillan; New York: Free Press, 1966).

McCalman, Iain, 'Newgate in Revolution: Radical Enthusiasm and Romantic Counterculture', *Eighteenth-Century Life*, 22 (1998), 95–110.

McCann, Philip, and Francis A. Young, *Samuel Wilderspin and the Infant School Movement* (London: Croom Helm, 1982).

McCord, James N., 'Taming the Female Politician in Early Nineteenth-Century England: *John Bull* versus Lady Jersey', *Journal of Women's History*, 13 (2002), 31–53.

McCormack, Matthew, *The Independent Man: Citizenship and Gender Politics in Georgian England* (Manchester: Manchester University Press, 2005).

McCrone, Kathleen, 'Feminism and Philanthropy in Victorian England: The Case of Louisa Twining', Canadian Historical Association, *Historical Papers* (1976), 123–39.

McClelland, Keith, 'England's Greatness, the Working Man', in Catherine Hall, Keith McClelland, and Jane Rendall, *Defining the Victorian Nation: Class, Race, Gender and the British Reform Act of 1867* (Cambridge: Cambridge University Press, 2000), 71–118.

Mack, Phyllis, *Visionary Women: Ecstatic Prophecy in Seventeenth-Century England* (Berkeley, Calif.: University of California Press, 1992).

—— 'Religion, Feminism and the Problem of Agency: Reflections on Eighteenth-Century Quakerism', *Signs*, 29 (2003), 149–77.

Mahoney, Maureen A., and Barbara Yngvesson, 'The Construction of Subjectivity and the Paradox of Resistance: Reintegrating Feminist Anthropology and Psychology', *Signs*, 18 (1992), 44–73.

Maidment, Brian E., '"Works in Unbroken Succession": The Literary Career of Mary Howitt', in Kay Boardman and Shirley Jones (eds), *Popular Victorian Women Writers* (Manchester: Manchester University Press, 2004), 22–45.

Malster, Robert, *250 Years of Brewing in Ipswich: The Story of Tollemache and Cobbold's Cliff Brewery, 1746–1996* (Ipswich: Malthouse Press, 1996).

Mandler, Peter, 'The Making of the New Poor Law *Redivivus*', *Past and Present*, 117 (1987), 131–57.

Manton, Jo, *Mary Carpenter and the Children of the Streets* (London: Heinemann, 1976).

Marcus, Jane (ed.), *Suffrage and the Pankhursts* (London: Routledge & Kegan Paul, 1987).

Markus, Hazel R., and Shinobu Kitayama, 'Cultural Variation in the Self-Concept', in Jaine Strauss and George R. Geothals (eds), *The Self: Interdisciplinary Approaches* (New York: Springer-Verlag, 1991), 18–48.

Martin, Mary Clare, 'Women and Philanthropy in Walthamstow and Leyton, 1740–1870', *London Journal*, 19 (1994), 119–50.

Marwick, William H., *The Life of Alexander Campbell* (Glasgow: Glasgow and District Co-operative Association, 1964).

Mascuch, Michael, *Origins of the Individualist Self: Autobiography and Self-Identity in England, 1591–1791* (Cambridge: Polity Press, 1997).

Matthew, H. C. G., 'Rhetoric and Politics in Great Britain, 1860–1950', in Philip J. Waller (ed.), *Politics and Social Change in Modern Britain: Essays Presented to A. F. Thompson* (Brighton: Harvester, 1987), 34–58.

Mavor, Elizabeth, *The Ladies of Llangollen: A Study in Romantic Friendship* (London: Penguin, 1971).

Meisel, Joseph, S., *Public Speech and the Culture of Public Life in the Age of Gladstone* (New York: Columbia University Press, 2001).

Midgley, Clare, *Women against Slavery: The British Campaigns, 1780–1870* (London: Routledge, 1992).

—— 'Slave Sugar Boycotts, Female Activism and the Domestic Base of British Anti-Slavery Culture', *Slavery and Abolition*, 17 (1996), 137–62.

—— 'From Supporting Missions to Petitioning Parliament: British Women and the Evangelical Campaign against *Sati* in India, 1813–30', in Kathryn Gleadle and Sarah Richardson (eds), *Women in British Politics, 1760–1860: The Power of the Petticoat* (Basingstoke: Macmillan, 2000), 74–92.

Mills, Anthony R., *Two Victorian Ladies: More Pages from the Journals of Emily and Ellen Hall* (London: Frederick Muller, 1969).

Mitchell, C. J., 'Women in the Eighteenth-Century Book Trades', in O. M. Brack (ed.), *Writers, Books, and Trade: An Eighteenth-Century English Miscellany for W. B. Todd* (New York: AMS, 1994), 25–76.

Moi, Toril, *What is a Woman? And Other Essays* (Oxford: Oxford University Press, 1999).

Moilliet, Andrew (ed.), *Elizabeth Anne Galton (1808–1906): A Well-Connected Gentlewoman* (Northwich: Léonie Press, 2003).

Morgan, Simon, 'Domestic Economy and Political Agitation: Women and the Anti-Corn Law League, 1839–1846', in Kathryn Gleadle and Sarah Richardson (eds), *Women in British Politics, 1760–1860: The Power of the Petticoat* (Basingstoke: Macmillan, 2000), 115–33.

—— 'Seen But Not Heard? Women's Platforms, Respectability and Female Publics in the Mid-Nineteenth Century', *Nineteenth-Century Prose*, 29 (2002), 50–67.

—— '"A Sort of Land Debatable": Female Influence, Civic Virtue and Middle-Class Identity, c. 1830–1860', *Women's History Review*, 13 (2004), 183–209.

—— 'From Warehouse Clerk to Corn Law Celebrity: The Making of a National Hero', in Anthony Howe and Simon Morgan (eds), *Rethinking Nineteenth-Century Liberalism: Richard Cobden Bicentenary Essays* (Aldershot: Ashgate, 2006), 39–58.

—— *A Victorian Woman's Place: Public Culture in the Nineteenth Century* (London and New York: Tauris Academic Studies, 2007).

Morris, Marmaduke C. F., *The British Workman Past and Present* (London: Oxford University Press, 1928).

Morris, Robert, J., *Class, Sect and Party: The Making of the British Middle Class, Leeds, 1820–1850* (Manchester: Manchester University Press, 1990).

—— *Men, Women and Property in England, 1780–1870: A Social and Economic History of Family Strategies amongst the Leeds Middle Classes* (Cambridge: Cambridge University Press, 2005).

Moselle, Boaz, 'Allotments, Enclosure and Proletarianization in Early Nineteenth-Century Southern England', *Economic History Review*, 48 (1995), 482–500.

Muirhead, Ian I., 'Catholic Emancipation: Scottish Reactions in 1829', *Innes Review*, 24 (1973), 26–42, 103–20.

Murgatroyd, Linda, 'Only Half the Story: Some Blinkering Effects of "Malestream" Sociology', in David Held and John B. Thompson (eds), *Social Theory of Modern Societies: Anthony Giddens and his Critics* (Cambridge: Cambridge University Press, 1989), 147–61.

Nead, Lynda, 'Mapping the Self: Gender, Space and Modernity in Mid-Victorian London', in Roy Porter (ed.), *Rewriting the Self: Histories from the Renaissance to the Present* (London and New York: Routledge, 1997), 167–85.

Neville, Graham, *Religion and Society in Eastbourne, 1735–1920* (Eastbourne: Eastbourne Local History Society, 1982).

Neville-Sington, Pamela, *Fanny Trollope: The Life and Adventures of a Clever Woman* (London: Viking, 1997).

Nicholls, David, 'Richard Cobden and the International Peace Congress Movement, 1848–1853', *Journal of British Studies*, 30 (1991), 351–76.

O'Gorman, Frank, *Voters, Patrons and Parties: The Unreformed Electorate of Hanoverian England, 1734–1832* (Oxford: Clarendon Press, 1989).

Oliver, W. H., *Prophets and Millennialists: The Uses of Biblical Prophecy in England from the 1790s to the 1840s* (Oxford: Oxford University Press, 1978).

Onslow, Barbara, *Women of the Press in Nineteenth-Century Britain* (Basingstoke: Macmillan, 2000).

Oram, Alison, 'Telling Stories about the Ladies of Llangollen: The Construction of Lesbian and Feminist Histories', in Ann-Marie Gallagher, Cathy Lubelska, and Louise Ryan (eds), *Re-presenting the Past: Women and History* (Harlow: Longman, 2001), 44–62.

Parker, J. Oxley, *The Oxley Parker Papers: From the Letters and Diaries of an Essex Family of Land Agents in the Nineteenth Century* (Colchester: Benham & Co., 1964).

Parrish, Constance (ed.), *Isabella Lickbarrow: Collected Poems* (Grasmere: Wordsworth Trust, 2004).

Parry, Jonathan, *The Rise and Fall of Liberal Government in Victorian Britain* (New Haven and London: Yale University Press, 1993).

Paston, George [Emily Symonds], *At John Murray's: Records of a Literary Circle, 1843–92* (London: John Murray, 1932).

Patterson, Alfred Temple, *Radical Leicester: A History of Leicester, 1780–1850* (Leicester: University College, 1954).

Paz, Denis G., *Popular Anti-Catholicism in Mid-Victorian England* (Stanford, Calif.: Stanford University Press, 1992).

Pedersen, Susan, 'Eleanor Rathbone (1872–1946): The Victorian Family under the Daughter's Eye', in Susan Pedersen and Peter Mandler (eds), *After the Victorians: Private Conscience and Public Duty in Modern Britain* (London: Routledge, 1994), 105–25.

Perkin, Harold, *The Origins of Modern English Society, 1780–1880* (London: Routledge & Kegan Paul, 1969).

Perkin, Joan, *Women and Marriage in Nineteenth-Century England* (London: Routledge, 1989).

Perry, Ruth, *Novel Relations: The Transformation of Kinship in English Literature and Culture, 1748–1818* (Cambridge: Cambridge University Press, 2004).

Peterson, Linda H., *Traditions of Victorian Women's Autobiography: The Poetics and Politics of Life Writing* (Charlottesville, Va.: University Press of Virginia, 1999).

—— 'Collaborative Life Writing as Ideology: The Auto/biographies of Mary Howitt and her Family', *Prose Studies*, 26 (2003), 176–95.

Peterson, M. Jeanne, *Family, Love and Work in the Lives of Victorian Gentlewomen* (Bloomington, Ind.: Indiana University Press, 1989).

Petersson, Sandra, 'Gender Neutral Drafting: Historical Perspective', *Statute Law Review*, 19 (1998), 93–112.

Philips, David, 'Evangelicals, Aborigines and "Land Rights": A Critique of Henry Reynolds on the Select Committee on Aborigines', *Australian Studies*, 17 (2002), 147–65.

Phillips, John A., *The Great Reform Bill in the Boroughs: English Electoral Behaviour, 1818–41* (Oxford: Clarendon Press, 1992).

—— and Charles Wetherell, 'The Great Reform Act of 1832 and the Political Modernization of England', *American Historical Review*, 100 (1995), 411–36.

Phillips, Nicola, *Women in Business, 1700–1850* (Woodbridge: Boydell Press, 2006).

Pinchbeck, Ivy, *Women Workers and the Industrial Revolution, 1750–1850* (London: Routledge, 1930).

Prince-Gibson, Eetta, and Shalom H. Schwartz, 'Value Priorities and Gender', *Social Psychology Quarterly*, 61 (1998), 49–67.

Prochaska, Frank K., *Women and Philanthropy in Nineteenth-Century England* (Oxford: Clarendon Press, 1980).

Proudfoot, Lindsay, 'Hybrid Space? Self and Other in Narratives of Landownership in Nineteenth-Century Ireland', *Journal of Historical Geography*, 26 (2000), 203–21.

Pugh, Patricia M., *Calendar of the Papers of Sir Thomas Fowell Buxton, 1786–1845* (London: Swift, 1980).

Purdue, A. W., 'Queen Adelaide: Malign Influence or Consort Maligned?', in Clarissa Campbell Orr (ed.), *Queenship in Britain, 1660–1837: Royal Patronage, Court, Culture and Dynastic Politics* (Manchester: Manchester University Press, 2002), 267–87.

Randall, Vicky, 'Gender and Power: Women Engage the State', in Vicky Randall and Georgina Waylen (eds), *Gender, Politics and the State* (London and New York: Routledge, 1998), 1–17.

Redstone, Lilian J., *Ipswich through the Ages* (Ipswich: East Anglian Magazine, 1969).

Rendall, Jane, *The Origins of Modern Feminism: Women in Britain, France and the United States 1780–1860* (Basingstoke: Macmillan, 1985).

—— (ed.), *Equal or Different: Women's Politics, 1800–1914* (Oxford: Basil Blackwell, 1987).

—— 'Women and the Public Sphere', *Gender and History*, 11 (1999), 475–88.

—— 'The Citizenship of Women and the Reform Act of 1867', in Catherine Hall, Keith McClelland, and Jane Rendall, *Defining the Victorian Nation: Class, Race, Gender and the British Reform Act of 1867* (Cambridge: Cambridge University Press, 2000), 119–78.

—— 'Who was Lily Maxwell? Women's Suffrage and Manchester Politics, 1866–1867', in June Purvis and Sandra Stanley Holton (eds), *Votes for Women* (London and New York: Routledge, 2000), 57–83.

—— 'John Stuart Mill, Liberal Politics, and the Movements for Women's Suffrage,1865–1873', in Amanda Vickery (ed.), *Women, Privilege and Power: British Politics 1750 to the Present* (Stanford, Calif.: Stanford University Press, 2001), 168–200.

Rendall, Jane, '"Friends of Liberty and Virtue": Women Radicals and Transatlantic Correspondence, 1789–1848', in Caroline Bland and Maire Cross (eds), *Gender and Politics in the Age of Letter-Writing 1750–2000* (Aldershot: Ashgate, 2004), 77–92.

—— '"Women that would Plague me with Rational Conversation": Aspiring Women and Scottish Whigs, c. 1790–1830', in Sarah Knott and Barbara Taylor (eds), *Women, Gender and Enlightenment* (Basingstoke: Palgrave Macmillan, 2004), 326–47.

Reynolds, K. D., *Aristocratic Women and Political Society in Victorian Britain* (Oxford: Clarendon Press, 1998).

Richardson, Sarah, 'The Role of Women in Electoral Politics in Yorkshire during the 1830s', *Northern History*, 32 (1996), 133–51.

—— '"Well-Neighboured Houses": The Political Networks of Elite Women, 1780–1860', in Kathryn Gleadle and Sarah Richardson (eds), *Women in British Politics, 1760–1860: The Power of the Petticoat* (Basingstoke: Macmillan, 2000), 56–73.

Riviere, Joan, 'Womanliness as a Masquerade' (1929), repr. in Athol Hughes (ed.), *The Inner World and Joan Riviere: Collected Papers, 1920–1958* (London and New York: Karnac, 1991), 90–101.

Robbins, Keith, *John Bright* (London: Routledge & Kegan Paul, 1979).

Roberts, David, 'The Paterfamilias of the Victorian Governing Classes', in A. S. Wohl (ed.), *The Victorian Family: Structure and Stresses* (London: Croom Helm, 1978), 59–81.

—— *Paternalism in Early Victorian England* (London: Croom Helm, 1979).

Rodgers, Silvia, 'Women's Space in a Men's House: The British House of Commons', in Shirley Ardener (ed.), *Women and Space: Ground Rules and Social Maps* (London: Croom Helm, 1981), 46–69.

Rogers, Helen, '"The Prayer, the Passion and the Reason" of Eliza Sharples: Freethought, Women's Rights and Republicanism, 1832–52', in Eileen J. Yeo (ed.), *Radical Femininity: Women's Self-Representation in the Public Sphere* (Manchester: Manchester University Press, 1998), 52–78.

—— *Women and the People: Authority, Authorship and the Radical Tradition in Nineteenth-Century England* (Aldershot: Ashgate, 2000).

—— 'Any Questions? The Gendered Dimensions of the Political Platform', *Nineteenth-Century Prose*, 29 (2002), 117–32.

—— 'In the Name of the Father: Political Biographies by Radical Daughters', in David Amigoni (ed.), *Life Writing and Victorian Culture* (Aldershot: Ashgate, 2006), 145–64.

Rogers, Nicholas, *Crowds, Culture and Politics in Georgian Britain* (Oxford: Clarendon Press, 1998).

Rose, Gillian, *Feminism and Geography: The Limits of Geographical Knowledge* (Cambridge: Polity Press, 1993).

Rose, Mark, *Authors and Owners: The Invention of Copyright* (Cambridge, Mass., and London: Harvard University Press, 1993).

Ross, Ellen, 'Survival Networks: Women's Neighbourhood Sharing in London before World War One', *History Workshop*, 15 (1983), 4–27.

Ross, Ishbel, *Child of Destiny: The Life Story of the First Woman Doctor* (London: Victor Gollancz, 1950).

Salmon, Philip, *Electoral Reform at Work: Local Politics and National Parties, 1832–1841* (Woodbridge, Suffolk: Boydell, 2002).

Sanders, Valerie, *The Private Lives of Victorian Women: Autobiography in Nineteenth-Century England* (London and New York: Harvester Wheatsheaf, 1989).

—— '"Fathers' Daughters": Three Victorian Anti-Feminist Women Autobiographers', in Vincent Newey and Philip Shaw (eds), *Mortal Pages, Literary Lives: Studies in Nineteenth-Century Autobiography* (Aldershot: Scholar, 1996), 153–71.

Sayer, Karen, *Women of the Fields: Representations of Rural Women in the Nineteenth Century* (Manchester: Manchester University Press, 1995).

Schwarzkopf, Jutta, *Women in the Chartist Movement* (Basingstoke, Macmillan 1991).

Seeliger, Sylvia, 'Hampshire Women as Landholders: Common Law Mediated by Manorial Custom', *Rural History*, 7 (1996), 1–14.

Selleck, R. J. W, *James Kay-Shuttleworth: Journey of an Outsider* (Ilford: Woburn Press, 1994).

Seymour, Charles, *Electoral Reform in England and Wales: The Development of the Parliamentary Franchise, 1832–85* (Newton Abbot: David & Charles, 1970; 1st publ. 1915).

Sharpe, Pamela, 'The Female Labour Market in English Agriculture during the Industrial Revolution: Expansion or Contraction?', *Agricultural History Review*, 47 (1999), 161–81.

Shattock, Joanne (ed.), *Women and Literature in Britain, 1800–1900* (Cambridge: Cambridge University Press, 2001).

Shepard, Alexandra, 'Honesty, Worth and Gender in Early Modern England, 1560–1640', in Henry French and Jonathan Barry (eds), *Identity and Agency in England, 1500–1800* (Basingstoke: Palgrave Macmillan 2004), 87–105.

Shiman, Lilian Lewis, '"Changes are Dangerous": Women and Temperance in Victorian England', in Gail Malmgreen (ed.), *Religion in the Lives of English Women, 1760–1930* (London: Croom Helm, 1986), 193–215.

—— *Women and Leadership in Nineteenth-Century England* (Basingstoke: Macmillan, 1992).

Simcoe, Ethel, *A Short History of the Parish and Ancient Borough of Thaxted* (Saffron Walden: W. Hart & Son, 1934).

Smith, Dorothy E., *Texts, Facts, and Femininity: Exploring the Relations of Ruling* (London and New York: Routledge, 1990).

Smith, E. A., 'The Yorkshire Elections of 1806 and 1807: A Study in Electoral Management', *Northern History*, 2 (1967), 62–90.

—— *Lord Grey, 1764–1845* (Oxford: Clarendon Press, 1990).

—— *Reform or Revolution? A Diary of Reform in England, 1830–2* (Stroud: Alan Sutton, 1992).

Smith, Hilda L., 'Women as Sextons and Electors: King's Bench and Precedents for Women's Citizenship', in Hilda L. Smith (ed.), *Women Writers and the Early Modern British Political Tradition* (Cambridge: Cambridge University Press, 1998), 324–42.

Smith, Margaret (ed.), *The Letters of Charlotte Brontë: With a Selection of Letters by Family and Friends*, i. *1829–1847* (Oxford: Clarendon Press 1995).

Smith-Dampier, J. L., *East Anglican Worthies* (Oxford: Blackwell, 1949).

Snell, K. D. M., 'The Sunday-School Movement in England and Wales: Child Labour, Denominational Control and Working-Class Culture', *Past and Present*, 164 (1999), 122–68.

Soja, Edward, and Barbara Hooper, 'The Spaces that Difference Makes: Some Notes on the Geographical Margins of the New Cultural Politics', in Michael Keith and Steve Pile (eds), *Place and the Politics of Identity* (London: Routledge, 1993), 180–202.

Sökefeld, Martin, 'Debating Self, Identity, and Culture in Anthropology', *Current Anthropology*, 40 (1999), 417–47.

Spicksley, Judith, 'A Dynamic Model of Social Relations: Celibacy, Credit and the Identity of the "Spinster" in Seventeenth-Century England', in Henry French and Jonathan Barry (eds), *Identity and Agency in England, 1500–1800* (Basingstoke: Palgrave Macmillan, 2004), 106–46.

Stapleton, Karyn, 'In Search of the Self: Feminism, Postmodernism and Identity', *Feminism and Psychology*, 10 (2000), 463–9.

Staves, Susan, 'Instruments, Votes and "Bribes": Women as Shareholders in the Chartered Companies', in Hilda Smith (ed.), *Women Writers and the Early Modern British Political Tradition* (Cambridge: Cambridge University Press, 1998), 259–78.

Stott, Anne, 'Patriotism and Providence: The Politics of Hannah More', in Kathryn Gleadle and Sarah Richardson (eds), *Women in British Politics: The Power of the Petticoat 1760–1860* (Basingstoke: Macmillan Press, 2000), 39–55.

Studer, Brigitte, 'Citizenship as Contingent National Belonging: Married Women and Foreigners in Twentieth-Century Switzerland', *Gender and History*, 13 (2001), 622–54.

Stunt, Timothy C. F., *From Awakening to Secession: Radical Evangelicals in Switzerland and Britain, 1815–35* (Edinburgh: T. and T. Clark, 2000).

Summers, Anne, 'A Home from Home: Women's Philanthropic Work in the Nineteenth Century', in Sandra Burman (ed.), *Fit Work for Women* (London: Croom Helm, 1979), 33–63.

—— '"In a Few Years we shall None of us that Now Take Care of them Be Here": Philanthropy and the State in the Thinking of Elizabeth Fry', *Historical Research*, 67 (1994), 134–42.

Sutherland, G., 'Administrators in Education after 1870: Patronage, Professionalism and Expertise', in G. Sutherland (ed.), *Studies in the Growth of Nineteenth-Century Government* (London: Routledge & Kegan Paul, 1972), 263–85.

Sweet, Rosemary, 'Women and Civic Life in Eighteenth-Century England', in Rosemary Sweet and Penelope Lane (eds), *Women and Urban Life in Eighteenth-Century England: 'On the Town'* (Aldershot: Ashgate, 2003), 21–42.

—— *Antiquaries: The Discovery of the Past in Eighteenth-Century Britain* (London and New York: Hambledon, 2004).

Swift, David E., *Joseph John Gurney: Banker, Reformer and Quaker* (Middletown, Conn.: Wesleyan University Press, 1962).

Tadmor, Naomi, *Family and Friends in Eighteenth-Century England: Household, Kinship and Patronage* (Cambridge: Cambridge University Press, 2001).

Taylor, Barbara, *Eve and the New Jerusalem: Socialism and Feminism in the Nineteenth Century* (London: Virago, 1983).

Taylor, Clare, *British and American Abolitionists: An Episode in Transatlantic Understanding* (Edinburgh: Edinburgh University Press, 1974).

Temperley, Howard, *British Antislavery, 1833–1870* (London: Longman, 1972).

Tew, Jerry, *Social Theory: Power and Practice* (Basingstoke: Palgrave, 2002).

Thoits, Peggy A., and Lauren K. Virshup, '"Me's and We's": Forms and Functions of Social Identities', in Richard D. Ashmore and Lee Jussim (eds), *Self and Identity: Fundamental Issues* (Oxford and New York: Oxford University Press, 1997), 106–33.

Thomas, Peter D. G., *The House of Commons in the Eighteenth Century* (Oxford: Clarendon Press, 1971).

Thompson, Dorothy, 'Women, Work and Politics in Nineteenth-Century England: The Problem of Authority', in Jane Rendall (ed.), *Equal or Different: Women's Politics, 1800–1914* (Oxford: Basil Blackwell, 1987), 57–81.

Thompson, Edward P., 'The Crime of Anonymity', in Douglas Hay, P. Linebaugh, and E. P. Thompson (eds), *Albion's Fatal Tree: Crime and Society in Eighteenth-Century England* (Harmondsworth: Penguin, 1977), 255–308.

Thompson, Francis M. L., *English Landed Society in the Nineteenth Century* (London: Routledge & Kegan Paul, 1963).

—— 'Town and City', in Francis M. L. Thompson (ed.), *The Cambridge Social History of Britain, 1750–1950*, i. *Regions and Communities* (Cambridge: Cambridge University Press, 1990), 1–86.

Thompson, Madeline, '"Distant Prospects and Smaller Circles": Questions of Authority in Maria Edgeworth's Irish Writings', in Joan Bellamy, Anne Laurence, and Gill Perry (eds), *Women, Scholarship and Criticism: Gender and Knowledge c. 1790–1900* (Manchester: Manchester University Press, 2000), 42–57.

Todd, Arthur C., 'An Answer to Poverty in Sussex 1830–45', *Agricultural History Review*, 4 (1956), 45–51.

—— *Beyond the Blaze: A Biography of Davies Gilbert* (Truro: Gilbert D. Bradford Barton, 1967).

Tosh, John, *A Man's Place: Masculinity and the Middle-Class Home in Victorian England* (London and New Haven: Yale University Press, 1999).

Turbin, Carole, 'Refashioning the Concept of Public/Private: Lessons from Dress Studies', *Journal of Women's History*, 15 (2003), 43–51.

Turley, David, *The Culture of English Antislavery, 1780–1860* (London: Routledge, 1991).

Turner, Ralph E., *James Silk Buckingham, 1786–1855: A Social Biography* (London: Williams & Norgate, 1934).

Twells, Alison, 'Missionary Domesticity, Global Reform and "Woman's Sphere" in Early Nineteenth-Century England', *Gender and History*, 18 (2006), 266–84.

Twycross-Martin, Henrietta, 'Woman Supportive or Woman Manipulative? The "Mrs Ellis" Woman', in Clarissa Campbell Orr (ed.), *Wollstonecraft's Daughters: Womanhood in England and France, 1780–1920* (Manchester and New York: Manchester University Press, 1996), 109–20.

Tyrrell, Alex, 'Making the Millennium: The Mid-Nineteenth Century Peace Movement', *Historical Journal*, 21 (1978), 75–95.

—— '"Woman's Mission" and Pressure Group Politics in Britain (1825–60)', *Bulletin of the John Rylands University Library*, 63 (1980), 194–230.

Tyrrell, Alex, *Joseph Sturge and the Moral Radical Party in Early Victorian Britain* (London: Christopher Helm, 1987).

Unger, Rhoda K., 'Imperfect Reflections of Reality: Psychology Constructs Gender', in Rachel T. Hare-Mustin and Jeanne Marecek (eds), *Making a Difference: Psychology and the Construction of Gender* (London and New Haven: Yale University Press, 1990), 102–49.

Valverde, Mariana, 'The Love of Finery: Fashion and the Fallen Woman in Nineteenth-Century Social Discourse', *Victorian Studies*, 32 (1988), 169–88.

Vansittart, Jane (ed.), *Katharine Fry's Book* (London: Hodder & Stoughton, 1966).

Vaughan, Eliza, *The Essex Village in Days Gone by* (Colchester: Benham & Co., 1928).

—— *The Stream of Time: Sketches of Village Life in Days Gone by*, 3rd edn (Colchester: Benham & Co., 1934; 1st publ. 1926).

Verdon, Nicola, *Rural Women Workers in Nineteenth-Century England: Gender, Work and Wages* (Woodbridge: Boydell Press, 2002).

—— '"Subjects Deserving of the Highest Praise": Farmers' Wives and the Farm Economy in England, c. 1700–1850', *Agricultural History Review*, 51 (2003), 23–39.

Vernon, James, *Politics and the People: A Study in English Political Culture, c. 1815–1867* (Cambridge: Cambridge University Press, 1993).

—— (ed.), *Re-reading the Constitution: New Narratives in the Political History of England's Long Nineteenth Century* (Cambridge: Cambridge University Press, 1996).

Vickery, Amanda, 'Golden Age to Separate Spheres? A Review of the Categories and Chronology of English Women's History', *Historical Journal*, 36 (1993), 383–414.

—— *The Gentleman's Daughter: Women's Lives in Georgian England* (London and New Haven: Yale University Press, 1998).

—— (ed.), *Women, Privilege and Power: British Politics, 1750 to the Present* (Stanford, Calif.: Stanford University Press, 2001).

Violi, Patrizia, 'Gender, Subjectivity and Language', in Gisela Bock and Susan James (eds), *Beyond Equality and Difference: Citizenship, Feminist Politics and Female Subjectivity* (London and New York: Routledge, 1992), 164–76.

Virgoe, Norma, and Susan Yaxley (eds), *The Banville Diaries: Journals of a Norfolk Gamekeeper, 1822–44* (London: Collins, 1986).

Wach, Howard M., 'Civil Society, Moral Identity and the Liberal Public Sphere Manchester and Boston, 1810–1840', *Social History*, 21 (1996), 281–303.

Wahrman, Dror, *Imagining the Middle Class: The Political Representation of Class in Britain, 1780–1840* (Cambridge: Cambridge University Press, 1995).

—— *The Making of the Modern Self: Identity and Culture in Eighteenth-Century England* (New Haven: Yale University Press, 2004).

Walker, Lynne, 'Home and Away: The Feminist Remapping of Public and Private Space in Victorian London', in Iain Borden, Joe Kerr, Jane Rendell, and Alicia Pivaro (eds), *The Unknown City: Contesting Architecture and Social Space. A Strangely Familiar Project* (Cambridge, Mass.: MIT, 2001), 296–311.

—— and Vron Ware, 'Political Pincushions: Decorating the Abolitionist Interior, 1787–1865', in Inga Bryden and Janet Floyd (eds), *Domestic Space: Reading the*

Nineteenth-Century Interior (Manchester: Manchester University Press, 1999), 58–83.

Waller, Philip J., 'Laughter in the House: A Late Nineteenth-Century and Early Twentieth-Century Parliamentary Survey', *Twentieth-Century British History*, 5 (1994), 4–37.

Walling, Robert A. (ed.), *The Diaries of John Bright* (London: Cassell & Co., 1930).

Waters, Mary A., *British Women Writers and the Profession of Literary Criticism, 1789–1832* (Basingstoke: Palgrave Macmillan, 2004).

Waylen, Georgina, 'Gender, Feminism and the State: An Overview', in Vicky Randall and Georgina Waylen (eds), *Gender, Politics and the State* (London and New York: Routledge, 1998), 185–205.

Webb, Beatrice, *My Apprenticeship* (London: Penguin, 1971: 1st publ. 1926).

Webb, Robert K., *Harriet Martineau: A Radical Victorian* (London: Heinemann, 1960).

Wells, Roger, 'Social Conflict and Protest in the English Countryside in the Early Nineteenth Century: A Rejoinder', *Journal of Peasant Studies*, 8 (1980–1), 514–30.

—— 'Rural Rebels in Southern England in the 1830s', in Clive Elmsley and James Walvin (eds), *Artisans, Peasants and Proletarians, 1760–1860: Essays Presented to Gwyn A. Williams* (London: Croom Helm, 1985), 124–65.

—— 'Mr William Cobbett, Captain Swing and King William IV', *Agricultural History Review*, 45 (1997), 34–48.

White, Daniel E., 'The "Joineriana": Anna Barbauld, the Aikin Family Circle and the Dissenting Public Sphere', *Eighteenth-Century Studies*, 32 (1999), 511–33.

Williams, Katherine S., 'The Public Law and Women's Rights: The Nineteenth Century Experience', *Cambrian Law Review*, 23 (1992), 80–103.

Wilson, Dorothy Clarke, *Lone Woman: The Story of Elizabeth Blackwell, the First Woman Doctor* (London: Hodder & Stoughton, 1970).

Winstanley, Michael, 'Industrialization and the Small Farm: Family and Household Economy in Nineteenth-Century Lancashire', *Past and Present*, 152 (1996), 157–95.

Winter, Alison, 'Harriet Martineau and the Reform of the Invalid in Victorian England', *Historical Journal*, 38 (1995), 597–616.

Wiskin, C., 'Urban Businesswomen in Eighteenth-Century England', in Rosemary Sweet and Penelope Lane (eds), *Women and Urban Life in Eighteenth-Century England: 'On the Town'* (Aldershot: Ashgate, 2003), 87–110.

Wolffe, John, *The Protestant Crusade in Great Britain, 1829–1860* (Oxford: Clarendon Press, 1991).

Woollacott, Angela, 'The Fragmentary Subject: Feminist History, Official Records, and Self-Representation', *Women's Studies International Forum*, 21 (1998), 329–39.

Yeo, Eileen Janes, *The Contest for Social Science: Relations and Representations of Gender and Class* (London: Rivers Oram, 1996).

Young, Iris Marion, *Throwing Like a Girl and Other Essays in Feminist Philosophy and Social Theory* (Bloomington, Ind.: Indiana University Press, 1990).

Zegger, Robert E., *John Cam Hobhouse: A Political Life, 1819–1852* (Columbia, Mo.: University of Missouri Press, 1973).

Electronic sources

Copeland, Edward, 'Opera and the Great Reform Act: Silver Fork Fiction, 1822–1842', *Romanticism on the Net*, 34–5 (2004): http://www.erudit.org/revue/ron/2004/v/n34–35/009440ar.html

National Portrait Gallery: http://www.npg.org.uk/live/search/portrait.asp?LinkID5mp00069&rNo50&role5sit

National Register of Archives: http://www.nationalarchives.gov.uk/nra/

Oxford Dictionary of National Biography: http://www.oxforddnb.com/

Snow, David, 'Collective Identity and Expressive Forms', Center for the Study of Democracy, October 1, Paper 01–07: http://repositories.cdlib.org/csd/01–07

Unpublished sources

Capern, Amanda, 'Women, Family and Land in Early-Modern Yorkshire', conference paper, Economic History Society, University of Reading, April 2006.

Index